THE
COMPUTER
SECURITY
HANDBOOK

RICHARD H. BAKER

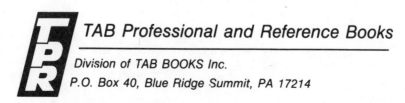

TAB Professional and Reference Books

Division of TAB BOOKS Inc.
P.O. Box 40, Blue Ridge Summit, PA 17214

FIRST EDITION

FIRST PRINTING

Copyright © 1985 by TAB BOOKS Inc.

Printed in the United States of America

Reproduction or publication of the content in any manner, without express
permission of the publisher, is prohibited. No liability is assumed with respect to
the use of the information herein.

Library of Congress Cataloging in Publication Data

Baker, Richard H.
The computer security handbook.

Includes index.
1. Computers—Access control. 2. Electronic data
processing departments—Security measures. I. Title.
QA76.9.A25B35   1985   005.8   85-14750
ISBN 0-8306-0308-5

Contents

Introduction

In the summer of 1983, a Milwaukee-based group of young computer hackers managed to find their way into the data banks of a bank, a hospital, the Los Alamos National Laboratory, and several other computers loaded with sensitive programs and data. It was a significant achievement.

The great achievement was not that they managed to break in. As the young raiders demonstrated, that was ridiculously easy. Their real achievement was that they suddenly made the computer-using community aware that their products were not as secure as they had thought. Called later to testify about how they had accomplished their feats of electronic breaking and entry, the young hackers painted a national picture of slipshod security. For example, said one member, the group often found that computer owners had never changed their passwords from the standard—and well-known—terms initially installed by the computer manufacturers.

Suddenly, it seemed the world was full of young hackers, taking electronic joyrides into randomly selected computers, endangering our defense, commerce, and privacy. Some raiders went farther than the Milwaukee group, stealing and altering important information.

Just as suddenly, the computer world has come to realize that its old attitudes about security aren't good enough. It is time to do something more. But what?

LITERACY A CURSE?

Until recently, every computer was delivered with a built-in safety feature: only a select few knew how to operate it. Programming was an arcane and aloof activity, practiced in isolation from those mortals who didn't understand it. Sure, knowledgeable computer users sometimes would apply their skills to creative forms of electronic theft and fraud, but like all kinds of computerized activity, this was only for the select few. Most of the people who juggled books still did it on paper. They didn't have the slightest idea how to do it electronically.

Then came the microcomputer phenomenon and the boom in computer literacy. Suddenly, it appears, nearly anyone who can buy an inexpensive home computer and learn a few things about how to use it can invade mainframes across the country, stealing secrets, learning confidential details of our private lives, and threatening the information on which we are building our society's future. The future, with its expanding data communication networks and home teletext systems, promises only to increase the damage a motivated hacker can do.

Consider the often-feared scenario in which a terrorist manages to hold us hostage with a well-placed nuclear bomb. In truth, the ultimate weapon may not be a bomb at all, but a microchip.

While everyone is waking up to this fact, it's time to realize this, too: Many organizations that hold information and programs in their computers fail to realize how valuable this information is. Actually, says security consultant Robert P. Campbell, there are very few systems that are *not* sensitive or critical.

Because so few users have grasped this point in the past, few have yet developed comprehensive security programs that try to define the critical information they are trying to protect and then take adequate steps to protect it.

That's not to say there has been no effort at all. In a series of articles on data security for the trade newspaper *Comuterworld,* Campbell points out that the industry has been working on security problems for at least 15 years. He also predicts it will take another 15 to 20 years to finish the job.

That isn't very good news for those who suddenly realized that they need better protection now. It gets better, though, because the awakened interest in security certainly will speed up the process. The first 15 years produced a substantial body of knowledge; we can now put to use the lessons we've learned so far.

A FULL-TIME STUDENT

Most learning has been done by the institution that has the most to lose: the United States government. The need for secure computers in the areas like defense and nuclear secrets has spurred research that has placed the government far ahead of most private users.

The government faces other security problems, too, as illustrated by recent flaps over the use of government data files. The Internal Revenue Service ran into opposition when it proposed using commercial mailing lists to search out laggard taxpayers. There was a similar reaction when the government wanted to use draft registration files to track down runaway fathers.

The main objection to the IRS proposal was that the information used to compile mailing lists is not reliable enough for law enforcement purposes. The draft file proposal had more fundamental constitutional implications. For example, could someone refuse to register for the draft on the basis of self-incrimination?

You probably don't have exactly the same kind of security problems the government has, but the government has no monopoly on computer security research, either. If we are to build effective security programs now, we must build them on the basis of what was done before, and the government has held a central role in the history of computer security research.

This book will pull the research of the past off the proverbial dusty shelf so you can put it to good use. It will examine the threats you face and the measures you can take against them. It will help you develop a plan, tailored to your own needs, to stop the criminals before they do any more harm.

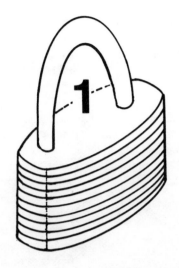

Security: It's More Than Fighting Hackers

For a brief but significant period in recent history, if you wanted to make a data processing security manager turn slightly pale all you had to do was mention the telephone area code of Milwaukee, Wisconsin.

That code provided the name for the 414 Group, a Milwaukee-based group of young computer hobbyists who generated national publicity by finding their way into the supposedly secure computers of businesses, hospitals, and government agencies. They gave a bad name to the term *hacker,* once used to describe an experiment-minded computer enthusiast, but now the common name for a computer trespasser. They spawned television shows like "Whiz Kids" and "Riptide," whose heroes perform impressive but unrealistic feats of unauthorized access.

Most of all, they made computer professionals realize that even a youngster with modest computer knowledge could penetrate systems. Suddenly it seemed as if every telephone line had a hacker at the other end.

Now that this incident has passed, it has become clear that, in a way, the hackers did us a favor. They made us aware of how vulnerable our systems are. In fact, marauding teenagers are among the least of our problems. There are much more serious threats from sources like these:

- ☐ Computer-related fraud, particularly by employees who work within the affected companies.
- ☐ Industrial espionage and the loss of trade secrets.
- ☐ Use and misuse of electronic fund transfers.
- ☐ The computerized invasion of personal privacy.

A special study committee commissioned by the federal Office of Technological Assessment (OTA) recently found 14 major areas of law and regulation that affect computer information systems, or are affected by them. The OTA list includes the individual right to privacy, freedom of information, First Amendment rights, the Fourteenth Amendment, the right to due process of law, and communication regulation, with particular emphasis on the AT&T breakup.

Areas where the systems are vulnerable to misuse include computer crime; patents, trademarks, and copyright infringement; the use of computer-generated evidence in court; liability laws; antitrust law; taxation; information available from the government; and government purchases of information systems.

As extensive as this list is, the OTA group feels it probably missed many others.

THE INFORMATION AGE

No one who has been involved with computers for any length of time needs to be told that we're in the process of an information revolution. All but the very young can recall when "transistorized" was a synonym for "miniaturized." The computer chip, in effect, is a transistorized transistor. Through this single, small device we are putting computer power into the hands of everyone.

As just one example of how far we've gone, pick up any computer publication that carries an interview with one of the field's "pioneers"—from 1970 or some equally ancient date. You're almost sure to find them saying that the computers on which they contrived to get a little time early in their careers had only a fraction of the power of those you can pick up today in a shopping mall.

The vast advances in computers and their use have been accompanied by equally rapid improvements in communication technology. Satellite transmission is now routine. The makers of teletext and videotext equipment have yet to find real markets for their products, but we have the technology. The type for this book has been set directly from the microcomputer disk on which it was written, and that's only the tip of an electronic publishing iceberg.

Coming Together

The real significance of the new technology, and major source of all our security problems, is in the combination of these closely related developments. When you combine the widespread availability of computers with rapid developments in the ways they can communicate with each other, you have vast new potential for good or evil.

The OTA study went on to point out that computers can be connected inexpensively to communication lines, making it possible to provide access economically to large computer data bases from anywhere in the country or the world. Networks of remotely sited computers provide services such as credit card and check authorization or airline scheduling to users nationwide.

Techniques for organizing and displaying information are improving, as are methods of instructing the computer to perform its tasks. This makes it easier for nonexperts to obtain usable information.

Information storage technology that is less costly and more compact makes it feasible to store large amounts of electronic information for long periods. It often costs less for electronic storage than for paper records, and access to specific items is faster and more accurate.

National Information Systems

Keep in mind that the OTA report represents a 1980 state of knowledge and is already a little outdated. Still, the study committee displayed some sharp foresight. It expressed concern, for example, over the use of national computer networks for airline scheduling and reservations.

More recently, the Civil Aeronautics Board expressed a more serious and direct concern: that the airlines operating these services were giving undue emphasis to their own flights in the computer displays they fed to travel agents. CAB has since adopted regulations that the criteria used to organize the displays be unbiased and well-publicized.

The airline systems represent only one type of what the OTA committee called a *national information system*. By way of definition, the committee included systems that are national in scope; are used to store, manipulate, and spread information about people or institutions; and are based on the use of computers and related information and communication technology. Focusing only on those areas where it felt the federal government had a substantial interest, the committee listed these examples:

- [ ] The National Crime Information Center (NCIC) run by the Federal Bureau of Investigation.
- [ ] An electronic fund transfer network between banks in the Federal Reserve System.
- [ ] Nationwide electronic mail services, including one operated by the Postal Service.
- [ ] Nationwide computer-based credit card and check authorization services.
- [ ] The computerized air traffic control system operated by the Federal Aviation Administration.
- [ ] Computerized military command and control systems.
- [ ] The computerized air reservation system.
- [ ] Computerized stock price reporting systems.
- [ ] Computerized data bases and information services, such as Dialog and The Source.

Many more information systems, such as local area networks and micro-mainframe links, are less than national in scope but present the same kinds of security problems. Their growth means these problems will grow along with them.

Problem Areas

On the basis of its study, OTA made these major findings:

- [ ] There are many laws and regulations, some overlapping and some at least potentially conflicting, that affect the operators of information systems. They also affect the users of information services and the subjects of personal information data banks.
- [ ] There is no strong trend or sentiment toward a uniform information policy that

could consider all the problems arising from the many possible uses of data systems.
- [ ] There is a lack of focus on information policy as such, and the emerging issues are not being directly addressed.
- [ ] Allowing the present situation to continue could inhibit many socially desirable applications of information systems and could create future policy problems in the future that are even harder to handle.

If anything, the trends reported a few years ago by OTA are continuing, particularly those items that reflect a lack of firm action. For example, in the wake of the hacking episodes, Congress and state legislatures have considered a wide variety of new computer crime legislation. Many bills have been offered; only a few have been passed. The same appears to be true on the private front, where business leaders recently have shown more concern for computer security but have taken few firm steps to control it.

INFORMATION IN CONFLICT

As the OTA committee points out, there are three different and fundamental types of values at stake in any kind of information security policy—personal interest in protecting privacy, the public interest in the information necessary to run government, and commercial interest in both obtaining and protecting business information. These often come into conflict.

Public versus Private Values. Freedom-of-information laws, which reflect a public value, can conflict with the private value of a right to privacy. For example, the government collects an extraordinary amount of information about its citizens, businesses, and organizations. Most is collected with a legitimate public interest in mind. Automated systems reduce the cost and time barriers that previously tended to protect this information, thus providing wider access to public records. This raises new questions about how much information should be available to the public.

Commercial versus Public Values. There is a similar conflict between government and commercial use of information. As information becomes a more valuable commercial commodity, there is increased tension between those who want to sell it through new information systems and those, like public librarians, whose traditional role is to treat information as a public good that should be available to everyone. There is a similar conflict between the desire of businesses to maintain confidential information and the government's interest in making available the information it collects through freedom of information laws.

Commercial versus Private Values. Here, as a major example, the value of a mailing list to a business conflicts with the needs of the people on that list to keep personal information in confidence. A recent manifestation of this conflict is a heated debate over the use of commercial mailing lists to catch income tax evaders.

SECURITY HAS MANY FACES

Preventing computer crime, then, is only one of many aspects of computer security. A security plan must protect all three kinds of values and—if possible—resolve conflicts between them. It must also protect them from all danger, not just theft or alteration by hackers. For example, the debate over IRS use of mailing list information has centered mainly on the accuracy of the information. A list sorted by income, occupation, or some other demographic factor may be reliable enough for a promotional mailing, but it may identify many innocent citizens as possible tax cheats.

Full computer security includes these things—and more.

Secure Data and Equipment. One of our first concerns is to keep the information in our computers from being stolen or altered. In the age of desktop and portable microcomputers, we must worry also about keeping the computer itself from being stolen!

Here, the three main sets of values—private, public and commercial—easily find some common ground. For example, it is in everyone's interest—yours, the government's, and the bank's—to make sure your electronic fund transfers go through safely and accurately and that no outsider taps your account.

It is also in everyone's interest to prevent the kind of invasive practices that made Milwaukee famous. A careless hacker could mess up the credit records of thousands of customers. Hackers penetrated the patient records of at least one hospital. They didn't alter any records, but they could have. If a nurse relies on an altered record to tell what medication a patient should have, the results could be fatal.

You don't have to steal or tamper with information to be dangerous. Think of the blackmail opportunities that must lie in the nation's banks of health and credit records. If an unauthorized person takes personal information from a file, it is the moral equivalent of wiretapping. Think of how a stock trader could profit from advance knowledge of data on a company's financial status.

Most individuals and businesses are just becoming aware of the need for computer security. The government has military, diplomatic, and commercial secrets to keep—and political reputations to protect. It has long been concerned with protecting its information, so most of the authoritative information now available on the subject was written either by or for a federal agency. It has taken a while for both the awareness and the information to reach a level of practical use in private business. Sometimes the lag is deliberate. Several years ago, the National Bureau of Standards developed a Data Encryption Standard (DES) for protecting data communication. It could have many private uses, too. But while the DES itself is public information, much of the federal expertise behind it is classified or in the hands of security-conscious agencies that don't want to spread the knowledge. As the OTA committee pointed out, no one has ever defined what role the federal government should take in publicizing this knowledge.

The same is true of possible federal programs to support private research on computer security, to set uniform security standards for nongovernment systems and certify security methods. The committee also notes this effect of the secrecy that surrounds the DES: Security restrictions on cryptographic research in colleges and universities tend to limit even the independent creation of data security technology.

Constitutional Rights. If private values are protected anywhere in our political and social system, it is in the Bill of Rights and other provisions of the U.S. Constitution. This is one area where the advocates of private values definitely have something to say. In particular, they've been concerned about invasion of privacy through improper use of computerized personal information.

Actually, the Constitution never mentions a right of privacy. The Supreme Court has said it exists by extension from guarantees that are more explicitly identified.

Lawyers can find few strong legal precedents for applying any of the listed constitutional rights to computers and data bases. For example, the First Amendment guarantees the rights to free speech, press, and religion. A major unresolved issue is how to preserve these rights in the new communication media that the computer has helped to develop. Equally important are old media that recently have been deregulated.

The central question is how to make sure these new outlets will serve as a "marketplace of ideas," open to all shades of opinion. Some argue for continued government regulation to make sure everyone has access to these media. Others point out that government regulation of the media is exactly what the First Amendment is supposed to prevent.

Another First Amendment problem is the idea that extensive data collection could be a type of surveillance that could dampen free speech and inhibit the expression of unpopular ideas. The collection of such information itself could have what the lawyers call a "chilling effect," on the listeners as well as the speakers. Consider, for example, a computerized list of people known to favor a minority political cause.

Then there is the Fourth Amendment, with its guarantee against unreasonable searches and seizures. Tapping a data base is a form of search and seizure, or the information could become a basis for issuing a search warrant. There's a similar problem with the Fifth Amendment's guard against self-incrimination.

Accuracy and Reliability. Another almost universal interest is the need for reliable information. The public, the government, and business have an intense interest in making sure the information placed in a computerized file is accurate.

It is inevitable that someone, somewhere will someday be sued for libel on the basis of false information stored in a computer data base. Short of that, accuracy is a major component of computer security. Protecting information requires a lot of time, effort, and, yes, money. We don't want to spend it to protect mistakes.

The Problem of Crime. Along with all these other problems, there is the one that probably worries us most: crime committed with the aid of computer. It can range from electronic trespassing to fraud and embezzlement with a 128K burglary tool. It is a problem too big to ignore. The spread of computers and of the knowledge of how to use them makes it an even greater danger.

And it is not the only problem. You can't fight crime and ignore the many other dangers that modern information systems have created. It is clear, though, that in the minds of many people—and perhaps in actual fact—computer crime is our biggest security problem.

OLD TRENDS—AND NEW ONES

Few things have moved as fast in the last 30 years or so as the computer. It's come through so many stages, we often have to wonder exactly which stage we're in at the moment. The changes in computers and how we use them have been shaped largely by technology, of course. There's been at least an equal influence, though, in the fact that as we gain experience with the new technology, we find new and better applications for it.

When Computers Were Big. In the 1950s, computers had something in common with automobile tail fins: They were big and kept getting bigger. Most computer users have heard about the early ENIAC and UNIVAC machines, with their rooms full of tubes and wires. Every advancement from that level of knowledge was an advancement in power and capacity.

In fact, there was a scientific "law" at the time which stated that if you doubled the price, you could get four times the computing power. That was computerdom's version of the "bigger is better" point of view.

Of course, computer designers were not providing size for its own sake. There weren't many computers in those days, and those that did exist were costly to own and operate. Economies of scale were important, and a pattern quickly developed in which an organization's applications would be pooled in a central computer that could support the scale and realize the economies.

Problems Develop. As much sense as this seemed to make at the time, it left two continuing problems. One was the "high priest" atmosphere in which data processors, the only people with keys to the great font of binary knowledge, lived in isolation from the people they served. Users had to fight their way through layers of bureaucracy, and DP departments developed a tradition of long delays between request and fulfillment.

A separate and more subtle problem was that scale is economical only to a point. In a computer, this was the point where a new application would require a major new program or some other costly new investment. The economies worked while you could run the same kind of application and program over and over, but diverse needs often must be answered by diverse computer resources. The big central machine wasn't always able to provide them as quickly or as cheaply as expected.

Noticing the Problem. It's not that these problems were overlooked and ignored. In fact, the 1960s produced two significant responses, both developed to overcome the basic problems of large cost and the need to keep a computer running almost constantly to justify the cost.

One approach was to make the computer available to more users through timesharing. A multitude of users could share the machine a few moments at a time—the moments adding up to an economical use of expensive computer time.

This was the economic response, but it produced another kind of effect: the realization that you didn't have to visit the computer to use it. You can make contact by telephone from nearly anywhere you happen to be. There is a direct link, not only from the user to the computer, but from early timesharing installations to the Milwaukee hackers.

The other response was the minicomputer. Early minis were neither small nor cheap by present standards, but they did make it possible for the user to sit down, more or less at a personally chosen time, and use the computer. This was direct contact—no waiting and no bureaucracy to penetrate.

This development established the point that a computer didn't require constant use to be economical. A smaller machine could be made inexpensive enough for only occasional use.

Modern Times. The minicomputer, of course, cleared a path for the personal computer boom and all that it means for security-conscious managers. The next trend appears to be in data communications: tying the micros to each other and to central mainframes and minis.

From a security standpoint, the challenge is this: the personal computer has given thousands of people the knowledge and tools to misuse your computer and your data. Modern communication systems make entry almost routine. People used to be amazed at the speed with which a computer could multiply. Now, unless you're careful, you can be equally amazed at how fast your problems multiply.

THE ANNALS OF CRIME BY COMPUTER

A California software company employee got involved in a pay dispute with his employer and left the company. The ex-employee soon turned up as the head of a new firm, marketing a product similar to the one made by his former employer.

That alone might give the ex-employer grounds

for a suit for stealing trade secrets, but the disgruntled former employee did more. He built an instant customer list from the comfort of his home, using a computer and modem to tap the ex-employer's confidential customer lists.

The software company discovered the thefts. Customers reported that they were being offered near-copies of the company's products at attractive discounts. A monitoring device installed on the computer soon traced the problem to its source, but not before the company had lost about 50 customers.

The International Association of Computer Crime Investigators, which reported this case, calls it unusual: The culprit was caught.

"Telemarketing" by Computer. A college-age computer whiz also had an eye for telephone technology. He developed a plan to acquire discarded equipment from a West Coast phone company and resell it to new users. The trouble is, he placed the orders illegally, by tapping into a phone company's computerized ordering system. He, too, was caught.

Then there was the engineering student who followed the script of the movie *War Games*—but did it for real. In a demonstration of how vulnerable the nation's military computers could be, he broke into an Air Force computer system. He was caught long before he could have begun the kind of nuclear brinksmanship depicted in the movie. When the young man was arrested, federal authorities also confiscated his computer.

Getting Along in Age. Computer crime, like love, is not entirely wasted on the young. A New York consultant cites the case of a company that installed a new computer to take care of its bookkeeping and payroll. A data entry clerk soon grabbed the opportunity to begin making out extra accounts payable vouchers.

It seems that before the computer had been installed, the clerk's work had been regularly audited by the company controller. Assuming the computer would be inherently honest, the company dropped the auditing practice after the new machine was installed. The computer was honest enough, but it still couldn't make up for a dishonest operator.

Another careless company had the distinction of starting a young hacker on a productive career. The company gave young Geoffrey Goodfellow a free account on its timesharing computer—and forgot about him. The company later discovered that Goodfellow had been roaming almost at will through the system. The accomplishment was so impressive the firm offered Goodfellow a job. He now puts his first-hand knowledge of hacking to good use with SRI International, a consulting firm on many of the government's computer security projects.

Growth Industry. Actually, computer crime still accounts for only a small fraction of the losses American business suffers to so-called white collar crime. Theft, embezzlement, industrial espionage, and counterfeit products all rank well ahead of computer crime. Still, the computer ranks as a major criminal tool for two reasons. First, it is the fastest-growing type of white collar crime, fueled by the equally rapid spread of computers and the knowledge of how to use them. And second, the computer lends itself to most other types of business crime. It increases the number of opportunities and makes it easier to capitalize on them. As SRI's consultants put it in a report prepared for the Justice Department, "Computers are engendering a new kind of crime."

In creating many new occupations, computers also have created many new kinds of criminals. It isn't just a matter of accountants juggling the books. Programmers, operators, and electrical engineers can get in on the criminal act.

Their methods also are new. SRI points out that a new jargon has been developed, identifying such illicit activities as data diddling, Trojan horses, logic bombs, super zapping, and asynchronous attacks. These new techniques are aimed at new targets: information on warehouse inventories, for example, or the growing supply of "electronic money."

To add even more to the problem, computer crime can be committed at nearly any time and with blinding speed. SRI says some computer crimes have been committed in less than three milliseconds—three hundredths of a second. It could be done from thousands of miles away—all the criminal needs is a telephone connection.

IS BUSINESS ASLEEP?

In one of several computer crime reports it recently prepared for the Justice Department, SRI International had this to say:

> Unfortunately, however, the business community, constituting all businesses, government agencies, and institutions that use computers for technical and business purposes, is neither adequately prepared to deal with nor sufficiently motivated to report this new kind of crime to the authorities. Although reliable statistics are as yet unavailable to prove this, computer security studies for the business community and interviews with certified public accountants have indicated that few crimes of this type are ever reported to law enforcement agencies for prosecution.

On the one hand, many businessmen complain that even when they do report this crime, prosecutors frequently refuse to accept the case for a variety of reasons, including their lack of understanding of the technology and their already heavy case loads. On the other hand, prosecutors and investigators indicate that the victims' records and documentation of crimes associated with computers in the business community are inadequate for effective prosecution.

How Criminals Use Computers

Computers have been used in most types of crime, including fraud, theft, larceny, embezzlement, bribery, burglary, sabotage, espionage, conspiracy, extortion, and kidnapping. A major problem facing enforcement agencies is that many people think of computer crime as something that is done only within the computer. Recent events have helped overcome this misunderstanding, says SRI, but they have added new complications of inadequate reporting by journalists who do not fully understand the technology.

SRI's experts suggest that we adopt the broadest possible definition of computer crime. Their suggested definition, for law enforcement use, is that

> [*Computer Crime is*] *any illegal act for which knowledge of computer technology is essential for successful prosecution.*

This definition was written to meet two major needs: to identify the broad scope of computer crime, and to make it clear that if we are to understand the crime, we first must understand the computer.

Computer crime certainly is not just white collar crime. It can include violent crime or activities that seriously endanger human life. One is the alteration of computerized medical records. An incident of that kind also finds its way into a television script, in a 1984 episode of "St. Elsewhere". There could be similar dangers any time someone alters the proper function of a computer that controls a sensitive process.

Computers play four major roles in crime:

☐ As an *object*. Criminals have destroyed programs and data and, at times, entire computers. One well-demonstrated way to cause damage is to shut off the power while material is in memory. A more subtle alternative might be to shut down the air conditioning on a muggy day.

☐ As the *scene* of a crime, such as altering the contents of a computer file.

☐ As the *instrument* of a crime. The computer often becomes the means to commit a high-tech crime that could be impossible without it. For example, a computer can be made to simulate a legitimate general ledger while its operator skims money off the real books.

☐ As a *decoy*. In such cases, the computer is used to intimidate or deceive, such as in false advertising for a computer dating service.

Table 1-1 is a detailed list of computer crimes and the losses they cause.

Long Criminal Record

Some form of computer crime probably has been around for as long as there have been computers. SRI cites incidents of computer abuse as early as the 1940s, with the first officially recorded incident in 1958.

The first federal prosecution for a computer-related crime, identified as such, was in 1966. The case involved the use of a computer to alter the records of a Minneapolis bank.

Until the last few years, though, the incidence of computer crime was low. An SRI study found only 669 incidents of computer abuse between 1958 and 1979. Of these, it said, only a small and unknown fraction produced hard proof of criminal activities. In fact, one research report, published in 1970, concluded that the level of computer crime was so small it wasn't really worthy of further serious study. A later study suggested that investigators and prosecutors should worry only whether a crime was a crime—the use of a computer to commit it was only incidental.

Even in the 1970s, though, some agencies were becoming concerned. In particular, the federal government worried about the number of computerized secrets it had to maintain. Law enforcement officials also began to take computer crime more seriously. The techniques of fighting computer crime have been part of the standard FBI training course since 1976.

That also was the year of the first Congressional hearings on computer crime, and the next year Senator Abraham Ribicoff (D-Conn.) introduced the first anticomputer crime bill. Many more have been introduced since, particularly in the wake of the Milwaukee hackers incident.

Investigators and prosecutors do often approach computer crime on much the same basis as they attack more traditional forms of crime. They may well find, though, that traditional crimes are being committed in nontraditional ways that require a better understanding of the technology and the ways computer criminals can exploit it.

WHAT'S BEING DONE?

When the U.S. House of Representatives approved a computer crime bill in mid-1984 it was a first: a measure that would penalize computer crime on a nationwide basis.

Congress had earlier passed, and the President had signed, a bill that directed the Small Business Administration to educate its clients about computer security. Where actually penalizing computer crime was concerned, however, neither Congress nor anyone else had acted officially to make computerized invasion illegal.

Earlier, Congress had considered many measures, dating back to the original Ribicoff proposal. Many state legislatures have considered similar legislation. The overall legislative record, though, is still primarily one of bills introduced. Few of them actually have been enacted.

For example, Congressman Bill Nelson (D-Fla.) had for several years been a major advocate of new legislation to curb computer crime. Nelson authored of a bill that would specifically make it illegal to tamper with a computer that falls in any way under the federal government's jurisdiction. This would include computers used in interstate commerce, those that are hooked into interstate communication networks, and the computers of federally regulated businesses such as banks.

For just as many years, Nelson's bill failed to make it out of committee—in fact, it was still there when the House suddenly rushed to pass a similar measure.

As a result of that flurry of activity, a limited computer crime bill was passed late in the 1984 session. It prohibits unauthorized access to a computer to obtain classified information or data protected by federal privacy and credit disclosure laws. It also forbids the disclosure or destruction of information in a federally owned computer.

This measure may be significant primarily for what it didn't do. Provisions that would have extended federal criminal law to protect most private computers were stripped from the bill in a House-Senate compromise. The Senate had not wanted to pass *any* computer crime bill that year.

There still is less than unanimous agreement

Table 1-1. Computer Abuse Cases.

Incidence and Loss by Type of Crime (Yearly)

Year	Type 1 Physical Destruction			Type 2 Intellectual Property Deception and Taking		
	No. of Cases; % of Total		Known Losses for Type 1	Av. Loss Per Case, Type 1	No. of Cases; % of Total		Known Losses for Type 2	Av. Loss Per Case, Type 2
1958	-	-	-	-	-	-	-	-
1959	-	-	-	-	-	-	-	-
1962	2	0%	-	-	-	-	-	-
1963	1	50%	2,000	2,000	-		-	-
1964	1	17%	-	-	2	33%	2,500	2,500
1965	-	-	-	-	1	13%	-	-
1966	1	33%	<1	<1	-	-	-	-
1967	2	50%	<1	<1	-	-	-	-
1968	1	8%	-	-	3	25%	7,203	3,602
1969	4	20%	2,000	2,000	8	40%	1,003	334
1970	8	21%	3,600	900	6	16%	6,843	1,369
1971	7	12%	-	-	20	34%	9,844	1,641
1972	17	23%	11,148	2,230	19	26%	180	30
1973	10	13%	4	2	26	35%	26,782	2,435
1974	7	10%	2,010	1,005	20	27%	2,197	439
1975	5	6%	115	58	21	25%	91,670	13,096
1976	5	8%	1,110	370	19	32%	49,465	7,066
1977	14	16%	2,252	322	16	18%	17,946	2,991
1978	10	24%	2,523	841	13	31%	300	50
1979	2	10%	-	-	11	55%	-	-
Total	97	14%	26,761	836	185	28%	215,932	3,322

Cases: Total known cases of this type in year, whether or not loss is known
Known losses: in thousands of dollars
Av. loss: Average for cases where loss is known

that legal action is needed against computer crime. The committee chairman who had jurisdiction over the Nelson bill expressed just such an opinion.

Other critics warned against overreacting to the hacking incidents. In the rush, they warn, we may unwittingly enact draconian penalties for innocent activities. The 1984 act's penalties for disclosing government information have come under attack because they might be used to penalize reporters or whistle-blowers who reveal evidence of govern-ment wrongdoing.

On the State Level

Several states have enacted computer security laws of their own. Florida was among the earliest, with a law written by Nelson when he was a member of the state legislature. About 20 states now have passed laws that make hacking a crime. Some of these go further, imposing added penalties

No. of Cases; % of Total		Type 3 Financial Deception and Taking — Known Losses for Type 3	Av. Loss Per Case, Type 3	No. of Cases; % of Total		Type 4 Unauthorized Use of Services — Known Losses for Type 4	Av. Loss Per Case, Type 4	Total Cases	All Types — Total Known Losses	Average Loss
1	0%	<1	<1	-	-	-	-	1		
1	0%	278	278	-	-	-	-	1	278	277
-	-	-	-	-	-	-	-	2	-	-
1	50%	81	81	-	-	-	-	2	2,081	1,040
3	50%	100	100	-	-	-	-	6	2,600	1,300
4	50%	126	63	3	38%	-	-	8	126	63
2	67%	28	14	-	-	-	-	3	28	9
-	-	-	-	2	50%	10	10	4	10	5
6	50%	5,251	1,313	2	17%	-	-	12	12,454	2,075
4	20%	6	2	4	20%	2	2	20	3,011	376
13	34%	8,910	810	11	29%	-	-	38	19,353	967
24	41%	5,943	540	8	14%	351	175	59	16,137	849
19	26%	3,090	257	18	25%	107	21	73	14,524	518
28	37%	206,274	11,460	11	15%	7	1	75	233,066	6,474
34	47%	3,952	158	12	16%	3	3	73	8,162	247
49	58%	6,513	176	9	11%	14	5	84	98,312	2,006
30	51%	2,026	78	5	8%	-	-	59	52,601	1,461
44	51%	47,501	1,319	13	15%	154	77	87	67,853	1,330
17	40%	12,384	826	2	5%	-	-	42	15,207	633
4	20%	200	200	3	15%	-	-	20	200	200
284	42%	302,661	1,462	103	14%	646	32	669	546,001	1,685

for manipulating data once a hacker reaches your computer.

Oklahoma has adopted a law its sponsors said was aimed primarily at "professional" computer criminals. It now is a misdemeanor in that state to gain improper access to a computer—a felony if you destroy, copy, or alter any records. One reason for the law is to make Oklahoma more inviting to high-tech industries.

Massachusetts, whose Boston suburbs are an eastern equivalent to California's Silicon Valley, has been considering a similar law. It would recognize two degrees of computer fraud—one aimed at hackers who simply gain improper access—the other providing stiffer penalties for more serious types of crime.

Still, fewer than half the states have adopted computer crime laws, and action at the federal level has long been delayed. Prosecutors often have had to rely on other laws that can serve the purpose, but were written with other kinds of crime in mind.

For example, one Milwaukee hacker was fined and placed on probation under a federal interstate commerce statute. Several people who tapped a law firm's computer to gain inside knowledge of pending stock price developments were charged with violating federal securities laws. Federal antiwiretapping laws also have been applied to computer cases.

In all, says Congressman Nelson, there are about 80 federal laws that could be used against computer crime, but none were written with the idea that computers would be used in those crimes. He feels they force prosecutors to make unnecessary adaptations, shoehorning laws into situations for which they never were intended.

Except for the temporary incentive of the Milwaukee episode, there seems to be some justification for the view that there is no real demand for an anticomputer-crime law.

In a survey of 200 members, the Data Processing Management Association found that 70 percent recognize a need for security. However, only 65 percent of their companies make regular budget allocations for computer security, and the average amount is only 2.7 percent of the corporate budget. One commenter described the effort as "lip service."

The computer professionals who belong to DPMA say they're well aware of the need for security and, in particular, of the large losses they risk from insecure systems. They've had problems, though, selling the idea to senior corporate management.

That appears to be a common theme: Many computer owners have not yet taken serious interest in security. Another sign of this attitude: Sellers of such products as encrypting software and antihacking insurance policies report disapppointingly slow sales of their products.

Waking Up?

There are signs of an awakening. The hacking incidents were easily forgotten once the publicity had died down, but they did sound an alarm. A more substantial warning may be inherent in the spread of microcomputers in both homes and businesses.

They give thousands of new people the means and opportunity to copy, alter, and sabotage your data. As they are connected in networks and with direct access to mainframe computers, your material becomes much more vulnerable.

The hackers may have been just the first—and least harmful—of a coming wave of computer invaders. No computer user can afford to be lax about security anymore. The need can only be more acute with every new computer that's shipped.

TRUSTING COMPUTERS TOO MUCH

Any assessment of your security situation must take this into account: we tend to trust computers. They are inherently honest and accurate, in spite of the many horror stories about malfunctions.

This point of view is accurate as far as it goes. We've been told, and probably have said ourselves, that most computer errors really are human errors. The problem is, the first people to ignore it often are the people most familiar with computers—those who use them regularly. We know the computer is basically a trustworthy device. We tend to forget about the fallible humans who operate them.

A tragic case in point was the 1979 crash of an Air New Zealand flight, killing all 257 on board. An investigation found that an automated flight plan fed into a computer-controlled automatic pilot had been changed just before the flight—without the pilots' knowledge. When visibility became poor, the pilots relied on the computer's instructions. Apparently, they thought they were over water, and flew into a mountain.

Blind faith in computers doesn't always have results as tragic as this incident, but it is a cause for worry in any security system. The more faith we place in computers, the more risk we take that the faith will be misplaced.

That's one reason several teen-agers were able to make their highly publicized invasions into supposedly secure computers. We learned, almost too late, that we had placed too much faith in the limited security systems of the past.

There are other reasons to be concerned.

Massachusetts banking authorities say they came within only a few days of having to close several banks after a computer malfunctioned at a data processing company that served more than 100 banks. The Defense Department's critical Arapnet network once went down when bad data in one of the system spread throughout the network.

Yet another reason to worry is that computers the decision to remove human controllers from the are being applied in more and more situations where there is no human intervention. A key element of the fictional scenario in *War Games* was missile silos, placing the firing systems on automated control. The Defense Department has not actually done anything like that, but it's being considered.

A more down-to-earth example: Many companies used to enjoy the services of clerks and accountants whose sixth-sense judgment could spot questionable items on the sheets. Sometimes these loyal employees would even save their employers from bankruptcy. More and more, though, these human safety valves, with their instinctive human judgment, are being replaced by computers.

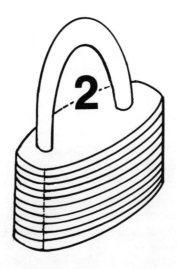

The Right Management

Approach to Security

Of the mushrooming number of personal computers now used by American business, more than 71 percent are connected to other personal computers or have access to the data in the company's mainframe computers. Yet only 19 percent of the companies that own these computers say they have developed security policies to protect the data in these linked computers.

Those are the results of a survey of 240 officers from 100 companies taken by Price Waterhouse for the National Association of Accountants. Of the executives surveyed, 81 percent said they have policies on purchasing microcomputers, and 74 percent said they have formal in-house training programs. But these are older problems now being solved, Price Waterhouse pointed out. In spite of all the publicity about the weaknesses found by youthful hackers, computer users in the survey had yet to give security the same kind of attention they have given other microcomputer issues.

NEW SURVEY, SAME RESULTS

This attitude may be costly. In a similar survey a few months later, the American Bar Association (ABA) concluded that "computer crime is a problem of substantial and growing significance." The ABA's Computer Task Force surveyed 283 companies and found that 72—nearly an even 25 percent—had suffered "known and verifiable losses to computer crime" during the previous year. Individual losses during the year ranged from a low of $145 million to a peak figure of $730 million. These were only the losses the companies were able to confirm, the ABA pointed out. The actual figures probably are much higher. Other conclusions from the ABA survey:

☐ Most respondents believe that private industry and individual users bear the major responsibility for controlling computer crime.

□ They also believe that the most effective way to prevent and deter computer crime is "more comprehensive and effective selfprotection by private business."

□ Members of top management underestimate their vulnerability to losses from computer crime and the likely magnitude of those losses.

□ There is a gap between computer technology and computer security, and it continues to grow.

In the words of the ABA report, "[the] proliferation of machines and knowledgeable users, along with recent concrete examples of the damage that can be caused by one person with one personal computer, provides disturbing and undeniable evidence that the scope and significance of computer crime, and its potentially devastating effects, are broad and deep."

The ABA also points out that computer crime is rapidly coming to be identified as *the* white collar crime. Many also see it as more important than other types of offenses, including such things as shoplifting and illegal immigration.

Gerald M. Ward, of Price Waterhouse, sees things much the same way, particularly with the spread of micro-mainframe links and computer networks. "Once you open up communication, you need to determine whether you have reasonable safeguards. There is clearly a trend toward more sophisticated application in telecommunications of microcomputers. Companies have done a very good job on acquisition and training," he says—but now they must place a similar emphasis on data security controls.

"There is a need to integrate microcomputers into a company's overall policy," Ward said. This process should include "ethics, security, password control, acquisition, and software."

Ward does feel that security policies should be "balanced against the increasing necessity for employees to have access to pertinent data. People have to be encouraged to use the system," he continues, "and it is a very delicate balance be-

tween making a system that is 'user friendly' and a system that is so secure no one can use it."

To achieve the right sense of balance, Ward suggests that you ask questions like this: "Do I have reasonable data security safeguards, with passwords and policies to insure that employee adhere to the security system?"

Within the need for balance, Ward sees a strong and growing need for better security. "The more computers we have," he says, "the more data files and the more need for policy in handling them."

Yet another survey, this one by the Data Processing Management Association (DPMA), concludes that while senior managers have become aware of the need for security, their concern is not always reflected in things like money, and top-level support.

Of the 200 DPMA members who responded to the survey, 70 percent said they feel their senior managers are aware of the importance of data security, but only 65 percent of the firms represented have specific budgets for the purpose. Among those that do, security accounts for an average of 2.7 percent of the corporate budget—barely a sliver of a pie chart.

WHY THE LAG?

On one hand, then, the typical company's lack of full data security puts it at a high risk of major loss. On the other, management seems to be aware of this, but doesn't seem to be doing very much about it. Why?

Bad press is one suggested answer. Charles Wood of SRI International points out that many computer crimes go unreported because the victims are companies that don't want the publicity. Banks in particular are anxious not to tell the world they have been victimized. Says Wood, "There's nothing like this kind of publicity to foster loss of confidence in your firm's ability to handle security."

This anxiety to avoid publicity may also inhibit many security programs. You might hesitate to install a security system that will be highly visible to the public because the system itself reminds your customers that there's a risk.

Security consultant Danny Bowers says most security incidents go undetected; of those that are, only one in 10,000 is ever prosecuted. The topic of security today, says Bowers, is much like the subject of sex was about 25 years ago, "a no-no subject." No one wants to be embarrassed or to have to admit a mistake.

Another reason for the lack of attention to security may be that many managers think it is purely a technical problem. "It's not," says Bowers. "It's a management issue." Bowers points out that most security problems are caused by people, not equipment. Human error and misuse account for at least half the incidents, including the most expensive ones, he says. These losses usually stem from poor procedures, carelessness, a lack of knowledge by employees, or from a general lack of controls.

He attributes another 20 percent of the losses to design and programming flaws, usually due to poor controls or documentation. Dishonest and disgruntled employees account for another 15 percent .

In short, according to Bowers' figures, at least 85 percent of all security incidents have human causes.

Another reason for the lax attention, Bowers points out, is the attitude "It can't happen to me." Not only can it happen, he says, but there's a 50-50 chance it will happen within the next year.

Other excuses, such as the cost of security, a need to address what are considered to be higher priorities, and a lack of time or money, also contribute to the lag.

"Management usually waits until the 11th hour to look at security," Bowers says. "Sometimes the 11th hour is too late."

WHY YOU NEED SECURITY

Considerations of the need for computer security usually begin with security against the telephone line invader. Unfortunately, they often end there, too. As we've seen from the cast of characters in Chapter 3, computer abusers have a variety of operating methods. As a matter of fact,

the telephone hookup ranks among the lesser risks, particularly when compared with the knowledgeable insider who knows how to tap the till while covering tracks.

Computers are not just electronic warehouses where you can stash information until you need it. They are dynamic facilities that use and process the information in many ways.

A computer can collect much more than the data it receives through the conventional keyboard process. Consider, for example, the bar code readers used at some retail checkout counters. They collect data that is used to retrieve, print, and add the price of each item. It would take only a small extension of this process also to subtract each item from the inventory and to compile data for a profile on how fast each item moves.

A similar application that has potential for security users is the door lock that reads the code on a user's entry card. Not only can this code be used to unlock the door—if it's a proper one, of course—but it can be used to compile a record of who entered the area and when.

In short, you can use a computer to collect information to be used in ways the subject may never suspect. Any such system is wide open to abuse and requires strict control of data collection and used.

Organizing Information

After you've collected the information, the computer makes it possible to apply it in new and inventive ways. Suppose, for example, you had the time and energy to enter the local telephone book into a data base management program. You'd probably set up separate fields for name, address, and telephone number.

Once you had compiled such a listing, you could begin a search based on the name of the party you're trying to reach and retrieve the address, telephone number, or both. That's probably the main reason you would set up such a file, and, many business users do exactly that. They don't type entire phone books, but they do compile computer listings of customers and contacts.

The computerized phone book would have other uses, too. Want to find out the phone number at a certain address? A search of your data base probably could produce it. Should you do such a thing? That's a little less clear. There might be some situations where using such a number would be a borderline ethical practice at best.

Computations

The machine is called a computer, so naturally it computes. It can whip through formulas and calculations at internal working speeds that might as well be instantaneous. The computer is particularly impressive when it takes only an instant or two to whip through a full blackboard-length formula.

This capacity, like all the others, is a source of security problems. For example, a "salami slicer" criminal technique described in the next chapter uses the computer's precise calculating ability to divert fractions of a cent into his own account—adding up hundreds of dollars in the process.

Communication

Data communication is a fast-growing field, with fast-growing opportunities for misuse. Although security leaks from the communication process have so far been lower than popular accounts would suggest, the potential for major losses certainly is there.

Consider, for example, the typical corporation that wants to hook a network of microcomputers to the mainframe so individual users can exchange and process the information in a central file. Any of the wired-in users, plus several outsiders, would then have the means to enter the system and steal or manipulate data.

Security, then, is much more than putting a password or a code scrambler on the telephone line. It requires that you address the full spectrum of computer uses. For every use, there is a possible misuse, and you must be on guard against all of them.

INNOVATION, SECURITY GO TOGETHER

In Lewis Carroll's famous scene, Alice finds it necessary to run ever faster just to stay in the same place. Anyone in business today probably feels much the same way. Today's research and development project is tomorrow's obsolete technology. For this problem, the computer is both cause and solution.

On one hand, computer and communication technology is moving ahead so rapidly a product can be obsolete within a few years. Consider the microcomputer field. No sooner had the 8-bit CP/M configuration been accepted as an unofficial industry standard than IBM came along with with a 16-bit MS-DOS setup that became the new industry standard. Unix or one of its variations may be next.

At the same time, the computer is the means to create much of the innovation that helps us stay ahead of the game. It has sharply reduced the lead time you need to get a product out of the lab and onto the market.

Computer-controlled processes also have helped overcome many productivity and quality control problems that have plagued American industry for the last few decades. It's probably no accident that electronics and agriculture, two fields that have shown major increases in productivity, also are this nation's healthiest export businesses.

Continued innovation is the key to success, and security is a necessary companion to any kind of innovation. It's as simple as this: a new idea is no longer new if someone else is able to steal and use it.

Even the Founding Fathers recognized this basic point when they wrote into the Constitution the foundation of the patent and copyright systems. Authors, inventors, poets—and programmers—are given legal rights to control how their creations are used and to collect the rewards of their work. If this kind of reward is available, the framers reasoned, the creators will continue to create.

Good computer security is just a high-tech extension of this 18th century logic. If you can't protect the programs and processes through which you do your own innovating, the return on your work will drop to zero—and it won't take a sophisticated spreadsheet analysis to make it obvious that innovation is no longer worthwhile. You need security to protect your ideas and keep up with the Red Queen in the wild race not to lose ground.

SECURITY REQUIRED BY LAW

If there's no other reason to establish a sound computer security program, there's always the law. Computers are governed by a large, varied, and growing network of laws and regulations. In its report on computer-based national information systems, the Office of Technology Assessment (OTA) found 14 areas of law and regulation that somehow involve themselves with computerized information.

There actually are many more. OTA cited only the regulations, statutes, and constitutional provisions that have widespread general application. If you're in a regulated industry like banking or insurance, there are many more requirements to be considered. Many demand that you maintain a secure computer system.

Take banking, for example. Your records must be accurate, customers' funds must be kept safe, and confidential information must be protected. All these requirements impose a requirement that you maintain a secure computer system. If the computer doesn't maintain the necessary level of accuracy and security, you can't hope to do it.

In any business, you face not just a single law or policy but a haphazard collection of legal and regulatory requirements. Among OTA's findings:

☐ There appears to be neither a strong trend nor sentiment at present among policy makers in favor of a uniform federal information policy that would encompass all the problems that could arise from the many possible uses of data systems.

☐ There are numerous laws and regulations, some overlapping and some potentially or actually conflicting, that directly and indirectly affect the users of information systems, the consumers of information services and the subjects of personal information data banks.

☐ There is a lack of congressional focus on

information policy as such, and consequently the emerging issues are not being directly addressed.

We Haven't Really Tried

One reason there is no central government policy on information is the First Amendment. It was written to guarantee free, unregulated exchanges of information and ideas. Any government action in this area carries the automatic threat that it could intrude on First Amendment rights.

Another reason is that no one has really tried to set up a central government policy. Various pieces of the computer security question are being studied in increasing detail, but few students have taken an overall view.

In his 1975 book, *Why Information Systems Fail*, Henry Lucas reported on a detailed quantitative study of how information systems affect corporate decision making, and on the problems connected with implementing a system. Other authors, like James Rule and Abby Mowshowitz, have done philosophical and historical analyses of automated information systems and their effects.

Several other authors have concentrated on particular subjects. Privacy has been one of the most thoroughly studied: the National Academy of Sciences; the Department of Health, Education, and Welfare; a Privacy Protection Study Commission; and a series of congressional hearings have dealt with the subject.

What the Rules Require

The laws and policies that do exist tend to focus on the design, use, and operation of information systems. They reflect concerns that the system does what's expected of it, reliably, securely, efficiently, and within the expected time. Fortunately, these tend to be the same kinds of things users worry about. The system designer who meets one set of needs probably will do well with the other at the same time.

These specific, often technical, requirements can have much broader significance. Take, for example, the recent incidents—outside the movie *War*

Games—in which air defense computers have falsely detected apparent missile attacks.

In a 1979 article, computer law expert Susan Nycum, who headed the OTA study committee, listed three hypothetical incidents where computers could be at fault: a midair plane crash caused by a fault in the control system, a subway train switched into the path of another oncoming train, and workers splattered with molten steel.

Two years later, Michael C. Gemignani, dean of science and humanities at Ball State University, suggested that Nycum's disasters weren't all that hypothetical. He listed several real events—including a near-collision of two airplanes, a computer error that closed some nuclear plants, fuel wasted during Skylab's final descent, and a false alarm of nuclear war—which were attributable in some way to computer failures.

All are cases in which the details of computer operations, the main subjects of laws and regulations, can literally have widespread impact. Areas of concern cited by OTA include:

- ☐ The safety and reliability of the air traffic control system.
- ☐ The reliability, security and controlability of military command and control systems, existing and proposed.
- ☐ The security of large-scale electronic funds transfer systems;
- ☐ The reliability, accuracy and responsiveness of the social security information systems.

In each case, notes OTA, we need secure, reliable operation—and face serious consequences if we fail.

Secondary Effects

These are only the primary effects. By increasing the amount of information we collect, and by making it easier to collect, store, and use, the computer can create new areas of conflict.

For example, the automated systems developed to store and spread criminal justice information can help bring arrests and prevent crime. It also spurs

legitimate worries about the individual rights of honest citizens whose names find their way into these systems. The use of electronic mail means speedier communication, and perhaps less privacy for our mail.

If anything, we face more rules in the future that will demand secure, reliable computer systems. Recent issues like the suggestion for a national identification card to help spot illegal aliens, the spread of electronic fund transfer systems, and the drive by some nations for a New World Information Order all present new things to worry about—with the possibility of new laws and regulations to deal with these worries.

TREAT INFORMATION AS AN ASSET

One of the ten "megatrends" identified by best-selling author John Naisbitt is the nation's switch from an economy based on products to an economy based on information. Naisbitt is merely the best-known of many writers who have identified that trend in the last few years.

As early as 1973, sociologist Daniel Bell, offered the theory that we are entering a "post-industrial period" characterized by trends like an emphasis on a service economy instead of on manufacturing, economic growth based on scientific discovery and technical innovation, and information used as a resource and commodity. As long range predictions go, Bell's ideas seem to have held up pretty well over the dozen or so years since he made them. That's particularly true of the last point: Information is now a valuable resource. Why else would someone try to steal it? We are in fact developing an economy in which information is among our most valuable resources.

Bell's other predictions are closely related to the growing value of information. Service industries are indeed growing in importance. Many, such as medicine, law, education, and the government, require large amounts of information. That need has spurred the technical growth, particularly in computers and communication.

At the bottom line, a corporation's greatest assets might not be its plants or its products but the information in its computer banks. It can be as important to protect an item of information as it can be to protect money or property.

To Be Feared?

Some experts worry that the emphasis on information, and on the technology to use and process it, holds a threat of potential danger. One is August Bequai, a Washington, D.C., attorney, who has been working on a book called *High Tech Terror*.

Bequai worries about the rise of an "informational elite," a group of technically oriented people who come to control computers and information channels. He is concerned in particular that these people will not always act with the public interest in mind. People who have had technical educations aren't often well-versed in the ethical and social implications of how they use the technology, Bequai points out.

Others take a more optimistic view. They stress the two points that it is not information technology that creates the problem but the choices that are made on how to use it, and that most problems arise because the new techniques have arisen in a framework of old institutions and attitudes. The postal and banking systems, for example, both are long-established institutions that have suddenly felt the impact of electronic communication and record keeping.

On this basis, Bell (among others) believes that new information technology broadens our choices, and we'll make the selections that fit our social and legal environment. A totalitarian society would design an information system to improve government control of its citizens; the monitoring system of George Orwell's *1984* is a fictional example. A democratic society would find that unacceptable and would press for a system that encourages a free exchange of information.

Bequai fears that it won't be so automatic. The technically minded people who would make up his information elite have been educated with "absolutely no grasp of history," he said. "We don't sensitize them to what white collar crime is or to

the way the political process in this country operates," he told an interviewer from the trade newspaper *Computerworld*.

The Nature of Information

No matter which side is right, information is becoming more important, and it becomes equally more important that we protect it. The industry that provides information services and technology has become a major part of the U.S. economy. More and more people need more and more information so they can function effectively.

In particular, information has become a significant economic commodity, but it has unique characteristics that make it different from the types of commodities to which we are accustomed:

☐ It can be reproduced, quickly and at low cost.

☐ When information is stolen, you are not usually deprived of its use. What you lose instead is the exclusive right to use confidential information.

☐ Information can be transported instantly to nearly anywhere.

☐ Its value is determined by its useful life, sometimes very brief.

☐ Its value does not add up. Two copies of the same information are not normally worth much more than one copy.

These unique characteristics have created many problems in a legal, social, and business system that is not yet truly geared to cope with the new order. Our institutions still are oriented primarily toward the commercial exchange of tangible products and services, not to the use—and misuse—of information.

The Security Challenge

This developing age of information presents whole new challenges to the manager who's concerned with computer security. The problem is much more than a group of teenage tinkerers. It is a major security problem, and it requires a thorough and serious approach.

Recognize that *information is an asset*, as valuable, and as well worth protecting—as any other kind of property. *Assess the threat* to this asset. Determine what kinds of information are vulnerable, to what kinds of threats, and from whom. Finally, choose the right *techniques and technology* to meet the specific threat.

Protecting Your Information Assets

Someday you may scan the annual report of some modern corporation and, under the assets section of the balance sheet, find an entry called "Information." As information becomes more important to the business world, enlightened managers will recognize its value, treat it as an asset, and try to maximize its value.

Information already represents a major investment for many firms. In financial institutions like banks and insurance companies, it is estimated that as much as 25 percent of the payroll is devoted to creating and maintaining just the information that's needed for routine business operations. That doesn't include the money needed to own and operate the information systems themselves. Probably less than 10 percent of the cost falls within the area traditionally identified as data processing.

If you invest so much in your information asset, it makes sense to try to get a maximum return from it. It also makes sense to protect this large and growing asset. The first step is to recognize information as the asset it is.

Traditional economists still resist this idea. They've been trained to think in terms of hard goods and, for the most part, have yet to adapt their thinking to the information age.

Accountants have established standard practices of charging the costs of data processing to various users and activities, but these don't really reflect the true value of the information you're trying to protect. A better system might be to add up these expenses:

☐ The costs of *creating* the information. This is primarily a labor cost, the salaries of the clerks and specialists who do the job.
☐ The costs of *maintaining and updating* it.
☐ The *production costs* you incur to make the information available and useful. These can include the major part of the system cost, plus the costs of printing, communication, and other activities.

Even this method has some conflict with accounting tradition. Labor costs normally have been reported in terms of cost per unit. You can't measure units of information, although some people have tried, and the amount of information doesn't necessarily reflect its value. The traditional allocation process doesn't work well with an uncountable asset like information.

A possible solution lies in the "information center" concept, similar to the idea of a profit or cost center. As manager, you compute the cost of creating, maintaining and reporting your information, then calculate the future return you expect to gain from it. This could be the return you expect from your research and development on a new product, or the costs you expect to save from the new efficiency your knowledge can help you gain.

This is your return on the information investment, a familiar and useful calculation that can give you a sound assessment of how much your information is worth. Its value is pegged to the earnings or savings you expect from it. With this assessment of the information's value, you can treat it as a capital cost, even amortizing it over a time period.

More important from a security standpoint, you can determine the value of what you are trying to protect. This could give you a new appreciation of the value involved. It also is a valuable guide to the amount of effort and expense you wish to devote to a security program.

THE HUMAN FACTOR

Computers don't commit crimes. As with other inanimate objects, the crimes committed by computer actually are committed by people who just happen to use computers for the purpose.

And most of those people work for your company. Sure, the long-distance hackers gained publicity and demonstrated our many weak spots, but the real threat comes from people within your own organization.

In fact, the greatest threat comes from people within your organization who have legitimate access to the computer. Some of these employees may be dishonest, and others may hold grudges. Either way, they can capitalize on their right of access to cause you untold grief, stealing information or fouling up important files.

On some detective show or another you've probably heard the elements of a murder conviction described as "motive, method, and opportunity." A motivated computer criminal who has access to your system certainly has the opportunity to hurt you, and the method will come easily.

The teenagers who invaded government and business computers hit their targets more or less by accident. Finding the password is at most an educated guess. By contrast, the insider knows the password. This type of computer criminal also has a good idea of types of projects, who has been working on what, and where to find the files.

The outsider has to probe for your weak spots. The insider already knows where they are. In this light, some experts feel, the growing numbers of microcomputers hooked up to corporate networks and mainframes don't really offer much additional danger that wasn't there in the first place. Many organizations already are using on-line terminals to gain access to mainframe files, notes Alvin Begun, a University of California systems analyst.

"If you don't have adequate mainframe security under those circumstances," he says, "chances are you won't have it with personal computers either. On the other hand, if you do have adequate security safeguards in a timesharing environment, personal computers probably won't be able to crack them."

By that reasoning, the personal computer won't have much effect on either the motive or—under a good security system—the method and opportunity.

Insiders Take Billions

According to the Research Institute of America, (RIA), computer-related white-collar crime claims a total "take" of about $70 *billion* every year. Of that, up to 75 percent can be attributed to insiders.

Bankers find their institutions particularly vulnerable to computer crime. The traditional picture of an embezzler is an innocent-looking clerk who quietly juggles the figures in a stack of large account books. The damage this old-timer could do was limited by the time it took to find and alter manually all the necessary figures.

Give this character a computer and see what happens. Millions of dollars can be sucked up in a matter of minutes. And it can be hard to detect. The "salami technique," in which a criminal siphons odd fractions of interest payments into a personal account is almost invisible, because every customer gets a correct payment. It's proven popular among embezzlers, perhaps for that very reason.

Security managers who encounter such techniques emphatically don't share the view that linked personal computers pose only a minor threat. They believe that as more people are given the means to commit fraud and other crimes, more will take advantage of the opportunities. They can hardly wait for the nationwide spread of home banking, which will place the potential in every household.

Complacency Doesn't Help

Meanwhile, the threat from inside remains the most serious, in large part because so many managers fail to take it seriously. Donn Parker of SRI International has collected information on more than 1100 cases of computer fraud and feels he has only begun to count. He bases that belief on what has become a familiar experience. Says Parker, "Every security review we have done has revealed a significant number of computer-related losses that have not been reported."

The fear of bad publicity again appears to be a major security problem. Many managers also appear to proceed under the belief that "our people would never steal."

As a result, in the experience of many security professionals, getting top management to take computer crime seriously, much less to do anything about it, is an exercise in frustration.

Help Wanted: Criminal

Many computer crimes begin the day an applicant applies for a job. Employers often screen their applicants inadequately, particularly when they're anxious to boost the staffs of growing high-tech companies. They don't take the time to do something as elementary as checking out their new employees. Ironically, many rely instead on lie detector tests. Questions about the tests' reliability have caused many would-be employees to challenge them. The consequences of a faulty test actually could be much worse for the employer.

Many employers continue to look the other way even after the employees are caught in security violations. Again, the inability to admit that you have a problem gets in the way of a solution.

It doesn't help, that white collar criminals often consider themselves to be honest, dedicated employees. Like the young hackers, they see beating the computer as a challenge to overcome.

Perhaps the ultimate barrier to a solution comes when the crooked employee goes to look for a new job: the employer who's been victimized may write a glowing letter of reference.

Handling the Human Problem

The time to begin dealing with the human aspects of security is before the employee is hired. An employee who will have access to the computer and its contents should be treated as a high-security employee and given the closest possible scrutiny.

Avoid sloppy hiring practices that fail to check out references and credentials and that rely too heavily on fallible tests. The Research Institute of America recommends that you take these steps to identify troublesome employees *before* you hire them:

☐ Make sure your application form provides enough detailed information that you can verify the applicant's statements and investigate items the applicant might try to gloss over.

☐ Check out all the information, including education and previous jobs.

☐ Check out the references. Do it by phone, not by a standard form letter.

☐ If the job will be particularly sensitive, hire an investigator to screen the applicants.

That's only the beginning, of course. Once the employee is on the job, you must make use of a system of internal control to protect yourself from computer crime.

Internal control is a term that enjoys a specific definition within the accounting profession, and it takes in two major kinds of control. *Accounting control* is probably the one you think of first. It concerns the procedures and safeguards needed to make sure your financial records are reliable. You should give yourself reasonable assurance that:

☐ Every transaction is executed in accordance with management's instructions and policies.

☐ Each transaction is properly recorded to permit the preparation of acceptable financial statements and to maintain a system of accountability for assets.

☐ No one should have access to an asset without specific authorization from management.

☐ The assets for which you are accountable are periodically checked against the assets actually in your custody.

Administrative control involves the organizations, procedures, and records you establish. They should be set up so activities proceed according to management's wishes and leave audit trails of accountability as they do so. It also includes most of the personnel controls designed to prevent losses due to the ever-present human factor.

Controlling the human factor involves a full range of security factors, including such basic security precautions as limiting access to sensitive data. You should also consider personnel controls like these:

☐ Provide clear job descriptions.

☐ Separate duties so no one has beginning-to-end control over the entire system. In a mainframe environment, systems analysts, operators, and data entry employees are separate positions, each working with only a part of the system. Control is more difficult in a microcomputer system where one person may take on all these functions.

☐ Enforce minimum-length vacations. This long has been a standard practice in banking. An embezzler usually needs frequent access to the books to keep covering up the thefts. An enforced vacation interrupts the criminal sequence.

☐ Have key employees bonded.

☐ Rotate employees among shifts, computers, or projects.

☐ Maintain logs of who uses programs and data files.

☐ Maintain physical security. Consider establishing areas where even programmers and systems analysts are not allowed to enter.

☐ Maintain a password system that will admit only those who have *current* authority to use the computer.

☐ Collect keys, identification cards, and other security items as soon as a departing employee leaves.

☐ Develop a motivation campaign to make all employees aware of your security needs.

☐ Establish a system of internal auditors, independent of any computer-using department.

SELLING SECURITY TO MANAGEMENT

"Okay," you say, "I'm convinced. We need better security for our computers. But the people upstairs don't see it as clearly as I do. They aren't convinced. How can I sell a security program to executives who don't understand how important it is?"

As security professionals from around the nation have busily been telling us lately, the greatest obstacle to better computer security comes from ranking executives who still don't feel it is necessary. Security is a human problem, and a major part of this problem is in the head office.

Managers who work directly with the computer system usually are well aware of their security needs. They have this in common with most computer criminals: they know the system and are well aware of its weak spots. The problem is to persuade senior managers who don't have this kind of firsthand knowledge.

Security consciousness is a state of mind, and your task is to instill the right attitude among the people whose moral and financial support you need.

A Sales Campaign

To sell anything successfully you need a well-developed sales campaign. That's just as true when you are trying to sell an idea as it is when you're selling a product. The object of this campaign is to make management more security-conscious. Plan your attack around these basic points:

☐ Let management understand the degree of risk the company faces from poor security.

☐ Present your case in terms of the kinds of business risks management already understands.

☐ Make the people who have custody of computerized information responsible for its security.

☐ Conduct a formal risk analysis.

Now let's take them one by one.

The Degree of Risk. Business computers exist in a constantly changing environment, and these changes bring new security risks. Look at the things that probably have happened within your own organization:

- [ ] Increasing numbers of people have microcomputers on their desks.
- [ ] More computing is done by end users and less by specialists in the data processing department.
- [ ] Networks and other forms of computer communication make your data more widely available to more people than ever before.
- [ ] Several applications may share a common data base.
- [ ] Employees (and, in fact, the general public) are becoming more at ease with the use of computers.

Watch Your Language. Your job is to point out these increasing risks to managers who may not fully comprehend the problem. The worst way to accomplish that may be to bury them in computer jargon. Even a chief executive officer can lack computer literacy—and many of them do. You must state your case, then, in language they *do* understand.

For example, instead of simply stating that inadequate security could invite data manipulation, emphasize the consequences of such an act:

- [ ] A reduced bottom line due to improperly used assets or misstated operating results.
- [ ] Management decisions based on incomplete or inaccurate information.
- [ ] Business operations interrupted by lost data or processing capacity.
- [ ] Confidential data open to access by competitors, investors, or employees.
- [ ] Possible legal difficulties involving privacy, corrupt practices, and other laws.

Assigning Responsibility. Make it clear to management that it is important not only to control access to the company's data but to make sure

it remains accurate, complete, and reliable. The best people to handle this task are the individuals and groups that have direct custody of the data.

One reason management may hesitate to accept your security program is a doubt that it will be effective. In the view from the head office, the computer system may look like such a large, interconnected entity it seems almost impossible to police its proper use.

The answer to that concern is to cut the system down to size. Develop and propose a plan that makes individual custodians responsible for protecting the limited amounts of data under their control.

Each custodian should have the authority to read, alter, and use the data. Each also should have the power to insist that other users abide by necessary security controls. The custodians, of course, will be responsible for installing and maintaining these controls. If the proper means are not available, the custodian should have the authority to request the necessary financing or other support.

Analyzing the Risk. A risk analysis is the heart of a security plan, and we will examine its detailed procedures later. A completed analysis also can be part of your sales campaign, because it shows management exactly where you are weak, and to what kinds of threats.

Your analysis might show that microcomputer users who have access to a network system have the ability to steal, modify and destroy valuable information. The analysis will assess the probability of such an event as well as the likely losses should it occur. The likely loss, weighted by the likelihood, then can be compared with the cost of effective security measures in a basic *cost-benefit analysis.*

A *risk assessment* will make such an analysis for every possible risk. The completed assessment should present a detailed picture of the risks you face and the measures that can deal with them effectively. Those are the black-and-white figures that any manager can understand.

You Do Need Support

"You must have the support of top management." That phrase is so common, and so generalized, it almost has become a business cliche. In this case, though, it is absolutely correct. You can't mount an effective security program unless you have top management behind you, with financial moral, and any other kind of support you need. Unless you are fortunate, though, the executive suite could easily be a pocket of ignorance where data security is concerned.

It's not that they're deliberately ignorant. Instead, they're waiting for you to demonstrate the need for security in the hard numbers that are the universal executive's language.

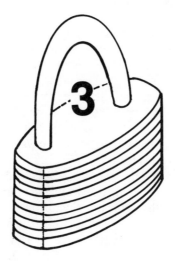

Find Your Weak Spots

A good security program begins with a thorough assessment of the threats you face. Before you can do an effective job of protecting your resources, you must identify the dangers against which you must protect them.

A threat assessment is nothing more than an organized process for finding your weak spots, or your *vulnerabilities* as the experts call them. You must learn three essential things:

☐ The *sources* of potential threats to your system.
☐ The *assets* vulnerable to loss.
☐ The *locations* of these risks.

As with so many other aspects of computer security, the government took an early lead in developing threat analysis techniques. Military users, of course, have been security-conscious about their computers from the time they first began to use them.

On the civilian side, active interest in security has been traced to a 1967 report, *Security and Privacy in Computer Systems*, based on a conference sponsored by the American Federation of Information Processing Societies (AFIPS). At about the same time, government monitoring of Vietnam dissenters raised new questions of personal privacy. To top it off, there was a well-publicized rash of computer crime in the 1970s.

In 1978, the Office of Management and Budget (OMB) published a memo outlining a comprehensive policy for establishing computer security programs in all nondefense federal agencies. Among other security measures, the report outlined a method for conducting a risk analysis. In its 1982 computer security report to the Justice Department, SRI International said this report is still "a well-conceived document worthy of general use."

MATURING AWARENESS

We might as well have the good news first. Your risk assessment should include the assets with which you can try to correct your weak spots, and you may have more of these assets than you think.

As SRI points out, a growing awareness of computer security problems has brought a degree of maturity to the field. SRI looked into the security practices of seven organizations, including an insurance company, two research centers, and several state and local government agencies. It found that practices like these are now "typically used."

General Management Recognition and Support. Top management at all seven sites was interested enough in security to cooperate fully with the SRI project teams. The companies and agencies had established policies that reflected this management concern.

Established Specialists in the Subject. Full-time security researchers and designers in computer science and technology were developing the idea of *trusted computer systems*, significantly more secure than current computers. Many consultants are active in the field. Specific computer security positions have been developed, and new employees are hired specifically for these positions.

Computer Security Officers. Either full- or part-time, have been appointed in the larger organizations. National conferences on computer security and privacy regularly draw 700 to 800 people, most of them security specialists and administrators.

Security Products at Reasonable Prices. Examples include physical access controls for computer centers, password systems, file access control programs, fire safety equipment, cryptographic systems, auditing tools, and uninterruptible power supplies. Sales representatives have become new sources of information and assistance on security practices.

Federal Standard for Cryptographic Protection. The Data Encryption Standard (DES), approved by the National Bureau of Standards, was being used in at least 25 products.

Formal Security Review Programs. Task group reviews of computer centers are becoming more common. OMB now requires that federal agencies conduct risk assessments at their computer centers at least once every three years.

Documented Loss Experience. Conference proceedings, books, and trade journals have published detailed descriptions of computer loss cases, including detailed descriptions of how the losses occurred. Several security consultants now maintain extensive files of reported cases of computer crime and abuse.

New Laws and Regulations. Congress and many state legislatures have considered computer crime laws. Existing statutes, such as privacy and corrupt practices laws, establish a need for controls.

Special Insurance Policies. These now are available to protect you against business interruption, errors, lost data, and criminal acts.

Numerous Books and Articles. These have dealt with computer security problems.

Specialized Auditors. The auditing profession has developed new techniques, and computer specialties, to detect computer abuse.

WHERE TO LOOK

This is a list of what others are doing, and not all these measures apply to you. Still, it does a lot to point out existing practices and principles and is a basis from which to judge your own progress. If an item applies to you, it may at least be worth considering. Considering the threats you face, you need all the assets you can find.

To some extent, the threats you face are yours alone, unique to your organization and operations. An insurance company, for example, would have a significantly different list of security needs than a hard goods manufacturer.

Even diverse users have many things in common, though, and established methods of control can serve the purposes of many kinds of operations. Most computers share at least most elements of a common list of danger sources, vulnerable material and critical locations. Table 3-1 lists the types of threats that are common to most users.

On the other hand you, or your type of business, may face some threats that you do not share with most other computer users. More likely you will be one of a particular *class* of businesses that shares a similar type of security threat. SRI found, for example, that banks, insurance companies, re-

- ■ Potential Threats
  - — Disgruntled or error-prone employees causing physical obstruction and destruction or modification of programs or data.
  - — Natural disaster such as fire, flooding, and loss of power and communications.
  - — Outsiders or employees making unauthorized use of computer services.
  - — Outsiders or employees taking computer programs, data, equipment or supplies.

- ■ Assets Subjects to Loss
  - — Facilities
  - — Systems equipment
  - — People
  - — Computer programs
  - — Data
  - — Data storage media
  - — Supplies
  - — Services
  - — Documents
  - — Records
  - — Public respect and reputation.

Table 3-1. Common Sources of Danger.

- ■ Common Environments at Risk
  - — Computer rooms containing computers and peripheral equipment
  - — Magnetic media (tapes and disks) libraries
  - — Job setup and output distribution stations
  - — Data entry capabilities
  - — Program Libraries
  - — Program development offices
  - — Utility rooms
  - — Reception areas
  - — Communications switching panels
  - — Fire detection and suppression equipment
  - — Backup storage
  - — Logs, records, journals.

search institutes, and criminal justice operations share a particular set of security problems. Table 3-2 lists examples of applications and associated risks that aren't common to all computer centers, but that might be present in yours.

Then there's the story of the company that built its computer center over a burning underground coal mine. Your center might lie just beneath an airport glide path. You might contract your computer work to prison inmates. You might be vulnerable to mice who chew critical cables. Or, your risk might be slightly less exotic. You have chosen to be an early user of a new and developing type of technology.

The best security precaution against risks like these is to avoid the situation in the first place. If you're already there, though, this isn't the time to second-guess the decisions that put you there. Instead, your review should acknowledge that you face a truly unique risk that may call for a truly unique solution.

Zero-Base Analysis

Risk assessments and security audits have much in common. They're often confused, and the differences may not always be very significant. There are some differences, though.

- ■ Processing and storage of personal data.
  - — Intentional or accidental disclosure, modification, destruction or use of personal data or records of their use.
  - — Violation of confidentiality rules, personal data regulations, or privacy laws.

- ■ Processing and storage of secret data (e.g., investigative, intelligence, trade secret, marketing, competitive).
  - — Intentional or accidental disclosure, modification, destruction, or use of trade secret or sensitive data or records.
  - — Violation of rules, regulations, or laws.

- ■ Processing and storage of financial data (e.g., account balances, negotiable instruments input/output, general ledger, accounts payable/receivable, payroll).
  - — Financial fraud or theft.
  - — Accidental financial loss such as lost interest.
  - — Failure to meet financial report filing dates and other fiduciary obligations.

- ■ Process control (e.g., controlling manufacturing processes, transportation, meal processing, inventory control, patient monitoring).
  - — Intentional or accidental modification, failure, or destruction of processes.

Table 3-2. Risks Found in Some Circumstances.

A security audit is much like a financial audit. It involves a review by, or at least for, owners and senior managers. Its purpose is to spot problems and shortcomings in an existing security systems, particularly failures that could create violations of laws, regulations, or policies.

A risk assessment is more a planning tool for a new or improved system. Its purpose is to identify threats, the assets in danger, and the places where controls are needed. Where the audit evaluates an existing system, the risk assessment takes a *zero-base* approach. It assumes that there is no security system in place now, or if there is, it's inadequate. It then identifies the weak spots as the first step in providing useful controls.

Table 3-3 is a review sequence recommended in the SRI report. As its authors point out, however, hardly anyone goes through such a detailed sequence of specified actions.

Most likely, you'll want to combine, overlap or even skip some of these steps. A common variation makes use of the computer you're trying to pro-

tect, going through a more detailed quantitative analysis than is called for in Step 6.

Study the list, because it can give you more insight into what the full assessment process should include. If you then decide to put some variations in your own procedure, you'll be working from knowledge instead of ignorance. Like old age, this system is better than the alternative of conducting no formal review at all, or to do so without understanding the full spectrum of possible security needs. A limited analysis leads inevitably to a limited response. A thorough study that explores every possible weak spot may turn up problems you wouldn't otherwise have solved for the simple reason you didn't know about them. Many companies that embark on full risk assessments find that they identify several serious problems early in the process. They are able to correct these shortcomings even before the review is completed.

Is All This Necessary?

When SRI visited its seven computer users—

and keep in mind, this was a few years ago—it asked the managers to describe the organization and methods they used to go through the entire process of developing a security system, including selecting, justifying, and in installing their systems. Not one of the surveyed organizations used a formal cost-benefit or risk analysis to help determine its security needs. A typical reaction from management was that these are "textbook" procedures: they work better in theory than in practice. They are too elaborate, the managers felt, and they were not cost-effective.

Another problem with quantitative techniques was a lack of valid data. Instead, the managers used informal and subjective techniques for assessing the pros and cons of particular security controls.

That's not to say the managers were careless or haphazard. Most described their techniques in terms like "prudence" or "common sense." Many said they looked at the practices of other organizations whose circumstances were similar to their own. SRI distilled their basic considerations to this key question: *Would a different manager in my place install and operate the same controls?* The factors they considered in answering this question included:

☐ Whether the controls were in use by other organizations with similar applications and equipment.
☐ Reported loss experiences.
☐ Whether they felt unique factors in their own organizations justified departures from the practices of similar groups.
☐ How much added security a measure could achieve.
☐ The laws and regulations they must observe.

Other Factors

Other, less distinct, factors also influenced the managers' decisions. In some cases, existing policies, procedures, or ethical standards were seen as useful substitutes for specific computer security techniques.

Outside parties also often influenced the managers. Some measures, for example, were taken with an eye to satisfy client needs. In that case, the requirements of the clients' organizations became the requirements of the surveyed firms. The users also often were influenced by the expected demands of auditors.

To the researchers' apparent surprise, the managers who responded so readily to outside influences and to the practices of similar firms did

Table 3-3. A Commonly Recommended Review Method.

The usual method of security review often described in the literature and in seminars includes combinations and various orderings of the following steps:

(1) Organize a task group to conduct the review; establish plans, assignments, schedules, budgets, and scope; obtain management approval and support of the plan.
(2) Identify the assets subject to loss; either determine their value, consequences of loss, and replacement value or rank their importance.
(3) Identify potential threats to the identified assets.
(4) Identify the controls in place or lack of controls that mitigate or facilitate the potential threats to the assets.
(5) Combine associated potential threats, assets subject to loss, and lack of mitigating controls; each triple of items constitutes a vulnerability.
(6) Evaluate and rank of vulnerabilities in terms of greatest to least expected potential loss; alternatively quantify risk for all or only the major vulnerabilities in terms of annual frequency of loss and single case loss in dollars to obtain annualized loss exposure.
(7) Identify actions and controls that would reduce the risks of losses to acceptably low levels.
(8) Recommend an implementation plan to reduce risk to an overall acceptably low level.
(9) Carry out the plan and establish ongoing security maintenance and improvements.

not actively seek out information about what is being done elsewhere. It came to them. Although the information that came their way often was useful, they didn't seem to feel it would be cost-effective to seek it out, at least for lower-cost items.

The managers invested in more research when they considered very expensive items like vaults and electronic lock systems. They would set priority lists and look for the most cost-effective choices within the field.

Still, SRI points out, these managers looked at their security systems almost exclusively in terms of cost. The managers seldom fully balanced costs against expected savings.

A BASELINE APPROACH TO PLANNING

In a true textbook case, you would make a detailed analysis of every vulnerable spot in your system, including a cost-benefit balancing of the losses you might face, versus the cost of guarding against them.

As SRI learned in its seven-company survey, real-world managers don't always follow the textbook. They're unwilling or unable to follow this detailed process of evaluation for every possible security risk and precaution. Many feel the evaluation process itself is not cost-effective, and it may not be necessary.

The SRI report also points out that all computer users have many security problems in common. Name the problem your assessment has uncovered. You probably share it with many other people. On that basis, SRI has developed what it calls a *baseline system* of security planning. It starts with the idea that many controls are so universal and have such proven value you should not have to justify their use in your own organization.

The only time you need go through the full process of analysis and justification is if you decide *not* to use one of these widely accepted controls. For example, you would be required to document a decision that a particular risk is too small, and its solution too expensive, to be used in your organization.

Three-Level System

The baseline controls represent the first of

three levels in the evaluation system. In theory, the need for baseline controls is so obvious you need not worry about formally identifying the weak spots, risks, or other factors. They are chosen simply on the basis of their wide acceptance and general effectiveness. Examples include:

- ☐ A secure area to house central computer facilities.
- ☐ A procedure to control physical access to computers.
- ☐ A way to maintain secure backup copies of programs and files.
- ☐ Logs and journals of computer use and performance.
- ☐ Built-in controls to prevent errors in processing.
- ☐ Fire detection and control equipment.

Baseline controls are also designed to meet common security *objectives*. These, too, are the goals nearly everyone shares, such as preventing unauthorized access, detecting improper use of the system, and avoiding violations of laws and regulations.

Selective Controls

A second level is made up of *selective controls*. Here, your objective might not be universally shared, but if you decide to pursue that goal, there is an established and effective way to achieve it.

This analysis need take you only far enough to determine that you should pursue the goal in question and that there is one obvious method for reaching it. Once you've accepted the goal, you can treat the established method as a baseline control. You need not take your analysis any further unless you decide *not* to follow conventional wisdom.

Special Controls

This is the third category, composed of needs and methods that truly are unique to your operation. You have the special need, and it demands a unique solution. Here—but only here—must you go through the full process of assessing your risks and justifying solutions.

The baseline approach, then, cuts things down to size and makes the analysis process itself easier and more cost-effective.

To use a cliche, it is not cost-effective to reinvent the wheel. The baseline approach suits the attitudes and practices of managers who do not feel it is worthwhile to make a full analysis of every possible security need, and who take many of their cues from successful methods used elsewhere.

This system is organized so you need go through the full procedure only if you decide to depart from the conventional way of doing things. If you have a common goal, or a well-established way to meet a unique goal of your own, you can accept and make use of what has been done before.

The idea that baseline controls are common to the computer security field does not mean that there is a fixed, standard list of such controls. The accepted procedures that make up baseline controls will change as the security field matures.

When SRI published its study in 1981, it was concerned primarily with access to mainframe computers. Now that personal computers have made significant inroads into the security picture, a pattern of standard control methods is being developed for them. As these are accepted, and as they fit your needs, they can be added to your list of baseline controls.

Other types of controls may become generally accepted through a process of increasing exception-taking. If enough people find ways to justify exceptions from standard lists, the exceptions will themselves become the standards.

There also is disagreement among various organizations, perhaps even within your organization, about which goals and methods should be included in a baseline system. It's also quite likely you will decide to use variations on standard techniques, tailoring them to your own needs.

The baseline system, then, depends on a uniform list of well-accepted goals and techniques. Yet there is no uniform list of well-accepted goals and techniques. There seems to be a bit of an inconsistency here.

The solution is to write your own list. Start from the common security controls later in this book. Pick those that fit your situation. Add the ideas you pick up from other publications and in your professional contacts. Stay alert for new developments in the field. With a little information and good judgment you probably can establish a valid baseline system for your own use.

ESTABLISHING YOUR BASELINES

Consider, for example, the baseline controls you might want to establish for a single, universal type of objective: controlling access to a computer room. There are many ways to meet that goal; some of them are listed in Table 3-4. This is a useful list of proven techniques, but it has two problems: there is the temptation to use it as a checklist instead of a planning guide. Do not just go down the list and verify that every item is in place.

Also, it tells you nothing about how well these individual controls would work *together*. A security system is just that—a system—not a collection of individual good ideas.

For example, items 1, 2, 6, 7, 9, and 13 are valid security techniques, but none of these would do the job by itself. Instead, they are intended to be integrated into an overall system. The last five items probably are necessary, but the value of other controls will depend on such things as traffic, the degree of risk, the level of security you want to maintain within the room, and the level of security in the area from which you are controlling access.

This list can be refined. In the process, you may cut it in half. The first version was a list of measures that might be used. The second, Table 3-5, zeros in on controls that are generally used in well-run computer centers.

This list develops the original checklist into a system of seven controls, less than half the size of the original but with more detail.

You'll have to add even more detail to fit these controls into your own system. Several, for example, call on you to specify who is responsible for access control or how often to test and audit the system. Before you can implement this plan, you also must add details such as construction specifications for the walls and windows—perhaps a

(1) Sign-in/out log
(2) Procedure to challenge the presence of a person
(3) Mechanically locked doors
(4) Electronically locked doors
(5) Guards at doors
(6) Badge-access areas
(7) Closed-circuit television (CCTV) monitoring of doors and areas
(8) Man-trap or turnstile doors (a pass-through isolation booth)
(9) Microprocessors for access monitoring
(10) Automatic physiological identification varification for access (e.g., geometry, fingerprint scanning, voice pattern analysis, signature dynamics analysis)
(11) Frequent test and audit of access controls
(12) Contingency plan for failure of access controls
(13) Policy and procedure documents for access control
(14) Administration of access controls
(15) Physical barriers (sturdy walls, windows, and doors).

Table 3-4. Common Methods of Access Control.

specification of high-impact glass. With these variations you can develop a baseline that not only represents a consensus in the field but also is adapted to your specific needs.

The process of establishing your baseline controls should go something like Table 3-6. You need not do all these steps in a single study by one individual or group. That probably is the best way to do it if you can, but it's not always practical. You can split up the job, both among people and groups and over different time periods.

For example, as a first priority you might assign one group to develop the baseline controls. Later, separate groups can work on the selective and special controls. You might also find yourself implementing special controls as new problems arise.

Because those new problems do arise, you should plan to repeat this process periodically. At the very least, keep a running record of your security activities and incidents. Computers are part of a fast-changing field, and it's important that the security system keep up with the changes.

WHO THREATENS YOUR SYSTEM?

The major threat to the integrity of your system does not come from teenage pranksters, unscrupulous competitors, or any other outside source. It comes from inside your organization, from disgruntled, disloyal, or dishonest employees who have both the means and the ability to cause you harm.

To assess your risks adequately, you must

Table 3-5. Refined List of Access Controls.

(1) Physical barrier access control (strong walls, windows and doors, access mechanism)
(2) Administration of access control (responsibility assigned to somebody accountable, recordkeeping, authorization activity)
(3) Frequent testing and audit (frequency specified)
(4) Contingency plan for failure of access control
(5) Policy and procedure documentation
(6) Identification and authentication of authorized accessors
(7) Constraints on unauthorized accessors

Table 3-6. Steps to a Baseline.

(1) Determine the scope of the review by identifying in gross form the facilities, people, equipment, supplies, computer programs, production processes, sources and destinations of data, and data files, and where stored and processed. Documentation must be collected, and supportive functions such as audit, safety, security, personnel, insurance and computer user departments must be identified. Potential threats need not be identified at this stage.

(2) Identify and document all existing controls and catalog them according to their purpose (control objectives). Include complete descriptions of all control variants.

(3) List additional control objectives, controls and control variants from current data security literature and from ideas collected from security review staff, managers, auditors, past audit reports and past security reviews. Catalog controls according to the control objectives and order the objectives from Step 2.

(4) Visit several other computer centers that are judged to have characteristics similar to yours and have effective data security. The number will depend on review resources available and opportunities. Visits should be arranged by an exchange of letter agreements assuring confidentiality and benefits for all parties from mutual exchange of information. In these visits identify the best controls, how they were justified, the cost-effectiveness, and the experience with them. Also identify controls that were rejected or that are not particularly effective and reasons for this.

(5) Synthesize information collected in Steps 1 through 4 into a baseline representative of control objectives, controls, and selected variants where no justification for their selection is to be developed other than citing general use. Also develop a selective baseline similarly where identification of purpose is needed to supplement information concerning limited use by other organizations. Categorize all controls and variants in both baselines according to whether they are currently installed, would cause a change to currently installed controls, are new controls, or are new controls that are not to be recommended (along with explanations).

(6) Perform potential threat, vulnerability, and risk analysis using current methods documented in the literature for those assets that would not be adequately (by consensus) protected by the baseline and selective baseline. There should be relatively few assets or issues remaining to be treated in this way. Reasons include new technology in use, unusual conditions, and possibly issues resulting from lack of concurrence on a baseline control or variant or where high cost of possible controls requires further justification.

(7) Make recommendations to management in three categories:
    A. Baseline controls where no justification other than general use is provided.
    B. Selective baseline controls where justification extends to a statement of purpose.
    C. Special controls where full and detailed justification is provided.

In addition, recommendations can be organized according to priorities for implementations: immediate, soon, future, and when other conditions make them appropriate.

---

know from whom they are likely to come. There are four basic classes of potential computer abusers:

☐ People who have physical access and the abilities to perform physical acts of theft or damage.

☐ People who have access and know-how to operate the equipment.

☐ Programmers who have access.

☐ People who have access and electronic engineering abilities.

There is an obvious common denominator: access to the system. It stands to reason that even the most talented computer criminal needs access of some kind. Except for physical access, that access need not be direct. Unprotected telephone lines make up the interstate highway system of computer abuse.

This suggests that the job of identifying potential abusers should start with identifying those who have access to the computer. You then can look for those who have the ability to make improper use of the computer once they get into it.

Table 3-7, based on an analysis prepared for the Justice Department, indicates the kinds of losses you might face from people in various occupations. The numbers from 1 to 5 indicate how much information someone in this position might be able to steal or damage. A rating of 5 indicates this person could get to virtually everything in your computer. A blank entry indicates the individual could affect virtually none of it. An entry of 3 indicates the person could affect up to 60 percent of

Table 3-7. Vulnerability by Occupation.

Acts
M—Modification   T—Talking
DE—Destruction   DN—Denial of use
DI—Disclosure

Vulnerabilities (Physical, Operational, Programmable, Electronic)	Occupations	Internal Data			Internal Application Programs		
		M	DE	DI	M	DE	DI
	Tape librarian						
	User tape librarian						
	User trans. & data entry operator	2	2	2		1	1
	Computer operator	1	5	5		5	5
	Peripheral equipment operator						
	Job set-up Clerk						
	Data entry & update clerk	3	3	3		4	4
	Facilities engineer						
	Operations manager	1	5	5		5	5
	Data base administrator	3	3	3			
	System programmer		5	5		5	5
	Applications programmer	1	1	1	2	2	2
	User programmer	1	1	1	2	2	2
	Programming manager	1	1	1	4	4	4
	Communication Engineer/Operator		5	5			
	Terminal Engineer						
	Computer system engineer						
	Security officer	5	5	5	5	5	5
	EDP auditor	5	5	5	5	5	5

Column header note: **Vulnerable Assets by Acts**

your information assets. The other numbers are scaled accordingly.

The table also shows the types of acts to which you are vulnerable in each case and the areas—physical, operating, programming, and electronic—in which you are vulnerable. These estimates assume that you have taken the normal baseline precautions and that they work about as well for you as they do for everyone else.

Application and user programmers are assigned relatively low scores in relation to their ability, because it's assumed your normal precautions would limit their access to the system. They shouldn't have access to current work being done in their system, and their work should be screened for possible security defects before it is fed into the computer.

One thing that is not considered is a combination of skills. An individual who has more than one ability has more than one way to damage your system. The same is true when two or more individuals with differing skills get together to attack your system. Using these figures, it's possible to rank occupations according to the degree of risk they present, as in Table 3-8.

Identifying the Suspects

This doesn't mean everyone in these occupations, or even most of them, are out to cause you damage. It merely indicates the types of people who have the greatest opportunity. They represent the greatest risks to be considered in your security evaluation. Studies of computer crime indicate the

Explosure Scale

blank	no effect
1	up to 20%
2	up to 40%
3	up to 60%
4	up to 80%
5	up to 100 %

Internal System Programs			External Data			External System Programs						Computer Equipment & Supplies			System Service	
M	DE	DI	M	DE	DI	M	DE	DI	M	DE	DI	M	DE	T	T	DN
				4	4		3	3		3	3		1	1		
				2	2		1	1					1	1		
			2	2	2		1	1					1	1		
	5	5	1	3	3								5	5	5	5
				3	3		4	4		1	1		2	2		
							4	4					1	1	5	
	5	5	3	3	3		4	4		1	5		1	1		
												1	5	5		5
	5	5	1	3	3		4	4		1	5		5	5	5	5
			3	3	3								1	1		
5	5	5							5	1	5		1	1	5	5
						2	2	2					1	1		
						2	2	2					1	1		
						4	4	4					1	1		
												2	2	2		
												1	1	1		
2	2	2										5	5	5		
5	5	5	3	3	3	4	4	4	5	5	5	5	5	5	5	5
5	5	5	5	5	5	5	5	5	5	5	5	5	5	5	5	5

typical computer criminal may also have the characteristics listed below.

Computer Criminals Tend to be Young. In one study of a group of computer abusers, the ages ranged from 18 to 46, with a median of 25. It's not quite certain why. The sponsors of this study suggest it's because the younger employees are recent graduates of colleges and universities where attacking campus computer systems is not only condoned but often encouraged. That may be an example of world-class conclusion-jumping. More plausible: The younger workers have not yet acquired a fully developed sense of professional responsibility. An effort on your part to help newcomers develop such an attitude could pay off in better security.

They are Among Your Best and Brightest Employees. These highly motivated people often find themselves overqualified for the routine type of work they often are called upon to do. This may help explain the rate of abuse among young workers, because they often come with great expectations to the most routine jobs you have to offer. Maintaining a good level of motivation and professional challenge, then, can also help avoid security problems.

They Often are in Positions of Trust. Most computer criminals do their damage during the course of their normal working routines, using systems with which they are intimately familiar. Any security plan should carefully monitor the activities of these people through close supervision and effective auditing. Table 3-9 lists the criminals and their victims in recent computer abuse cases.

Table 3-8. Risk Levels of Occupations.

Greatest risk
  EDP auditor
  Security officer
Great risk
  Computer operator
  Data entry and update clerk
  Operations manager
  Systems programmer
Moderate risk
  Computer system engineer
  Programming manager
Limited risk
  Application programmer
  Communication engineer/operator
  Data base administrator
  Facilities engineer
  Peripheral equipment operator
  Tape librarian
  User programmer
  User transaction and data entry operator
Low risk
  Terminal engineer
  User tape librarian

(Occupations in Alphabetical Order Within Risk Level)

Table 3-9. Relationship of Occupations to Victims.

Perpetrators Occupations	Victims
Teller	Large bank
Accountant	Computer service
Company owner	Small manufacturing company
Time-sharing user	Time-sharing computer system
Business programmer	Small bank
Systems programmer	State, government agency
Computer operations and systems manager	Financial institutions
President of a firm	Electronics supply company
Business manager	Large manufacturer
Sales manager	Large retail service organization

They Often Have Help. In about half of all computer crime cases, the criminal conspires with some other party. Sometimes the crime requires more skill and access than any individual holds. Other cases involve an employee working on the "inside" in partnership with an outside party.

Computer abusers also often have certain attitudes in common. One problem stems from a phenomenon called *differential association,* or the willingness to accept small deviations from normally accepted standards. The small variations can escalate into major crimes. For example, a service bureau was victimized by programmers from a competing firm who started by playing games on the bureau's computer, moved up to checking the bureau's customer lists, and eventually stole a complete program.

Then there's the *Robin Hood syndrome.* Among computer criminals interviewed by researchers, most expressed the moral view that it is wrong to harm an individual but all right to victimize a large organization. One embezzler, for example, was careful never to take more than $20,000 from any one account, the limit of federal deposit insurance at the time.

Game playing is another common characteristic. Many computer abusers are attracted by the challenge of trying to beat your security system. They also tend to believe that there's nothing wrong with using an idle computer for nonofficial purposes. Taken to an extreme, this idea leads to an elitist syndrome: The criminals believe their expertise uniquely entitles them to play with the computer.

Search For Antagonism

It often takes more than one person to commit a computer crime, but investigators have found there are some classes of people who make unlikely collaborators because they do not work well together.

Table 3-10 shows the types of complaints people in jobs listed across the top row are likely to have against people listed down the side. It shows the types of problems these groups are likely to have with each other. If you consider the table for a while, you also should be able to see areas where

Table 3-10. Potential Antagonistic Relationships.

From → To	Operators	Programmers	Media Librarians	Data Entry Clerks	Source Data Preparers	Users	Vendors' Maint. Engineers
Operators	Complaints	Job failures, failure to report errors.	Unrecorded removals and submissions			Job failures Failure to report errors.	Misuse of equipment Failure to report errors
Programmers	Poor program design. Misleading or absent instructions.		Misleading or absent instructions.	Poor input formats. Poor instructions.	Poor input formats. Poor instructions.	Lack of problem understanding Poor documentation.	Programs Improper use of equipment
Media Librarians	Slow or incorrect media selection.	Loss of media incorrect labelling.				Loss of media	Poor handling of media
Data Entry Clerk	Data errors causing reruns	Data errors unanticipated in program design Program entry errors	Loss of media assigned to them			Data entry errors causing erroneous output	Misuse of equipment
Source Data Preparers	Data errors causing reruns	Data errors and out of range data not anticipated in program design		Poor legibility on data forms		Data errors causing reruns and incorrect output	
Users	Inconvenient run schedule demands Poor job instructions	Unclear or absent problem specifications. Inconvenient program change demands	Misleading or absent instructions	Inconvenient work schedule demands	Poor instructions. Inconvenient work schedule demands		
Vendors	Inconvenient equipment maintenance schedule Equipment failures	Equipment failures		Inconvenient equipment maintenance schedule Equipment failures			

people in some specialties *depend* on those in other jobs—prime candidates for collaboration.

The fact that one or more persons have the characteristics listed in this section does not mean they should be regarded as prime suspects in a computer crime case.

Use these factors instead as points to consider in your analysis and in the resulting security plan. These are the points where human characteristics make you vulnerable and where you should consider controls to reduce your weaknesses.

WHERE ARE THE WEAK SPOTS?

Along with knowing who poses a danger to your computer system's integrity, you must know where they might strike. Every system has two sets of weak spots. They are found among various *functions* of the system and at an equal variety of physical *locations*.

Functional Weaknesses

An analysis of computer abuse cases for the Justice Department produced a list of eight functions (Table 3-11) where data processing systems tend to be most vulnerable. They are:

Poor Controls over Manual Handling of Input and Output Data. This is by far the single most vulnerable spot. It shows that your data assets are most seriously exposed before they are put into the computer or after they are retrieved. This is when the information is most accessible, and the criminal needs little computer expertise to obtain it.

The message here: extend your security program beyond the boundaries of the computer. Protect valuable data in whatever form it appears —paper and punch cards, as well as disks, tapes, and in the computer's memory.

Weak Physical Controls. Sometimes none at all. This is an invitation to crime, and the criminal won't necessarily give you the courtesy of an RSVP. Even a motivated criminal can be stopped and deterred by an effective physical security system.

Of course, any security system has its limits. The Justice survey found four cases in which attackers had used firearms. Three of these incidents were political disputes; the fourth was committed by a frustrated employee.

Inadequate Operating Procedures at Computers and Terminals. A knowledgeable criminal who gains full access through a keyboard is in position to do a lot of damage. Countermeasures against this type of activity include separating staff duties, establishing dual control over sensitive functions, setting up a system of staff accountability, a security information program, and carefully written operating instructions. Backup

Table 3-11. Functions Vulnerable to Computer Abuse.

Vulnerable Functions	Number of Cases	Percentage of Cases
Manual handling of input/ output data	147	41
Physical access to EDP facilities	46	13
Operations procedures	43	12
Business practices	41	11
Computer programs usage	33	9
Operating systems access and integrity	24	6
Time-sharing service usage	19	5
Magnetic tape storage	9	3
Total	362	100

systems and disaster plans can help limit the losses.

Weak Business Ethics. Sometimes the computer criminal is not an individual but an entire company. Many of the cases documented for the Justice Department have involved things like fraud, intimidation, theft, and industrial espionage, carried out in response to management's business decisions. At times, management may encourage this behavior; in other cases, lower-ranking employees go overboard to extremes their superiors didn't anticipate. Either way, a firm policy, enforced from the top, should be to discourage computer abuse no matter at whom it is directed. Compete—but do it fairly.

Poor Program Controls. Poorly written programs often include points of entry that criminals can exploit. We'll see examples of these "trapdoors" when we discuss the methods computer criminals use. In other cases, criminals have used the programs themselves as entry tools. This usually happens because the program lacks one of several vital controls: labeling programs to indicate ownership, formal development methods that include testing and quality control, separating the responsibility for parts of sensitive programs, making programmers accountable for their work, and safe storage of programs and documentation. Regular audits should compare operating programs with the master copies.

Operating System Weaknesses. This has been a particular problem for timesharing services. The criminals take advantage of design weaknesses and bugs in the operating systems to get past the access controls. They'll often search for bugs or for shortcuts put in by the programmers.

Impersonation. This is the hacker's field, getting past access control systems by pretending to be an authorized user. The main cause of failure here has been failing to protect password lists or leaving them open to educated guesswork. The movie *War Games* depicted one common failing: a password visibly connected with its creator. (The young computer user correctly guessed that it would be the name of the programmer's deceased young son.)

Inadequate Controls Over Media. The survey, which concentrated on mainframes, reported several cases in which the criminals gained access to magnetic cases. Improperly stored microcomputer disks pose an even greater invitation to abuse.

Physical Locations

The functions that are vulnerable to computer abuse are related, of course, to the physical locations where you will find the weak spots (Table 3-12). The most vulnerable locations according to the survey, are listed below.

Data and Report Preparation Areas. These locations correspond to the preinput and postoutput functions as major criminal targets. Areas include data conversion, job setup, output control, and distribution and transportation. Not included in this group are the input and output areas connected with on-line remote terminals.

Computer Operation Centers. These targets include all the locations that house operating computers or peripheral equipment.

Areas With no EDP Functions. Computer crime often takes places in areas such as management, sales, and business offices.

On-Line Systems. The spread of personal computer networks will probably increase your security problems here.

Programming Offices. Areas where programmers create and store their work are vulnerable.

Data and Output Handling Areas for On-Line Terminals. These are counterparts to the similar areas for direct computer operations. Again, expect some growth due to micros.

Media Storage Facilities. This is yet another area where personal computers can create problems. The greater the number of computers, the greater number of locations where disks and other media must be protected.

On-Line Terminal Operation Areas. Again, the ranks of on-line terminals is being swelled by network-connected personal computers.

Central Processing Units. Little damage

Table 3-12. Locations Vulnerable to Computer Abuse.

Vunerable Functional Locations	Number of Cases	Percentage of Cases	Total	
			Number of Cases	Percentage of Cases
Data and report preparation	120	33		
Terminal areas	14	4	134	37
Computer operations	95	26		
Terminal areas	10	3	105	29
Non-EDP	44	13	44	33
Computer systems	7	2		
Terminal systems	33	9	40	11
Programming	27	7	27	7
Magnetic tape storage	12	3	12	3
Total	362		362	100

actually takes place here. Usually it is physical sabotage or manipulation of the operating system.

Preventing Accidents

In spite of their many labor-saving advantages, computers still involve a great many people, many of whom are doing precise, detailed types of work. Mistakes will happen in this kind of atmosphere. Most data processing managers know this, and it presents two kinds of problems.

First, it can be hard to tell the difference between an accidental loss and an intentional one. In fact, some abusers have closed what little gap there is, finding errors in their favor and taking advantage of them instead of reporting or correcting the mistakes.

The real problem here, though, is that when something goes wrong you tend first to suspect that it's a hardware problem or a "bug" in the program. This is a convenient reaction because it often lets you blame a vendor, an outside programmer, or an inanimate piece of equipment. Only after you have eliminated these possible outside causes do you take a look inside your own operation and open yourself to the possibility that the loss was intentional. Many computer abusers thrive on their superiors' unwillingness to face facts.

The second problem is that, unlike security precautions, the computer industry has been working almost from the beginning to prevent and correct errors. Most programs try to anticipate the mistakes their human users will make and have error-trapping routines to keep the error from causing damage.

It's natural to believe, then, that the many precautions you have established against errors will also protect you against intentional acts that have the same effect. They won't.

Remember, your opponent probably is a knowledgeable person who knows these error-trapping techniques at least as well as you do. That means they'll be evaded early, easily, and often. The security controls you implement must be specifically suited to their purpose: protecting your system from intentional acts.

Using Natural Forces

Among the major area of vulnerability is the proverbial act of God. We'll deal with natural disasters later in the chapter on disaster planning. Meanwhile, though, it's important to watch out for the intentional act that appears to be a natural disaster. Just as some criminals will take advantage of an error or disguise their activities to look like a mistake, others will create or capitalize on what seem to be natural disasters (Table 3-13).

For example, in the 1960s, magnetic fields were identified as major sources of danger to data stored on tapes and disks. Sure enough, in 1962 a disgruntled employee in a New York office tried to sabotage a tape reel by holding a magnet next to it. There was no significant damage, but only because the magnet had not been large enough or close enough. One way the employee might have succeeded would have been to use a bulk tape eraser, which obviously does have the power to do that job. Keep these in secure storage.

Radio and x-ray signals could have similar effects, but again they must be strong and close. This alone may help alert you to the difference between deliberate and accidental damage.

If the apparent natural force is strong and close enough to do real damage, but only to an isolated area, it's time to start looking for human, not natural, causes.

TYPES OF COMPUTER CRIME

One reason your system has so many potential weak spots is that computer criminals have developed a wide variety of techniques. Below are some of the recognized ways in which modern computer criminals work.

Data Diddling

This is one of the simplest, safest, and most common ways to commit a crime by computer. It's a simple matter of altering the data in a computer, and it can be done at nearly any time: while the data is being entered, while it is stored, and when it is retrieved. An example: a timekeeping clerk was responsible for filling out the work-hours records of about 300 railroad employees. He noticed that each data entry included both the employee's name and number, but when the computer processed the payroll it referred only to the number. It even used the number to look up the employee's name and address. Meanwhile, outside the computer hardly anyone used the numbers. All the manual processing of payroll records was done by name.

It would be gratifying to report that this employee notified the railroad of an opportunity for fraud in the payroll system, but he didn't. Instead, he took advantage of the system to give himself some "overtime." He would prepare overtime entries for the computer, using the names of employees who frequently worked extra hours, but putting his own employee number on the form. The computer then would issue him a check for the extra time. It was several years before an auditor

Table 3-13. Dangers Due to Natural Forces.

Extreme temperature		
Hot weather	Cold weather	Fire
Gas		
War gases	Commercial vapors	Humid air
Steam	Wind	Tornado
Explosion	Smoke	Dust
Liquids		
Water	Rain	Flood
Ice	Snow	Sleet
Hail	Chemical solvents	Fuels
Projectiles		
Bullets	Shrapnel	Powered missiles
Thrown objects	Meteorites	Vehicles
Earth movements		
Collapse	Slides	Flows
Liquefaction	Shaking	Waves
Cracking	Separation	Shearing
Electromagnetic discharges		
Electric surge	Electric blackout	Static electricity
Microwaves	Magnetism	Laser
Atomic radiation	Cosmic waves	

thought to ask about the unusually high figures on the clerk's W-2 forms.

Here was a crime that cost the company thousands of dollars, committed by a clerk who actually had little inside knowledge of the computer. He just took advantage of a loophole in the administrative system.

A simple solution to this problem would have been to combine the names and numbers, perhaps adding the first three letters of the employee's name to the number used in the computer. Other defensive techniques can include:

☐ Comparing the totals of newly entered items with the proper figures for those items.
☐ Using check digits embedded in other numbers. There are several ways to do this. One of the simplest would be to add the digits in an employee's number and add the last number of the sum. For example, employee number 123456 adds up to 21. Put it into the computer as 1234561.
☐ Program the computer to kick back entries that are outside a specified range. You could ask it to reject a date that is not a payday, for example, or a figure that is well

above the employee's normal pay. The questioned amount may indicate fraud, or it may come legitimately from unusual amounts of overtime. In either case, the computer would let you check it out.

☐ Another simple technique that might be used as a spot check is to compare the data in the computer with its source material or a separate entry of the same data used as a control (Table 3-14).

The Trojan Horse

Like its namesake, this technique is sneaky. The criminal sneaks instructions into a program so the computer performs an unauthorized act, but appears to be running correctly (Table 3-15).

In the hands of a clever programmer, instructions like these can easily be hidden in the thousands of lines that make up a major program. Even if you find them, you still won't know who put them there. There still are some ways, though, to combat this technique.

Keep a backup copy of the original program listing. If you suspect you've been the victim of a Trojan horse, compare the backup with the version now running in the computer. This could be a time-

Table 3-14. Detection of Data Diddling.

Detection of Data Diddling		
Potential Perpetrators	**Methods of Detection**	**Evidence**
Transaction participants	Data comparison	Data documents Source
Data preparers	Document validation	Transactions Computer-readable
Source data supplies	Manual controls instrumentation analysis	Computer data media Tapes Cards
Nonparticipants with access	Computer validation and verification exception	Disks Storage modules
	Reports analysis	Manual logs, journals, and
	Computer output	exception reports
	Integrity tests	Incorrect computer output

Table 3-15. Detection of Trojan Horse Crimes.

Potential Perpetrators	Methods of Detection	Evidence
Programmers having detailed knowledge of a suspected part of a program and its purpose and access to it	Program code comparison Testing of suspect program Tracing of possible gain from the act	Unexpected results of program execution Foreign code found in a suspect program
Employees Contract programmers Vendor's programmers Users of the computer		

consuming process that requires expert help. It's also important that you keep the backup copy up-to-date with any changes you make in the operating program.

If your search turns up a Trojan horse, you may not know who is responsible, but the search for a culprit has been narrowed. Your suspect is someone expert enough to have altered the program and who had the necessary access.

Another possible technique is to run the same data through another version of the program and compare the results. This will work best if you have some initial idea of the kinds of manipulation for which you are looking. And while a difference in the data can indicate that you have a Trojan horse *somewhere,* you still must locate both the alterations and the responsible party.

The Salami Technique

This practice gets its name because the criminal takes only a thin slice at a time from any one source, adding up a substantial score by stealing from many sources.

In a bank, for example, the criminal might deduct 10 or 15 cents from each of 100 accounts. No alarms are set off within the system, because no one element suffers a significant loss. What's more, if the money is transferred to the thief's own account within the system, there is no large withdrawal to be accounted for. When the thief removes the accumulated money from this account,

it all seems quite legitimate. The assets could be small items from an inventory instead of pennies from a bank account.

A variation on this technique is called the "round down" system. To use this method, the thief must have access to a computer system in which large numbers of financial accounts are processed. The process also must involve multiplication, as it does when interest payments are calculated. Another requirement is that the resulting figures be expressed in fractions of less than one cent and use a "running remainder." SRI offers this example.

A savings account in a bank may have a balance of $15.86. Applying the 2.6 percent interest results in adding $0.41236 ($15.86 × .026). Thus, $15.86 + .41236 = $16.27236.

Because the balance is retained only to the nearest cent, it is rounded down to $16.27, leaving $0.00236. What is to be done with this remainder? The interest calculation for the next account in the program sequence might be the following: $425.34 × 0.026 = $11.05884. This would result in a new balance of $436.39884 that must be rounded up to $436.40, leaving a deficit or negative remainder of $0.00116.

The net effect of rounding in both these accounts, rounding down to the calculated cent in the first and adding one cent in the second, leaves both accounts accurate to the nearest cent and a remainder of $0.0012 ($0.00236 − $0.00116). This remainder is then carried to the next account calculation, and so on. As the calculations continue, if the running remainder goes above one cent, positive or negative, the last account is adjusted to return the remainder to an amount less than one cent. This results in a few accounts receiving one cent more or less than the correct rounded values, but the totals for all accounts remain in balance.

This is where the creative computer programmer can engage in some treachery to accumulate for himself a fancy bit of change and still show a balanced set of accounts that defies discovery by the auditor. He merely changes the rules slightly in the program by accumulating the rounded down remainders in his own account rather than distributing them to the other accounts as they build up.

If rounded down correctly, the results would look like Table 3-16. Note that some accounts have been rounded upward and others downward. With a little inventiveness, though, the result could look

like Table 3-17. This time, the only accounts that have been rounded are those where it was necessary to round them downward to replenish the floating remainder. Any adjustments made when the remainder exceeds a whole cent are saved and applied to the last account in the program—the programmer's own.

The programmer netted three cents for his attentions to these 18 accounts. Were there 180,000 accounts, he would have pocketed $300 for the day's work.

It's almost impossible for an auditor to catch this practice except by a careful check of the programmer's personal account. Even then, the account may not be in the programmer's real name.

One way to watch for this technique is to be alert for a sudden change in an employee's financial habits. Monitor work habits, too, because this technique requires a great deal of maintenance time. Keep employee accounts under strict scru-

Table 3-16. Example of Rounded-Down Accounts.

Old Balance	New Balance	Rounded New Balance	Remainder	Accumulating Remainder
$ 15.86	$ 16.27236	$ 16.27	$ 0.00236	$ 0.00236
425.34	436.39884	436.40	(0.00116)	0.00120
221.75	227.51550	227.52	(0.00450)	(0.00330)
18.68	19.16568	19.17	(0.00432)	(0.00762)
∘ 564.44	579.11544	~~579.12~~	(0.00456)	(0.01218)
		579.11		(0.00218)
61.31	62.90406	62.90	0.00406	0.00188
101.32	103.95432	103.95	0.00432	0.00620
∘ 77.11	79.11486	~~79.11~~	0.00486	0.01106
		79.12		0.00106
457.12	469.00512	469.01	(0.00488)	(0.00382)
111.35	114.24510	114.25	(0.00490)	(0.00872)
∘ 446.36	457.96536	~~457.97~~	(0.00464)	(0.01336)
		457.96		(0.00336)
88.68	90.98568	90.99	(0.00432)	(0.00768)
∘ 14.44	14.81544	~~14.82~~	(0.00456)	(0.01224)
		14.81		(0.00224)
83.27	85.43502	85.44	(0.00498)	(0.00722)
127.49	130.80474	130.80	0.00474	(0.00248)
331.32	339.93432	339.93	0.00432	0.00184
37.11	38.07486	38.07	0.00486	0.00670
∘ 111.31	114.20406	~~114.20~~	0.00406	0.01076
		114.21		0.00076
$3294.26	Total	$3379.91		

Table 3-17. Rounded-Down Accounts Diverted to Programmer's Account

Old Balance	New Balance	Rounded New Balance	Remainder	Accumu- lating Remainder	Pro- grammer's Remainder
$ 15.86	$ 16,27236	$ 16.27	$ 0.00236	$ 0.0000	$0.00236
425.34	436.39884	436.40	(0.00116)	(0.00116)	0.00236
221.75	227.51550	227.52	(0.00450)	(0.00566)	0.00236
18.68	19.16568	19.17	(0.0098)	(0.00998)	0.00236
○ 564.44	579.11544	579.12	(0.00456)	(0.01454)	0.00236
		579.11		(0.00454)	
61.31	62.90406	62.90	0.00406	(0.00454)	0.00642
101.32	103.95432	103.95	0.00432	(0.00454)	0.01074
77.11	79.11486	79.11	0.00486	(0.00454)	0.01560
457.12	469.00512	469.01	(0.00488)	(0.00942)	0.01560
○ 111.35	114.24510	114.25	(0.00490)	(0.01432)	0.01560
		114.24		(0.00432)	
446.36	457.96536	457.97	(0.00464)	(0.00896)	0.01560
○ 88.68	90.98568	90.99	(0.00432)	(0.01328)	0.01560
		90.98		(0.00328)	
14.44	14.81544	14.82	(0.00456)	(0.00784)	0.01560
○ 84.27	85.43502	85.44	(0.00498)	(0.01282)	0.01560
		85.43		(0.00282)	
127.49	130.80474	130.80	0.00474	(0.00282)	0.02034
331.32	339.93432	339.93	0.00432	(0.00282)	0.02466
37.11	38.07486	38.07	0.00486	(0.00282)	0.02952
○ 111.31	114.20406	114.20	0.00406	(0.00282)	0.03358
		114.23		0.00076	0.00000
$3.294.26	Total	$3379.91			

tiny, particularly if the employees have the skill and access they need to employ this scheme. Try to remove at least one of the several conditions this scheme requires. Remove more if you can. Ask your auditors about any doubts you might have (Table 3-18). The technique predates computers, and most auditors are familiar with it. Even if they can't find hard proof, they can point in the right direction.

The Superzap

The user of this technique applies a legitimate tool in an illegitimate way. In fact, it takes its name

Table 3-18. Detection of Salami Techniques.

Potential Perpetrators	Methods of Detection	Evidence
Financial system programmers	Detail data analysis	Many small financial losses
	Program comparison	Unsupported account buildups
Employee Former employees Contract programmers Vendors' programmers	Transaction audits	Trojan horse code changed or unusual personal financial practices of possible suspects
	Observation of financial activities of possible suspects	

from a utility program used in most IBM mainframe computers.

In any protected computer system you'll occasionally need something that will override the built-in security measures. SRI calls it a "break glass in case of emergency" or "master key" procedure. The computer may stop, malfunction, or need attention that your normal procedures and access methods don't allow. You sometimes need a universal access program to bypass the security system and get at the heart of the problem.

This is a necessary tool, but a dangerous one. Its use should be restricted to system programmers and maintenance people who absolutely must have it. However, many companies store copies of the program in libraries where they are open to anyone who knows where they are and how to use them.

In one case, the managers of a New Jersey bank discovered that the system they normally used to correct errors in account balances wasn't working properly. This system had been overlooked during an equipment changeover, and it had become obsolete and prone to errors. As a result, the computer operations manager began using a superzap program to override the faulty system and make the corrections.

In the process, the manager discovered how easy it was to make changes in the system, without the usual controls and audit records. He put this knowledge to work, switching money into the accounts of three friends.

Unlike clever users of the salami technique, the manager took enough from one customer's account that the customer noticed the shortage. A quick response by bank officials led them to the manager and his friends.

That's about the only way you'll discover a fraud of this kind. An experienced programmer with the means to override most security controls can make changes that won't be detected in the normal course of operations. Most application programs aren't written to detect the kind of changes such a person would make. The only person likely to notice a problem is a user like the bank customer who is able to compare the current data with past reports. Even then, it's easy to conclude that the discrepancy was a data entry error.

One way to protect yourself is to maintain "father" and "grandfather" copies of each file processed with the operating program. You then can check the new version against the previous ones for any differences that shouldn't be there.

Maintain records of who uses the computer and when. If there is a discrepancy, check the use records, particularly for the times just before and just after the application program is run. That's the most likely time for a superzap (Table 3-19).

Trapdoors

A large program often will have built-in breaks, where you can check the output at intermediate stages of the operation and insert additional instructions to make the program work properly. These *trapdoors* are intended as debugging tools, but they are open to misuse.

Table 3-19. Detection of Superzapping Crimes.

Potential Perpetrators	Method of Detection	Evidence
Programmers with access to superzap programs and computer access to use them	Comparison of files with historical copies	Output report discrepancies
	Discrepancies noted by recipients of output reports	Undocumented transactions
Computer operations staff with applications knowledge	Examination of computer usage journals	Computer usage or file request journals

Table 3-20. Detection of Trapdoor Crimes.

Potential Perpetrators	Methods of Detection	Evidence
Systems programmers	Exhaustive testing	Computer output reports that indicate that a computer system performs outside of its specifications
Expert Application programmers	Comparison of specification to performance	
	Specific testing based on evidence	

In particular, a thief could use such an opening in an operating system to insert a routine that could be used to override normal security controls, in much the same manner as superzapping.

Because trapdoors are intended for use primarily when the program is being developed, most are removed before it goes into regular service. Some are left in, though, for the sake of later program maintenance. Your thief may already be active at this stage, leaving a place in the program for later manipulation.

There also are times that poor program logic leaves an inadvertent trapdoor. Or, the computer's circuits may provide an unseen opportunity. An undocumented combination of commands could allow the system to be compromised. That's exactly how one programmer made use of a trapdoor which allowed him to transfer control of the program into a region normally used to store data. This meant the computer would respond to instructions formed by the data entered. All the programmer had to do was to enter a string of data that was translated into program commands. The commands let the programmer use hours of free time on a timesharing computer and gain access to the files of other users.

In another incident, several automotive engineers in Detroit discovered a trapdoor in a commercial timesharing service in Florida. Through it, they managed to find the password assigned to the president of the timesharing company. With this, they obtained free use of several programs that were supposed to have been protected as trade secrets.

Both of these violations were discovered purely by accident, and no one knows how many other users might have taken advantage of the openings. There is no direct technical way to discover a trapdoor, and only expert programmers can find one at all.

The best way to guard against trapdoors is to try to prevent them. Monitor your program listings and have them checked by outside experts to make sure there are no remaining traps. Then proceed on the assumption that you have found and closed all but one (Table 3-20).

Logic Bombs

A *logic bomb* is the offspring of a Trojan horse by way of a Hollywood screenplay. In one case, these instructions were secretly inserted in an operating system. At 3 P.M. on a specified date two years later, the confession of a crime would appear on all 300 terminals connected to the system. The program then would crash. The culprit arranged, of course, to be many miles away at that date and hour.

In another case, a programmer arranged for automatic retaliation should he ever lose his job. Removing his name from the payroll would remove *everyone's* name from the payroll.

Because a logic bomb is usually inserted with a Trojan horse technique, your lines of defense are much the same. Another way to detect a logic bomb: When it goes off, you'll probably know it (Table 3-21).

Asynchronous Attacks

A computer used from multiple terminals is

Table 3-21. Detection of Logic Bombs.

Potential Perpetrators	Methods of Detection	Evidence
Programmers having detailed knowledge of a suspected part of a program and its purpose and access to it	Program code comparisons	Unexpected results of program execution
	Testing of suspect program	Foreign code found in a suspect program
Employees	Tracing of possible gain from the act	
Contract programmers		
Vendor's programmers		
Users of the computer		

designed, of necessity, to handle one job at a time. Incoming requests for processing are handled individually, in a predetermined order, to maintain a complete separation between these operations, so one user's data doesn't appear on someone else's screen. The *asynchronous attack* overrides the separation mechanism to gain access to someone else's operation.

In one simple example, many long programs have periodic checkpoints at which the user may stop for a while and resume later. These checkpoints require that the program and data be kept in storage for later use. The attacker who enters the system at this point can easily alter the program or steal the data.

Most crimes of this type are much more complex. This helps, at least, to narrow the list of people who know how to do it. The main method of detection is by checking out any unexpected deviations from the output you expected (Table 3-22).

Scavenging

After a computer finishes a job, it doesn't always fully erase all the information it processed. Some may be lurking in the machine's memory or on disks or tapes. Most microcomputer users probably have had experiences in which they encounter traces of old files on disks that supposedly had been erased. In fact, routines designed to restore accidentally erased files work by searching for these ghosts of data past. The same method can be use for less noble purposes.

This was exactly the technique applied by one customer of a Texas timesharing service used by several oil companies. The customer would request that when its jobs were run, the data be recorded on a temporary storage tape. An operator began to notice through signal lights on the console that the customer would "read" the storage tape before any new data was entered on it. The suspicious operator reported the discovery, and an investigation found

Table 3-22. Detection of Asynchronous Attacks.

Potential Perpetrators	Method of Detection	Evidence
Sophisticated advanced system programmers	System testing of suspected attack methods	Output that deviates from normally expected output or logs containing characteristics of computer operation
Sophisticated and advanced computer operators	Repeat execution of a job under normal and safe circumstances	

the customer was scavenging information its competitors had recorded earlier on the same tape.

Unlike some kinds of computer crime, scavenging often doesn't require specialized knowledge. A pair of Florida newspaper reporters, checking the opportunities for computer crime, found critical information on printouts in a trash can. In Wisconsin, another reporting team found the password for a state government computer system posted on a bulletin board. Notes, printouts, and even carbon paper can help a scavenger, who need not even enter your system to take advantage of it.

The paper trail can be used in reverse, however. Should you feel confidential information has been taken from your system, the basic technique is to try to trace the problem to its source (Table 3-23).

In one such case, the suspect information was itself found on a printout. From numbers on the paper, an FBI agent was able to trace it first to the company that had made it, and then to the computer center where it had been used. From there, the numbers led directly to the particular job and programmer involved.

Leakage

Here we have the kind of intelligence gathering practiced by the James Bonds of our information society. It makes use of subtle clues and bits of information to leak information from a computer. Among the more exotic ways information could slip out are:

☐ A report that contains large blocks of numbers is altered so the sensitive information is slipped into the blocks.

☐ A printout is manipulated so the sensitive information is contained in lines of a certain length.

☐ Tape reels on a large computer move clockwise and counterclockwise to represent the binary digits 0 and 1. It's possible to steal the information by tracking the movement of the reels.

☐ A sound tape recording of a printer at work, replayed at low speed.

Most other forms of computer crime—particularly scavenging, logic bombs, and Trojan horses—can be sources of data leaks. Keeping records of computer use and previous versions of the data can help you trace the source of leaked material. Also on your side: In many of the leakage methods, the thief must be physically present to record the leaked data (Table 3-24).

Piggybacking and Impersonation

This is another type of crime that doesn't necessarily require an expert. It involves getting past your security system, either physically or electronically, by using the authorization of a legitimate user.

It can be as simple as this: One of your operators arrives at a security entrance to find a frustrated-looking person standing there with arms

Table 3-23. Detection of Scavenging Crimes.

Potential Perpetrators	Method of Detection	Evidence
Users of the computer system	Tracing of discovered proprietary information back to its source	Computer output media
Persons having access to computer facilities and adjacent areas	Testing of an operating system to discover residual data after execution of a job	Type font characteristics
		Similar information produced in suspected ways in the same form

Table 3-24. Detection of Crimes from Data Leakage.

Potential Perpetrators	Methods of Detection	Evidence
Computer programmers	Discovery of stolen information	Computer storage media
Employees Former employees Contract workers Vendor's employees	Tracing computer storage media back to the computer facility	Computer output forms
		Type font
		Trojan horse or scavenging evidence

full of tapes, printouts, or other official-looking material. The nature of the material doesn't matter much. It just needs to look official and keep the impostor from reaching for a key or punch in an access code. "Could you give me a hand?" the impostor asks. The unthinking employee agrees to help, and the impostor slips into the computer room.

Good security education is the main safeguard against this kind of invasion. Employees should be warned not to let people they don't know, or who don't carry clear authorization, into a secured area. Posting guards at these entrances might help. Some companies have installed turnstile entrances that let only one person through at a time.

Piggybackers usually are more inventive than expert. One young impostor posed as a magazine writer and was given a full public relations-style tour of a telephone company's computer facilities. He learned enough about the security system to steal more than $1 million worth of equipment.

A more sophisticated form of piggybacking uses a second terminal to impersonate the terminal of an authorized user. This is most useful in systems that depend on automatic verification of the user's identity. The thief will hook another terminal into the same line as the authorized user's. Waiting until the user is away, the thief will use the added terminal to enter the system. When the terminals are hooked up in this fashion, the automatic verification system can't distinguish between the real ter-

minal and an impostor's.

Then there's the impostor who pulled off an electronic version of the old "bank examiner" scam. He used this method to take thousands of dollars through automated bank teller machines (ATMs).

ATMs normally use customer identification cards with coded magnetic stripes. The customer inserts the card and enters a personal identification code. The machine will respond only if the personal code identifies the authorized user of the card. The thief would steal the access cards, then phone the customers, pretending to be a bank security official. He found the customer's card, but he also wanted to catch the thief. For this he needed the customer's personal identification code. The customers would invariably give out the numbers—and later would find large sums missing from their accounts.

Yet another version is to learn the system by which passwords and access codes are determined. If your code depends on some physical characteristic of the authorized user, or is based on something only the right people are supposed to know, unauthorized users easily can learn and imitate these characteristics.

A detailed log is one of your best protections against impersonators. It can be recorded automatically or manually by a guard. It can tell you who supposedly has used the computer at what times. If there is a pattern of unauthorized access, it usually will show up on the log (Table 3-25).

Table 3-25. Detection of Impersonation Acts.

Potential Perpetrators	Methods of Detection	Evidence
Employees, former employees, vendors' employees	Access observations	Logs, journals equipment usage meters
	Interviewing witnesses	
Contracted persons	Examination of journals and logs	Other physical evidence
Outsiders		
	Specialized computer programs that analyze characteristics of on-line computer user accesses	

Wiretapping

Wiretapping would seem to be a major security threat. A raider simply could use well-known technology, available from nearly any electronics store, to tap a telephone wire or intercept a microwave relay.

Actually, says SRI, at the time it compiled its Justice Department report there were *no verified cases* of computer wiretapping. One reason, SRI suggests, is that wiretapping requires a major capital investment by the thief. Other means are cheaper.

Still, the rapid spread of data communication can leave you increasingly vulnerable to wiretapping techniques should someone decide to try it. There are also some kinds of raiders, (industrial espionage experts, for example) who might be willing to go to the expense. The best defense is probably to transmit your most sensitive information in code, using one of the many data encryption programs now available (Table 3-26).

Simulation and Modeling

Here's one for the TV scriptwriters: A master criminal uses his own computer to set up an electronic simulation of a real program, then substitutes his version for the real thing.

It's been done in real life. An accountant set up a duplicate of his company's accounting and general ledger system on his own computer. He would use this computerized clone to enter various kinds of data to examine the "what if" effects of his embezzlement activities. By running his own system in reverse, he was able to determine the changes he must make to the real books to cover up his acts.

In another case, an insurance company used a spreadsheet-type of model to determine the effects of various levels of sales. Someone used the system to create 64,000 fake policies and introduce them into the company's working system.

This kind of activity requires someone with a knowledge of simulation and modeling techniques,

Table 3-26. Detection of Wiretapping.

Potential Perpetrators	Methods of Detection	Evidence
Communications technicians and engineers	Voice wiretapping methods	Voice wire tapping evidence
Communications employees		

Table 3-27. Detection of Simulation and Modeling Techniques.

Potential Perpetrators	Methods of Detection	Evidence
Computer application programmers	Investigation of possible computer usage by suspects	Computer programs Computer program documentation
Simulation and modeling experts		Computer input
Managers in positions to engage in large, complex embezzlement		Computer produced reports
		Computer usage logs and journals

but this person is not necessarily the criminal. SRI reports several cases in which programmers were led into these schemes with no idea that their work was being used illegally.

A better clue might be the large amount of computer time a scheme like this requires. Again, logs of computer use can be valuable. Also check the customer logs of available timesharing services and look into the recent business dealings of suspects. This method is less valuable than it used to be, though, because much of the required modeling now can be done with spreadsheet programs on home microcomputers (Table 3-27).

IN SUMMARY

A risk analysis should identify the risks you face and the proper means to reduce them. Among the factors to consider in your analysis:

☐ The roles played by the computer systems in your company.
☐ The value of your data assets.
☐ How seriously you will be affected by downtime.
☐ How vulnerable your data assets are.
☐ The appropriate degree of protection to provide.

Here are some of the most common measures to consider:

☐ Assign a specific individual to manage data security.
☐ Issue written security policies.
☐ Conduct frequent, unannounced, audits and inspections.
☐ Keep all tapes and disks in secure storage, whence they can be signed out only by authorized users.
☐ Classify files in terms of their sensitivity to the company. Give the highest protection to the most sensitive material.
☐ Maintain a user log of those who use the system by way of personal computers or remote terminals.
☐ Establish and maintain a carefully designed password system.

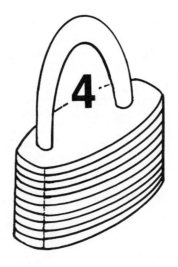

Open Sesame:
Controlling Physical Access

"Knapsack" was the code name of a computer access control system thought to be the equal, at least, of the best security control systems available, but about 50 times faster. Its inventors proudly offered a $1000 prize to anyone who could crack the Knapsack code.

It took two years, but the prize finally was claimed by Ernest F. Brickell, of the Sandia National Laboratories in Albuquerque, New Mexico. Most of that time, Brickell explained, was spent trying to determine *how* the access code was computed. Once he crossed that barrier, he programmed a supercomputer to break the code in about an hour.

Things could be worse. Not every would-be computer abuser has two years and a supercomputer to devote to cracking your access codes. Even then, the payoff might not be worth it. No doubt Brickell was more interested in meeting the challenge than in the $1000. Computed per hour of the code-cracker's work, it would give new meaning to the term "minimum wage."

The real point of Brickell's accomplishment is this:

You can make physical access difficult.
You cannot make it impossible.

A hard-to-crack access code like Knapsack can give you a strong measure of access control. The time, cost, and difficulty involved will make many people conclude that, unless you are trying to protect something truly valuable, it just isn't worth the effort.

Don't make the mistake of assuming that any method is absolutely unbreakable. Brickell said a key to his success was the discovery that the Knapsack code was a relatively simple mathematical formula disguised as a difficult one. He admits he would not know how to break an access code that actually uses the more difficult formula—but someone else might.

KINDS OF COMPUTER SECURITY

There are three main approaches to preventing

access to your computer: *physical security*, which restricts direct access; *procedural controls*, which control use of the computer system; and *technical controls*, which are built into the system itself. A threat assessment considers much the same types of possible weak spots. These categories represent the tactics you can apply to these areas of vulnerability.

Passwords and access codes, which probably are the most familiar kinds of computer security, are examples of the physical controls to be discussed in this chapter. Later chapters will deal with procedural and technical tactics. None of these techniques will be the "one-and-only" answer to your security problems. Look at them as components in an overall security strategy. The exact mix will depend on what you are trying to protect and the environment in which you are trying to protect it. If you have assessed properly the threats you face, you will have a basis on which to decide which mix of techniques should be used.

What the Right Protection Can Do

If you select the right combination of protective measures you should be able to:

- [ ] Ward off threats to the welfare of your company.
- [ ] Establish different degrees of access, depending on the needs and responsibilities of each user.
- [ ] Hold users clearly responsible for their own computer use.
- [ ] Maintain a clear separation between users, programs, data files, and other resources.
- [ ] Identify attempts to misuse the computer or evade its protective measures.

The central purpose of any security program is to protect your resources and assets while allowing maximum use and flexibility to authorized users. You can choose from a variety of physical, procedural, and technical controls. With proper selections, you can put your computer users into a type of maze. At each corner, the system evaluates the user and type of access, if any, for which they are authorized. If the evaluation is positive, the user is sent in the proper direction. Otherwise, the unauthorized entrant is repelled or misdirected.

In such a maze technique, the user usually first encounters a set of physical protections such as passwords. These can identify the user and admit only those who are authorized. Next, a set of procedural controls will read the user's identification and determine what level or types of access this person should have. Technical controls then can insure that the access is limited to proper programs and files.

Back up the built-in security system with written policy and procedure statements. Explain the types of assets you feel it is important to protect. Spell out each employee's responsibility for protecting specific kinds of information. Explain the operating requirements for using the computer. This kind of information will help prevent accidental security violations. More important, it helps make the employees aware of your security requirements, why they exist, and how to work within them.

When most people think of computer security, they think first of physical security. Many physical security techniques are traditional security methods: locks, guards, badges, and other means to limit access to your computer and its valuable contents.

Good physical security, though, will go beyond the traditional techniques and back them up with technology to match the computer you are trying to protect. Electronic keys or video cameras, for example, can back up or even replace a human security guard. The physical techniques you implement also can help in other areas, protecting against disaster, for example, or against errors and crashes.

What Physical Security Can't Do

Physical security measures can serve three main purposes. First, they can *control access to your equipment and data*. Locked doors, passwords, and similar techniques restrict access, keep authorized people from entering security-sensitive areas, and impede their access to valuable information.

Second, they can *protect the computer site*, particularly its structures and surroundings. The basic idea is to extend circles of protection outward from the central computer location.

Third, they can *protect against hazards* that can damage the computer or its contents. These hazards include unintentional access by untrained and unauthorized people.

Electronic surveillance and access controls can augment a physical security system, but high technology can also add to your physical security problems. This is particularly true with the advent of remote terminals, personal computers, and networking systems.

Your computer system is no longer confined to a central location that is relatively easy to protect. You still might have such a location for your central processing unit, but other elements of the system can be scattered around a building, a plant site, the nation, or even the world. You no longer can concentrate your efforts on a single operating site.

Your job is also made more difficult as computers change in size and function. It's possible, for example, that major elements of your computer system will soon become indistinguishable from major elements of your telephone system. This is one of many ways in which computers are becoming interrelated with other equipment. This makes the computer system more vulnerable to abuse and misuse, and it is a particular challenge to the physical elements of your security program.

New ways of storing data also present new physical security challenges. The microcomputer diskette is a major example: It started with a diameter of 8 inches, then shrunk to 5 1/4, and some versions are now little over 3 inches. It becomes easier all the time to slip several hundred pages of valuable information into a shirt pocket or the hidden corner of a briefcase.

Even when you're dealing with larger items, physical security can be difficult. It's not all that hard for someone to steal a tape from an unprotected library or to walk out with pages of valuable documentation on how to alter or manipulate your programs. The ever-present office photocopier and the COPY command of a microcomputer operating system probably rank very close to each other as threats to your security.

A physical security system must protect data as well as equipment—in fact, protecting the data easily could be the more important objective of the two. Sometimes it escapes in the most obscure ways: Discarded printouts, used printer ribbons, and passwords left visible on monitor screens are common sources of loss.

Another major danger is that some people become such familiar figures around a computer facility they are allowed to move around at will, even in places to which they should not have access. Think of it this way: If you were an outsider looking for ways to steal or sabotage your data, you probably would look for exactly such a person to do the job.

Recognize the Limits

Perhaps the best thing we can learn from these new challenges is that we must recognize the limits of traditional physical security methods. They can do part of the job, but there is no way they can do all of it.

Good physical security will continue to be necessary, but the day is long past when it can meet all your needs. Instead, consider physical security in combination with other types of techniques as part of an overall computer security system.

Computer complexity is a complex field. It requires a hard look at what physical security methods can—and cannot—accomplish in the new Information Age.

TYPES OF PHYSICAL SECURITY

A central feature of most physical security methods is that they distinguish in some way between authorized persons and those who are not. There are three basic ways to make this distinction:

☐ By what the person *knows*. This can be a password, a more complex access code, or some simple identifier. One simple but effective question: your mother's maiden name. Don't automatically assume, though, that this can automatically identify the authorized individual. A relative also would know the name, as would an industrial spy who has looked it up.

☐ By something the person *has*. This could be a security badge or an electronic key card.
☐ By who the person *is*. Some new security systems identify an individual by a fingerprint, a voice characteristic, or a written signature. Others will read the shape of a hand or even the pattern of blood vessels in the eyeball.

As usual, all have their limits. The first depend heavily on the individual's willingness not to reveal the key knowledge or share the access badge. The third group involves costly hardware that probably can be justified only for the highest security needs.

The most common physical security measures usually are tailored to the type of protection you need: equipment and data, the computer site, or disaster relief and recovery. Among the techniques used for equipment and data are:

☐ *Physical access controls*, including passwords, numerical access controls, security badges, magnetic card readers and biological detection methods.
☐ *General security controls*, including guards and sign-in logs.
☐ *Remote terminal security*, including locking devices and surveillance by closed-circuit television.

For site security, there are:

☐ *Fire control systems*, including alarms, extinguishers, fire-resistant construction, and smoke and heat detectors.
☐ *Water damage controls*, such as waterproof equipment covers, water-tight ceilings, and under-floor drains.
☐ *Secure heating, ventilation and air conditioning*. This includes proper maintenance and housekeeping, adequate design and construction, and the availability of backup systems.

A later chapter will cover disaster recovery in detail. The major physical security methods for the purpose revolve around the use of backup sites.

THE PERILS OF PASSWORDS

Not all access code systems are as hard to crack as Knapsack. The hackers who made Milwaukee famous went about their work with ridiculous ease. The first step was to dial the local telephone number of Telenet, one of several telephone networks that make reaching another computer nearly as easy as reaching another telephone.

Once they hooked into the system, Telenet asked them which remote computer they were trying to reach. They didn't know and didn't care. Each system hooked to the phone network has its own identity code. The young raiders simply punched in a few likely sounding numbers to see what they would get. What they got were places like the Los Alamos National Laboratory, a nuclear research center, and the Sloan-Kettering Cancer Center in New York City.

The Not-So-Secret Password

The Sloan-Kettering computer was used to plan and monitor patient treatments, and it was protected by a password system. One available password was one which the computer's manufacturer had installed to allow access by maintenance technicians. As Groucho Marx used to say, "It's a common word, one you hear every day." And the Milwaukee youths knew it.

The standard maintenance passwords used by computer manufacturers are a common item of exchange on the fringes of the home computer hobby. When the computers are installed, the new owners are advised to change these widely known passwords, but often don't bother. Among other things, they want to provide easy access for their own maintenance workers.

Sloan-Kettering's computer service director told the *New York Times* that the hospital's computer responded to one of the common maintenance passwords. The unit had been programmed, though, so the password would provide access only to a few elementary functions that were necessary for service work. It was supposed to block access through the maintenance password to critical information and functions.

It didn't. Once they had gained access via the maintenance door, the young invaders found themselves in the same type of computer they had used in high school data processing courses. Using their knowledge of this system, they overrode the access-limiting program to roam at will through the hospital's data. They managed to shut down the computer twice. Both incidents were late at night and no patients were harmed, but hospital officials said they spent "a month of man-hours" trying to track down the source of their problems.

Since this incident occurred, we have learned that it was by no means unique. The world is full of such raiders, all with the potential to do serious damage to programs and privacy. Many have more sinister motives than testing the limits of a teenager's world. For example, when a *Newsweek* reporter infiltrated the hacker network for a story, his subjects retaliated by penetrating the records of a credit bureau and devastating his credit rating.

The young people who do such things have shattered three comfortable old assumptions about computer security:

- [ ] The assumption that, except for computers that protect defense secrets or large amounts of money, few people ever would want to gain access to your computer.
- [ ] The assumption that a password offers adequate protection and that it's not necessary to change even widely used passwords and access codes.
- [ ] The assumption that few people have the technical knowledge to gain access to your computer or to manipulate the information inside it.

Wanting In

The fact is, many people might want to get into your computer—and know how to do it. Computerized theft and fraud now are recognized as major white collar crimes. Stealing data is a standard technique of industrial espionage. Even young hackers who have no evil intentions can cause catastrophic damage.

The password system is one way to protect yourself, but it's far from foolproof. A password is like any other kind of secret: hard to maintain—and infinitely harder as more and more people know about it. More seriously, many passwords have lost their effectiveness through the unthinking complacency of their owners. The computer owner who fails to change a widely known maintenance password doesn't just risk trouble. It's an open invitation.

Much of the complacency has its origins in the high-priest atmosphere in which data processing professionals worked before personal computers came into widespread use. Until then, computer knowledge was a special kind of expertise, held only by knowledgeable insiders who were given expensive toys to play with. No mere mortals need apply.

Now it's possible to buy a primitive computer for less than $100, and a full-featured microcomputer system for about half the cost of a well-equipped new car. The expansion of computer literacy has given thousands of people the means to use computers and manipulate programs and data. Ironically, one of the major problems in bringing computers to management is the attitude of many executives that using such a device is "beneath" them.

Most of the world's newly computer-literate people use their knowledge properly and privately, but many do not. It is no wonder, then, that after the Milwaukee case received its wide publicity the makers of computer security products reported that customer inquiries nearly tripled. As the marketing data of one such service put it, "The chiefs go to the data processing managers and ask, 'Are we exposed?' When they found out the answer is yes, the phone starts ringing."

BUILDING A LIMITED ACCESS ROUTE

The traditional computer password demonstrates a basic principle of computer security: most problems are caused by people, not machines.

On a technical level, the password has its limits. You can put one into effect with a simple IF/THEN/ELSE routine. IF the user offers the right password, THEN the computer will acknowledge it; ELSE the computer will not respond. Even better, it will try to trace the call. Even more sophisticated password systems often are written as add-ons to the basic control systems of the computers they protect. Nothing this simple will stand up against a determined raider.

The simplicity exists because of the human factor. On one hand, any password system you devise must be designed to be used by ordinary people. The more complex you make the system, the better security it will provide. At the same time, though, the harder it is for your own people to use it.

This kind of user-friendliness may be important, for example, if your system must be used by a roomful of inexperienced clerks or if you are selling a service to paying customers, neither group will respond well to a system that forces them through a complex series of access codes. You'll be asking for even more trouble if you take the sensible precaution of periodically changing the passwords.

Some computer experts are coming to believe that user-friendliness is overrated. This may be particularly true if you achieve it at the expense of security. Even so, there is an obvious trade-off to be made here: your interest in security against the interests of legitimate users. There are limits to the amount of unfriendliness you can build into the system, and these translate into limits on how secure you can make the system.

The human factor also shows up in the type of carelessness that the Milwaukee incident uncovered. People assume that a password provides automatic protection, and once you have installed one, there's nothing more you need do to protect your security. We've recently had some painful lessons in how wrong that assumption can be. The system will not wait like Ali Baba's treasure cave until the right party comes along with the magic words to open the door. Others will try to open it, too, and some will succeed.

The Basic Technique

In spite of its limits, the password still stands as what might be called the "entry-level" computer security technique. It holds that position for a good reason. Lack of a password can stop many casual raiders. That's a valuable asset if you recognize its limits and use it only as part of a larger security program.

One additional part of that program is to maintain a high level of security over the passwords themselves. Release them only to employees who have both the need and the clearance to use them. Change the passwords regularly to guard against leaks.

Two newspaper reporters in Madison, Wisconsin, recently conducted a test of how easy it is to break into the state government computer center there. As most of these tests seem to have gone recently, they found it easy. An official of the computer center later complained that someone out to embarrass the department must have slipped the reporters the password. Not so, said the state's attorney general. He had monitored the test. The reporters used a password they had found posted on a bulletin board.

After prosecuting a major case of credit card fraud, an assistant U.S. attorney in the Washington, D.C., area said he was alarmed at the ease with which the suspect had gained access to the personal records of credit card holders. In one instance he was able to obtain the passwords for a major department store's credit records by posing as a credit bureau employee.

The home computer is the "burglary tool of the future," said the prosecutor. He made this comment after accepting a plea bargain from a suspect pleading guilty to one of an original list of 13 charges of fraud. In all, said the prosecutor, the suspect had used information obtained from personal credit records to charge more than $50,000 to other peoples' accounts. Like many other computer criminals, this suspect had exploited a big weak point in any protective system: simple human carelessness.

Securing the Security Measure

You must guard against human failings, if the password is to be an effective security device. With proper precautions to maintain its secrecy, it can help you deny access to anyone who lacks the knowledge to evade it. It's a good initial barrier of the type that helps keep honest people honest.

It won't do you much good, though, if you don't give it the care it deserves. If you post it in public view or give it out to too many people, it can become no good at all. In fact, it can be worse than no good. The invader who steals or evades a password often can do so without a trace. You can suffer a serious loss and never know it until the intruder has disappeared.

MAINTAINING DEGREES OF ACCESS

One modem that connects computers with telephone lines comes with its own built-in password system. In fact, it has two. The modem won't process a call unless you give it one of the two authorized passwords.

The first password is for ordinary users. The modem's owner can designate up to nine destinations that are open to those who enter this password. The second opens up the ability to change or delete critical information within the system. This password would be given only to a select subgroup of authorized users who also are authorized to make such changes.

There are many other types of multilevel password systems. They exist because you often need more than one level of access control. You probably don't want data entry clerks to have the ability to change programs or gain access to trade secrets or other critical information.

Take a payroll system, for example. Only a selected few people should have the authority to alter individual pay rates. Otherwise, you run the serious risk of a do-it-yourself pay raise. However, you also probably have several clerks who need access to the system to enter time card data or print W-2 forms. You need a system that will grant the clerks enough access to do that job while you place more critical pay information under a higher degree of security. It is not always enough that an access control system give a simple yes-or-no answer. It also must make sure that those who are granted access to the system can reach only the information and functions they legitimately are entitled to use.

This, too, is a field where complacency has been rampant. There is the story a clerk who for many years ably and honestly kept the firm's financial records. Each regular audit produced nothing but praise for her accuracy and efficiency. Then the company switched to a computerized system that included a built-in audit check in place of the periodic reviews. The company learned later that with the help of the computer—and the absence of the human auditors—the clerk had quietly taken the company for thousands of dollars.

That was a case of giving too much access, even to a trusted employee. Your access control system should be set up so that even someone who is given a high degree of access to sensitive material is not readily able to exceed that authority.

Even most split-level access control plans divide up only large classes of people. The modem's split between supervisors and ordinary users is typical. The obvious shortcoming is that such large-group plans limit your ability to tailor the access rights you wish to grant to individuals who should receive them.

At the same time, there has been a tendency to subdivide the types of information to which an individual is given access. Where once an employee was granted or denied access to a particular file, the access rights now may be granted record by record or even by individual data items. The small subdivisions being created on the data side are a clear mismatch with the large groups covered by most control systems. Add to this the growth of networks in which multiple users share resources. The result is a major problem.

It's almost impossible to police every bit of data to make sure it is available only to the proper users. This is particularly difficult when the data in question is intended for use by supervisors. Once a supervisor has been given access to one type of privileged information, it's hard to effectively deny access to other privileged information as well.

This problem has spawned several attempted solutions. As usual, none of them is perfect. Again, the basic problem is that the more effective an access system, the more barriers it presents to honest, everyday users.

One method is an elaborate built-in auditing system. It may not keep unauthorized people from obtaining confidential data, but the system will let you know if they do. Another approach is to split the data into separate systems or programs, with controlled access to each. This runs contrary, though, to the modern concept of a central data base management system, and it has a built-in danger. If you do not adequately control access to every element of such a system, it actually could be less secure than the system it replaces.

Then there is a menu-driven approach, which presents a user with a list of authorized functions from which to choose. This helps keep the user from wandering off unsupervised into other parts of the system.

A method that ultimately may solve the problem produces software that can be certified against a particular set of security standards. The customer can determine what security needs the program and its data must meet. The vendor will produce a program designed to meet those needs.

The biggest drawback to this technique is that we have not yet perfected the art of writing this kind of software. Most importantly, customers are only now waking up to their security problems. To a large extent, they still don't know what standards they should set for the vendors to meet.

Research in this area might proceed along the lines of a classification system set up by the Defense Department's Computer Security Center. The center has the specific assignment of developing more trustworthy security systems and evaluating available products for their ability to protect sensitive data.

The center's classification system recognizes four basic levels of security. At the top, adequate protection is built into the system. It needs only minimal added security. At the other end of the scale, the equipment is considered untrustworthy without extensive physical and environmental protection.

Most available computers are near the bottom of that scale. Until recently, most commercial users had assumed there was no need for anything that approached a military level of security. One result is that the Defense Department is forced to operate its computers at well below peak efficiency to give the necessary add-on security a chance to work. Civilian users are likely to choose efficiency over security, which may be one reason we have seen so much computer abuse lately.

ALTERNATIVES TO THE PASSWORD

When Ernest Brickell broke the Knapsack access code, he had to find which of 100 numbers, each 60 digits long, could be added together to produce a particular 62-digit sum. As he demonstrated, it was difficult but not impossible.

Knapsack is an example of a public key encryption code that uses advanced mathematics to scramble your data, something like the signal from a pay-TV service. It gained its name because the mathematical principle involved is something like trying to make optimum use of your carrying capacity when packing for a hike. It is more advanced than the Data Encryption Standard endorsed by the National Bureau of Standards, but less complex than the code developed by RSA Security Corporation.

The RSA code is generally considered the most secure available. It works with more than 100 digits, and Brickell says he sees "no known way" to break a code that long. He knows how to crack systems of up to 70 or 80 digits, but he also points out that the level of difficulty increases tenfold for every 10 added digits.

These are some of the high-tech alternative controls being developed to replace or supplement passwords and more conventional access restrictions. Their cost and difficulty makes them suitable only for the most vital kinds of information, and as has been demonstrated, even the best are not infallible. There also are other, more conventional means to replace or supplement traditional physical controls.

Badges and Other Identification

Physical access to a computer room is normally controlled by some form of personal identification. The most common version is the security badge.

Several kinds of badges have been developed, many using advanced electronic techniques. Among them, the *photo ID badge* is by far the most common. It's also vulnerable to counterfeiting, theft, and loss. Laminated cards discourage some substitution of pictures and other tampering, but they don't prevent it entirely.

One way to make a photo badge more reliable is to keep a second badge at the guard station where the employee checks in. The guard verifies the employee's identity, keeps the employee's badge, and gives the employee the badge kept at the desk. The badges are swapped again when the employee leaves. The advantage is there's one badge that, ideally at least, never leaves the premises.

An *optical coded badge* uses a geometric pattern of spots laminated into the badge. They can be seen only under infrared light and are hard to counterfeit.

An *electric coded badge* carries its own printed circuit. The guard can test the circuit by slipping the card into a standard card edge connector. It's simple to decode and counterfeit the circuit, however.

A *magnetic coded badge* uses a pattern of magnetic spots. It is moderately difficult to counterfeit or alter this type of badge, but the coding is vulnerable to exposure to magnetic fields.

Magnetic coated strips now are commonly used on credit cards. In fact, the American National Standards Institute has established a pair of alternative standards for them. Unfortunately, tampering and duplicating are easy.

Passive electronic coding uses a built-in circuit that absorbs certain radio frequencies generated by the badge reader. The badge need only be placed near the testing device to get a reading of which frequencies are absorbed. As happens so often, though, ease of use also means ease of abuse.

An *active electronic badge* reader supplies power to the badge by magnetic induction and reads an encoded serial number. The unit will automatically read the badge of any employee who passes. It also can keep a log of entries.

Advanced Access Controls

The password is intended to identify positively anyone who seeks access to the system. Its weakness in doing that has inspired attempts at several other kinds of access control. One that has attracted a lot of attention is a *callback system*. When a user tries to dial into the system, the computer reads the password and determines the normal user of that code. The computer then cuts the connection and dials the password holder's number. The assumption, of course, is that an unauthorized caller would not be at that location.

This system is attractive because it screens the outside caller who might otherwise slip past the security system. Unfortunately—and inevitably—this system has some weak spots, too. One problem is that any assumption can sometimes be wrong. This system assumes that only an authorized user will answer that user's phone. That wouldn't be true if, for example, an employee from the next office manages to slip into the authorized user's terminal location.

In other words, this system identifies the location, not the individual. It cannot positively insure that the proper person is there at the time. Another problem is that a callback system can be seriously clumsy for users who must gain access several times a day.

Another alternative is the *smart card* like those used in ATM banking terminals. It's possible to encode a considerable amount of information in a modern card. A chip inside the remote terminal can be programmed to verify that the right person is calling from the right place.

Still, it isn't not perfect. The card system again suffers because the system identifies the card, not the person. It's practical only when you can maintain strict control over access cards or, as with a bank card, the user has a strong motive to do so.

Designers have been working on some new approaches to access control, including ways to identify voice patterns, fingerprints, signatures, and eyeballs. All are still experimental and are too limited, expensive, or time-consuming for most applications.

Consider, too, the personal privacy problems of registering someone's fingerprints or eyeball vein patterns in a system which itself might be vulnerable to improper access.

ASSESSING SITE SECURITY

Don't be confused. Data communication and other recently developed techniques mean you can no longer rely just on physically securing the computer site itself. That doesn't mean, that site security is no longer important. It's still an important component of the overall security package.

In fact, the increasing use of communication can have one security advantage. It becomes more feasible to locate your major computer facilities at some distance from other operations. That means you will have fewer people in the vicinity and fewer problems trying to control traffic. It also means a fire or other emergency in the main building will not as readily endanger the computer center.

In planning your site security there are a number of factors to consider, such as

- ☐ Location
- ☐ Site characteristics
- ☐ Fire protection systems
- ☐ Supporting systems such as power and air conditioning.

It Doesn't Pay to Advertise

One of the simplest beginnings to a site security program is to remove any signs that point to the data center. Those who are authorized to use the center should know where it is. Those who aren't, don't need to know.

In that light, the only people who would find the signs really useful would be illicit users, who would be told exactly where to go to begin their dirty work. If you *must* have direction signs for some reason, post them outside the main flow of traffic. Make the unauthorized user seek some other way of locating the room—like asking directions from a security guard. While you're getting rid of signs, don't forget any listings that might be found in building directories.

If you have the luxury of picking a site, look for a place that is not susceptible to damage from natural forces like wind, floods, or earthquakes. Try not to install your sensitive electronic gear in the path of blowing sand.

Build to suit the location. There's hardly anywhere on earth that a basement location is suitable for a computer. If the equipment isn't quickly drowned by a storm or bursting water pipe, it could slowly rust to death. Remember this bit of news from the insurance industry: More computer damage claims are due to water damage than any other source.

Fire in any kind of electronic equipment will do a lot of expensive damage before it can put out much heat. That means you'll need highly sensitive fire detection devices in the computer center. Standard sprinkler systems usually are set to go off when the temperature at the ceiling reaches about 165 degrees Fahrenheit. Your fire detector should be set much lower: 130 degrees tops, and lower if you can manage it.

Don't install a system that will douse your equipment with water; that gains nothing over letting the fire burn. Although it is expensive and has been criticized as unreliable, most authorities recommend Halon equipment. Put water sprinklers in noncomputer rooms, particularly those where paper is stored. Halon would do a poor job on a fire in such an area. If possible, combine the fire detection system with alarms that will warn of power or air conditioning failures. Wire the system to shut down operating equipment before the Halon is discharged.

A Secure Floor Plan

The layout of your building will have a big effect on its security. Most authorities recommend, at most, two entrances: a door for employees and a loading dock for supplies, etc.

From each entrance to the computer area itself there should be a single route, easy to monitor and used by no one else. One company found that questionable access to its computer fell sharply when it moved a terminal that had been stationed at a major intersection of office traffic. Try to make each person pass through successive layers of security.

Unfortunately, the barriers that restrict unauthorized people will restrict your regular workers much more often. You'll have to compute a tradeoff between access for workers and restrictions on others.

Backup systems for your power and air conditioning can keep the computer running when everything else goes down. Again there's a trade-off, though, because backups are expensive. Whatever support equipment you install, establish a strict preventive maintenance program to improve its reliability.

PICKING YOUR TACTICS

As with every aspect of security planning, the first step is to assess your needs. Then develop a security plan designed specifically to meet them. That plan will be a mix of the right kinds of tactics.

The computer security experts at SRI International compiled for the Justice Department a list of possible tactics, evaluating them for their effectiveness against particular areas of vulnerability. The National Bureau of Standards has compiled a similar list. Here are the major control strategies the two agencies considered. Not every one will be right for you—in fact, the list includes some sets of alternatives. At the same time, there probably is no one selection that will do what you need. Analyze your needs and find out where you are vulnerable. Then examine these recommended tactics and decide which best fit your situation.

Passwords

This is the basic means of access control, and we've already discussed it at length. As the SRI and the Justice Department note in their report, passwords are used so commonly there is almost no standard way to manage them.

Normally, the report suggests, each user should have his or her own password. Occasionally, a group of people will share the same password, but the most secure method is to let each user select a password known only to the user and stored in the system. It's a good idea to clear personally selected passwords through a computer security administrator to make sure the chosen terms are appropriate and not easy for someone else to guess.

An alternative is to let the computer generate passwords at random and assign them to the users. Or, the security administrator could invent the access codes and make the assignments. Yet another variation is to assign a user an initial password, which the user should immediately change.

If you use a group password, you'll have to change it every time someone leaves the group, particularly if that person is also leaving the company. Passwords should be changed regularly in any event; the more privileged the user, the more often the password should be changed. Change passwords, too, when you find any sign the system has been entered or compromised.

Watch out for security leaks in the process of assigning the passwords. Have a trusted employee deliver the password in a sealed envelope directly to the assigned user, or face to face in a private meeting. A sealed carbon-paper envelope of the kind often used for customer statements could be ideal for this purpose. Get a receipt, acknowledging that the user has accepted the password and the responsibility for using it properly. Keep password records only in a well-protected master file within the computer system. Never save paper copies.

Inevitably, someone will lose or forget an assigned password. In that case, assign a new one and purge the old password from the system. Table 4-1 summarizes the strong and weak points of most common password systems.

One method of password administration sug-

Table 4-1. Password Strengths and Weaknesses.

gested in the Justice report is a system in which the computer automatically generates passwords, using a random letter/number generator. Deliver them to the users in sealed envelopes.

This system has some built-in safeguards. If a user expects a new envelope but receives none, that's a signal something is wrong. The best response usually is to cancel the missing password. Do the same if the envelope shows signs of tampering. Table 4-2 assesses the strengths and weaknesses of this system.

The user-generated password is an alternative assignment method in which users can change their own passwords at any time they log onto the system. This method requires that you install some way to keep anyone else from changing a password. It might be a program element the user could activate, or the ability to change could be available only when the user first logs on and establishes an authorized identity. This precaution would be needed, for example, when a user has to leave the terminal briefly and does not want to log off. Without it, a passerby could walk in and alter the password.

The password changing program should also require that the user enter the new password twice. If the two versions don't match, allow for a limited number of retries, but don't give an unauthorized user a chance to keep on trying until he finally gets it right. Consider this system when the users are parts of a scattered network and delivery of sealed envelopes would be impractical. Table 4-3 summarizes the benefits and drawbacks.

Restricted File Access

Any file whose compromise or modification

Table 4-2. Assessing Automatic Generation.

Table 4-3. User Generation.

would be a serious loss should be protected by a password system, the Justice report recommends. That should include restricting the *type* of access allowed: read-only, add-only, modify, change the access controls, change the file name, or some combination of these.

There are commercial file access control systems available for some makes of systems. Similar controls are built into the operating systems of some other brands. The system should include a journal of access activity, including an exception report that would note such things as unauthorized attempts to reach specific files. Like most other kinds of control, this system relies on effective administration in such areas as assigning passwords and access rights. Table 4-4 summarizes this technique.

Control the Controls

You should establish a formal procedure to be used when anyone wants to have a new kind of access to the system or to change the existing control methods. Prepare a standard request form to be submitted to a computer security coordinator.

Give the successful requester a written permit that specifies the conditions of the access and the user's other privileges. Have the user sign a document indicating that he or she understands the conditions. Table 4-5 assesses these tactics.

Control Use of Terminals

One of the best ways to keep unauthorized users out of your computer is to keep them away from the terminals in the first place. The simplest way is simply to keep the door locked. If that doesn't seem sufficient to protect your sensitive information, consider locks that can be used to shut off the terminals themselves. There also are locking devices to keep terminals and microcomputers from being removed. Table 4-6 assesses these controls.

Log-On Procedures

You can limit unauthorized access by setting up a standard procedure for logging onto the system. In effect, the user who knows the procedure has a kind of extended password.

This is no time to be user-friendly. The system

Table 4-4. Restricted Access.

Benefits
The written conditions and signed documents help establish an understanding of the type of access you are granting. They impress the user with the limits and help discourage violations. This procedure also defines the duties of your access coordinator and of the users.

Drawback
This system can create a mountain of paperwork, and its bureaucratic procedures may be excessive for a small, informal organization.

Table 4-5. Assessing Access Administrations.

should expect the user to complete a full identification sequence before it makes any response that isn't absolutely necessary. It should do nothing, either, to correct an improper entry. Until the user has completed the entire sequence successfully, the system should not identify itself or display a prompt that's any more helpful than, say, the A > of a standard microcomputer operating system.

After the user has properly completed the sequence, the computer can issue an effusive welcome to the system. Until then, it should display a stolidly blank screen.

At a minimum, the expected sequence should include the assigned password plus some other kind of personal identification such as the user's name or account number. Better yet, also expect the user to enter a correct, unprompted code for the file or program to be used.

Make sure the screen display does not show the password as it is entered. Try to avoid any command that would send a password to a printer.

Then, in case it should happen anyway, provide for immediate repeated overprints that will quickly make it illegible.

Give the user a chance to correct mistakes, but three consecutive wrong entries should disconnect the telephone line. Hang up, too, if there is an excessive delay before the user enters the password or other information. Include a recordkeeping system that keeps track of log-ins and produces exception reports of improper or unsuccessful attempts.

Another tactic suggested in the Justice report is not to cut off all unauthorized access. Instead, provide something innocuous for the unauthorized user to play with while an alarm alerts you to the invasion. It may have been this kind of advice that uncovered the Milwaukee group. One of the raided computers offered a video game that kept the youngster busy long enough for a telephone trace.

Another good idea is to display after a successful log-in the time and date of the user's last

Table 4-6. Rating Terminal Use Controls.

Strong Points
Locks have a strong psychological effect. Coupled with other well-enforced security procedures they help make employees more security-conscious.

Weak Spots
Locking and unlocking can be a time-consuming burden, particularly when the terminal gets only occasional use. In many cases, though, you can open the lock at the beginning of the working day and leave it that way until you close for the night.

Table 4-7. Log-In Controls Evaluated.

access. This could alert the user to unauthorized use of the password. Table 4-7 summarizes the advantages and drawbacks of these methods.

Other Tactics

Other ideas suggested in the federal reports include:

☐ Store passwords in code within the computer.

☐ Prepare a signed agreement that details the user's rights and responsibilities.

☐ Bill all computer use to the user's department. This gives the department head a chance to check for unauthorized access.

☐ Maintain logs and documentation of all program changes.

☐ Restrict access to utilities that could bypass the security system.

☐ Control access to system documentation.

☐ Keep detailed records of access to particularly sensitive files.

☐ Maintain a log of any commands that would modify programs or data.

☐ Establish special passwords, modified *daily*, for the most critical data and users.

☐ Require secondary passwords for access to particularly sensitive material.

☐ Automatically disconnect unneeded access lines during off hours.

☐ Modify your hardware and software so it will not recognize systemlike prompts from a terminal. This can keep an invader from gaining access by making the system believe the messages are coming from the computer instead of the terminal.

☐ Determine normal use patterns for authorized individuals and departments. Note and check out any significant exceptions.

EVALUATING PHYSICAL SECURITY

An ideal physical security system would minimize the number of false alarms and maximize the number of true alarms. It would be hard to deceive, evade, or counterfeit. It would be inexpensive to buy and operate. It also doesn't exist. Every security system is a compromise between good and bad features. The real test is whether you can enjoy most of the advantages and avoid most of the drawbacks in your own circumstances. Analyze your needs and tailor a solution to meet them.

The answers to these questions can help you determine whether you have established an adequate physical security program for your needs:

☐ Is your physical security program part of a larger overall plan for the total security of your computer system?

☐ Have your systems and methods kept up with changes in technology—particularly the advent of personal computers?

☐ Have employees been made fully aware of both their rights to computer access and the restrictions under which they must work?

☐ Have you included adequate security provisions in the design and construction of new facilities?

☐ Have you provided ways to limit fire and water damage?

☐ Is a single person clearly in charge of monitoring security and access controls?

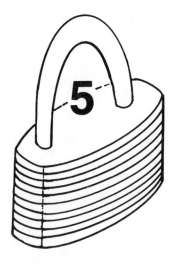

Building Secure Procedures

Any kind of pigeonholing system faces the problem that the pigeons stubbornly refuse to stay in their assigned places. That is certainly true of the three major kinds of computer security: physical, procedural, and technical. They frequently overlap and interlock. You may have noticed, for example, that the last chapter's discussion of physical protection methods often became involved with the procedures for operating and managing the physical systems. Physical protection also involved some technical safeguards.

This illustrates a major point: An effective security program must be a well-planned combination of all available types of methods. You can't rely on one type of protection while ignoring the other two.

The three-way breakdown is useful, though, to discuss and understand the range of tactics available to you. While you often may think of security first in terms of physical controls, the procedural elements of your program can be just as important.

THE ROLE OF PROCEDURAL SECURITY

Thoughts of procedural security may not always come leaping to mind, but secure procedures have a central place in any good computer security system. Procedural security, also sometimes called *administrative security,* deals with the human element. The best physical and technical methods are of little value if your employees do not use them properly. More important, is the fact that you can use procedural methods to build computer security into the way your employees conduct your overall business operations. At the same time, you can minimize the degree to which security measures interfere with full, productive use of your computers.

At its heart, procedural security is a set of management and supervisory controls. It includes rules for the use of computers and data and ways to detect unauthorized use. These controls are applied throughout the computer system, including:

☐ Data input.

Table 5-1. Strong Points of Procedural Controls.

☐ Data processing.
☐ Program development.
☐ Output.
☐ Communication.
☐ Storage.

Because it covers the entire range of computer operations, procedural security becomes an integral part of your business. You'll consider it when hiring employees. Many operating controls will be based on security considerations. Auditing and supervisory techniques will be designed with security in mind. With this overall emphasis by management, you can establish a secure computer system, and back it up with adequate checks and balances, *as an everyday management activity.*

It should be clear by now that any one security technique is a mixture of strengths and weaknesses. Tables 5-1 and 5-2 illustrate the mixed blessings of procedural techniques. You can't fully protect a computer by any one method or any one of the three major approaches. Procedural methods are valuable primarily because they strongly back up

the other two and help keep other controls in proper working order.

Recent surveys have uncovered what might qualify as a latent complaint by data processing managers. Top management is concerned about security, the DP people agree. They wonder, however, whether their superiors are as fully concerned as they ought to be. Several of the surveys mentioned in Chapter 2 came to essentially the same conclusion: top management *thinks* it gives adequate support to computer security, but its actual support often falls seriously short of the need.

This lack of attention increases your vulnerability. If you don't insist on secure procedures, rigidly observed, you are open to loss from such things as sloppy operating procedures, open access to computers, unprotected data storage, and insecure communications.

You depend on your computers. You have no choice but to actively oversee their secure operation. Computer security should occupy a central position in your list of business objectives.

Whatever other security methods you choose,

Table 5-2. Things to Watch Out For.

their effectiveness will depend on how well you provide continuous control over your data, equipment, and employees. Procedural controls will include such considerations as your organizational structure, the quality of supervision, and your ability to detect and correct abuses.

SET YOUR OBJECTIVES

Any good plan starts with a list of the goals to be met. This is particularly important with procedural security because it covers such a broad range and should be integrated with so many other aspects of your operation.

Establishing a Need to Know

The rapid changes that computers have brought to the business world have strained traditional lines of supervision and control. Established lines of authority are crossed easily and often. Computers, and the need to secure them, require that your organization be structured to avoid these problems. A first objective of your new structure should be that it divides individual jobs and duties on the basis of the particular employee's *need to know*.

Traditional organization patterns still can be applied here. It is common, for example, to have one person conduct a financial transaction and to appoint separate supervisors and auditors to monitor it. Whenever possible, separate job duties to provide a system of checks and balances. The person who does the work should not be the same employee who checks it for accuracy.

It isn't always easy. A small company must use more generalists and fewer specialists. The personal computer puts the entire range of computing functions on a single employee's desk. These cases call for closer supervision of the employees and more frequent reviews of their work. You also can restrict the access over personal terminals and computers to information in the central storage unit.

Tailor Your Access Controls

A second objective, related to the first, is to tailor your access controls to ensure that your data is available only to the limited number of people you authorize to use it.

This is largely a matter of managing your use of physical access controls, tailoring them to your specific needs. After you have structured your job assignments on the basis of checks, balances, and a need to know, you must set up a control structure that will maintain the necessary limits and separation.

One basic way is a multilevel password system that will restrict an authorized employee only to the data and programs that are necessary to the job assignment. The design of your access controls should depend on:

- ☐ *Who* must use the system? Which employees will be granted access?
- ☐ *What* purpose requires the access?
- ☐ *When* is it needed? You might be able to limit access to specified times.
- ☐ *Where* will the employee require access? Will this be a local or remote terminal or a personal computer?
- ☐ *How* is the information to be acquired and used?

Journalists should recognize these as the traditional five elements of a basic news story, applied to another use where they work just as well.

Promote Use Along with Protection

It is possible to take security to extremes. If they interfere with easy, productive use of the computer. Some of this is necessary, but it is possible to go so far the information is almost impossible to use because it's so well protected. At that extreme, the security feature defeats itself.

On the other hand, look at the incentives you give your employees. They're usually under strong pressure to produce, both in quantity and quality. The security shortcut often can help boost their output. Supervisors, their own reputations enhanced by productive employees, overlook or even encourage these security lapses. Employees are allowed or even encouraged to share passwords or use other means to bypass access restrictions. Necessary security tasks like making backup copies are postponed or avoided.

The first is an extreme; the second is a common problem. Both should be avoided. It requires a reasonable balance between security and efficiency. Procedures must not be so difficult or time-consuming that there is a strong incentive to evade them.

At the same time, security should be made as important as production. Keep employees and supervisors informed about their particular security responsibilities. Your evaluations of individuals and departments should include proper use of required security procedures. Tell your department heads:

Increased production is of no value if it is offset by a major loss due to lax security.

and be sure you understand it yourself.

Provide an Integrated Program

You need to combine a variety of approaches into an overall program. Procedural methods can serve as vital links in doing this. Good procedures will reinforce other security measures, making them more effective and helping them to work in combination.

It can work the other way, too. If your procedures are not strictly observed, your other controls can be seriously undermined. Employees who swap passwords or supervisors who fail to monitor operations properly can leave you as vulnerable to abuse as if you had no security program at all.

Security should be part of the overall management picture. Observing a security procedure should be just as important as any other job requirement. Let your people know they will be judged accordingly.

Put Security Where It Is Needed

Well-tailored procedural controls also let you aim your security programs directly at the operations that are in most need of attention.

Payroll. This is often the first place a computer criminal would look. Follow that lead, and emphasize payroll in your security plans. Dishonest employees have programmed computers to inflate their paychecks, pay for work not done, continue to pay employees who have left the company, and even to pay nonexistent employees. Even without this kind of dishonesty, a payroll system is vulnerable to calculating errors.

Accounts Receivable. Another vulnerable area, where a dishonest employee can send out fake invoices for sales never made. Many companies pay these invoices without checking their own records. The employee pockets the proceeds. Other sources of possible trouble are an employee's failure to credit properly a receivable or to follow up a customer's complaint of being overcharged. That complaint could mean an error—or a padded bill with a dishonest employee claiming the excess.

Accounts Payable. A big source of risk in accounts payable is to be on the receiving end of a fake invoice and pay the bill without checking. Payments can be made without proper authorization or support. Employees could buy or sell important assets without recording them.

Inventory. This is a prime area for computerization and thus a prime candidate for fraud and error. One computer manufacturer recently discovered that thousands of dollars worth of parts had disappeared with no trace or record. The computer showed them in a warehouse. The warehouse was empty. It's not certain whether the items were stolen or whether the fault was in the computerized inventory system. Either way, poor procedures probably contributed to the loss.

Many of these activities are traditional business crimes performed in years past without the aid of modern data processing. Computerization has made them easier, particularly because businesses that install computers often do away with manual audits and controls.

These controls are even more important in the information age. Proper security of your computerized business assets should be a major business objective.

THE KEYS TO SECURE PROCEDURES

Most procedural security measures are based on two established principles—the keys to effective security procedures.

Make Each Employee Personally Accountable. If a sensitive transaction is being made, you should be able to identify the person responsible and hold that employee personally responsible for the results. You can log the use of passwords and connect the holders with the transactions for which the passwords were used. Audit trails also identify individuals with transactions. You also can use such traditional methods as checking control totals against the actual results.

It Should Take More Than One Person to Commit a Fraudulent Act. This is based on the same principle as checks that require two signatures or safe deposit boxes that need two keys. Don't leave an opportunity for a single criminal working alone. Make the improper user face the risk and difficulty of bringing at least one other person into the scheme.

Good Procedures Made Better

Even good procedures can sometimes be made better. If you keep these points in mind, you can put a keen edge on your program:

Some Files Are More Sensitive than Others. They deserve protection according to their value as an information asset and the amount of damage an unauthorized user could do.

A User Doesn't Have to Know All the Procedural Controls. Unless they are applied to a particular task. Many controls, like logging the employees activity or verifying a data input can be done without visible on-screen activity. These controls should become visible only when someone tries to evade them.

Maintain Audit Trails to Show Who Conducts What Transaction. This is a proven way to assign responsibility for correct, proper methods.

Keep in Touch with Your Security Force. Management holds the primary means to control computer misuse, but when unusual activity or some other sign makes you suspect you have a problem, let security know immediately.

A good procedural security program should include:

- [ ] A *written policy* that spells out employees' responsibility, provides a means to detect violations and has enough management control to make sure it is properly implemented.
- [ ] Existing management controls should be *reviewed regularly* to make sure they have kept up with the development of your computer systems.
- [ ] Your procedures should *maintain control* over processes, computer use, and access to programs and data.
- [ ] Require *regular tests* of your security system to make sure it is adequate and employees are observing the proper procedures.
- [ ] Be prepared to *take action* against anyone caught misusing the system. This can range from minor disciplinary action to criminal charges if necessary. Be ready to take this action even if it might mean bad publicity for the company.
- [ ] Management officials and members of the technical staff should *stay in touch* to discuss security needs and problems.
- [ ] Include security provisions in any *purchase agreement* for new computers or software.

Controls Built Into the Organization

The organizational controls in your security policy should define exactly who is authorized to what, and under which conditions. Maintain individual accountability and assign check and balance functions to different people. Set up supervisory and review systems to monitor each employee's use of your computer resources. Computerization usually reduces the number of checks and balances you have over the operations of the business. That means your level of security must increase.

Work department by department. Establish controls over both the uploading and downloading of sensitive data. Establish procedures to be used when entering the system. Encrypt the most sensitive data, and keep track of which individuals have access to the code. Make sure the system identifies everyone who uses it, including the time and the programs and files used.

All these measures are designed to maintain the integrity of your data and to assign accountability to each user. A department can determine that all work is properly processed, without improper alterations.

Be particularly sure that only authorized employees are allowed access to central data base files, and then only to the files necessary for that employee's job. Once in the file, restrict what the employee can do with it, such as read-only access or a restricted ability to add new data. The people who use the data should not be the same people who are authorized to make major changes in it. If you can't do that, substitute more active supervision and monitoring.

Personnel Controls

These controls deal with the people who make up your company, starting when they are hired and extending until—and even after—they leave. You may not think of it in this way, but your hiring procedures are part of a computer security program. Check out the references and records of everyone you hire. Many employers don't. This is an open invitation to crime and industrial sabotage.

Nondisclosure agreements are becoming a standard job requirement for people who work with computers. IBM, for example, obtains signed agreements not to reveal its trade secrets even after the employee has left the company. When employees have moved to competing companies, IBM has gone to court several times to enforce its agreements.

Other precautions against abuses by your employees include mandatory vacations that keep each employee away from the computer for at least two weeks at a time. An employee who is trying to cover some fraudulent use of the computer usually will have to cover the tracks more often than that. Regular and mandatory job rotations also can make it difficult to engage in long-term abuse.

The departing employee presents a particular problem. Whether the employee resigned or was fired, there may be some resentment that could return in the form of a sabotaged computer. The passwords of departing employees should be canceled immediately. Give a particularly close check to their recent activity records. Increased access time or the use of unusual files or programs may indicate that the ex-employee has been up to something.

Your employees' privacy is an important concern, too. Any file that contains individual information about an employee—payroll and personnel records are the prime examples—should be treated as highly sensitive. Except when it is necessary (to process the payroll or to evaluate the employee, for example), this information should be available only in the form of broad statistical data from which no individual can be identified.

A clear policy statement on employee rights informs the employees of where they stand. It reassures them that information about themselves will be protected. It also discourages searching for data on other employees.

Programming Controls

Controls in this class direct the way in which programs and procedures are written. The employees involved here are programmers, analysts, and other highly skilled people. For example, you should establish a set of standards for writing programs that traps errors and otherwise helps maintain the integrity of their data. A program should resist use in any way that can threaten sensitive data. It should not allow uncontrolled access to important data files or financial transactions.

You can enforce these standards through a continuing review process. Make sure any program or procedure developed is strictly for legitimate company purposes. Otherwise, you could find yourself harboring a well-programmed routine that would quietly strip your computerized resources, putting false records in their place, without anyone's knowledge. You also should conduct regular reviews of your program structures, software development techniques, access controls, and authorization techniques.

Operating Controls

These are the rules to be observed when entering, changing, or using data. The procedures should be set up to check entries against normal value ranges, trapping errors and deliberate incorrect entries. The employees should be held strictly accountable for the data they enter and use.

This aspect of the security system also includes the means to detect and correct errors and to hold the appropriate employees accountable for them.

Staying in Control

This has not been a list of alternatives from which you can make selections. You should implement *all* the procedural controls, excepting only those that clearly don't apply to your situation.

Many of these controls also require periodic reviews to make sure they still are in place and working as they should. It is your job to make sure that the monitoring and control functions continue to help maintain your security goals.

GOOD TRAINING IS IMPORTANT

The department heads at one recent training session were a bit surprised to be served fortune cookies along with their seminars. When the first cookie was opened, the reason was obvious. The message inside read, "Ill fortune will befall one who shares password." Other cookies contained messages (minus the pidgin Chinese) like these:

- [ ] Choose a password no one else can easily guess.
- [ ] Change your password at least once a month.
- [ ] Information on customers is to be treated

in strictest confidence.
- [ ] You are responsible for anything done under your password.
- [ ] Log off before you leave your terminal.

This was a gimmick, although probably an effective one, designed to remind these experienced people of their data security responsibilities. It was devised by Carolyn Crowson, security manager for Seattle First National Bank, as part of an overall information and education program to make all employees more security-conscious—and to keep them that way.

As Crowson points out, educating employees to think of data security as important should be one of your major priorities. The procedures you put into place must be executed by people. The people must be trained to observe these procedures. They'll also require regular reminders of their duties and responsibilities.

What Training Should Accomplish

A good security training program should meet these objectives:

- [ ] New employees should learn the company's computer security policies and procedures.
- [ ] More experienced employees should develop a greater understanding of why the procedures are in effect and how they are implemented. Better understanding usually brings better compliance.
- [ ] Managers should gain more knowledge of security policies and techniques.
- [ ] Managers also should be able to make effective decisions, directing effective security measures at the specific threats they face.

Formal training is only one way to educate employees about their roles in the security program. There are many ways to provide both formal training and regular refreshers. Again, look for the methods that work best in your organization. Some possibilities include:

- [ ] Data security articles in company publications.
- [ ] Management letters distributed to department heads and other managers at various levels.
- [ ] Have your staff prepare security articles for trade journals in your field or in computer industry publications. For example, the computer industry newspaper *Computerworld* regularly solicits articles on your in-the-field experiences, particularly if you've been able to solve a problem of some kind.
- [ ] Establish a password awareness program to teach the importance of password security. It could include a "bumper sticker" type of message on a computer terminal, reminding the user of one password protection rule. You also could provide more detailed explanations in brochures or bulletin board notices.

Use Existing Programs

Computer security can easily be added to many existing training and orientation programs. Normally, all you need do is to write a data security module to be inserted into the appropriate programs.

These modules could be tailored for use in various types of training: employee orientation, management training, technical training, and project management programs are all good places to add material on data security.

Security training courses are obvious candidates for data security material. At Seattle First National Bank, for example, a robbery training course required by law has been fleshed out to include material on data security. Crowson says that program has had a direct impact in detecting and preventing attempted fraud in wire transfer transactions. Any orientation course can include an awareness program to emphasize the importance of computer security.

Developing Material

Some employees will need more specialized training. For example, auditors, programmers, project managers, and similar employees will need detailed training in security. These should cover the company's main areas of vulnerability, emphasizing the available solutions to these problems.

Take advantage of any in-house resources you have, or can develop, for preparing and presenting training sessions. Look in particular for people who can prepare strong visual presentations, like video tapes. Don't try to make the same presentation cover everything. Consider the nature of your audience, and prepare a program directly related to these employees' needs and responsibilities. Test your initial presentations on pilot audiences to get their reactions. Use that experience to polish your act.

Remember, training is expensive. It requires good materials, and it takes people away from their jobs. Make sure you prepare a sound program that will effectively help employees do their part on the computer security system.

Subjects and Format Choices

Depending on the needs of the audience, a computer security training program should include these topics:

- [ ] The company's *physical security* system, including the procedures employees should follow when passing security checkpoints.
- [ ] Procedural security measures, again emphasizing the proper actions you expect employees to take.
- [ ] Security controls built into the system and how to use them properly.
- [ ] The legal and social needs for security, including privacy, trade secrets, and liability problems.

Don't limit yourself to the traditional training process of an instructor who lectures a room full of students. Consider all forms of communication. Use those that best get the message across. Among the possibilities are:

- Workshops and seminars.
- Video tape and other visual presentations.
- Written materials, including books, reports, and specialized publications.

WHAT A GOOD PROGRAM REQUIRES

An ideal procedural program should have these characteristics:

- It should be *nondiscretionary*. Employees should have no practical choice but to observe the prescribed procedures.
- It should be *automatic*. The controls should be a built-in part of normal working procedures.
- It should *not be a problem* to authorized employees who do their jobs properly.
- It should *sound a warning* when the system is used improperly.
- It should be *self-monitoring*, depending as little as possible on constant supervision. Human monitoring is an important part of the process, but the system should not be designed so an error could slip past at some moment when the supervisor is not available.
- It should leave room for *innovations and new developments*.

It is not easy, nor even always possible, to meet all these demanding criteria. But come as close as you can. Don't make the common mistake of assuming that traditional management controls will automatically work in a computerized setting. This is a quick invitation to false security. Don't make the follow-up mistake, either, of assuming that controls developed primarily in a mainframe setting will automatically work for microcomputers and communication networks. As we'll see in a coming chapter, these present an entirely new set of security challenges.

Another mistaken assumption is that the program you have in place will continue to be good enough. As computers and security techniques advance, the program that seems adequate may actually be seriously deficient. Keep abreast of new needs and techniques, and make sure your program does the same.

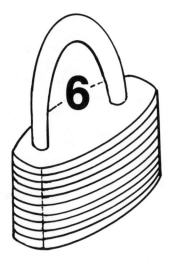

Built-In Security

Two men were arrested recently at a Connecticut airport, where they were trying to buy tickets to Hawaii. Stuffed into their clothing was about $15,000 that, police charged, had been taken in nearly 250 separate withdrawals in a single night from automatic bank teller machines in nearby Springfield, Massachusetts.

The two aroused suspicion at the airport, because they carried no luggage and planned to pay cash for their tickets—a standard profile of airline hijackers. It was only later, after police checked with banks in the vicinity, that the computerized loss was discovered.

NO PROTECTION IS AUTOMATIC

As police later reconstructed this incident, one of the two men had stumbled upon an input code that allowed him to make repeated cash withdrawals from the ATMs operated by a Springfield savings bank. The transactions somehow were not registered by the system as withdrawals.

The two men and a teenager then went on a one-night spree, making the mass withdrawals from eight different ATMs. The bank knew nothing until it it opened Monday morning to find itself nearly $40,000 short. After the arrests at the airport, police also arrested the teenager and confiscated a car he apparently bought with his share of the proceeds.

This case illustrates an important point to remember when planning a security program. Banks know their ATMs can be vulnerable to crimes like this. Accordingly, these units have some of the most elaborate built-in security systems ever devised. Yet there was at least one flaw, and someone was able to exploit it. Even the best built-in security systems can be beaten.

No form of computer protection is perfect. Each has weaknesses that reduce its effectiveness. Your objective is to build a system of security measures that compliment each other and offset each other's shortcomings.

In spite of its own shortcomings, as illustrated

in the ATM case, the technical security you can build into the system itself is an important part of the package.

Looking Too Good?

Technical security, of the kind that's built into the computer or its software, is an attractive means of protection. In fact, its biggest fault may be that it looks *too* good.

Promising advances have been made in the methods of technical protection. The best of these methods literally make the computer protect itself. This does have this one big drawback: people have to use the computer. Like other forms of protection, technical security measures tend to pose difficult barriers to legitimate users. They're also hard to apply to modern developments like microcomputers and networks.

Even so, technical methods can play a big part in your overall security program. In fact, technical security has become more important as computers have become more vulnerable. The more functions a computer will perform, the more flexibly programs are designed, and the more involved in computer operations, the more you need good technical security as part of your package. Table 6-1 illustrates a paradox: you must make full use of advanced computer technology to protect yourself from the losses this same advanced technology makes possible.

The Growing Role of Technology

There is one school of thought among security experts that we have relied too much on technical fixes and have paid too little attention to other measures that might be more effective. The increased use of personal computers in business has brought more attention to technical protection, however.

You hardly can establish a locked computer

Table 6-1. Technical Developments and Responses.

Development	Vulnerable Areas	Technical Needs
Computer processors have become faster and more complex.	Passwords may be bypassed before the system can detect it.	High-speed identification methods.
More people know how to use the computer.	Unauthorized employees can gain access to sensitive information.	Multiple levels of access control.
More people have technical computer knowledge.	Programs modified to bypass normal controls.	Use input-output protection to isolate users.
Micros and remote terminals have decentralized computer operations	More opportunities for improper access.	Isolate users and regulate their access.
Information has been centralized in data base systems.	More opportunity for manipulation or misuse of data.	Allow access only to authorized files.

room for all your micros. When nearly everyone has access to a computer, it becomes harder to monitor compliance with your rules and procedures. That means technical security is of increasing importance, particularly when you link all the desktop micros into a communicating network.

Strictly speaking, it's impossible to build a perfectly secure computer. The protective technology one person can design, another can defeat. It's never safe to assume that any particular combination of hardware and software is secure against some new or unexpected type of attack.

It is possible, though, to design technical protective measures that will protect you against most types of crime and abuse. Often the technique requires more ingenuity than it does money. Technical solutions, then, can often be very cost-effective.

A MATTER OF DEFINITION

Built-in security is a combination of controls within your hardware, software, and communication systems. As you can see from Table 6-1, their purposes are similar to those of the physical and procedural methods discussed earlier. All three types of systems interact and support each other. The three basic types of technical security also overlap and work together:

- [ ] *Hardware controls* are used to make sure the operating system functions properly and to control access to the programs and data.
- [ ] *Software controls* are used primarily to identify users and control their access. They also let you monitor use of the system.
- [ ] *Communication controls* are applied to networks, modems and other communication system components to control access and the flow of data over the system.

All work together to help improve your security. Sometimes they are combined, such as when security controls are built into the *firmware* of read-only memory.

Technical Security Goals

Most technical security methods are aimed at one or more of the objectives listed below.

Maintain the *integrity* of your computer system and its contents. The computer should do its job correctly and consistently. Your data must be reliable, and your programs must process it without error. These qualities can be important in such functions as payroll, inventory, and finances. Poor integrity can leave you open to fraud, theft, and embezzlement.

Keep sensitive information in *confidence*. This is largely a matter of access control. The information in your data base files often is critical to the operation of your business. It may include critical financial details or trade secrets which, if not protected, can have a critical effect on your business. You also must be careful to protect the privacy of personal data on your employees and customers.

Make the computer's services *available* whenever they are needed. You certainly know the perils and frustrations of a computer that goes down. Good technical controls can help you minimize that problem, protecting the system from sabotage, accidents, misuse, and even poor design.

It's Not Always Easy

Technical security measures have yet another thing in common with their physical and procedural counterparts. No matter how badly they are needed, there always seems to be some reason they cannot be applied immediately and to their full effect. Usually it is because they get in the way of normal business operations.

Employees, and even managers, aren't always willing to support the security effort, particularly when it interferes with the ease or productivity of their work. You aren't always able to exercise the close supervision good security often requires. Then there is the common problem of a budget that simply doesn't have enough money for all the security measures you would like to have in place.

In fact, you easily could find that your programmers and technicians can easily create all the technical security measures you want. Your real problem will be to overcome the many conflicts you will encounter between your need for security and the other goals of your business. For instance, access control requires, at a minimum, a delay while the user enters and the computer responds. Then consider the costs and delays you face should someone lose a password. Encryption can protect data—but at the expense of delays, difficulties, and reduced operating speed. It's hard to accept these problems, particularly when you depend on your computer for quick decisions.

The only way to resolve these conflicts is to set priorities. Determine how important security is to you, compared with other goals such as efficiency and productivity.

The priority you give to security will depend in part on how much value you place on the competing functions. Compare this with the value of the information you are trying to protect. You may find that security deserves a higher priority than you'd thought.

WHERE TO USE TECHNICAL SECURITY

Technical security often is designed to serve many of the same purposes as physical and procedural methods. This doesn't mean, that they duplicate each other. Instead, your approach should be to make these techniques work in tandem, complementing each other. For example, the physical requirement for a password can be backed up by procedures that protect its security and require its use, and by built-in features to prevent evasion and misuse.

Technical security methods may do many of the same jobs as other techniques, but they do them in different ways. Some of the major applications of technical security techniques include:

- ☐ *Separating* the material to which a user is allowed access from other resources inside the system.
- ☐ Protecting one user's data from *other users*.
- ☐ Controlling access from *remote locations*.
- ☐ Defining and enforcing *levels* of access control.

☐ *Monitoring* the system for improper use.

Maintaining Separation

Some of the most sensitive information your business maintains is the personnel file. It contains data that must be kept in confidence, both to protect the employees' privacy and to avoid the disruption and jealousy that could infect your organization should someone know the details of everyone else's personal and economic life.

You can use technical methods to help protect information like this. The information should be *compartmentalized* within the computer's active memory and its storage facilities. Place the data in small, segregated files. Then use hardware and software techniques to restrict a user's access only to those small chunks of information that individual needs to do the job. Access to particularly sensitive files, like the personnel records, should be on the basis of a strict need to know. Then have the computer provide only the data that is needed to be known.

You can include these restrictions in programs, which allow the holder of a certain password or other identification code access to material in a specified file. You also can use technology to control access to particular computers, peripherals, or stored media. The available methods can include controls on access to information within the computer memory, or you can block unauthorized users from operating certain procedures.

Isolating Users

If there's one file more sensitive than your personnel records it is your collection of payroll data. If there's one file that is harder to protect, payroll is it. The problem: you must maintain security at the same time your payroll clerks work with this file—all of it—every pay period.

Again, separation is the basic technique. An employee's ability to alter payroll data should be limited to prevent such common criminal techniques as crediting extra time or even creating phony employees.

Another level of separation is needed, too. You

must include blocks that keep the data called up by a payroll employee from becoming available to someone else who logs onto the system at the same time. Once the payroll operation has been finished, the data should be cleanly purged from memory.

The separation techniques will also be effective in protecting you from accidental access as well as deliberate acts.

Securing Remote Terminals

The need to restrict access only to certain blocks of data is closely related to the need to limit access. The network setting is one place where this could be important. Take, for instance, a sales force operating out of several branch offices, all connected to your central computer by a communications network. Each sales office maintains its own file of customer records.

Where is this system vulnerable? Let's say a competitor should become interested in finding out who your best Chicago-area customers might be. It would take only a little computer and communications expertise to tap into your network and get a look at the customer files. The competitor may find an unprotected terminal or learn the dial-up access procedure for your computer. While he's at it, he can get Denver and Atlanta, too.

This means you're entire communication system must be secured. One way is to encrypt the customer file data (do your password files, too). Or you could use a callback routine to identify either the individual or, more likely, the authorized terminal. You might also use the physical security techniques of patrols or cameras around the terminals and other access points.

Setting Levels of Sensitivity

Many of the elements of a security system tend to define each other. How you separate employees according to their needs for various data also largely defines how you will separate the data into "compartments" for access by the authorized employee.

Many access control software programs work by compartmentalizing the files according to *levels of sensitivity*, much like the military system of Top

Secret, Secret, Confidential, and so on. An individual is cleared for access to information at a certain level, and that access right is connected in the computer with the user's access code. To reach a file at a certain level, you must give a password that reflects your access to material on that level.

Leaving an Audit Trail

A good security system will not stop at access control alone. It also should keep a record of its work. Anyone who tries to gain access—successfully or not, legitimately or not—should leave a distinct trail of electronic footprints. The system should tell you who was there, when, and what they did.

Pay particular attention to the use of your most sensitive files. If you see *any* reason to suspect a problem, check it out right away.

SOME TYPICAL APPLICATIONS

If the functions and applications of technical security sound a lot like the functions and applications of other kinds of security, you're right. All are intended to do much the same set of tasks. Your technical measures should back up your physical and procedural techniques, and all three should reinforce each other as elements of a total security program.

Backing Up Passwords

You may have discovered in Chapter 4 that passwords aren't as effective as you had thought. If so, you're probably in the majority. Many managers, particularly those who aren't well-versed in computer technology, play a one-round mental game of word association. The clue "security" brings the quick response, "password." And it never goes much farther than that.

A password is effective only as part of a large security program, and then only if it is managed well. It makes sense, too, to back up the physical and procedural aspects of a password system with technical controls.

A fundamental technical control for passwords

is a routine that will keep the password from being displayed on a screen or printer. At the next level of sophistication, the system should encrypt the files that contain password assignments. A system that can generate random passwords for assignment to their users is another example of technical support. Or consider this possibility: a microcomputer program that controls access in the same way many such programs are now protected against copying.

Restricting Remote Access

As the hacker community has demonstrated, the telephone lines coming into our computers are major sources of damage and disruption. The networks that connect remote terminals and computers are highly vulnerable to security problems. Technical controls alone can't block all unauthorized access but like everything else, they can contribute to the cause.

An automatic dial-back system is one technical feature that can help close a major opening to crime and misuse. There also are devices to determine without the callback that a remote device hooked to the computer is actually one of yours. If the terminal is not one you've authorized for access, the system might be able to locate it and close down its access.

Of course, controls like these identify the hardware, not the user, and they still leave you vulnerable to an unauthorized person misusing an authorized terminal, or even an authorized user on an authorized terminal doing an unauthorized act.

That only illustrates what by now should be a familiar point: don't depend on one technique alone—or even one type of technique alone. Use them in combination to back each other up.

A SECURITY SHOPPER'S GUIDE

Because technical security is largely a hardware/software solution, establishing this part of your security program will largely be a matter of obtaining the right kind of hardware and software.

Of course, writing a check isn't all there is to it. Good security requires that your purchases be evaluated and that you fit them into your overall security scheme. They will do no real good if they don't suit your individual needs. You also must expect to take some steps on your own.

There is a wide variety of security products on the market, enough to cover most of your technical security needs. This list is neither complete nor necessarily representative, but it does indicate some of the types of products now on the market:

☐ Comprehensive mainframe security packages designed to work with the system's existing operating system. This is the type of system purchased by banks and other large, highly security-conscious organizations. (Example: Top Secret, by CGA Software Products.)

☐ Gnosis, a program designed particularly to guard against programmers who write programs to evade security measures. The package, still under development at last report, also isolates users and material in timesharing and multiple user systems. (Tymeshare Inc.)

☐ Sherlock, a multifeatured protection system that authenticates messages, encrypts information, and organizes the information access in network systems. (Analytics Communications Systems, Reston, Virginia.)

☐ Lazerlock is a software program designed for personal computers as well as larger units. You can call for a security check at any chosen point in the program, and the user must use a hand-held decoder to continue. (United Software Security, McLean, Virginia.)

☐ Fiber-optic communication cables, which generally are more secure than conventional electronic links.

☐ Communication by infrared light beams. These can be made so small they are almost impossible to locate and intercept.

Rating System Established

There is a wealth of software and equipment

on the market to help you improve your system's security. But how well does it work? To help you answer that question, there now is a standard rating system for computer system security. Called the Trusted Computer System Evaluation Criteria, it was developed by the Federal Government with help from the Institute of Electrical and Electronics Engineers (IEEE) and the Association for Computing Machinery (ACM).

One part of the rating system is a list of six fundamental requirements a secure system should meet. A second major part is a rating system that ranks systems and components according to the level of security they provide.

Because the evaluation criteria were first published in 1983, several equipment manufacturers have applied to the government's Computer Security Center to have their products evaluated and assigned to one of the system's security classifications. Other manufacturers are expected to develop additional products that will help meet the classification system.

Of course, these classifications will be useful mainly to companies that are buying complete new systems. You still can use the same guidelines, though, to evaluate your existing system and its individual components.

According to the evaluation criteria, a secure system should meet these requirements:

- [ ] It must implement an *explicitly defined security policy*. This policy should describe fully how you wish to grant access to information.
- [ ] All information should be *classified according to its security level*.
- [ ] Every individual who is authorized to use the system should be *positively identified* and granted access only to *designated processes*.
- [ ] Any action that might affect security must be *recorded*.
- [ ] The hardware and software components of the system should be designed so each can be *evaluated independently*.
- [ ] Provide as much protection to your *security*

mechanisms as you do to the information it is supposed to guard.

Systems Classified for Security

Based on how well a system meets these requirements, the evaluation guide will place it in one of four classes, according to the level of protection it offers.

Class A. The most secure, they must have a secure, verified design based on a formal model of an established security policy. The hardware and software must work together to ensure that the policy is constantly enforced. The main requirement for this class is a verification system to guarantee that the security functions will work as intended.

Class B. These systems also implement a formal security policy, and they maintain separate levels of sensitivity. Systems in this class control all access by users, and they maintain extensive audit trails. Some systems in this class have reference monitors to direct proper access to sensitive material. Some also contain formal mathematical models for the security policy.

Class C. These systems provide access on a need-to-know basis, either by the individual or by members of designated groups. Each authorized group or user is recognized by a unique identification code. A subdivision of this class adds features that keep authorized users from scavenging data from memory or storage, identifies each user, and establishes an audit trail.

Class D. These systems fail to qualify for any of the more secure classes. Users of these systems rely primarily on procedural and physical controls.

Security by Default

An important feature to look for in any security system: It should offer security *by default*, not as the exceptional condition.

Under a system of *security by exception*, you must decide, item by item, which files and activities the system should protect. This requires a long decision-making process with the ever-present possibility that you might forget to cover something important.

A system of security by default initially covers everything in the system. Then, if you decide it is not necessary to secure a particular file you can exclude it from the security coverage.

An exception system might be the right choice for a small user who wants to protect only a few sensitive files. For larger systems, a default system is much easier to manage. It also insures that if you make a mistake in a coverage decision, you err on the side of safety.

Security by default also protects newly created files from the moment they enter the system. This eliminates the chance someone will neglect to secure an important new file.

A MODEL FOR SECURE SOFTWARE

Software plays at least as great a role in security as hardware. Proper software design is particularly important to controlling the types of information a given user is allowed to retrieve. The basic technique: design a program that shows the user as little as possible, although, of course, enough for the user to do the job at hand.

A method to design such a program was developed a few years ago by the National Bureau of Standards, with the help of other government agencies and private firms. It's called the *Hierarchical Development Methodology*. Fortunately, it also can be called HDM.

Programmers who work in the discipline called structured programming are familiar with the top-down method of constructing a program in individual modules or subroutines. HDM might be called a top-down, bottom-up, meet-in-the-middle method.

HDM is something like those childhood word games in which you were given a word ("there," for example) and were asked to subtract one letter at a time, each letter forming a new word. The final word in the sequence is supposed to be "e." The proper solution is, "here," "her," and "he."

This oversimplified puzzle is also an oversimplified explanation of HDM, but it illustrates the main point. The most primitive version of your program is the unrefined data. It then is processed by

a series of subroutines, each building on the results of the last, until you reach the highly refined version that serves as the user interface. The user sees only what you want the user to see: a restricted view comparable to a single letter of one word.

In a data base system, the interface is a particular *view* of the data. The program will relate the user's password or other identification to the particular items, and their arrangement, to which the user is allowed access.

Let's say you have a data base with columns called EMPLOYEE, SALARY, and SUPERVISOR. A user sends a query into the system, which (in the language of dBASE II) would look like this:

LIST ALL EMPLOYEE FOR
SUPERVISOR = 'KELLY'

The system would first check to see if this particular combination of data is authorized for use by the person whose identification was issued. In this case we can assume the individual is authorized. The system would display a list of the employees under Kelly's supervision.

But suppose this same user decided to vary the query a bit:

LIST ALL EMPLOYEE, SALARY
FOR SUPERVISOR = 'KELLY'

There's a bit of a difference here. Now the request is for both the names and the salaries of Kelly's people. Chances are the user's authorized views do not include the salary listing. In that case, the system should be geared not to respond.

The best way to do this would be to separate the data bases. Create one file that lists employees and their supervisors. Set up a separate file with the pay information. Give access to each file only to those people who absolutely need to know its contents.

There is much more to HDM. It's a complex system designed for large operating and data management systems where security and reliability are important. It does provide a useful model, though, for anyone who wants to design security into software.

CONSIDERING ENCRYPTION

The first thing you might do with an encryption system is to give away a key to the code. That is indeed the basis of one of the best-recognized encryption systems now available: the public key system, in which you provide a key to outside users who feed data into your system. You can receive information from anyone to whom you give the key to the system.

But what would keep these people from using the same key to decode information you don't want them to have? It's simple: There is a second key. You use one key to encode the information, the other to decode it. Naturally, you only give out the first one. Then, in the words (almost) of Muhammad Ali, "Data checks in. It doesn't check out.'

The public key system, introduced in 1976 at Stanford University, has since gained recognition as a legitimate state-of-the-art system in computer security. It has had a major impact on the art of encrypting data. Encryption, in turn, is picking up new attention, particularly as a way to maintain security over communication networks.

The natural alternative is a single-key system, in which there is only one key for both encoding and decoding. Naturally, you have to keep the key itself under tight security. Probably the leading single key codes now available are the Data Encryption Standard (DES), developed by the Bureau of Standards, and IBM's own code system, called Lucifer.

The leading systems set up a mathematical challenge similar to that of the Knapsack code discussed at the beginning of Chapter 3. DES uses a 56-bit key, designed so it can be deciphered only by trying every one of an unmanageable number of computations. As the Knapsack incident illustrated, this can be done, but it requires the right combination of time, equipment, and expertise.

Security experts consider a code like DES suitable only for short-term protection. For longer term protection, or if you need the best possible security, they recommend coding schemes that re-

quire multiple passes through the codes written into a DES chip.

The public key system offers several advantages over the single keys. For one thing, you don't have to worry about protecting the public key. You also can do such things as placing electronic "signatures" within the system to identify users and trace their activities.

On the other hand, there is no particular advantage over single-key systems if everyone who feeds data into the encrypted files also is authorized to retrieve and use that material.

Access Control. In particular, both systems must be backed up by some form of access control to identify authorized users of your decoding key. The system must be able to distinguish an authorized user from someone who has stolen the code or has managed to crack it. The system should also control access to multiple levels of security. Other qualities of a good encryption program are:

- ☐ It should work *transparently*. It should inhibit normal and efficient operations as little as possible, and the process should not be overtly visible to users.
- ☐ It should be *automatic*. Data saved on disks, tapes, and other off-line media should be encoded as it is recorded, and this information should be deciphered only as it is retrieved by authorized users.
- ☐ It should allow individual users to place *private data* under individual codes, independent of the automatic process.
- ☐ If used in an extensive communication network, it should provide for *managed distribution* of the keys.

A Less Expensive Alternative. Not all your information, and perhaps not even much of it, may need the full protection of encryption systems like DES or public keys. These are expensive to obtain and time-consuming to use. Don't subject yourself to this continuing expense unless the data you are trying to protect is worth it.

There is at least one less costly alternative. *Data compression programs* are a simple form of encoding data so it requires less storage space. In the process, it also puts your material under a simple encoding scheme that must be decoded to use. It's not as hard to crack as the more sophisticated systems, but it could be useful when a cost-benefit comparison doesn't justify the more secure methods.

Two Ways to Lose. An encryption system has two main weaknesses. The first is that only the most complex codes are unbreakable—and perhaps not even these. Less sophisticated codes yield to less sophisticated code-cracking.

The more likely source of loss is that the code itself will be compromised. Your most sensitive information deserves a strong protection system. A strong system, in turn, demands that you protect the access code itself. This is a human factor, and you must take adequate steps to control it. An encryption system also requires the help of a good access control system.

Encryption also can produce a false sense of security. Be careful not to assume that it is the answer to all your problems or that once installed it will continue to provide security without regular checkups and maintenance.

WHERE SECURITY COULD BACKFIRE

Technology can help solve many security problems. It also can create one. In fact, technical security methods automatically bring with them the key to their own failure. That key lies in the human reaction to technology. We focus so much on the ability of technical methods to protect our computers that we expect too much. We believe the security we build into the systems will do the entire job, and we may neglect other forms of protection.

In particular, warns one security consultant, many managers who build security into their systems fail to realize that these are only parts of a security plan that must extend far beyond the system itself if it is to be successful.

Some managers, says the consultant, feel that because they've installed the "best security money can buy," it is enough. They don't bother to go through the entire process of assessing their risks, developing a plan that will meet those risks, and selecting security methods that will implement the plan.

No system, no matter how good, can offer full protection by itself. Don't lull yourself into thinking that you have no weak spots. They are inevitable. And someone whose attitude is far from complacent may be looking for them.

A TECHNICAL SECURITY CHECKLIST

The federal security criteria and ratings provide a good basing point for any evaluation of your technical security plan, planned or existing. Here are some other points to consider:

☐ Your risk analysis should include an assessment of the degree of technical protection you now enjoy—or lack—with particular attention to networks and communication lines.

☐ Look into special access control software, checking it for useful application to your specific needs.

☐ Design the system to detect and trace unauthorized access attempts.

☐ Make sure you don't rely too heavily on passwords. Back them up with other types of controls.

☐ Establish a firm security policy, and make sure all your controls are useful for implementing that policy.

☐ Set standards for including security considerations in the design, development, and modification of software.

☐ Consider encryption techniques for sensitive data.

☐ Make sure you protect your security provisions as well as you protect other elements of the system.

☐ Check out the security features of any new equipment or programs you buy.

Strong Points to Use

By planning carefully, you can use many security devices and procedures to overlap one another, thus increasing security, saving money, and simplifying security procedures. Look for the following advantages:

- [ ] Built-in security measures often can automate security routines that otherwise would be slow and clumsy.
- [ ] Technical security measures are an integral part of the system. They aren't just added on to it.
- [ ] They can overlap and reinforce other types of security measures and the technical measures built into other parts of the system.
- [ ] Their operation usually is automatic; they require no special effort by the operator.

Problems to Avoid

Technical security measures can easily be overemphasized at the expense of other types of security. You need a mix of security techniques, arranged to reinforce each other. Watch for these problems:

- [ ] Installing technical measures can give you a false sense of security.
- [ ] Particularly if they are poorly designed, technical security measures can interfere with efficient use of the computer.
- [ ] Built-in devices are vulnerable to tampering by knowledgeable users. If so, their work probably will be well hidden. You may not learn about it until serious damage has been done.
- [ ] A technical security device can protect only the part of the system in which it is installed. Other parts, particularly communication lines, remote terminals, and microcomputers, may remain unprotected.

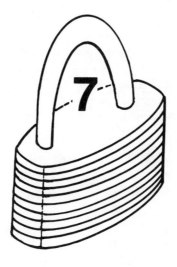

Protecting the Microcomputer

When a small Arizona electronics company decided to computerize its records, it found that a microcomputer was fully adequate for the purpose. Equipped with a hard disk, the micro had all the capacity needed to manage the company's financial records, prepare management reports, manage a parts inventory data base, and do some incidental word processing on the side.

With that much capacity, the company's management began to wonder what else this computer could do—and they came up with one frightening possibility.

The location chosen for the computer was near a well-used path through the building. About 50 people from half a dozen different departments regularly passed that way. The computer was a familiar, widely used model; many of the passers-by probably knew how to use it. Given a few unwanted moments at the keyboard, and any of them could devastate the company's records.

The company did keep a tape backup of the contents of its hard disk. Even so, correcting or replacing the records would be a disruptive, time-consuming process. To add to the problem, it was possible the invasion could go undetected for a critical period of time.

Accordingly, the company began to look for a solution to its problem. That solution turned out to be a password system.

NEW PROBLEM, OLD SOLUTION

The company installed an accessory board (a Stoplock IIR by SDI, Inc.) that has a password system built into its circuits. With the board in place, a user must enter an authorized password to use the computer, and the number of password holders has been limited to seven. The board also records an audit trail of access attempts and can print out a record of the computer's use.

In other words, this company found a traditional solution to a growing modern problem. The spread of microcomputers has presented serious new challenges to computer security. The problem here was typical: a computer full of sensitive data sitting in a highly exposed location.

That's true of many microcomputers, minicomputers, office automation, and other small systems, say computer security experts. Users buy these units for what they consider to be small-scale use. They fail to realize that they are acquiring large-scale security problems. If there is a basic rule of microcomputer security, it would be this:

> *A small computer requires the same kind of security as a large computer—only more of it.*

Most computer security techniques have been developed with mainframes in mind. They are designed to protect large units with extensive files of critical information. There are a few mainframe techniques that can't be readily adapted to micros. Many of the physical protection techniques devised for mainframes are based on having a single computer in a room, or even an entire building, dedicated to its care and feeding. The techniques that protect these locations can't be adapted readily to the micro on every desk.

But that's the exception, and even then standard methods may be easier to apply than you think. Most mainframe security techniques can be—and must be—adapted to the personal computers in your organization. At most, the need only be adapted to their new, decentralized purpose. For example:

- ☐ A *password* system must be as fully developed as the access control system for a larger computer, including proper administration to make sure the passwords are not leaked or shared. Even with a system like the circuit board protector, you must assign passwords that someone else cannot easily guess, and you must change them regularly.
- ☐ You must maintain an *audit trail* to keep track of who has been using the system, when, and for what.
- ☐ You must *separate* the tasks performed by individual users and the types of data to which they have access. This is reasonably

easy when each user has a truly personal computer with which to work. It becomes much harder when the computers are shared or hooked together in a network.
- ☐ Most of all, you need a *security policy* that recognizes personal computers as important elements of your system.

THE CHALLENGE OF MICROCOMPUTER SECURITY

There is one significant difference between microcomputer and mainframe security. Micros make it easier to bypass the usual security and management controls that can be imposed over their more centrally controlled big brothers. They make it harder to limit access, control activity, and segregate duties. A 1983 report by Price Waterhouse identified these particular security threats from the spread of microcomputer use:

- ☐ Financial records can be modified, and you will have no record that it has been done.
- ☐ Limited storage space may mean some records are not kept in great enough detail.
- ☐ Access to information on microcomputer disks—hard or floppy—is not easily controlled.
- ☐ Users may keep inadequate records and backups of their files and activities.

Vulnerable spots like these mean that having a personal computer in the office is like having your own in-house burglary tool. After all, it is the tool used by so many hackers on their cross-country invasions of defense computers, credit records, and medical computers.

The micro's vulnerable spots also have a frustrating ability to multiply. A password that slips out today may be on a hacker's bulletin board tonight, available to thousands of would-be raiders. That's exactly what happened when the password to a major retail chain's credit records was compromised.

It was a month before someone told the company what was happening. By then, illicit users had run up unknown numbers of false credit card charges and had access to the credit records of about 90 million people.

Personal computers multiply your security problems because they multiply the number of sources from which a threat could arrive. What's more, the spread of small computers has been accompanied by the widespread knowledge of how to use them. Where once you had to watch out only for a few knowledgeable computer specialists who worked in an easy-to-control environment, nearly anyone now has, or can easily get, the knowledge to bypass your controls and get into your system. Computers make it easier to conduct many business operations that used to be nothing but boring drudgery. They also have made it easier for computer criminals to compromise these processes.

Take accounts receivable for example. Anyone who's done this process manually would probably add the Youngmanesque "Please." A computerized receivable system can eliminate an intricate, cumbersome process—or at least make it a lot easier for the operator who must do it. The computer also can eliminate the many opportunities for error that go along with manual data entry.

But for everything the computerized system lets you do, it also provides an opportunity for mischief by someone else:

- [ ] You can quickly enter payments, credits, and other changes to a customer's account. The criminal can take this same information out.
- [ ] You can make instant credit decisions by calling the customer's record to your personal computer screen. Someone else can make instant alterations the same way.
- [ ] You can transfer data from the receivables system to other programs such as financial and inventory records. A raider can follow the same route to these other accounts.

To shore up widely scattered weak spots like these, you must include the personal computer in your basic security assessments and policies. Treat the micro like an integral part of the system. That's what your enemies will do.

A POLICY FOR MICROCOMPUTER SECURITY

A sound security policy, properly implemented in practice, gives you a first big advantage over anyone who tries to misuse your computers. To put it simply: You were there first. A good policy lets you anticipate raids on your computer instead of just reacting to them. Elements of a good security policy for small computers include:

- [ ] It should be based on an *overall company plan* for computer security. Think of small computer security as a major element in the larger plan.
- [ ] Include provisions for *communicating* your policy and enforcing it.
- [ ] Include security in your *purchasing* plans. Try to avoid random selection of microcomputers or office automation products that don't work well together. A unified system lends itself to a simple, uniform set of security procedures and equipment. It might also qualify for volume discounts on both purchases and maintenance agreements. Include provisions for cost/benefit analysis of prospective purchases. Once you have the equipment, put it to use maintaining an inventory of all your computer resources.
- [ ] Explain clearly and completely each employee's *responsibilities* for security. Observing proper security procedures should be part of each employee's job requirements.
- [ ] Explain the *reasons* for your controls, including their legal basis.
- [ ] Set *standards* for the use and management of computer resources.
- [ ] Provide *central support* to help small-computer users do their work more efficiently and securely. Make security and proper use an important part of the train-

ing program. Make sure there is help available in case of trouble. The employee who learns to use the computer properly, and who doesn't encounter repeated bugs, is more likely to observe policies and avoid dangerous shortcuts.

☐ Write and post separate notices applying the overall security policy to *each department*. Specify what the workers in each operation should do to help maintain the security system.

Set Priorities

Employees must take responsibility for their use of the computer, proper or improper. That responsibility should extend to supervisors and managers, too. Ideally, you should create a sense of ownership. People who are responsible for a certain file should come to feel that file is *theirs*. That should mean, of course, that it is theirs to protect and maintain, not to manipulate.

Set priorities for the data to be protected and the proper safeguards to be installed for its protection. And don't limit your view to the data that is stored and used within your area of responsibility. Look beyond the office walls to the data transmitted to and from your department. Data transmission lines are among the weakest links. They're even weaker if you forget them in your planning.

Get Involved

There are fewer managers these days who feel it is "beneath them" to operate a computer themselves, but there still are many who don't use computers regularly and who rely primarily on other operators. Even if you don't personally use a computer very often, it is important that you gain a basic understanding of how the equipment works and the role it plays in running your operation.

Don't be afraid to ask questions, either of your own support staff or of the dealers who supply the equipment. Both are supposed to be there to help you. Take advantage of it. In particular, you can use your own experience and knowledge to help establish procedural security standards. It takes

more management than technical skill to decide what duties should be separated and what an employee needs to know. You also can set up the policies and procedures for managing passwords and other procedural elements.

In a Supporting Role

The technical and physical requirements of small computer security may require other kinds of specialized knowledge, but a manager's touch still is required.

Assigning responsibilities, scheduling and budgeting activities, and analyzing the cost-effectiveness of a security plan are important management activities that organize the work of your technicians. It takes a good management head to build good organizational support for the full security program and to integrate security into all the company's operations.

SECURITY TECHNIQUES FOR MICROS

The security techniques for protecting small computers aren't all that much different than those for larger, centrally located units. They just must be adapted to the widely scattered physical locations in which microcomputers and other desktop units are stored.

Physical Security

This is an area where it's easy to give up before you even get started. Certainly, physical control of a scattered group of small units isn't as simple as building a protective ring around a central computer, but it's not that much different, either.

Consider this: There have been few computer crimes in which the criminal has walked right up to a working mainframe to do the damage. In nearly every case the criminal has worked from a distance, entering the computer electronically over its communication lines. That's exactly your major problem with an automated office or microcomputers connected over communication lines.

Then consider this: Many physical security techniques start with the basic locked door, backed up by other means to limit access. Microcomputers used in sensitive applications also can be gathered into a central place where access is easier to control.

It's not so different after all.

The lock and key is the basis to another leading security approach: simply locking the computer. There are many locking devices available that will secure the computer to a table or lock up the keyboard when the unit is not in use.

Another lock should control access to any disks that contain sensitive data. On one hand, a microcomputer disk is such an efficient storage device for its size, your collection of all the company's most important records could go out the door in a briefcase—and not even a well-filled briefcase. On the other hand, the disk's convenient size makes it easy to lock up your stored data. Whether the disk is convenient to you or to the thief depends on how reliably your information is kept in secure storage when it is not in use.

A physical security program also should take into account the special *hazards of office living*. It's been said—by the many who've gained first-hand knowledge—that a spilled cup of coffee is a devastatingly efficient way to ruin a keyboard. Even a puff of cigarette smoke can do a surprising amount of damage if directed to the wrong place—like a hard disk.

One of your major small-computer security problems will be to protect them from all the hazards in their environment. This doesn't just refer to the traditional Big Three of fire, flood, and electrical disturbances, although any of the three can readily do in a micro.

The real hazards to microcomputer operation are the little things. One of computerdom's great disaster stories tells of the disk full of painstakingly created data that was wiped out by a magnetic paper clip dispenser. If the magnet didn't do the damage, an ill-placed piece of dust could have.

A computer really never was designed to exist in the typical office environment. It is sensitive (perhaps unduly so) to radio speakers, fluorescent lights, coffee, smoke, and dust. You must be equally sensitive in searching out these sources of possible trouble and isolating the computers and disks from them.

Welcome to the strange concept of "coffee break productivity." Give your employees ample opportunities, and strict instructions, to take their breaks somewhere else. Light up, if you must, at the same time. Just don't do it near the computer. Then, check out the fire and flood protection. And don't hesitate to invest in electric surge protection and uninterruptible power supplies.

Procedural Methods

If you think it's hard to implement physical security around a microcomputer, it may be even harder to implement any kind of effective procedural security program. But it's necessary. The basic security problem of a microcomputer is that it's so easy for anyone with a microcomputer and some new-found computer literacy to overcome any of the controls you have built into or around your system. Procedural controls help you meet this risk.

Effective procedures may be difficult, but they aren't impossible. Listed below are some ways to attack the problem.

Develop *accountability* for computer use. This should be the main goal of your procedural control system. With computers in the hands of so many new users, it's important to make it clear that the users are totally responsible for their data, equipment, and passwords.

When a file is used in an individual computer, this can be easy. When users are hooked up to central processors or shared storage systems, it can become infinitely difficult. This is why it should be an important part of your training program. Include continuing notices and information on bulletin boards, in employee publications, and through other means.

A system of user accountability also can help you implement controls to help maintain the *integrity* of your data.

When many people use the same file, it often can be impossible to control the accuracy and proper use of that file. One way to make users responsible for their own work is to establish a procedure through which users make themselves and their intentions known before they can work with data from a central file. This check-in can be built into the system, or it can be as simple as being required to check out the disk from a library under the supervisor's control.

Another is a variation on batch processing techniques. Each user who makes additions or changes to a central file enters these changes first onto a disk in the user's own computer. At the end of the day or some other appropriate period, the material from the disks is transferred into the central file. The disk files then are kept for their value in auditing. If you find the disk from which a questionable entry came, the employee who used that disk is clearly the leading suspect.

As an alternative, each entry added to the central file could be flagged with enough information to identify its source. Make sure, too, that everyone is required to make backup copies of their work and to keep necessary logs and documents.

Procedural controls for microcomputers also should reinforce the *password* system. Here again, the microcomputer you are trying to protect is part of the problem. It can be used to generate random password attempts, or a clever user can bypass the security control system.

Even the length of a password is important. Make it at least four letters—below that, the odds of guessing are just too great. Other general types of password controls work just as well with micros. A user who makes an error entering a password should be given only two or three more attempts to do it right. Don't let passwords appear on the screen or printer. Maintain tight security over the password file itself.

A fourth procedural control for small computers is a *monitoring* system to help detect unauthorized activities. There are several microcomputer activities where you can effectively direct a surveillance system.

One of these is the use of on-line systems. If the system keeps track of users—as it should—it is then up to you to read those reports once in a while.

Bring the employees themselves into the monitoring system. Each employee who logs on should be shown the last data and time the employee's password was used. The employee who suspects a misuse should be encouraged to report that suspicion instantly. In the same way, give each employee a regular printed log of a week's or a month's computer use.

Part of the employees' personal responsibility for their use of the computer should be the responsibility to report discrepancies in these use records. Many employees will respond favorably to this kind of responsibility. For those who don't, have fair but firm job rules in place to require that they uphold their areas of responsibility.

Technical Methods

As with other forms of protection, technical controls are not a full answer to your problem, but they are part of it. That's particularly true with micros where the scattered locations and the increasing sophistication of their users make technical solutions harder to implement and easier to evade.

Within these limits, there are several technical solutions that can contribute to your overall strategy.

You will need technical means to back up your *access control* system. The system should have internal controls to identify users, screen out the unauthorized, and restrict what authorized users are allowed to do. The internal controls also should shut down the system if someone makes more than two or three tries to enter a proper password.

Another effective built-in control is one that shuts down a terminal automatically if there is no activity within a certain period. This limits the risk that someone will take advantage of an open, unattended terminal.

Technical controls also can contribute to your controls over access to designated files. Encryption is a useful technical method, particularly for your most valuable data. Don't forget the encrypting effects of data compression programs, which are available for microcomputer data files. Built-in controls also can help impose identification and access procedures for the use and transfer of data and establish audit trails.

Another valuable built-in control is an error-checking mechanism that tests to see if an entered figure is within a certain range. A simple example is a date-checking routine that would reject an entry like February 30. You can apply the same idea to your payroll system. You should know, for example, the total amount you normally need to meet a payroll. Add allowances for vacations, normal overtime, and other contingencies. Program the computer to sound an alarm should a total payroll exceed that figure. It could mean nothing. Then again, it could mean that someone is trying to pad the payroll.

This kind of built-in control also helps you maintain the reliability and accuracy of your data. Another technique that can help is an automatic mechanism for backing up microcomputer data. Tape backup of a hard disk's contents is a leading example.

SIGNS OF A GOOD PROGRAM

Perhaps the best test of a good microcomputer program is the simple answer to this question: Have you checked up on your micro security program lately?

Small computers add new dimensions to your security problems, and they're not always easy to solve. The best sign that you have a handle on this slippery problem is the simple fact that you give micro security the serious, regular attention it deserves. Other elements of a good program include:

☐ Security considerations are included in your *purchasing* specifications.
☐ You have adequate controls to *limit access* to both files and equipment.
☐ You have an up-to-date *inventory* of your small computers and their programs and files. You know what they are, where they are, and how they are protected.
☐ You provide adequate *supervision* to make sure employees observe established procedures, particularly those that segregate and isolate their access to sensitive information.
☐ Employees, supervisors, and managers all are given *personal responsibility* for their computer use. This responsibility should be clearly communicated and enforced, preferably with a written notice or agreement.
☐ The system keeps adequate *records* of computer use, and you regularly review these records.
☐ You have adequate provisions for *backing up* your data.

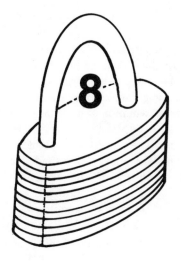

Securing the Network

A telephone tap can pick up more than a suspicious conversation. One tap was placed on the telephone line between a bank's computer and a remote automatic teller machine. The tapper soon picked up and deciphered the codes used to control access to the ATM. Using the stolen codes, the tapper stripped the machine of about $80,000 within half an hour. Fortunately, it was only play money.

The telephone tapper/ATM robber was Stephen Leibholz, who had been hired by the bank to test the security of its ATM system. His company, Analytics Communications Systems, markets the Sherlock encryption system. He has taken a natural interest in the security features of ATMs and other computer networks. He knows, for example, that if you choose "Snoopy" as a password, you will have chosen a common term known to nearly every hacker in the land.

Leibholtz also had these points to make in a 1983 interview with *Computerworld*:

☐ Fewer than 2 percent of the companies whose computers are vulnerable to intrusion have anything more than password security.

☐ The average bank robbery yields about $9000. The average computer crime takes about $650,000.

☐ Most computer crimes since 1972 have involved penetrating passwords.

THE MOST VULNERABLE SPOT

What experts like Leibholz don't have to tell us is that the proverbial weak link in any computer system is its communication link. The rapid spread of local networks and micromainframe connections means that miles and miles of weak linkage are being strung throughout the nation's office buildings. These buildings are connected to other buildings by a telephone system that itself is far from secure.

Protecting your computers, then, will be largely a matter of protecting the communication system that links them. It does little good to protect the computer if the network is vulnerable. On the other hand, if you protect the network, you've done much of the job of protecting the computer.

In a way, a network offers some security advantages, particularly for multisite companies that use distributed data processing. These are less vulnerable to a fire or earthquake, for example. That modern hazard, a terrorist attack, would be less likely to hit the entire network. But that's about the only security advantage they have. The more communication links you have, and the more distance they cover, the greater the problems of securing them properly.

Communication networks can take many forms, and their numbers and variety seem to multiply daily. For most discussions, they are grouped into three main types:

- [ ] The traditional links between a central processing unit and remote terminals. This group has expanded recently into micro-mainframe connections.
- [ ] The local network (technically, local area network or LAN, but if it's local, it must be in the area). This is typically a network of microcomputers whose users share and swap resources over communication lines.
- [ ] The external telephone network, including the conventional phone system and other types of public communication services.

All three types of communication networks are highly vulnerable points. Access is easy, and the results are hard to detect.

GREATER USE, GREATER RISK

It isn't just that these networks are strung out all over the place—although they are. John M. McQuillan, who heads a Cambridge, Massachusetts, consulting firm, points out that new forms of data communication bring together many computer-related activities that previously had been handled separately.

One example: The formerly separate fields of data processing and office automation often are now hard to distinguish from each other. Add microcomputers and hook everything into the telephone system, and you have one multifaceted system where you formerly had at least four.

One result has been to combine and multiply the risks associated with each of these previously separate components. A second has been to increase the number of communication channels that must be secured. A third is to blur old departmental distinctions within the organization. Where once you might have been responsible for the security of a single computer or a small shared-facility network, you now must watch out for a small communications conglomerate within your own company.

Familiar organizational patterns are being broken down, McQuillan points out, and the distinctions will be blurred even more as microcomputers move in. Almost anyone in the office will have computing and communication power—to be used well or otherwise.

This sense of diffusion within the organization can easily outstrip the company's ability to manage it. Management includes security. Just as your expanding communication net requires tighter and better management, its impact on the organization can seriously curtail your ability to do it.

Electronic mail may offer the newest threat. It's yet another communication system that has many points of access and a number of vulnerable spots. Sure, it's convenient to send a sales order to be filled immediately or to receive reports with the most up-to-date information possible. But don't send a salary schedule by electronic mail. Don't transmit a facsimile of the blueprints for a major new product. Don't send sensitive information about your employees or customers. At least don't do so without encrypting it first.

These rules could apply to any communication link whose security is not absolutely certain. The first rule of communication security is to be careful what you send over the network. Don't assume it is safe from compromise. Assume that whatever you will transmit will arrive shortly on the desk of the person you would least want to receive it.

COMPLACENCY HURTS

One reason communication networks have been

so wide open to invasion is that their users don't understand how vulnerable they are. That kind of naiveté is behind Stephen Leibholz' statement about the vast majority of users who rely solely on password systems. Many of them don't know any better.

Even the users who would seem to have the most to lose—bankers involved in ATM networks and electronic fund transfer (EFT) systems—sometimes seem complacent about the threats they face. A poll taken early in 1984 of bank security officers indicated they feel the threats to their institutions from electronic crime are more potential than real. These same security officers indicated a feeling that the technical security now available is adequate to cope with the threat.

In fact, through 1983 only two successful thefts had been reported from EFT systems. One was in Japan, the other in Switzerland. No American banking institution had yet been held up through the EFT system that switches funds between institutions, or if it had, it was keeping quiet about it.

ATMs, the ubiquitous street-corner cash dispensers, are something else. Security agents hired to test the systems have found them easy to penetrate. So have some criminals. Some security experts have pointed to this embarrassing combination: Business leaders have been calling for more laws to restrict the spread of computerized crime while failing to take adequate security measures of their own. Speaking at a 1984 conference on security, Alan Grossman of Dow Jones, warned computer users to make sure their own security systems are adequate before they ask Congress or their state legislatures for help.

Another speaker at the same conference, Bette Steiger of Reference Technology, cast the same problem in terms of effective law enforcement. Even if the laws are adopted, she pointed out, it is hard to enforce them where security provisions are lax.

HAVE A PLAN AND A POLICY

The key to protecting a computer network is to protect the computers that are hooked into it. This means the protection measures that work for a central processing unit on one end of a communication link and a micro or remote terminal on the other also serve to protect the linked pair. The same is true if micros and peripherals are linked in a local network.

In other words, just as mainframe security measures can be adapted to the booming world of microcomputers, the combination of mainframe and micro security can be adapted to protect the complete network.

Get Networks into the Plan

The first of these items is one to be adopted, not adapted. Any assessment of your vulnerable spots should include an assessment of your highly vulnerable networks.

Find these spots, checking both the communication lines and the physical locations they connect. Figure out what would happen to the company should someone exploit this weakness. Identify the controls, both baseline and optional, that can be used to counter the threat.

In the process, make a detailed diagram of all the physical facilities in your system, including the wires, glass optics, and other lines that serve as communication links. Identify the uses of each element and the policies under which it is operated. Not only does this give you a complete inventory of your linked resources, it gives you a better picture of your system and could indicate some ways to save costs.

Then include these vulnerable communication links in your overall security plan. Look at:

☐ How much the company relies on communication, and how much it is likely to do so in the future.

☐ What kind of data is to be communicated over the network.

☐ Who will use this data, and what they will be allowed to do with it.

☐ The value of the data you are trying to protect.

☐ How much you can budget to protect this data.

Resources for Network Assessments

The system diagram is one resource you can use to assess your position and plan for adequate network security. In one case it uncovered some mysterious extra communication lines that appeared in none of the original system documents. Tracing these lines led to a pair of employees who had installed their own lines into their employer's computer and were using it to run their own timesharing bureau.

Include site plans in the security check. Remember that most of your network security measures will deal with the computers, not the lines, and a poorly protected site will be the familiar weak link. Access control and restricting individuals' use of particular files should also be part of the review.

THE SECURITY LESSONS FROM ATM

Few computer networks are as vulnerable to loss, or risk such large losses, as banking's growing network of automatic teller machines (ATMs). Naturally enough, these machines offer some leading examples of network security techniques.

A typical ATM transaction begins when the user inserts an authorization card into a reader on the terminal. This is the first level of access control, in which the system decides whether it has been given the card of an authorized user.

Next, it tries to link the card with the user. It asks for a personal identification number (called a PIN) that only the authorized user should know. In effect, a PIN is a password. At this second level of access control, the ATM checks whether the PIN it has been given identifies the same customer as the card. If not, the terminal often will swallow the card, and you can get it back only after some serious explanation to a bank officer the next morning.

At a third level of access, the system reads the transaction the customer wishes to make and checks to see if there are sufficient funds in the account. The comparable check in a business computer system might be to see whether the user is authorized to use a particular data file.

This type of access control may be only the beginning of ATM security. Banks now are under orders from the Treasury Department that they must meet by mid-1988 new requirements developed by the National Bureau of Standards for access to financial institution computers. At the same time, their transmitted messages must meet the federal Data Encryption Standard for protecting transmitted data.

While all this is being accomplished, ATMs also stand as remarkable examples of units that manage to combine high security with user-friendly operation. They prove the two don't necessarily have to be conflicting goals. Bankers use their ATMs not only as transaction machines but as sales tools. Future ATMs may rival video games in their use of graphics, touch screens, and other customer-attracting features. They'll also be found in growing numbers in convenience stores, service stations, and perhaps even workplaces.

The federal government has indicated that it would like to start moving payments of all kinds through ATMs. Some day, government workers may collect their salaries and retirees their Social Security through street-corner terminals. This would be only a logical extension of the direct deposit system through which Social Security and other government payments travel the EFT system directly to their recipients' bank accounts.

There's still one problem, though. Federal officials aren't convinced ATMs have yet been made secure enough for that purpose.

BORROWING FROM MAINFRAMES

You can also take several tips from the mainframe world on how to protect computer networks. Many microcomputer networks are not designed with security as a high priority. It's not unusual for the system to allow every user access to every file, with no controls at all. That makes for a versatile system, but it also is very insecure.

A typical mainframe, on the other hand, usually has security built into its operating system. The system software controls the sharing of data and programs. It often includes a user table that identifies authorized users and their access rights. This access can be only for certain purposes, such as read-only, execute, add, or modify. Software controls the sharing of data and programs. Each time a user requests material, the request is checked against the authorization table. The request is granted only if everything matches up.

A mainframe security system can assign classification levels to both users and data and check for a match before it lets the material be used.

Translated to Networks

It's not always easy or even possible to transfer all these mainframe techniques to a micro network. The general ideas can be adapted, though. Concentrate on using the *principle* of the mainframe method instead of the specific technique.

For example, consider the general principle of access control. Password systems can easily be added to micro networks. Several existing network systems have password systems built in.

Another available technique is the identification card similar to the one a customer uses in an ATM. A card reader is attached to each work station. The operator inserts the card, and the computer reads an electronically coded message. No match, no computer.

Procedural security programs are useful no matter what kind of computer you are protecting. A basic principle of network security is that no one person should have 100 percent access to everything. As with mainframe procedures, segregate employees and authorized files. Try to arrange the system so it would take more than one person to commit an offense. An auditing program is another procedural method that can check up on how the system is being used.

Among built-in security measures, a modem with a built-in callback provision is one good method. Even simpler are incoming telephone connections leading only to a single computer, isolated from the network and containing no sensitive large files. Authorized files can be left in this computer, and it can be set to record incoming material. The

new data would be transferred to other computers within the net.

Some Principles to Follow

Whatever specific techniques you decide to use, the National Bureau of Standards and other security authorities recommend that you observe these principles:

- [ ] The controls should be part of a *comprehensive program* of security and risk management.
- [ ] Every user should be *uniquely identified*.
- [ ] The controls and the degree of protection they offer should match the value of the resources you are protecting.
- [ ] An appropriate control device should avoid *two kinds of errors*. Most security programs are mainly concerned with what researchers call a Type 1 error: admitting someone who is not authorized. You must also beware of the Type 2 error: refusing someone who *is* authorized.

The Encryption Dilemma

Encryption can present some particularly difficult problems for a cost-conscious security manager. Under most normal cost-benefit standards, this is an option to be used only where the files to be protected are unusually valuable. Its care and feeding is expensive, so it may not be practical for files of limited value.

On the other hand, it is the only known way to protect data while it is in transit between your secured computer stations. If this data is at all valuable, you may have no choice but to accept the cost of encryption. There is new equipment to buy, and then you'll need people to run and maintain it.

Make your decision carefully and consider all the costs. For example, an encryption system almost always reduces the system's response speed. Someone must maintain responsibility for protecting the encryption key. That's a particular problem if you have multiple users and a single key system. For networks, a public key system would let users encode their own work. without the separate key necessary to decode it.

KEEPING AN EYE ON THINGS

As we'll see in Chapter 18, auditing is an essential part of a computer security system. It's your assurance that things are working as planned. It's particularly important for networks, where the chances of loss are so high. With micros and networks spreading rapidly, you need all the assurance you can get.

Of course, audits are connected with Internal Revenue and other equally unpleasant thoughts, so they will not be warmly accepted by the people who are being audited. This may be doubly true of microcomputer users who feel, with some justification, that their machines are supposed to set them free of the type of restraints an audit represents.

There's another psychological problem, too. Business people are conditioned to abhor bad news, particularly about themselves. Business has a very bad tendency to try to control information for the sake of looking good. An audit report almost always contains bad news about somebody. It also means that you'll have to spend some money to correct the problem.

But cheer up; things could be worse. That's what an audit is all about. A defect reported now can be corrected. It's better than learning about it when a competitor steals valuable data or you are slapped with a liability lawsuit. An investment in security now, even at the expense of those who run afoul of the auditors, could have a big payback later.

The same is true about prosecuting computer criminals. Many companies hesitate, afraid their reputations will suffer because they managed to become victims. If you don't take firm action to secure your networks, you'll suffer a lot more than that.

Computer networks, particularly when they involve microcomputers, can multiply your security problems as they multiply their own numbers. If personal computers are involved, they even provide the means to evade their own security.

Don't let the nature or the magnitude of the problem frighten you. That basic principles of computer security apply, no matter what kind of system you have. Assess your situation, develop a sound plan to shore up your weak spots, and develop a package of established security measures. There's no mystery about protecting networks. There's some hard work, though.

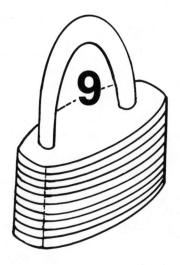

Beyond Security:
Meeting Legal Obligations

About two weeks after the nation had finished celebrating its bicentennial, a Vermont building contractor met with his banker to discuss future financing for his work. To his surprise, the banker pulled out a notice from a reputable credit reporting service. It said the contractor had recently filed for bankruptcy. Naturally, the contractor was granted no loan that day.

The credit report was an error. The bankruptcy petition had actually been filed by a former employee of the contractor. But before all that had been straightened out the incident had become a landmark case. The court ruled that the credit bureau was guilty of libel, and the erroneous report was not protected under the First Amendment.

No matter how the Supreme Court decided that issue, this case and others like it ask a serious question. To what extent are you legally responsible for the accuracy and security of the information in your computers?

This is only one example, although probably the leading one, of a problem that takes you beyond security precautions that are designed to protect your interests. You also can be held responsible for protecting the interests of the employees, customers, and other parties who are the *subjects* of your computer files.

WHERE YOU COULD BE HELD LIABLE

There are many ways in which you could be held liable for the accuracy and reliability of your computer system, and the list seems to be growing all the time.

There has been a surplus of cases in recent years in which innocent people have been tossed into jail because a computerized criminal information system falsely identified them as wanted fugitives. Part of this problem has been laid to laxity by the police in using the computerized information (a procedural problem); part of it also appears to lie in inaccurate information in the computer (a technical matter).

A Louis Harris poll early in 1984 showed that more than three-quarters of all adult Americans worry about computerized information that could invade their privacy.

After a major New York bank installed an electronic mailing system that linked more than 500 personal computers, it found many employees afraid to use the system to its full capacity. They were afraid the system would not provide adequate protection for their confidential and personal messages.

Dr. Willis H. Ware, a Rand Corporation computer security expert, suggests that you should be held legally liable for contributory negligence should someone else be victimized because your computer is unlawfully entered.

More Problems Coming

In its 1981 report on national information systems, the Office of Technology Assessment expressed a common view: Things will get worse, not better. OTA found a number of developing problems:

☐ New technology, and new applications of existing techniques, will produce new kinds of information files, all carrying the threat of misuse and faulty security.
☐ The individual who furnishes information for one purpose—a credit application, for example—can be surprised to see this information retrieved and used later by someone else for an entirely different purpose. The Harris poll uncovered a similar concern. Most respondents believed it would be easy to put together detailed computerized dossiers of their employment histories, purchases and travels.
☐ Computers have made surveillance easier. The OTA group worried that even a legitimate use, such as screening for improper telephone calls by employees, could easily be abused. It could raise the issue of civil rights in a new form, the report suggested.

Many Standards Already Exist

In these comments, OTA was concerned mainly with the impact of computers on the right of personal privacy. This is only one of many sets of ways in which you may be responsible to outside interests as well as your own. There are many federal laws and regulations that could impose this kind of external responsibility. Among them are:

☐ Securities and Exchange Commission (SEC) regulations. There have been several cases in which computer files have been misused to gain information for insider trading and other improper activities. SEC also is officially worried about the use of computer files to influence decisions by stockholders.
☐ The federal Privacy Act. It applies mainly to federal agencies, but it also suggests standards for private organizations to follow.
☐ A host of banking laws and regulations, including Federal Reserve rules that govern *all* credit transactions and electronic fund transfers.
☐ Regulations on foreign trade and other overseas activities. A leading manufacturer recently paid $1.1 million in fines after one of its customers turned out to be an agent of the Soviet KGB. Exports of many computer products are restricted for national security reasons.
☐ Product liability laws.

At the familiar bottom line is the fact that more and more people are doing more and more to demand that your computer is secure and reliable. And it's not just for your own protection.

WHAT ARE YOUR LEGAL REQUIREMENTS?

In its report to the Justice Department on computer security techniques, SRI International pointed out that many security managers take a follow-the-leader approach. They tend to rely on the proven, established controls that everyone else uses.

There are at least a couple of reasons for that. One is the simple fact that proven techniques are just that, proven techniques. Another is the legal duty of care. Whether you regard a programmer as a professional, a skilled technician, or something else, the work will be judged against the prevailing practices in the field. The obvious safe course is to let these practices prevail in your own work, too.

You can be held liable for the losses another party suffers through an act of malice on your part, or because you recklessly disregard the consequences of what you do. The average careful person isn't likely to have either of these problems. The real legal danger for most people is from failing to take due care for the interests of the other party.

In such a case, the first requirement is that you observe the accepted standards of your field. That may not be enough, though. The computer industry's established practices may form an initial frame of reference against which to judge your own efforts to maintain accuracy and security, but the circumstances may demand that you go even further. In fact, you can learn something from an unfortunate tugboat captain.

The captain's story goes back to 1928, when his tug, the *T.J. Hooper*, ran into a storm while towing a string of barges along the New Jersey coast. Two of the barges sank, and before this disaster at sea had run its course it had become a landmark court case.

In a ruling by the famed federal judge Learned Hand, the tug's owners were held responsible for the loss because they had failed to put a weather radio aboard the *Hooper*. The weather radio was a new high-tech device in 1928, but a few ship owners had installed them. Several skippers who heard the weather reports the day before the storm prudently headed for port while the *Hooper* sailed blindly into disaster.

It didn't matter, said Judge Hand, that the weather radio was an innovative device and its use was not yet an established industry practice. "A whole calling may have unduly lagged in the adoption of new and available devices," said the judge,

"and there are precautions so imperative that even their universal disregard will not excuse their omission."

That ruling has strong implications for people who work with today's innovative technology. It's not enough just to observe standard practice if there is some further step you could take to avoid the damage.

Judge Hand did recognize that we can't always predict and prevent every possible problem. It is our responsibility, though, to provide some form of relief from the unexpected. In nautical terms, he put it this way: "We need not hold that a barge is necessarily unseaworthy because she leaks in a gale; the heaving and straining of the seams will often probe weak spots which no diligence can discover. It is, however, just against this possibility that pumps are necessary."

Debugging a program is much like building a ship. There are times that, in spite of your best efforts, you won't discover a weak timber or a program bug until it turns up under the stress of long-term service. Your duty is to do your best to find and correct the weak spots before they cause trouble. It is also your duty to stand behind your product when the weak spots do appear—in other words, give your customers some pumps.

What Kind of Care Is Due?

The kind of care you owe the other party depends on the circumstances, and there are very few firm guidelines. In a case similar to the *Hooper* incident, it was argued that an airline should have installed radar to prevent a collision. That was in 1948, and the court rejected the argument because a commercially feasible radar system had not yet been developed.

In 1977, another airline was held responsible for the loss suffered by a bank in a robbery of the airline's storage room. The airline had taken the standard precautions of posting an armed guard in front of a locked, unmarked door, but the court ruled in this case that taking those industry-standard measures was not enough to relieve it of responsibility.

The requirements are even less clear in applying the legal concept of due care to computer services. One point is reasonably well established: the basic requirement of due care doesn't change just because a computer is involved. In other words, a computer error is no excuse.

For example, a finance company repeatedly received notices from its computer that a customer's car payments were past due, and it forwarded these notices to the customer. Twice, the customer came in with canceled checks for the disputed payments, but the computer continued to report them as overdue. Finally, on the basis of the computer reports, the finance company repossessed the car. When the shocked customer sued for damages, the company claimed it was the equally innocent victim of a computer error.

The court didn't buy it. "[The finance company] explains that this whole incident occurred because of a mistake by a computer. Men feed data into a computer, and men interpret the answer the computer spews forth. In this computerized age, the law must require that men in the use of computerized data regard those with whom they are dealing as more important than a perforation on a card. Trust in the infallibility of a computer is hardly a defense when the opportunity to avoid the error is as apparent and repeated as was here presented."

"It is clear," says SRI, commenting on this decision, "that excessive reliance on computer data without proper safeguards to ensure the reliability and accuracy of the information may constitute the failure to exercise due care, and in some cases may even result in the award of punitive damages," above those the courts grant to cover the actual loss.

Professional Standard?

SRI believes that at a minimum "there is clearly a duty to exercise reasonable care in using computers." Depending on the contract terms involved, "a higher standard of care may be required of suppliers of computer services." If programmers and other experts offer professional services to their clients, they may also be held to professional standards of care and performance.

This point is drawn from one of the many cases in which an installed computer and program failed to do the job its buyer expected. The buyer argued that from the time the system was installed, through the unsuccessful debugging process, and until the parties broke off their relationship, the vendor was in the role of a professional, much like a physician or lawyer. As a professional, the customer continued, the vendor was guilty of malpractice.

The court rejected that argument, as several other courts also have done. As SRI points out, though, the decision actually was a refusal to acknowledge a professional relationship under the circumstances of this particular case. Different facts could produce a different decision. Being treated as a professional could have its advantages, though. It is less likely you would be held to strict liability for losses that are not necessarily your fault.

The strict liability doctrine has been developed primarily for physical goods. Under the traditional legal approach, it would not apply to work you do under a contract for professional services. There are two main problems here. First, legal experts strongly disagree about whether data processing should be treated as goods or services. Second, traditional legal approaches don't always lend themselves very well to new technology.

SRI suggests a third approach, in which the decision is not automatic: Make an ad hoc decision in each case whether it involves sales or services and, thus, what kind of liability there might be.

None of this offers firm guidelines to the security manager who would rather avoid the fine details by keeping the case out of court in the first place. There are two things that you can do to help stay out of this legal maze.

First, do everything you can to make sure your information is accurate and your product reliable. Don't settle for the standard, conventional approaches. If there is something you can do to improve your performance, do it.

Second, have a serious talk with a knowledgeable attorney about the types of products or services you offer, the language of your contracts, and your resulting status under the various liability laws. There are many choices to be made, and most of them are tradeoffs. Make sure you understand exactly what you would gain or lose from each option.

YOUR RESPONSIBILITY FOR ACCURACY

Regardless of the standards of care and liability to which you are held, one thing is clear: You must do your best to make sure any information that comes from your computer is accurate, before you rely on that information.

The mistaken repossession was a case in point. Another example is found in the periodic reports required under federal securities laws. Company management has a duty to maintain accurate records, and anyone else has a duty to verify the information management supplies.

Various provisions of securities laws impose liability for making false or misleading statements, or for leaving out significant information. A company reporting to the Securities and Exchange Commission (SEC) has a legal duty to maintain accurate records and prepare accurate reports from them. Many other laws also require accurate record-keeping.

After an embezzlement cost a bank $21.3 million, for example, a stockholder in the bank filed suit. The suit claimed in part that management had failed to institute internal controls that were required by law—and might have prevented the loss.

Certainly, you should maintain a control system that makes sure your computer produces accurate and reliable information. These include controls on who can gain access to the computer and on who can use or alter the information stored inside. Audit trails should be established to create written evidence of who made what transaction. Both techniques will be discussed in coming chapters.

SRI has this advice: "Electronic record keeping systems are only as trustworthy as the people who use them, and it is imperative that a security system be established to help preclude unauthorized persons from gaining access to the computer or altering information in the system."

THE LAW AND LIABILITY

Some insurance companies now offer what they call *computer malpractice* policies. Their purpose is to protect computer owners from claims that arise from computer-created errors. Actually, says Boston attorney Robert P. Bigelow, "Malpractice is a fancy term for a particular kind of negligence." Strictly speaking he explains, anyone who acts negligently in building, selling or programming a computer could potentially be held liable for any financial or physical losses that occur when the system doesn't work the way it should.

So far, says Bigelow, computer errors have produced only a few negligence suits and even fewer successful ones. That's primarily because negligence is hard to prove. Still, in this litigation-conscious era, many computer users do worry about the risks they face from computer malfunctions. After all, an error could put a company out of business, and if the error was due to your mistake, the resulting lawsuit could put *you* out of business.

When there's a fear of such large losses, the insurance industry will not be far behind, offering policies against those losses. The malpractice policies now being offered are in addition to the general liability policies most companies carry. They're designed to protect against risks that can't easily be seen or anticipated.

For example, a software company might sell a program that not only fails to work properly but destroys some of the user's vital data in the process. If the user can demonstrate a serious loss and prove that the software supplier was negligent, the supplier might have to pay for such things as the cost of replacing the lost data and the user's financial problems while the information was not available.

Suits like this might become more common, many experts believe, as more and more small businesses turn to microcomputers to manage their finances. Unlike the traditional corporate computer buyer who has staff experts to help decide on mainframe purchases, the small-business owner tends to rely heavily on the promises made by computer and software sellers. Judges also tend to be more sympathetic to smaller users.

Protecting yourself against liability and other legal problems is a major part of computer security, and it is a part you should not ignore. Security isn't just a matter of protecting yourself from the misdeeds of outsiders, or even of your own employees and associates. To err is human, and one major part of your security program should be to protect yourself from your own mistakes. It is also important to protect yourself from other kinds of legal liability, like invading someone's privacy or violating a constitutional right.

A complete computer security program must consider *every kind of loss you might suffer*. A lawsuit may be unlikely, but should it come, and should you lose, it could be a serious loss. Guard against this kind of loss just as strongly as you would protect yourself from other kinds of losses.

LEARNING FROM MISTAKES—THE HARD WAY

In 1977, a mortgage company that held a $28,000 note found the debt wiped out by the Arkansas Supreme Court. Due to a computer error in calculating the payments, the company had inadvertently charged a usurious rate of interest. It was an honest mistake, but the company still was penalized.

This is just one of many ways in which a computer and its software can malfunction, often with disastrous results. Take, for example, a typical situation in which a programmer makes an error. The programmer is reasonably skilled and had no intention of causing any harm, and any warranty on the program has elapsed by the time the damage is done. Even under these reasonably favorable circumstances, computer lawyer Susan Nycum lists at least five different ways the programmer or the employer could be held liable for the results.

Express Warranties. The company that agrees to supply a program or service signs a contract with the user. In microcomputer practice, the

contract usually is a license agreement that spells out the conditions under which the customer may use the program. It also usually specifies the terms under which the company offers a warranty on the product.

Such warranties usually have stated limits. They are valid only for 90 days, or some other time period, and they are typically limited to replacing the defective program. The company will voluntarily accept no liability for any ill effects on the user's software or business—*consequential damages* in legal terms. Usually, says Nycum, provisions like this are enough to protect the company from consequential damages, but that may not always be the case.

In particular, she says, you could be held liable for any promises you make, or even suggest, *outside the contract*. For example, if your advertising suggests a certain level of performance, your product had better provide it. You also could be held liable if the bug slipped through a quality control program that wasn't up to normal standards. In circumstances like these, the company could even be held liable for damages to someone other than the customer.

Implied Warranties. Not all warranties are written into contracts. The law also imposes implied warranties to meet the interests of public policies. There are two major types of implied warranties. *Merchantability* means that the program should be suitable for the general types of purposes for which computer programs normally are used, and *Fitness* requires that the program also be suitable for the customer's specific intended use.

You can *disclaim* these warranties in the contract, a tactic that sometimes works and sometimes doesn't. State laws vary on this subject. You also might avoid liability if the customer makes a belated complaint, misused the program, is also guilty of negligence, or if the user voluntarily assumed the risk of an accident.

Third Party Contracts. You might find yourself liable to someone other than your customer. If a third party suffers loss due to a fault in your program, that party might have the right to sue. The basis of such a suit would be an argument that the program really was written for the third party's benefit.

Nycum feels few third-party suits could succeed, though, unless the program actually was written to be *used* by the third party. What this actually means in practice is that if you are sued, it probably will be for some other reason.

Negligence. This isn't based on any kind of contract. The basic question is simply this: Did you do anything, or fail to do anything, that caused harm to someone else? If so, you can be liable for that harm.

On the other hand, if you can demonstrate that the harm came from some other reason—a power surge, perhaps, or bad input by the customer—you can just as easily avoid liability.

This is based on an old common law theory: You owe your customer a certain minimal *duty of care*. Just what that duty might be depends on the circumstances.

Most likely, says Nycum, the programmer will be held to a standard of care typical of the profession, i.e., doing what most members of the profession would do. Or, because programmers lack full recognition as professionals, the standard might be that of a trained expert. If so, the programmers might find themselves in much the same position as accountants, for whom there are established limits to their liability to third parties.

Another possible standard is that, in some circumstances where a computer could cause airplanes to collide or nuclear plants to go out of control, the courts might consider the program to be an inherently dangerous instrument. If so, its use would require the highest possible degree of care.

Nycum also classes this idea as unlikely. More realistically, she says, such a program would probably be treated like a painter's scaffold: dangerous only when it's improperly built or used.

Strict Liability. This is a legal catch-all under which you could be held liable even after exercising all possible care. While this may sound unfair on the surface, it is based on three sound principles:

☐ If you make a product, you're in a better position than anyone else to reduce any hazards, and you should be given every possible incentive to do so.

☐ Some problems can't be completely removed. In that case, you can distribute the cost of the necessary insurance among all your customers.

☐ A person who is seriously injured isn't always able to prove negligence by the responsible party.

This is the theoretical foundation of a modern legal phenomenon, The *product liability suit*. The idea is that if you are held strictly liable for the performance of your product, you'll make good use of your unique ability to avoid errors, and you'll take out insurance on any liability you can't absolutely prevent. You'll also be expected to warn your customers of any such remaining hazards. There's also a legal precedent for imposing liability for defective design, and a faulty program easily could be considered a bad design.

AVOIDING LIABILITY

The standard way to reduce your liability for a defective product is to include a disclaimer in the contract. Talk with your attorney about the right language for your particular needs, but a typical disclaimer has three major clauses that read something like this:

The supplier does not make any express or implied warranties, including but not limited to the implied warranties of merchantability and fitness for a particular purpose. In no event will the supplier be liable for consequential damages, even if the supplier has been advised of the possibility of such damages.

The customer agrees that the supplier's liability hereunder for damages, regardless of the form of action, shall not exceed the total amount paid for the product. This shall be the customer's exclusive remedy.

THERE ARE NO UNDERSTANDINGS, AGREEMENTS, REPRESENTATIONS OR WAR-

RANTIES, EXPRESS OR IMPLIED (INCLUDING ANY REGARDING THE MERCHANTABILITY OR FITNESS FOR A PARTICULAR PURPOSE), NOT SPECIFIED HEREIN, RESPECTING THIS CONTRACT OR EQUIPMENT HEREUNDER. THIS CONTRACT STATES THE ENTIRE OBLIGATION OF SELLER IN CONNECTION WITH THIS TRANSACTION.

At some time or other, lawyers point out, all of these typical clauses have saved someone's hide. The first tries to limit the extent of any warranty the company might offer. Its main object is to disclaim any warranties other than those the supplier has specifically ordered.

In the second provision, the customer agrees to accept a limit on the amount of damages should the program prove faulty. In this case, the limit is to refund the price of the program.

The third clause, usually capitalized, makes the point that if there is any agreement between the seller and the buyer, it has been written into the contract. Verbal agreements, and most important verbal misunderstandings, don't count.

Clauses like these work in some cases, and are useless in others. In one of the first court cases to involve a computer warranty, a Pennsylvania automobile dealer contracted with a major computer firm for both the hardware and software to process the dealer's business records.

The system was installed with great hopes, and the dealer canceled its contract with the timesharing service it had been using. A year later, though, the new system still wasn't working right. The supplier's representatives still were working hard and earnestly trying to solve the problems, but the dealer was experiencing serious problems of his own. He rejected the machine and sued for damages.

Although the contract included most of the standard disclaimers, the court made a substantial damage award. The basis of its ruling was that the dealer never had accepted delivery of the computer. The court also held the supplier to a verbal promise, not included in the contract, that it would provide programming services to the dealer.

One conventional legal response to this deci-

sion was that the supplier should have included in the written contract a section that disclaims any oral promises that might have been made. A more reasonable view would be not to make any promises you aren't prepared to keep. A similar approach to the total problem of liability would be to provide the necessary contract disclaimers. They might help and can't hurt. More important, do everything you can to make sure your products work properly.

PRIVACY AND OTHER PERSONAL RIGHTS

The Internal Revenue Service (IRS) has a problem. It feels, with some justification, that self-employed individuals are major sources of tax losses because they don't report their full incomes. One big reason for the problem is that none of the established income reporting systems, such as Form W-2 or the information returns on savings account interest, give IRS an adequate way to check the tax returns against other income reports.

Seeking to fill this gap, IRS has launched several plans. In one, the agency has purchased commercial mailing lists targeted at high-income recipients and is checking the returns of people on the mailing lists. In another, it is asking state licensing agencies to report on people who take out occupational licenses or register expensive cars. IRS also would be part of a plan under which government agencies would have almost unlimited instant access to the computerized records of seven major credit bureaus.

These plans have run into strong opposition. To a large extent, the opposition is based on the general idea that the government should not have unrestricted access to information about our private lives. It stems from abuses in the Vietnam era, when it became apparent that just the collection of personal information could inhibit the free expression of unpopular views.

A right of personal privacy appears nowhere in the Bill of Rights, or anywhere else in the Constitution, but the Supreme Court ruled in 1965 that it does exist, inherent in other specified rights, including the First Amendment's right to free expression. There is legitimate reason for concern that the unrestricted collection and use of personal information could run afoul of the Constitution, and not just where IRS is concerned.

The Big Problem is Accuracy

That's only one dimension of the problem. Testifying before the House Judiciary Subcommittee on Civil Liberties, Robert Ellis Smith, editor of the *Privacy Times*, strongly opposed the widespread use of credit bureau reports. Invasion of privacy was a major concern, of course, but what he called the "most shocking aspect" of the plan was that the credit reporting business "has a poor reputation for maintaining the accuracy of its information."

The mailing list plan encountered similar opposition, and it came from members of the mailing list industry itself. The names that appear on a high-income mailing list are mostly those of high-income people, industry members pointed out, but the selection process is similar to the statistical technique used in public opinion polling. It includes a significant margin of error.

That means many of the names are there by mistake, the list managers said. The lists are considered accurate enough for commercial purposes, but the managers expressed doubt that they should be used in tax law enforcement. Many innocent people could find themselves facing IRS investigations.

These developments put two separate but related burdens on anyone who maintains computerized information about private individuals. You must be careful that you do not improperly invade your subjects' privacy in collecting, using, or spreading your information. This includes protecting it from unauthorized access. You also must take care that any information you publish is accurate. At the extreme end of this process, there could be a libel suit.

Issues of Long-Standing

Problems of personal privacy existed long before the computer. Table 9-1 summarizes just some of the developments in recent history. These have raised a multitude of issues, including these:

Government Intrusion. This is the extent to which the government can intrude—physically or electronically—in the lives of individuals. The subject of the 1965 Supreme Court decision, it affirmed the right of married couples to practice birth control, thus overturning a Connecticut statute that prohibited it.

Communication Surveillance. This can be defined as the government's right to intercept communication by reading mail and monitoring telegraph traffic, by wiretapping telephone conversations, or by using "mail covers" to keep records of who sends letters to whom. This issue is becom-

Table 9-1. Significant Milestones.

c.1964	Proposal for a National Statistical Center and the resulting public debate on privacy and government data systems—culminating in a series of congressional hearings.
1967	Alan Westin's influential book *Privacy and Freedom*.
1970	Fair Credit Reporting Act—provisions regarding credit records on individuals
1971	Arthur R. Miller's book *The Assault on Privacy: Computers, Data Banks and Dossiers*.
1972	National Academy of Sciences report: *Databanks in a Free Society*.
1973	Health, Education and Welfare Secretary's Advisory Committee on Automated Personal Data Systems report: *Records, Computers and the Rights of Citizens*.
1974	Family Educational Rights and Privacy Act controlling access to educational records.
1974	Privacy Act of 1974 enacted.
1977	Privacy Protection Study Commission report: *Personal Privacy in an Information Society*.
1978	Right to Financial Privacy Act of 1978 enacted to provide controls on release of bank information.

Significant Milestones in the Development of Privacy Issues. Source: Office of Technology Assessment

ing more important with the development of new computerized communication systems.

First Amendment Rights. These are the rights that guarantee a free, uninhibited exchange of ideas.

Privileged Communication. This is the traditional right of professionals to receive personal information in confidence, and the less-well-established right of news reporters to withhold the identities of their sources.

As the OTA committee observed after it compiled this list, "These examples not only convey the historical nature of privacy debates, but also the extraordinary range of issued encompassed by the term."

Where computers are concerned, the range hasn't been quite as broad. The issue of the government's use of information in private files has only recently been raised. Before that, the main discussion was concerned with private use of the same computerized collections.

Congress has considered several other privacy issues in the last few years. They include wiretapping, psychological testing of government employees, and the use of lie detectors.

The problem has become so large that, early in 1984, a subcommittee of the House Committee on Science and Technology recommended that a national commission be established to examine it. As proposed, the commission would "examine the vast set of interrelated issues surrounding the security and privacy of computer/communications systems, especially those that transcend either the jurisdictional boundaries of federal, state, and local government agencies or public and private sector interests."

LEGAL LIMITS ON DATA COLLECTION

In an attempt to limit the amount of data collected by government agencies, Congress specified in the 1974 Privacy Act that any collected data must be "relevant" to the reasons for which it is collected. That has proven to be a weak provision. A study commission found that government data collection decreased after the law took effect, but not by very much.

A 1980 dispute between the Labor Department and a major insurance company brought private information collections sharply into the picture. Labor was investigating possible charges that the company had engaged in discriminatory hiring. As evidence, it requested the company's computerized personnel records.

This case is still unresolved but, whatever the final result, the company's computerization of its records is significant for two reasons. First, without the computerized files, the Department of Labor probably would never have made such a sweeping request. The task of analyzing the same information on paper records would have been nearly impossible.

Second, computer technology might lend itself to a negotiated settlement, in which the company can tailor the information it releases to meet the government's needs without endangering the privacy of its employees.

In a similar fashion, the computer has added new elements to the overall privacy debate. It once was assumed that the information collected about an individual was given up voluntarily, and usually as a *quid pro quo* in exchange for some reciprocal benefit. Filling out a loan application in order to get the credit is a classic example.

More recently, though, privacy experts have been concerned with information collected without the subject's knowledge. The computer makes it easier to store, analyze, and trade this kind of information. The systems that can spread information about an individual also have a particular capacity to spread misinformation.

The Mailing List Problem

The mailing list is an example of how things have changed. At one time it was considered a reasonably benign type of information collection. At worst it did no harm. Now, however, the picture is different. Even without the IRS program, private users have put pressure on mailing list suppliers for a greater degree of selectivity. They want specialized lists of high-income people, for example. In response, list-making has become more sophisticated.

A political solicitation list may contain information about a person's memberships, religious beliefs, charitable contributions, income, and support for various causes. A modern political organization could use such information to predict your likelihood to support a certain candidate or issue. A targeted mailing list could be prepared accordingly.

Controls Lacking

Even before the IRS episode the OTA committee noted, "Such personal information, which is often collected without the consent of the subject through the exchange or purchase of mailing lists . . . assumes the character of a political dossier. It is not clear that existing controls, either over the use of such data systems for purposes beyond computing mailing lists or over the original collection of the information, are adequate to deal with the increasing capability modern technology offers to collect data and compile such lists."

Advancing computer technology will expand this kind of information collection, the OTA group predicted. "Print-of-sale systems are an example of this trend. A sale made at a store and recorded through a terminal will collect a variety of information about a customer, such as what was purchased, the exact time and location of the transaction, and possibly the customer's financial status. This will not only be recorded at the bank . . . but may also be retained by the store management for its own use, or perhaps even sold to third parties."

Once it reaches this open market stage, there are few controls over its further distribution and use—or misuse. Credit bureaus and mailing list operators sell information. Once it has been sold, they have no control over how it is used. Managers of large corporate information systems face the same kind of problem, particularly if many employees or even outside users have access to the data.

The problem is not just adequate security against unauthorized use, but *adequate control of authorized use.* Your security system must be concerned with who is authorized to use your data, and what uses they may make of it.

The challenge will grow as we develop data communication systems with easy access over internal communication lines. A local area network, one of the simplest and most centralized forms of data communication, still offers multiple-user access to large amounts of data, which is exactly what such a system is designed to do. Your system should be as effective against these authorized users as it is against unauthorized raiders.

OTHER RIGHTS AT STAKE

Privacy is just one of the individual rights a computer security manager may have to protect. The government currently faces a serious First Amendment question of how and whether to regulate new electronic means of communication, either as the relative freedom of print media or the regulated atmosphere of broadcasting and communication utilities like telephone and telegraph companies, or the Postal Service.

The AT&T breakup (and all the confusion it has brought) actually started with a simple idea: A company which has a monopoly on the means to *carry* information should not also be in the business of *originating* that information. There's too much danger it would favor its own information sources and would block transmission of competitors' data. That idea obviously has been put into practice imperfectly, but it is a major part of the First Amendment debate.

Also important to a data security manager is the Fourth Amendment, which forbids unreasonable search and seizure. The OTA group found three major problem areas here:

☐ The use of personal and statistical data contained in automated information systems as a justification for search and seizure. For example, a police officer might feed the known characteristics of a suspect into a data base full of personal information on a great many people. The system then would provide a list of people who have those characteristics.

□ The seizure of information as personal property, particularly when it appears in electronic form.

□ The use of automated information systems as a tool for search and seizure operations.

COMPUTER CRIME AND THE LAW

The problems you have with computer crime are shared with your lawyer. Attorneys trying to prosecute or defend computer criminals face complications like these:

□ There are new types of abuses that don't fit neatly into existing laws.

□ Traditional definitions of crime (theft is a major example) can be much different when computers are involved.

□ The need to obtain high-tech evidence can complicate, or even stop, many criminal prosecutions.

Most studies of computer crime had dealt with the acts of individuals or small groups against larger organizations. Some lawyers have noted, though, that an organization can just as easily use the computer to take advantage of customers or clients. For example, electronic billing and fund transfers, and even supermarket bar code scanners, are susceptible to fraud.

In addition, computer systems are used to make many decisions that affect people's lives, from political apportionment to setting pollution standards and assessing the effectiveness and safety of a new drug. There will certainly be a temptation for some interests to misuse these systems for their own purposes.

REGULATING COMPUTERS

The AT&T case represents an attempt by the courts and the Federal Communications Commission to draw a line between two classes: services and technology. The FCC decided communication services should continue to be regulated, but the technology to originate and process information

should not. It was a good idea in theory, regardless of its outcome in practice. That is part of the constitutional problem, of course, but it also relates to the regulatory problems the computer can create both for the government and for you.

Banking presents at least two regulatory challenges. Some large banks have developed elaborate data processing systems to support their operations. They've found that the sale of their systems and services to smaller banks can be very profitable sidelines.

In the banks' view, of course, selling such services is a natural extension of their normal banking activities. Timesharing service bureaus take a much different view, that the big banks are using their massive financial resources to enter an entirely new field, in competition, of course, with the bureaus.

An allied problem is that of branch banking. Computers and electronic communication systems are breaking down many of the barriers that long have restricted the spread of branch banks and have served as barriers to interstate banking. An electronic fund transfer can speed a transaction to a distant central office before you can say, "This bleeping machine didn't return my card."

The rapidly growing electronic mail services present even more problems. There's the natural danger of unauthorized access, but even authorized access raises some legal problems. For example, the "mail cover," in which investigators check the envelope but not the contents, has been accepted as an activity that requires no search warrant. In electronic mail, though, there's no real distinction between the "inside" and the "outside" of the letter.

WHAT CAUSES CRASHES?

Computers are now being bought by people who know little or nothing about how to use them. A computer isn't just a household appliance you can plug in and use right away. The computer is really a huge bank of tiny switches that are either on or off. The ways in which the program and the user manipulate these switches determine how the computer does its work. An error at any point in the process can cause the system to crash.

Sometimes the crash is due to an error by the operator. At others, it might be an outside factor like a power failure. At still others, the problem might be with the computer or the program. There are four main points at which you can introduce an error into a program:

☐ When the basic algorithm, or program structure, is created.
☐ When the programmer codes the algorithm into a high level language like C or COBOL.
☐ When the compiler or interpreter translates the programmer's work into machine language.
☐ When the machine language program actually operates the computer's internal switches.

What all this means is a practical application of Murphy's Law: Whatever can go wrong, will. The sheer numbers of codes, instructions, and switches present a multitude of possibilities for error.

Even this doesn't exhaust the possibilities for a computer-connected lawsuit. Many people have found themselves in court when their products didn't do what the customers expected.

An overstated sales pitch is one way to make a sale that leads to the courtroom, but customers can be disappointed in many more subtle ways. For example, a program's practice in rounding off figures could mean many dollars to some users. Or the program may work properly but take an unacceptable length of time to complete.

WHAT CAN YOU DO?

The first and best way to avoid this situation is to do everything within your power to make sure a program you file or you maintain is efficient and bug-free. Plan it well, and test it thoroughly. There's no test that can give ironclad assurance it will catch all the bugs. It can't hurt, though, to be able to show that you met all the expected standards for program testing. It can hurt even less if

you've exceeded them.

The second method—and next to the best—is to include the right language in your customer contracts. A contract disclaimer can't turn falsehood into truth, or vice versa, but it can help guard against those risks for which you have no other means of protection.

A third method: Communicate with your customers and employees. Make sure you understand what they expect of you, and that they understand what you can do. In particular, avoid overzealous sales pitches that can create false expectations.

If you are selling a computer-related product or service, communication also is important after the sale. If something does go wrong, do your best to reach a mutual settlement *before* someone takes the case to court.

EXPAND YOUR PROTECTION

Protecting yourself from liability problems is much like protecting yourself from any other kind of computer security problem. In protecting your own interests, you also do a lot to protect the people whose names, data, and interests are represented in your files.

Good security is only a start. It isn't enough to protect your files from errors and misuse caused by someone else's improper activities. You also must protect yourself and others from errors that are not due to someone's misuse. To meet your full legal and moral responsibilities to the outside world, do your best to make sure the system is accurate and reliable under any circumstances you might encounter.

Start With Good Maintenance

You probably appreciate the value of a sound preventive maintenance program for your major mechanical and electrical equipment. Well-scheduled prevention can catch small problems before they grow into big emergencies. The same preventive attitude should be the first step toward a reliable computer system.

You've no doubt heard, or perhaps have first-hand knowledge, of how a misplaced speck of dust can mess up a floppy disk or cause a hard disk to crash. Its effects on mainframe disks can be just about the same, but usually larger. It stands to reason that dust control should be one of the first items on any preventive maintenance program for computer media. Good housekeeping thus becomes an element of a computer security program. It's doubly important if there's a hard disk in the picture. The dreaded head crash that destroys 10 kilobytes at a single blow can usually be avoided simply with good maintenance.

Regular physical checkups are important to your media. If you find dust, tears or rough edges, copy the contents to a sound disk or tape, immediately if not sooner. Check the media storage, too. Make sure your disks and tapes are protected from dirt, magnetic fields and other hazards.

One thing you might not have thought of: Clean out your disk boxes and other storage containers. Their object is to keep dust out. But dust and other bits of debris often find their way inside anyway. A regular cleaning can prevent some major damage.

A Healthy Environment

Beyond that, filters in the ventilating system and similar measures can help reduce the risk. While you're at it, establish and enforce the necessary rules to keep food and drink out of the computer room—and out of the computer.

These are examples of environmental controls that are necessary to your computers' welfare and reliability. Cooling, ventilating, and electrical systems designed specifically for computer use may cost more than their household or office counter-parts, but they also must perform better and more reliably. A shutdown in the air conditioning could be uncomfortable to you. It could be devastating to your computer.

That's exactly what happened when the cooling system failed at a major airline's computer reservation system. The computers shut down and took millions of dollars worth of business with them. At least two securities exchanges have suffered major losses for similar reasons.

Your computer may not handle the major volumes that these enterprises require, but your resources are valuable to you. Compare that value closely with the cost of proper environmental controls. Even short of a computer that goes down like the *Titanic*, you could suffer from rust, corrosion, condensation, deteriorated media, and premature failure of your circuit boards.

The air conditioning system that's adequate for personal comfort may not be adequate for your computers. Check to make sure it has the capacity and reliability you need. Look for durable components, selected for long life, mounted in shock-resistant enclosures that open easily for service access. Look for similar features in other building equipment. Then let the computer help protect itself. Set it up to monitor the state of its environment and to turn the right switches or sound an alarm when things go wrong.

One Final Security Method

Then don't forget one of the simplest and most fundamental security procedures of all: Make a backup copy of everything. Sure, it's elementary. It's so elementary we tend to forget. Remembering could save a lot of trouble.

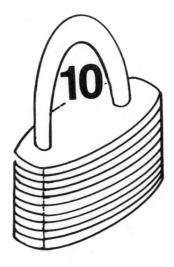

A Disaster Need Not Be Disastrous

Only a skeleton data processing staff was on duty one Sunday morning in 1983 at the West Coast headquarters of a major food processor. Suddenly a transformer caught fire in the building's basement. It was only a small fire, but it released a cloud of toxic gas that forced the company to evacuate its computer center. It would be nearly a year before local health officials would let them reoccupy the building and rebuild their center.

This company did well under the circumstances. Within a day, it was able to scrounge backup computer services from several business neighbors, and officials said they didn't miss a single order.

The data processing staff spent the next year in temporary quarters in six scattered locations. Personal contact and interoffice communications suffered badly, and managers had reason to sigh in relief when they finally moved back into a refurbished central facility.

In March, 1984, a major winter storm hit much of the East Coast, knocking out power in many areas and leaving the service that remained full of spikes and interruptions. After the lights flashed several times at a North Carolina textile company, the data processing manager found that *all* his disks and data had been destroyed. The computer and its contents had controlled a 24-hour-a-day packing and shipping operation.

While service technicians repaired the damaged equipment, the manager put his contingency plan into effect. Smoothly, and with only a few hitches, the shipping center fell back to a manual system until the computer was back in service.

Meanwhile, at a Massachusetts manufacturing plant, the same storm knocked out power to the computer just as it was being prepared to run the payroll. After learning the power would not be restored for several days, staff members retrieved backup tapes of the payroll data and took them to a sister company's computer in Rhode Island.

As it turned out, power was restored in time to run the payroll on the Massachusetts computer, but the storm provided a good training exercise, and officials were relieved to learn that they had been well prepared.

The many statistics kept by insurance companies include these sobering odds:

If your company suffers a major disaster, it has only one chance in three of surviving.

That's only an overall average. The smaller the company, the more the odds will be tilted against you. A large company with multiple computers and locations can simply shift its data processing work to some other part of the system. For a smaller company, a disaster of similar magnitude could wipe out everything you have.

A good disaster plan helps you make your own odds. You're no longer subject to laws of chance that are stacked heavily against you. Instead, you can put your future in your own hands.

THE VALUE OF BEING PREPARED

Neither of these plans was very elaborate. The North Carolina firm had simply prepared in advance to exist, if necessary, without its computer. The key element for the Massachusetts company was that it had the backup tapes. Larger companies, or those whose computers are more critical to their operations, may need more detailed and full-scale backups.

The important point is that you do *something*. Disaster can strike at any time and from sources you'd never expect. What computer center manager expects a toxic gas attack? You should have a plan in effect to recover from any disaster, no matter what the source, as quickly and painlessly as you can.

Protect Micros, Too

Disaster planning is important no matter how large or small your operation, and it is by no means limited to central computer resources.

When a major fire struck the Washington, D.C., headquarters of the U.S. Postal Service, it didn't affect the postal system's main computer center, which is in Raleigh, North Carolina. The service also had developed a disaster plan that it used to restore its communication system. The service also cleaned and restored to service most of the 1200 personal computers that had been hit by the fire.

There was still this one major problem: The fire damaged thousands of computer disks and there were few backups. Even disks that had been kept in file cabinets and flip-top files were covered with fine grit. At least 4000 disks had been warped by the heat.

The service was able to clean and copy many of the dust-covered disks, but at last report was still looking for a way to salvage the warped ones.

Think of It as Insurance

Disaster planning is a kind of insurance. When you face a risk, the prudent thing to do is to insure against it. A disaster is just that kind of risk. We have come to depend on our computers. The possibility that we could lose them is a risk against which we must protect ourselves.

In fact, if you ask an insurance carrier about disaster coverage, it will probably insist, as a condition of its coverage, that you take adequate steps to prevent the loss. There are several ways to minimize a risk.

Avoid It. This is the simplest and most effective. Protect your equipment and data against any kind of risk you can reasonably anticipate. A good security plan is a major part of this protection. Include protective measures against natural disasters, storms, and even deliberate sabotage.

If You Can't Avoid It, Reduce It. It isn't always (or even often) possible to eliminate a risk completely. It still makes good sense, though, to do what you can to minimize the risk.

Try to Control the Damage. Should the disaster happen in spite of your best efforts, be prepared to limit damages.

If All Else Fails, Learn to Live with It. Have a contingency plan ready to be put into practice. If you have a limited budget, concentrate on protecting the resources that would be hardest to replace. You might also assume a risk that is unlikely to happen.

All four elements have their places in a good disaster plan. You can't anticipate every possible disaster, much less avoid them all. To some extent, a disaster control plan must count on reducing some risks, confining the effects of others, and accepting still others. The plan should be based on a cost-benefit analysis that weighs both the likelihood and the seriousness of any particular loss.

PLANNING FOR THE WORST

First, of course, it's necessary that you have a plan. While it is true that any plan is better than no plan at all, a good plan is better yet.

There are two main elements to a good disaster plan: to minimize the *impact* of a disaster on your ability to conduct business, and to enjoy a *speedy recovery* to normal operations.

Assess the Threats

Just as with any other element of a computer security plan, the first step should be to assess the threats you face. Among the most common disasters that can strike a computer system are:

- [ ] Fire
- [ ] Power failures and fluctuations in the available power supply
- [ ] Interference from outside electrical sources
- [ ] Interruptions in gas, water, and other utilities
- [ ] Mechanical failures
- [ ] Sabotage

Determine the possible consequences of these disasters. Among the leading possibilities are these:

- [ ] The loss of vital business records such as accounts receivable, customer orders, or product development plans.
- [ ] The loss of communication systems.
- [ ] The possible failure of computer security systems.
- [ ] The inability to use important programs.
- [ ] An extended period of operating at less than normal efficiency.

Your control and recovery plan should be based, then, on an assessment of what you stand to lose and how you might lose it. It should present an organized approach to containing the damage, getting back into operation, and (as a longer-term goal, but as soon as possible) resuming full normal operations. It should also be based on a thorough comparison of the costs and benefits.

A Set Sequence of Events

It has been estimated that the average company can remain in operation 4.8 days after its computer goes down. That's more time than you may have thought you had to get a backup plan into operation, but it's probably less time than you'll need if you haven't already developed an adequate contingency plan. Then too, your company may not be average.

After a disaster, the company will go through a predictable series of events. They will happen with or without a plan. It's much better, of course, that you plan them instead of just letting them happen. Major steps in the sequence include:

- [ ] The disaster itself.
- [ ] The immediate response. Employees on the scene should begin a standard response procedure that will include protective measures to minimize the damage and notify key officials. These officials then will supervise the formation of a recovery team.
- [ ] An assessment of the impact. Determine what you've lost and what you must do to recover.
- [ ] Get back into operation. Have backup resources available to replace both your data and the equipment you need to process it. Get the company into an emergency operating mode as soon as possible.
- [ ] The full recovery. Replace and repair damaged resources, and get back to full normal operation.

The Goals of the Plan

Another major element of your disaster control

planning is to decide exactly what you hope to accomplish. The major objective, of course, is to get back into operation again, as quickly, smoothly, and inexpensively as you can.

Within that overall objective are several component goals that include the specific details of what you hope to do.

First, you must develop a plan that can readily be *implemented*. When the time comes, you will have to execute your plan, probably under the worst possible circumstances. Develop it with ready implementation in mind. Make regular trial runs so you can be sure the plan will work, and your employees will know what to do.

You must restore *vital operations and resources* as quickly as possible. You must get the company operating again as soon as you absolutely can, even if it is initially on a limited, emergency basis.

Finally, your plans, and the post-disaster resources you will use, must be *compatible* with your normal operations. Assuring this kind of compatibility can be a difficult proposition, because you may not have identical equipment and other resources available as a backup. Achieving it could be the key, though, to restoring your most critical operations.

Actually, nothing here will be easy. You face a complex problem of trying to find adequate backup resources that will replace, in a useful way, those you might lose in a disaster. You might find yourself renting time on a different type of computer than the one you normally use or hooking up to a completely different type of communication system.

This will mainly be a management problem, though, not a technical one. The most common reason disaster plans fail is that the company looks for technical solutions and pays too little element to the need for good management.

Your success will depend primarily on how well your people contribute to the effort. Even before the disaster, you must convince them to maintain adequate backup copies of their work. You and other managers must learn to anticipate a disaster, not just to react to one.

WHAT MAKES A GOOD PLAN?

As a Philadelphia insurance company learned after a major fire, the human factor can affect a disaster plan in totally unexpected ways. Security consultants who were called to the scene found the insurance firm's senior executives in varying states of shock. It would be several days before the people who must lead the company out of the disaster would again become the decisive, effective executives they normally were.

The consultants involved had written a disaster plan for the company—in fact, it had written several. But this incident proved the adage that the best-laid plans of mice and men are usually just about equal. They hadn't planned on the executives' limited ability to take charge.

The plans also did not account for one major short-term contingency: At the time the fire broke out, the company was three days away from completing its conversion to an entirely new system. Both computers were left entirely useless. A data processing subsidiary that might otherwise have provided a backup had recently moved and was not available.

A new plan was devised on the spot, and it worked. The job of recovery was divided into six chunks, each of a size that even a dazed executive could manage. One person was put in charge of each operation. The six areas were:

☐ Securing the site, restoring records, and overseeing salvage work.
☐ Communication and information, including notifying the public and heading off rumors.
☐ Negotiating with the insurance carriers.
☐ Locating a new facility.
☐ Acquiring new equipment.
☐ Restoring normal operation.

Prepare to Fail

The plan worked, and the company enjoyed a healthy recovery. Its success illustrates what might be the most important feature of any good disaster plan:

It should provide for its own failure.

No matter how hard you try, and you should try hard, no plan can cover every possibility. No one at this company anticipated that the fire would break out in the middle of a conversion, and with no relief in sight. Yet one of the first things salvaged was a workable plan.

The fact that plans had been developed, even if they weren't directly useful, probably helped. Even when an unexpected problem forces you to change or abandon a plan, you should be able to build or adapt from your existing plans to meet the actual circumstances.

Your plan should include a built-in means to make this adaptation. Provide an administrative mechanism to review your situation and make adaptations as they are needed. If for some reason you must build a whole new plan from scratch, your original should at least establish a method for doing that.

Beyond that, the plan should include a variety of available options. The proper response to a limited emergency is not the same as the right way to handle a total disaster. Give yourself a list of possible actions, and provide the means to take them. Then, in an emergency, you can select the individual actions that best respond to the situation at hand.

Other Qualities to Have

Other elements of a good plan include provisions to *test and refine* the plan. It should call for regular training exercises. If these show any need for improvements to the plan, make them. There also should be provisions for *maintaining* the plan—employees should be trained to execute their roles in the recovery process—and there must be support from *top management*. That's a cliche, but it's true.

THE PLANNING PROCESS

Developing a disaster plan is a major project in its own right, involving many complex decisions about costs, benefits, probabilities, and contingen-cies. Perhaps the best way to develop a plan in these circumstances is a *system development life cycle* approach. This is simply a matter of working from beginning to end, one logical step at a time.

The first step should be a thorough cost-benefit analysis. Assess the threats and their likely consequences. Determine the value of each resource you are trying to protect, and compare with the cost of protecting it.

As a second step, decide which activities and resources are most vital to your operation. Set priorities that will emphasize the most essential resources first.

Both considerations—protecting the most valuable resources and those most vital to your operation—will form the basis of the third step: actually developing the plan.

Identifying the Dangers

You can't proceed very far with any of these three steps until you know what dangers you face. You can't anticipate every disaster, nor can you tell in advance what the results of even a predictable disaster might be. Still, you can develop an idea of what is likely to happen. There's a good chance your plan will fall close enough to actual events to serve as a springboard for an effective response.

Consider the types of disasters most likely to happen, and for each work up a scenario that includes the likely length of the interruption (If it is unknown, say so), the operations that might be affected, and the types of equipment you might have to repair or replace.

For each possible scenario, determine what you would require to recover. Applying the priorities you have determined based on the value of the resource and how essential it is, lay out a step-by-step recovery process, including:

☐ The priority of each activity.
☐ Who will take charge.
☐ Procedures for notifying key personnel.
☐ How to implement a backup plan.
☐ The location of the command post and other key operating centers.

Testing Your Plan

Before you proceed any further, examine each element of the plan. Each possible response should specify:

☐ *What* must be done. The plan should provide as many details as possible about the exact procedure to be followed. Even if you must adapt these procedures to meet actual disaster conditions, these details will give you a place to start.

☐ *When* must it be done. Establish the proper sequence of each step. If a deadline is required, or if the step is a prerequisite to some other action, specify these requirements clearly.

☐ *Who* must do it. Someone must be in overall charge of the recovery effort. And, as was done in the Philadelphia disaster, each major operation should have an individual who is fully responsible for completing it. Also identify the staff resources to be assigned to each person.

☐ *How* it should be done. Describe the methods to be followed and the standards to be met.

☐ What is *needed* to do the job. Determine the amount of money, people, and other resources that must be applied to the task.

FINDING BACKUP RESOURCES

The North Carolina company that switched to a manual system when its computer went down is an example of one of the simplest possible types of backup resources: doing it with whatever you have left.

Certainly, any backup resources that you can develop and maintain within your own organization could be the easiest and least expensive solutions to your problem. The one big requirement is that they survive the disaster.

You may require something more, and that could easily mean you must depend on outside resources, either in other branches of your own organization or from sources beyond the company.

There are several possibilities.

Cooperative Agreement. There's a tradition in the newspaper industry—one episode of "Lou Grant" was built around it. If one newspaper suffers a disaster that knocks out its printing facilities, another newspaper usually will furnish its resources to help out—even if the other paper is a direct competitor.

Computer users could try to arrange something similar. You could form a mutual aid agreement with other computer owners. If one goes down, the others will temporarily pick up the slack. This can be a useful, inexpensive option. The main problem is to find other companies whose systems are compatible with yours. You also must acknowledge that this is just an arrangement to maintain your most vital operations through the worst early days. It's not likely that anyone would have the unused capacity to support an entire second company over a long term. That means you must identify your most critical priorities and make mutual arrangements to handle them.

Hot and Cold Sites. In a scene that resembled a "bugout" from "M*A*S*H," the computer staff of a Los Angeles-based restaurant chain suddenly found itself working in Dallas for a few days.

The occasion was a test of the company's ability to establish operations in a remote site should its main facility suffer an earthquake or some other disaster. The plan called for quickly relocating the operation to a part of the country not likely to be affected by the same disaster.

Several services have been set up, offering themselves as disaster relocation centers. In other cases, a company may establish its own. The center may be a *shell* or *cold site,* offering only a building with the necessary electrical and communication connections. The building is designed so necessary equipment can be installed quickly.

The more popular option is the *hot site,* where the vendor has a computer system already set up and running. This is a costly option, and you must be careful to find a compatible system. Many companies are choosing it, particularly when large amounts of money are at stake.

Service Bureaus. These timesharing services can offer capable backup support to many companies that cannot afford more permanent backup options. This could be a good choice if your main need is to get a batch job done in a hurry. Otherwise, it may not be too efficient, particularly if many other disaster victims are also demanding the service.

Duplicate Facilities. The Massachusetts company that hauled its backup tapes to Rhode Island made use of a duplicate facility that happened to be available in an affiliated company. It shows you don't have to be big to maintain this kind of backup, but you do have to be part of a fair-sized organization.

Such a company can set up a mutual aid system within its own subsidiaries and affiliates. The systems and procedures may well be much alike, solving compatibility problems and giving you most of the advantages of working in-house.

If money is an object, the developing network technology may give you a low-cost alternative. You can simply direct your work to a part of the network that is still in operation. You may face problems of limited capacity, but you should be able to get your most important work done.

TESTING THE PROGRAM

"The first test will not, in all likelihood, go well." That's a promise from John P. Murray, former director of management information services for the Rayovac Corporation. However, Murray explains, that's why you carry out the test in the first place.

Murray is one of many computer security experts who share one big worry: Even among companies that have developed disaster plans, few have tested their plans to find out what's wrong with them.

The choice of words is deliberate. You do not test your plan to find out whether it has any defects that must be corrected. You test it to find out what defects still require your attention.

The work of developing an adequate disaster plan literally never stops. You must test it regularly to find its weak spots and train the employees who

must implement it in an emergency. You also must continually update it to account for new equipment and techniques. If you install a new bank of microcomputers, for example, a plan originally developed for a central mainframe will not be much good.

The Charmed Third Try

In a *Computerworld* column, Murray described his own experiences. His company, centered in Madison, Wisconsin, conducts an annual exercise in which the data processing operation is relocated to a backup site near Chicago.

The first year, he reported, nothing went well. The staff was able to get the operating system to run, but it was unable to produce any useful work. The second year, several test production runs were successfully completed, but lack of a full communication system kept the test from being a success. The third year, everything finally went well.

As Murray pointed out, though, the first two tests could not be classed as failures. Each taught lessons that were applied to the succeeding years' improvements.

Another company, General Electric, recently established a corporate hot site for its varied divisions and affiliates. It's designed to be used when needed by any operating group that suffers a disaster.

The backup center staff conducts tests twice a year to make sure the center is ready. The individual subsidiaries are encouraged to test their own contingency plans just as often.

A program that hasn't been adequately tested is a program that easily could fail when you need it the most. This is true of plans much less elaborate than the major corporate programs just described. Depending on the type of plan you have, there are several ways to test it.

G.E., for example, conducts full-scale disaster simulations, testing the staff's performance against deadlines for restoring particular operations. These probably will give you the best picture of how well the system and staff would respond in a real emergency.

A less disruptive alternative is to walk through

Table 10-1. Disaster Plan Checklist.

How well could your company function if a disaster struck *right now*?
Is your plan adequate to recover the information, communication links and other assets connected with personal computers?
Do you know the kinds of disasters that are most likely to affect you?
Have you assessed the probabilities and the consequences of each?
Are one or more responsible persons assigned specific responsibility for establishing and maintaining a disaster control plan?
Have you developed specific policies on how to conduct disaster control and recovery?
Has your plan been adequately tested, and is there a plan for regular tests?
Are changes in the plan adequately explained to the people who will be involved?
Do you know exactly what to expect at your backup site?
Do you have adequate backups to all your material, and are they stored in a safe place?

the plan at night or on a weekend when you have the chance to stop and deal with any hitches that develop. The problem with this approach is that real emergencies don't proceed at convenient times, nor can they be handled at leisure.

Evaluating the Results

The test of a good program is whether it adequately protects and restores the functions you have identified in the plan, particularly the high priority ones. The results of the test should tell you how close you have come to this goal.

Use the plan itself as a checklist. Go over each function and see how well the system actually performs with respect to that need. Note the areas that need improvement. Then improve them.

Don't limit your examination to the computer system alone. Include related functions such as communication lines and instruction manuals.

Determine, too, whether all the information in data bases and other storage can be retrieved.

The human element is an important part of the system, too. Make sure all the employees who will be involved in executing the plan have been thoroughly trained in their duties. Use the plan as a training guide, and include disaster control in every appropriate orientation and training program.

Points to Consider

Table 10-1 is a checklist of points to consider in planning a disaster relief program, or in evaluating your present one. The results may not make you feel very comfortable. Nearly every plan has shortcomings of some kind, and even the good ones require regular checkups and maintenance.

Treat it as a learning experience. It's a whole lot better than learning the hard way—in a real emergency.

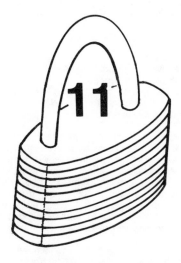

Eighty-Two
Control Tactics Analyzed

A security program is really an organized collection of tactics, tailored to the organization's vulnerable spots, the value of the resources to be protected, and the cost of implementing each tactic.

Here are 82 possible tactics to consider for inclusion in your own plan. You can't possibly adopt all 82 of them; some will not fit your needs, and many which do fit will not be cost-effective. You must select those that are best for your needs.

The list is taken from *Computer Security Techniques,* a report compiled for the Justice Department by SRI International. The tactics are organized according to the baseline system. Table 11-1 provides a detailed explanation of the listings.

PHYSICAL SECURITY

Baseline

1. Control Title: **Assets Accountability
   Assignment**

2. Objective: Prevent asset responsibility loss.

3. Description: Specific data producers, computer users, and computer center staff are assigned explicit ownership or custodial accountability and usage rights for all data, data handling and processing capability, controls, and computer programs. This can be done by establishing policy; establishing meaning of ownership, usage, and custodianship; and requiring that forms be completed and logs made designating and recording such accountability for data and programs and copies of them in all locations and for specified times. For example, one organization has a set of booklets for each data activity area stating ownership, usage, custodial, and control requirements. Another organization has this information as part of its policy manual.

4. Variables: Owners, users, custodians, data, programs, responsibilities, accountability, sanctions.

Table 11-1. Listings Explanations.

1. Control Title: A descriptive name for the control.
2. Objective: Control objective stating the type of adversity dealt with.
3. Description: A paragraph describing the idealized control function but based on observations at the field sites.
4. Variables: Variant specifications to be determined in particular cases.
5. Strengths: The particular positive values of the control in the field sites.
6. Weaknesses: Undesirable effects of the control such as creation of additional vulnerabilities or failure to reduce target vulnerabilities.
7. How to audit: Role of the auditor in testing and reporting the effectiveness of the control.
8. Purpose: Which security functions are performed, namely, deterrence, detection, prevention, or recovery.
9. Control area: Indicates the particular area of EDP environment in which the control is implemented, namely, computer center, application system, system development and maintenance, computer system and management.
10. Mode: Type of control and way in which the control is implemented or executed, namely, manual procedures, hardware, computer operating system, computer application programs, or policy.
11. Area of responsibility: Functional activity in an organization having responsibility and accountability for assets that the control protects, namely, user, security, legal counsel, audit, management, insurance, safety, personnel, computer security, quality assurance, computer program development and maintenance, computer operations, input control and output control.
12. Cost: Cost of the control and its operation on a scale of low, medium, and high. A low cost control would probably not appear as a line item in an annual budget. A medium cost control would be a line item, and a high-cost control would have a material effect on a computer center budget.
13. Principles of note: Strongly exemplified control principles, namely, cost-effectiveness, simplicity, override capability, independence from need for secrecy, least privilege, entrapment, independence of control and subject of control, minimal exceptions, compartmentalization and defensive depth, minimal dependency on shared mechanisms, completeness and consistency, instrumented, accepted and tolerated by personnel, sustainable, auditable, and facilitation of accountability.

5. Strengths: Accountability for assets is basic to their security. Accountability assignments also make clear who is responsible and accountable for each control and its effectiveness and overall adequacy of protection.

6. Weaknesses: If accountability assignments are not kept up to date with changes in assets and organizations, confusion and a loss of accountability can occur. Strict accountability can result in a structure that inhibits one owner from assuming responsibility for another's assets when emergencies or sudden changes occur.

7. How to Audit: Questionnaires and interviews should be used to assure accountability of all assets and discover any inconsistencies or lack of awareness of assignments in compliance with policy.

8. Purpose: Prevention

9. Control Area: Management

10. Mode: Policy

11. Area of Responsibility: Management

12. Cost: Medium

13. Principles of Note: Accountability

Baseline

1. Control Title: **Confirmation of Receipt of Documents**

2. Objective: Prevent disclosure, taking, or unauthorized use of documents.

3. Description: The confirmation process consists of verification of receipt of documents. Confir-

mations of delivery can be made by obtaining master files of names of input/output documents and their addresses, performing a selection of a sample of addresses by running the master file on a computer separate from the production computer or at least at a time different from normal production work. Confirmation notices and copies of the documents are then sent to the addresses to confirm that the documents are correct and that they received the documents as expected. Confirmation of smaller volumes of documents can be easily done on a manual basis. Receipt forms are used by recipients of particularly sensitive documents and returned to the sender to confirm correct report distribution and encourage accountability.

4. Variables: Area of responsibility, type of reports, frequency, sample type and size, acceptable percentage of response, exception action, forms design.

5. Strengths: An audit department's use of confirmations to determine the correctness of customer's balances in banking is well known. The use of confirmations in the insurance industry is also occassionally practiced. This suggests the possibility of extending the confirmation techniques as a general control to be used in a wide range of applicatins. Receipts increase assurance of confidentiality. Printing receipt forms embedded in a computer output to be returned to senders may be more efficient.

6. Weaknesses: The possibility of building the confirmation process into the application may not be desirable, since it might compromise the independence of confirmation control. Return of forged receipts can be accomplished. Failure to trace and recover missing receipts can cause rapid deterioration of control.

7. How to Audit: This control is used as an audit

tool. Review number and nature of confirmation—related activities for costs and benefits. Sampling of receipts and sensitive report deliveries can confirm correct procedures.

8. Purpose: Detection

9. Control Area: Application system, computer center

10. Mode: Manual procedure

11. Area of Responsibility: Audit, output control

12. Cost: Medium

13. Principles of Note: Auditability, accountability, instrumentation.

---

1. Control Title: **Data Accountability Assignment to Users**

2. Objective: Prevent asset responsibility loss.

3. Description: Users are formally assigned the responsibility for the accuracy, safekeeping, and dissemination of the data they handle. If the data processing department does not handle data properly, then it is up to the users to require corrections. Organizationally, users provide a data processing department with the resources to assist them with their functions. In terms of controls, users should be able to tell data processing what is required in terms of data accuracy, relevance, timeliness, handling procedures, etc.

4. Variables: Identification of users, responsibilities, documentation of procedures, policy.

5. Strengths: Explicit accountability ensures cor-

rect processing. Failures can be identified more easily.

6. Weaknesses: Users may not be knowledgeable enough to determine that data are inaccurate or improperly handled. This control requires that users have at least a fundamental understanding of computer security and privacy issues and controls. This may run contrary to many current organizational structures, where data processing in some sense controls the users.

7. How to Audit: Review organizational assignment of responsibilities for computer security and privacy matters. Discuss with both user and data processing management their mutual responsibilities regarding computer security and privacy. Review procedures in which users correct records, control the dissemination of records, and otherwise actively participate in the enforcement and design of computer security controls.

8. Purpose: Prevention

9. Control Area: Management

10. Mode: Manual procedures

11. Area of Responsibility: User

12. Cost: Low

13. Principles of Note: Simplicity, independence of control and subject, accountability.

Baseline

1. Control Title: **Suppression of Incomplete and Obsolete Data**

2. Objective: Prevent modification, disclosure, or unauthorized use of obsolete or incomplete input output data.

3. Description: Dissemination and use of incomplete and obsolete data are prevented or restricted by directive of the organization. This directive must be implemented by data receivers that are to be processed, converted, or stored by reasonableness checks within application systems and by output control and dissemination activities.

For example, in criminal justice information systems, access to nonconviction and arrest data that are one year old or more and do not contain a disposition, is restricted to certain types of requesters. The same concept (i.e., if a record is incomplete or outdated it should not be disseminated) can be applied to other applications besides criminal histories. Such data may also be selectively restricted by requester type.

4. Variables: Means of invoking directions, identification of relevant types of data, violation or exception actions, sanctions, recovery from disclosure.

5. Strengths: Prevents decisions from being based on outdated and/or incomplete information. Prevents the privacy of a data subject from being violated (in the above example, if the individual were to be acquitted, the arrest information would not be disseminated). Allows data bases to be updated (old and irrelevant information may be deleted), thus reducing operating costs and potentially increasing performance.

6. Weaknesses: Prevents decisions from being made on the best information available (a worse decision might be made based on no information than on partial or outdated information). Lack of automatic means of detecting incomplete or obsolete data makes directives difficult to enforce.

7. How to Audit: Review dissemination policies and procedures for reasonableness and compliance with regulatory, statutory, and civil requirements. Review procedures to block dissemination of certain types of information. Review procedures to expunge records from certain data bases.

8. Purpose: Prevention

9. Control Area: Management

10. Mode: Manual procedures

11. Area of Responsibility: Input/output control, users, management, development.

12. Cost: Low

13. Principles of Note: Completeness and consistency.

---

1. Control Title: **Discarded Document Destruction**

2. Objective: Prevent disclosure, taking, or unauthorized use of documents.

3. Description: Input/output documents, including any human readable documents or nonerasable computer media (carbon paper, punch cards and tape, one-time-use printer ribbons), should be reviewed for potential loss sensitivity and appropriately destroyed when no longer needed. Appropriate protection of materials awaiting final disposition should be used. Logging of all actions to ensure an audit trail and adherence to rules is essential. Strict assignments of tasks and accountability are essential. Documents such as obsolete system development materials, test data and manuals, and obsolete criminal histories should be considered.

4. Variables: Secure storage facilities; method of destruction, e.g., mechanical (shredding), chemical, or burning; logging method; marking documents for disposition.

5. Strengths: Provides complete accounting for all documents. Reduces exposure to loss in facilities and trash. Makes facilities less cluttered and reduces fire hazards. Reduces cost of storage.

6. Weaknesses: Expensive errors could result from discarding valuable documents. Sensitive documents are concentrated in one area and in one activity.

7. How to Audit: Examine trash for sensitive documents. Examine sensitivity criteria for appropriateness. Observe storage and destruction areas. Do sample confirmations of destruction based on destruction log.

8. Purpose: Prevention

9. Control Area: Computer center

10. Mode: Manual procedures, hardware (shredder)

11. Area of Responsibility: Input/output

12. Cost: Low

13. Principles of Note: Least privilege, completeness, and consistency.

---

1. Control Title: **Personal Data Input/Output Inspection**

2. Objective: Prevent disclosure or unauthorized use of personal information.

3. Description: An organization that receives or disseminates data bases from or to outside sources should have an input/output control group. This group checks the data bases when they are received and disseminated. It checks for the inclusion of improper data fields, such as individual names and social security numbers. Also, more sophisticated checking of the relational aspects of the data field is done to determine whether individuals can be identified by combining information from multiple fields. The group screens all files to be received and investigates anomalies. A log is kept of all activity.

4. Variables: Organization, specific rules, approval and logging forms.

5. Strengths: Potential privacy and confidentiality problems are caught early before data are made available to outsiders. This group also examines data to see that they meet the organization's standards with respect to items such as format, content, and value.

6. Weaknesses: High-level people are required to review the data bases.

7. How to Audit: Compliance review of existing data bases and review of criteria used by the group to evaluate the data bases.

8. Purpose: Prevention

9. Control Area: Computer center

10. Mode: Manual procedures

11. Area of Responsibility: User

12. Cost: Medium

13. Principles of Note: Independence of control/subject, compartmentalization, accountability.

**Selective
Human Subjects of Research
or Processing**

1. Control Title: **Human Subjects Review**

2. Objective: Prevent disclosure and unauthorized use of personal information.

3. Description: An independent review board (Human Subjects Review Board) reviews all proposals in an organization concerning treatment of subjects in studies. The board is made up of members of the parent organizations, some from the department in question, and some from outside the department. The charter of the board is to determine whether the subjects of a study will be put "at risk" or "at a disadvantage" because of participation in the study.

   The manner in which individual privacy (date confidentiality) is handled is a key issue. The board reviews the original plans of the project, the mode of operation, and justification of any risks to ensure that the potential benefits of the activity outweigh the potential costs. The board also has the responsibility to evaluate the staff decisions. The reason for this evaluation is that not all problems can be anticipated by the board. Three areas of qualifications are examined: (1) sensitivity to issues of privacy; (2) personal values; and (3) general competence and ability to cope with unforeseen problems. All decisions are documented.

4. Variables: Organization, criteria for acceptable activities, powers.

5. Strengths: An independent review is made at the beginning of the project. The review is made by peers and includes intangible factors.

6. Weaknesses: Control depends on the quality of board members, and sometimes not all problems are found.

7. How to Audit: Review minutes of the board meeting and any privacy problems that do occur.

8. Purpose: Prevention

9. Control Area: Management

10. Mode: Manual procedures

11. Area of Responsibility: Users

12. Cost: Medium

13. Principles of Note: Independence of control/subject, accountability.

Baseline

1. Control Title: **Proprietary Notice Printed on Documents**

2. Objective: Prevent disclosure or unauthorized use of documents.

3. Description: Sensitive and valuable documents have a classification (e.g., "sensitive," "private," "proprietary," "confidential," "for authorized parties only") or an explicit warning indicating that the information is the property of a certain organization, that it should be handled according to special criteria, that it is not to be used for certain purposes, etc.

   One site chose to print confidential in the middle of the page; although this made reading a bit more difficult, it prevented people from cropping the record and photocopying it to remove any indication that it was confidential. Another approach is to have the computer print appropriate words on only sensitive output. (This has the advantage of warning display terminal users that the information should be specially treated.) Policies and procedures must also be written.

4. Variables: Selecting documents, wording, how printed, rules of use, owner's interest.

5. Strengths: This control reduces ambiguity associated with the use and dissemination of sensitive information, provides concrete evidence that steps were taken to control information (this may be of use in court), and can be used to control use of proprietary software. Likelihood of privacy violation can to some extent be avoided or lessened. Use of copyright or trademark laws may reduce unauthorized distribution and useage of sensitive information.

6. Weaknesses: Errors of omission become more severe.

7. How to Audit: Examine samples of output to see that they contain an appropriate notice. Discuss the wording of such notices with legal counsel. Determine that the notice cannot easily be stripped from the output.

8. Purpose: Deterrence

9. Control Area: Computer center, application system

10. Mode: Manual procedures, application system, computer system

11. Area of Responsibility: User, legal, computer security, operations, input/output.

12. Cost: Low

13. Principles of Note: Minimization of exceptions, compartmentalization, acceptance, sustainability, auditability.

Selective
External Input of Incomplete Information

1. Control Title: **Completion of External Input Data**

2. Objective: Prevent modification, disclosure, or unauthorized use of obsolete or incomplete input/output data.

3. Description: If missing essential data are still missing beyond a time limit, take steps to obtain the appropriate data. Within the criminal justice environment, a request for disposition information is issued when a particular record has remained incomplete beyond a time limit.

4. Variables: Types of external data, time periods, method of completion, forms design.

5. Strengths: Acts as an error correction/detection control identifying records for which important information is still missing after a certain period of time (the update could have been misplaced, processed incorrectly, inadvertently omitted, etc.) Preserves personal privacy, ensuring that incomplete records, which may have misleading decisions based upon them, are reduced. The control also helps keeps records up to date.

6. Weaknesses: Administrative overhead associated with requests for information, when the information may not yet be available, may be a burden to the data supplier who may not be able to easily provide the information requested or who may not provide it because it is too costly. Unless data suppliers have a good reason for providing additional information, they may ignore requests for additional information. Information providers may no longer be able to provide information (due to funding and other reasons). Resolution may involve significant liaison efforts and problems in different levels and branches of government.

7. How to Audit: Review policies and procedures for requesting additional data. Identify certain records (preferably based on a random sample) that are in need of followup and determine that the proper requests have been made.

8. Purpose: Prevention, detection

9. Control Area: Computer center, application systems

10. Mode: Manual procedures, application system

11. Area of Responsibility: Users, computer operations, development

12. Cost: Low

13. Principles of Note: Independence of control and subject; completeness and consistency; instrumentation.

Baseline

1. Control Title: **Low Building Profile**

2. Objective: Avoid destruction of assets and business interruption.

3. Description: Buildings housing computer systems and the computer facilities should be unobtrusive and give minimum indication of their purpose. There should be obvious signs identifying computing activities outside or in-

side buildings. Buildings should look impressive and ordinary relative to nearby buildings. Building lobby directories and company telephone books should not identify locations of computer activities except for offices and reception areas that serve outsiders (users, vendors, etc.) and are located separately from operational areas. Physical access barriers, including access control signs, should be reasonably visible, however.

4. Variables: Building materials, windows, location relative to other functionally related areas, prestige and image value, safety.

5. Strengths: A low profile reduces the likelihood of attention by destruction-minded outsiders. Such attention tends to be directed away to other more visible targets.

6. Weaknesses: A low profile may reduce business promotion values and inconvenience visitors, vendors, delivery people, and others who have a legitimate need to find computing facilities.

7. How to Audit: Observation by those familiar with computing locations. Tests by persons unfamiliar with computer locations.

8. Purpose: Deterrence

9. Control Area: Computer center

10. Mode: Manual procedure

11. Area of Responsibility: Management, security

12. Cost: Low

13. Principles of Note: Avoidance of need for design secrecy, completeness and consistency, least privilege.

1. Control Title: **Physical Security Perimeter**

2. Objective: To avoid destruction of assets and business interruption.

3. Description:The physical perimeter within which security is to be maintained and outside of which little or no control is maintained should be clearly established. All vital functions should be identified and included within the security perimeter. Physical access control and prevention of damage immediately outside security perimeters should be carefully considered.

   For example, physical barriers should extend to the base floor and to the base ceiling around sensitive areas. Areas beneath false floors and above false ceilings must be controlled consistent with the control of working areas between them. Important equipment, such as electrical power switching and communication equipment and circuits, must be made secure and included within the security perimeter.

   Employees and on-site vendors should be made aware of perimeters on a least-privilege basis. The perimeter should be easily discernible, simple, uncluttered, and sufficiently secure relative to the value of assets inside the perimeter. Drawings and specifications of the perimeter should be available and used for planning any facilities changes. Additional barriers between areas with different security requirements within the exterior barrier also should be established.

4. Variables: Placement of perimeter, perimeter barriers

5. Strengths: Consistency and completeness in physical security will ensure maximum protection. Modification of facilities can be made without compromising security.

6. Weaknesses: Cooperation among all parties involved may break down and limit effectiveness. An obvious perimeter may attract undesirable attention.

7. How to Audit: Physical inspection of security perimeters should be done periodically, and physical barriers should be tested.

8. Purpose: Prevention

9. Control Area: Computer center

10. Mode: Hardware

11. Area of Responsibility: Security

12. Cost: High

13. Principles of Note: Completeness and consistency, minimization of exceptions, isolation, compartmentalization.

---

1. Control Title: **Placement of Equipment and Supplies**

2. Objective: Avoid destruction of assets and business interruption.

3. Description: Equipment, such as telephone switching panels and cables, utilities, power and air conditioning plants, computer devices, and supplies, such as paper, cards, chemicals, water, tapes, and disks, should be placed or stored to ensure their protection from damage and minimize the adverse effects they may have on other items. Dust, vibration, chemical effects, fire hazards, and electrical interference are produced by some equipment and supplies, and they should be kept separate from equipment and supplies effected by these phenomena. Items requiring special safeguards should be isolated to reduce the extent of required safeguard coverage. In multifloor buildings, vertical as well as horizontal proximity should be considered.

4. Variables: Equipment and supplies, nature and extent of separation requirements and limitations, functional relationships.

5. Strengths: Cost of protection can be reduced. Damage can be reduced and isolated. Traffic can be reduced in some cases.

6. Weaknesses: Distances and barriers between functionally related items may reduce efficiency. For example, small supplies of paper may be needed close to printers because of the remoteness of the primary storage. Traffic problems may arise, such as the need for access within the security perimeter by telephone repairmen.

7. How to Audit: Observe placement of equipment and supplies and conduct vulnerability analysis.

8. Purpose: Prevention

9. Control Area: Computer center

10. Mode: Hardware

11. Area of Responsibility: Computer security, operations

12. Cost: Medium

13. Principles of Note: Control and subject independence, limit of dependence on other mechanisms.

---

1. Control Title: **Emergency Preparedness**

2. Objective: Prevent human injuries and other damages from contingencies.

3. Description: Emergency procedures should be documented and periodically reviewed with occupants of areas requiring emergency action. Adequate automatic fire and water detection and suppression capabilities are assumed to be present. Reduction of human injury is the first priority, followed by saving other important assets. Emergency drills that enact the documented procedures should be periodically held. It should be assumed that occupants of an area in which an emergency occurs do not have time to read emergency procedures documents before action. Procedures should include activation of manual alarms and power shutoff switches, evacuation routes, reporting of conditions, safe areas for regrouping, accounting for all occupants, use of equipment such as fire extinguishers to aid safe evacuation, and actions following complete evacuation. A hierarchy of emergency commands should be established with backup assignments.

   Emergency drills should be organized to minimize loss of critical activities such as computer operation. Close supervision of drills by managers who are aware of practice or real emergencies is necessary. Large, clearly visible signs providing basic directions are required. For example, locations of fire extinguishers, portable lights, and emergency switches should clearly be identified with signs that can be read from likely positions of occupants. First aid kits should be available in regrouping areas. Emergency food, water, tools, waste disposal, waterproof equipment covers, communication and sleeping supplies should be available for prolonged emergencies. All civil ordinances and insurance policy requirements equipment.

4. Variables: Frequency and extent of drills and briefings, content and location of written procedures, manual alarms and switches, evacuation routes and regrouping areas, signs, command assignments, amount and locations of emergency equipment.

5. Strengths: The safety of occupants from injury is the primary purpose of this control. Employees will have more positive feelings about their employer's concern for their welfare, and alertness to potential emergencies is maintained.

6. Weaknesses: Drills can become too commonplace and not taken seriously. Emergency equipment and supplies can deteriorate. Written procedures become obsolete. Emergency switches can be accidentally or maliciously activated.

7. How to Audit: Observe drills, review written procedures, check signs and equipment.

8. Purpose: Prevention

9. Control Area: Computer center

10. Mode: Manual procedures, hardware

11. Area of Responsibility: Computer security, operations

12. Cost: Medium

13. Principles of Note: Override capability, completeness and consistency, acceptance by personnel, sustainability.

Baseline

1. Control Title: **Security for Sensitive Areas during Attended Periods**

2. Objective: To avoid destruction of assets and business interruption.

3. Description: Sensitive areas during unattended time should be made physically secure with locked doors, significant barriers, and automatic detection devices for movement or natural disaster losses. Periodic inspection by guards and closed-circuit TV monitoring are also important. In addition, sensitive areas not generally visible to others should never be occupied by a lone employee for safety and prevention of malicious acts. Some computer-related work areas such as the computer room are occupied by employees at all times. Other areas and some computer rooms are left unattended for varying periods of time from several hours per day to only 1 or 2 days, such as holidays, each year. Safeguarding when employees are present and not present represents significantly different security requirements.

4. Variables: Detection and suppression equipment (vendors of equipment can assist in selection), guard inspections, periods of unattended time.

5. Strengths: Adequate control of unattended areas will ensure consistency of security.

6. Weaknesses: Unattended sensitive areas are particularly vulnerable, and automatic monitoring may not be sufficiently comprehensive to cover all contingencies.

7. How to Audit: Auditors should periodically inspect unattended areas during times in which they are unattended.

8. Purpose: Detection

9. Control Area: Computer center

10. Mode: Manual procedures, hardware

11. Area of Responsibility: Security

12. Cost: Medium

13. Principles of Note: Universal application, completeness and consistency, instrumentation.

---

1. Control Title: **Areas Where Smoking and Eating Are Prohibited**

2. Objective: Avoid destruction of assets and business interruption.

3. Description: Smoking and eating are not permitted in computer equipment areas. Prevention requires signs, written policy, enforcement, and penalties rigorously applied. In addition, personal grooming to eliminate long hair and loose clothing should be voluntarily practiced to avoid interference with moving parts of peripheral equipment and personal injury.

4. Variables: Designated areas, signs, policy.

5. Strengths: In addition to obvious benefits, prevents smoke detection and water detection alarms from being triggered unnecessarily; also increases worker productivity somewhat.

6. Weaknesses: Poses an inconvenience for employees; may require the establishment of a separate lounge area. If lounge area must be outside the security perimeter around the computer room, physical access to the computer room may be comprised. Heavy smokers may not be able to work in this environment. Disciplinary measures will need to be defined and enforced.

7. How to Audit: Observation that this policy is actually being followed.

8. Purpose: Prevention

9. Control Area: Computer center

10. Mode: Policy

11. Area Of Responsibility: Operations

12. Cost: Low

13. Principles of Note: Acceptance by personnel.

---

1. Control Title: **Minimize Traffic and Access to Work Areas**

2. Objective: Prevent unauthorized access to sensitive areas.

3. Description: Employee and vendor work areas and visitor facilities should be located to minimize unnecessary access. Persons should not have to pass through sensitive areas to reach work stations. Sensitive functions should be placed in low traffic areas. Traffic points through security perimeters should be minimized. Employee convenience facilities such as lavatories, lounges, lockers, and food and drink dispensers should be located to minimize traffic through barriers and sensitive areas. Toilets outside of security perimeters, such as in lobby and receiving areas, are essential. Areas with many work stations should be separated from areas with few work stations. For example, computer peripheral equipment requiring human operation should be in rooms separate from computer equipment requiring little human attention.

   Access authorization should be granted on a privileged basis. Three access levels can be granted: general, limited, and by exception. General access is granted to those whose work stations are in a restricted area. In a computer room, this includes computer operations, maintenance staff, and first-level supervisors. Limited access is granted for specified periods of time to those responsible for performing specified preplanned assignments, such as

auditors, security personnel, and repair of construction crews.

   Finally, exceptions can be made in emergencies as long as those having access are escorted and after which extraordinary measures are taken to ensure integrity of the area. Application programmers no longer need access to computer rooms except on an emergency basis. Systems programmers need access on a limited basis. Visitors should be restricted entirely from computer rooms unless be exception and are accompanied by a high-level manager who explicitly accepts responsibility and is personally accountable. Other sensitive areas, such as programmers' offices, job set-up areas, and data entry work areas, should be similarly restricted to authorized access. Signs identifying limited access areas should be posted, and rules should be strictly enforced.

4. Variables: Functional relationships of computing activities, work assignments, logging accesses, building constraints, worker efficiency, space size requirements, security level differentials, and assets values.

5. Strengths: Unauthorized physical access is one of the greatest security vulnerabilities and is effectively reduced by careful placement of computing activities. Potential for criminal collusion is reduced. In addition, worker efficiency and productivity can be increased when interaction and communication among employees engaged in different activities are not essential. The number of security officers can be decreased.

6. Weaknesses: Employes and managers may resent restricted movement. Reduced interaction and communication among creative people may reduce their performance.

7. How to Audit: Observe traffic and work areas, study functional relationships, and perform traffic analysis.

8. Purpose: Deterrence, prevention

9. Control Area: Computer center

10. Mode: Hardware

11. Area of Responsibility: Security, management

12. Cost: Low

13. Principles of Note: Least privelege, minimization of exceptions, accountability, sustainability.

---

1. Control Title: **Physical Access Barriers**

2. Objective: Prevent unauthorized physical access to sensitive areas.

3. Description: Physical access through a security perimeter from a less sensitive area to a more sensitive area or between areas where different privileges apply must be limited to as few openings as possible. The remaining barrier between openings should be made of sufficiently sturdy materials to resist entry. Openings should have entrance controls consisting of one or more of the following methods.

   ☐ Sign in/out log.
   ☐ Challenge of unauthorized entry by authorized persons.
   ☐ Challenge access by posted signs.
   ☐ Mechanically or electrically locked doors.
   ☐ Guards (local or remote using CCTV).
   ☐ Mantrap (double) or turnstile doors.

   In computer centers, limited access should be maintained for all areas except public entry lobbies, lavatories, lounges, food areas, and all areas outside of the outermost security perimeter. There should be a central administration of access throughout a computer center. Procedures must be documented and include exception condition procedures. Emergency exit doors must be provided for safety and to comply with ordinances and insurance requirements.

4. Variables: Location of access, type of access constraints, authorization procedures, logging accesses, strength of barrier materials.

5. Strengths: Access control prevents unnecessary movements of people as well as unauthorized accesses for security purposes. The practice of a secure procedure for gaining access maintains a vigilance and security awareness among authorized persons. It also discourages malicious persons.

6. Weaknesses: Controls reduce efficiency. There is a danger of mismatching stringency of controls and actual needs. Sustaining adequate levels of effectiveness is difficult unless automatic barriers are used.

7. How to Audit: Frequent testing by making unauthorized access attempts (without force) and challenging a sample of persons in limited access areas should be done.

8. Purpose: Prevention

9. Control Area: Computer center

10. Mode: Manual procedures, hardware

11. Area of Responsibility: Security

12. Cost: Medium

13. Principles of Note: Least privilege, override capability, completeness and consistency.

---

1. Control Title: **Remote Terminal Physical Security**

2. Objective: Prevent unauthorized access to sensitive areas.

3. Description:Physical access barriers,accountability for use, and resistance to visual and electromagnetic monitoring of terminals and local communication loops are maintained and periodically reviewed consistent with security of the computer system being used from the terminal. Terminals are frequently owned or are under the control of computer users and often do not come under the jurisdiction of computer centers supplying services. Therefore, this control is directed to users or indirectly to computer center employee functions as liaison to terminal users and has the authority to disallow system access from any terminal where acceptable controls are not in place. Signed agreements are used to enforce the requirements.

   Resistance to visual or electromagnetic monitoring can include line-of-sight barriers to prevent reading of displays from a distance and placing terminals sufficiently removed from a security perimeter so that electromagnetic emanations would be costly to monitor. Securing of work papers and terminal media should also be ensured. Locks on terminals, clearing of work areas after use, and bolting of terminals to fixed objects might be considered.

4. Variables: Barriers, usage logging, distance to security perimeter, control of visual media, terminal locking mechanisms, mechanisms to prevent removal of equipment.

5. Strengths: Security consistency can be maintained over all system use. Losses are probably more likely to occur around terminals and during usage because people in positions of trust concentrate at terminals. Security reviews by computer center security staff facilitate independence and objectivity.

6. Weaknesses: Cost of security, remoteness, and informal environments make controls difficult

to maintain. Portable terminals increase difficulty of security.

7. How to Audit: Review remote terminal inspection reports. Examine usage logs at terminals and compare with system-produced logs. Conduct surprise audits at selected sites where problems are reported.

8. Purpose: Detection, prevention

9. Control Area: Computer center (and its extensions)

10. Mode: Manual procedures

11. Area of Responsibility: Computer users

12. Cost: Medium

13. Principles of Note: Least privilege, completeness, and consistency.

Selective
Large Staff, High Traffic, Many Outsiders

1. Control Title: **Universal Use of Badges**

2. Objective: Prevent unauthorized access to sensitive areas.

3. Description: To control access to sensitive data processing facilities, all persons are required to wear badges. Different color badges, including photos in some cases, are used for employees, visitors, vendor representatives, and those employees requiring temporary badges (used when employees have forgotten or lost their badge). All persons are required to wear their badges in conspicious places on their person; visitors, and in some cases everybody, could be required to leave an item of identification such as a driver's license at the front desk when they are issued a badge.

   The decision to require badges depends on

business practices, numbers of people, amount of traffic, and other access controls in use. For two or three people in an area with little traffic, the need for badges in that area may be precluded. However, minimization of exceptions may warrant their use. Positive badge administration is essential. Disciplinary action should result from infractions of the rules.

4. Variables: Type of badges, administration, use of card keys, areas and people affected.

5. Strengths: Quick visual inspection should allow management, auditors, and others to determine whether someone is authorized to be in sensitive areas and if so, what their status is. Badge color codes can also designate work areas. Unauthorized parties are prevented from gaining access and causing harm (violating someone's privacy, causing damage to expensive equipment, harming employees etc.). Separation of duties and unnecessary visiting restrictions are strengthened when badges restrict the movement of employees within data processing facilities.

6. Weaknesses: Unless universally and continuously enforced, this procedure may provide little security.

7. How to Audit: Visually check the use of badges and the extent to which they control access to restricted areas. Examine logs of visitors to make sure that proper badges were issued, that proper records (time in, time out, name, badge number issued, etc.) are kept.

8. Purpose: Prevention, detection

9. Control Area: Computer center (and its extensions)

10. Mode: Manual procedures

11. Area of Responsibility: Security

12. Cost: Medium

13. Principles of Notice: Override, overt design and operation, least privilege, universal application, instrumentation, minimization of interruptions.

---

1. Control Title: **Alternative Power Supply**

2. Objective: Avoid destruction of assets and business interruption.

3. Description: A power supply independent of the public utility source for uninterrupted service is provided by batteries charged from public utility power providing a few minutes of independent power or by an independent power source such as a diesel generator for long durations. An alternative source of energy, such as a diesel generator without batteries but with adequate power quality regulators, can be used when uninterrupted service is not important, but long durations of outrage are harmful.

   This control is needed only where power is sufficiently unreliable relative to the seriousness of computer failure or unavailability. The location, environment control, and access security are important to ensure integrity of the alternative power equipment and fuel. Periodic full tests are important for maintenance. Some organizations use the independent source as the primary supply and the public utility as a backup. One organization has located a new computer center at a site between two public electric power grids and obtains power alternatively from both to reduce the likelihood of public power failure.

4. Variables: Type and size of alternative supply, switching equipment, location of equipment and fuel, computing equipment and facilities to be supported, testing frequency.

5. Strengths: Electrical damage to computer equipment and loss of data can be prevented with uninterrupted power supplies.

6. Weaknesses: The cost may be prohibitive for large systems.

7. How to Audit: Auditors should require a demonstration of alternative supply use. An independent power engineer should be called in for periodic inspections. Fuel supplies should be checked periodically for supply levels, quality, and safety.

8. Purpose: Recovery

9. Control Area: Computer system

10. Mode: Hardware

11. Area of Responsibility: Computer security

12. Cost: High

13. Principles of Note: Limit of dependence on other mechanisms.

Selective
Severe Physical Access Constraints

1. Control Title: **Delivery Loading Dock Access**

2. Objective: Avoid destruction of assets and business interruption.

3. Description: The loading dock area is made secure with the use of a window and an intermediate holding room. The window is used by truck drivers when they wish to speak to someone from the facility, have receiving papers signed, and gain authorization for access to the intermediate holding room. An employee from the inside can release the lock on a door opening on the loading dock from the holding room. The truck driver can then unload supplies or other items onto the dock and into the holding room without having access to any other areas of the building. When the delivered material is entirely within the holding room, and when the delivery man has gone, the outside door can again be locked by the employee at the receiving window. Then an inside door leading to the holding room can be unlocked and opened for the movement of the material to its proper storage/use location.

4. Variables: Facility layout, staffing in area, volume of materials.

5. Strengths: Prevents unauthorized persons from gaining access to facilities through the loading area. Allows receiving clerk to stay physically separated from the driver/delivery men (employee safety is the concern here). Permits received materials to be inspected in a locked room prior to movement to operational and storage areas of a data processing center. A bell at the receiving window can be used to summon a clerk, thus eliminating the need for the window to be manned on a full-time basis.

6. Weaknesses: Holding room may take up a large amount of floor space, which could be used for other purposes. Receiving window, related doors and locks, plus additional walls incur additional costs. Only large data processing centers may have the volume of deliveries to justify such an expenditure.

7. How to Audit: Examine facilities to make sure that the appropriate loading dock access controls are in place. On a surprise basis, watch a delivery to make sure that specified procedures are being followed.

8. Purpose: Prevention

9. Control Area: Computer center

10. Mode: Manual Procedures, hardware

11. Area of Responsibility: Security, operations

12. Cost: High

13. Principles of Note: Simplicity, least privilege, independence of control and subject, universal application, sustainability.

---

1. Control Title: **Separation of Equipment**

2. Objective: Prevent damage to equipment.

3. Description: Different types of computer equipment (central processors, disk drives, tape libraries, terminals consoles) each require different environments for optimum operation and different numbers and types of people in attendance. Therefore, they should be placed in different rooms with appropriate separation walls, distances, and accesses. For example, printers create dust and vibration from paper movement and should be separate from disk and tape drives that are sensitive to air quality and vibration. Central processors are normally unattended and should be in a low traffic environment.

4. Variables: Equipment configurations, size of spaces available, traffic patterns.

5. Strengths: Reduces repairs, avoids excessive environment and traffic controls.

6. Weaknesses: Increases expenses of facilities changes when new equipment is acquired.

7. How to Audit: Participate in facilities design. Review usable space.

8. Purpose: Prevention

9. Control Area: Computer center

10 Mode: Hardware

11. Area of Responsibility: Computer security, operations

12. Cost: High

13. Principles of Note: Simplicity, sustainability.

---

1. Control Title: **Inspection of Incoming/Outgoing Materials**

2. Objective: Prevent unauthorized taking and facility damage.

3. Description: Certain materials and containers are inspected, and entry or departure is restricted. Within constraints of all applicable laws and personal privacy, guards would prevent movement of materials and inspect contents of closed containers into and out of sensitive areas. Materials may include tapes, disks, listings, equipment, recorders, food and beverages, chemicals, and such containers as lunch boxes and briefcases. Some unneeded materials could be kept stored outside for later retrieval by owners. Authorization forms may be used to control movement. Spot checks and posted signs rather than continuous inspection may be sufficient.

4. Variables: Materials, authorization, degree of inspection.

5. Strengths: Prevents unnecessary or dangerous materials from entering areas. Reduces suspicion of otherwise trusted persons. Reinforces restrictions or unauthorized persons.

6. Weaknesses: May reduce employee efficiency and freedom.

148

7. How to Audit: Observe inspection post activity. Attempt violation of rules (with great care).

8. Purpose: Prevention

9. Control Area: Computer center

10. Mode: Manual procedures

11. Area of Responsibility: Security

12. Cost: High

13. Principles of Note: Consistency and completeness, sustainability, acceptance by personnel.

---

1. Control Title: **Isolation of Sensitive Computer Production Jobs**

2. Objective: Prevent compromise of data.

3. Description: Some production systems, such as those producing negotiable instruments or processing personal information (as in organized crime intelligence files) are sufficiently sensitive to potential loss to require special handling. Such systems should be run on dedicated computers or only share computer systems with harmless or other trusted applications. For example, data communications access might be shut down during such a job. Some sensitive systems may be run at times when general activity is minimal, such as on Sundays, and run by an operations team especially held accountable for the operation. Extraordinary physical and computer security measures may be taken during the job run. Special marking may be done of all materials used.

4. Variables: Selection of sensitive applications, operational circumstances during job runs, operations staff selection, identification of materials used.

5. Strengths: Concentration of security resources is possible. Minimizes exposure to sources of loss. May increase operational efficiency.

6. Weaknesses: May introduce inefficiencies in scheduling production. Targets for compromise become obvious.

7. How to Audit: Rank and compare sensitivities of all production jobs. Observe special production runs and check on compliance with documented procedures.

8. Purpose: Deterrence, prevention

9. Control Area: Computer center

10. Mode: Manual procedures

11. Area of Responsibility: Operations

12. Cost: High

13. Principles of Note: Least privilege.

---

1. Control Title: **Protection of Data Used in System Testing**

2. Objective: Prevent compromise of data.

3. Description: Application and test programmers usually need test date to develop, debug, and test programs under development. In some cases, small amounts of fictitious test data can be generated independent of users and production data. However, many application programs require significant amounts of test data that are exact copies of a full range of production data. Test data are frequently obtained as samples or entire files of production input data

currently being used or recently used for the application being replaced or as output from other preprocessing computer programs. There is sometimes significant exposure by providing real, current production data to programmers.

Often data can be obtained from obsolete production input data files, but in some cases even these data may be confidential. Customers for whom production programs are being developed should be made aware of the exposure problem, and advice and assistance should be obtained in producing test data in the least confidential but expedient manner. Sensitive test data should be treated with the same care as equivalent production data. In any case, development and test programmers should not be given access to real production files in a production computer system except in the case of emergency and then under highly controlled conditions.

4. Variables: Selection of test data procedure, physical and logical handling of test data.

5. Strengths: This control can greatly reduce the exposure of an organization to a wide range of errors, omissions, and intentional acts. It also imposes a beneficial discipline on development and test computer programmers.

6. Weaknesses: Providing separate test data may be particularly expensive and not necessary in every case. Good decisions require the knowledgeable participation of customers for whom computer programs are being developed. This is sometimes difficult to obtain. Test data may also not be sufficiently representative. Production runs masquerading as test runs to expedite work is a possible problem.

7. How to Audit: Auditing requires a detailed knowledge of programming and testing practices and detailed observation of the software development life cycle.

8. Purpose: Prevention

9. Control Area: Operations

10. Mode: Manual procedures

11. Area of Responsibility: Development

12. Cost: Medium

13. Principles of Note: Least privilege.

Baseline

1. Control Title: **Correction and Maintenance of Production System**

2. Objective: Protect against unauthorized program or data modifications.

3. Description: In spite of implementation and strict enforcement of security controls and good maintenance of application and systems programs, emergencies arise that require violation or overriding of many of these controls and practices. Occasionally, production programs will fail during production runs on the computer. This may happen on second and third shift, during periods of heavy production computer activity. If a failure occurs in a critical application production run, it is frequently necessary to call upon knowledgeable programmers to discover the problem, make a change in the production computer program, make changes in input data, or make decisions about alternative solutions (e.g., reruns using previous versions of the production program).

When such emergency events occur, all necessary and expedient measures must be taken including physical access of programmers to computer and production areas, access by such programmers to data files and production programs, correction of production programs, and ad hoc instructions to operations staff. During any of these activities, it is necessary for a trusted individual in computer application production work to record all of the events as they occur or shortly thereafter.

Following the termination of the emergency, programmers should be required to make the necessary and ordinary permanent changes that may have been made on a temporary basis during the emergency and document the emergency actions. This usually requires updating and testing production programs and the normal process of introducing tested updated programs for production use. After an emergency and before permanent corrections have been made, the production application program should be treated in a suspicious mode of operation requiring increased levels of observance by users, production staff, managers, and possibly EDP auditors. These extra efforts should continue until confidence has been built up in the production activities through acceptable experience.

4. Variables: Emergency maintenance procedures, documentation of actions, past recovery procedures.

5. Strengths: Flexibility in handling emergency production situations and having security—related procedures and continuing levels of security at highly vulnerable times is important.

6. Weaknesses: Providing a formal method of handling emergency repair may encourage the excessive use of emergency repair procedures.

7. How to Audit: This control should be audited during emergency work periods by assigning EDP auditors to oversee emergency procedures and production work using patched computer programs. The basis of decisions to make emergency repairs should be examined for correctness and consistency.

8. Purpose: Recovery

9. Control Area: Computer center

10. Mode: Manual procedures

11. Area of Responsibility: Operations

12. Cost: Medium

13. Principles of Note: Override, least privilege, accountability.

Baseline

1. Control Title: **Computer User Trouble Calls Logging**

2. Objective: Prevent overlooked security problems and detect potential adverse side effects of changes to computer systems and other elements of the operating environment.

3. Description: All calls from users and staff regarding problems with a computer and communications systems are logged detailing the caller's name, the time and date, and the nature of the problem. A brief disposition report is then prepared for each problem report. A manager reviews each of the problem disposition reports to determine that the problem has been satisfactorily resolved and also to determine that there are not any adverse impacts of the solutions provided (e.g., a correction of the operating system may have some side effect with a security or privacy implication). The reviewing manager also determines whether or not the responding operating person taking care of the problem was within bounds of authority. Simple requests for information are not considered problems within this procedure.

4. Variables: Logging assignments, forms design, review process.

5. Strengths: This practice forces user and staff liaison people to justify their actions and to

151

document each correctional action that they have taken. The log can be analyzed by performance monitoring and by system development people for possible improvements of the current operating environment.

6. Weaknesses: Preparation of logs and brief reports is time consuming and takes talented and knowledgeable people away from their other duties. Users may abuse the problem reporting system whenever they wish to get operation management's attention.

7. How to Audit: Review a sample of logs detailing all problem reports received. Examine problem disposition reports. Interview managers who review the disposition reports.

8. Purpose: Prevention, detection

9. Control Area: Data center

10. Mode: Manual procedures

11. Area of Responsibility: User (responsibility to report problems); operations.

12. Cost: Medium

13. Principles of Note: Instrumentation, accountability, auditability.

1. Control Title: **Independent Control of Audit Tools**

2. Objective: Prevent interference with auditing.

3. Description: Audit programs, documentation, and test materials are kept in secure areas by the internal auditors. Audit programs do no remain in the data center tape library. The audit programs are not kept on disk or in any other way kept on the system where they might be subject to tampering.

4. Variables: Storage area, materials stored, auditors accountable.

5. Strengths: Preserves independence of auditors.

6. Weaknesses: It may be inconvenient for auditors to keep their materials in a secure place. An installation may have a policy that no tapes are to leave the tape library unless they are to be transferred to another computer center; this practice would then require exceptions to such rules.

7. How to Audit: Ascertain that all audit materials are maintained under the direct control of auditors, not the persons being audited.

8. Purpose: Prevention

9. Control Area: Computer center

10. Mode: Manual procedures

11. Area of Responsibility: Audit

12. Cost: low

13. Principles of Note: Independence of control and subject, least privilege.

1. Control Title: **Limited Use of System Utility Programs**

2. Objective: Prevent unauthorized program or data.

3. Description: Most computer installations have one or more system utility programs capable of overriding all or most computer system and application controls. In some computer installations, one such computer program is called Superzap. In one large computer installation,

five such utility programs were found. These programs should be controlled by password or kept physically removed from the computer system and the program library and physically controlled so that they are available only to a limited number of trusted, authorized users. Occasionally, if the programs are made available on-line, they can be protected by special passwords required for their use. Changing the name or password frequently is another way to better safeguard these on-line programs.

4. Variables: Utility programs in use, residence of utility programs, operating system features.

5. Strengths: Limitation of availability of system utility programs forces programmers to use more accepted means of accomplishing their purposes that can be more safely done under the controls of the system.

6. Weaknesses: Limitations in the use of existing utility programs may encourage programmers to develop their own programs that are not under the same controls as the utility programs.

7. How to Audit: Operational audits should include the examination of physical and internal computer control of utility programs.

8. Purpose: Prevention

9. Control Area: Programming and maintenance

10. Mode: Manual procedures, computer operating system

11. Area of Responsibility: Operations

12. Cost: Low

13. Principles of Note: Override, least privilege.

_____

1. Control Title: **Tape Management Avoiding External Labels**

2. Objective: Prevent loss, modification, or destruction of data assets.

3. Description: A tape management system can be used to keep track of all tapes using a serial number appearing on the tape reel. Serial numbers may contain storage rack location information as well as a serial number. Operators handling the tapes do not know the contents of the tapes because the identity of the data set owner, creation and update dates, data set names, and like information are recorded only on internal (machine readable) labels. The software package for managing tapes contains an index of serial numbers and the corresponding label information. An up-to-date copy of the index relating serial numbers and tape information is maintained at off-site storage location(s).

4. Variables: Tape management system, volume of routinely processed tapes, special handling.

5. Strengths: Provides operators with no more information than is necessary to do their jobs, thus preventing potential abusive acts that were made possible because these data were available to the operators. Operators are presented only with a request to mount, dismount, etc. certain tapes with provided serial numbers. Reduces operator errors associated with mounting the wrong version of a data set, the wrong user, etc. A tape management system can be used to monitor operator performance as well as control the tape library. Persons in the tape library or machine room cannot learn the nature of the data on a tape simply by examining the reel.

6. Weaknesses: lack of functional labels may increase errors.

7. How to Audit: Trace the steps taken to mount and dismount a tape reel from the initiation of a request to the actual performance by the operator. Examine data available to the operator to determine that confidentiality is not lessened by unwarranted exposures.

8. Purpose: Prevention

9. Control Area: Computer center

10. Mode: Computer operating system

11. Area of Responsibility: Operations

12. Cost: Medium

13. Principles of Note: Cost effectiveness, simplicity, least privilege, independence of control and subject, instrumentation, sustainability, auditability.

---

1. Control Title: **Separation of Test and Production Systems**

2. Objective: Prevent loss, modification, disclosure, or destruction of data assets.

3. Description: When an organization is large enough to have need for more than one computer, there is a distinct advantage to limiting the development and test to one computer system and production work to another computer system. Further separation of activities can also be achieved by using multiple production systems and even multiple test systems where each application is run on a separate computer system. Likewise, each group of programmers could do testing on separate computer systems. The cost benefits of large size and high memory capacity would be lost, but applications could be more nearly matched to the appropriate size of computer and memory. Compilers may be moved to the test system.

4. Variables: Size of test and production workloads, available computers, location of development staff.

5. Strengths: Separation of systems reduces the possibility of accidental or intentional programmed access to production files and programs. It separates the duties of operations staff from development staff and reduces the likelihood of system crashes on the production system. The data processing organization can orient the systems configurations and mode of operation to that of the specific purpose of the system. This also forces a more formal approach to the movement of test systems to the status of production systems. The test computer can also provide backup for production computers.

6. Weaknesses: The increased complexity of operating more then one computer for different purposes increases other loss exposures. Operating systems and configurations will require compatibility.

7. How to Audit: This control can be audited to ensure that the production system is not being used for test or programming development purposes and that the test system is not being used for production purposes by examining usage logs and sampling output reports and the use of output.

8. Purpose: Prevention

9 Control Area: Computer center

10. Mode: Policy

11. Area of Responsibility: Operations, Development

12. Cost: High

13. Principles of Note: Control and subject independence.

Baseline

1. Control Title: **Contingency Recovery Equipment Replacement**

2. Objective: Recover from business interruption.

3. Description: Commitments should be obtained in writing from computer equipment and supplies vendors to replace critical equipment and supplies within a specified period of time following a contingency loss. Some vendors will commit to replacement of their products within a reasonable period of time and will specify that period of time as a committment.

   For example, in one computer installation a vendor agreed to replace a central processor within five days and a second processor, if necessary, within 10 days. The paper forms supplier agreed to deliver a two-week supply of all special forms in the same time frame. In contrast, other vendors would not guarantee replacement times but would only indicate that best effort would be provided with a priority over other normal product deliveries. Emergency ordering procedures should be established as part of a contingency recovery plan.

4. Variables: Willing vendors, delivery time constraints, content of binding letters of agreement.

5. Strengths: Vendor commitments provide a means of planning alternative data processing until equipment and new computing capabilities have been restored.

6. Weaknesses: The legal value of vendor commitments is not known. A payment in return for commitments may be required. A false sense of security may be produced because other contingencies may interfere with vendor commitments.

7. How to Audit: Auditors should periodically confirm the validity of agreements to be sure that they are still in effect. Agreements should be reviewed with legal counsel. Commitment periods should be checked relative to other contingency recovery plans.

8. Purpose: Recovery

9. Control Area: Computer center

10. Mode: Policy

11. Area of Responsibility: Management

12. Cost: Low

13. Principles of Note: Sustainability, accountability.

Baseline

1. Control Title: **Computer Systems Activity Records**

2. Objective: Detect unauthorized system use.

3. Description: Most computer systems produce a number of system activity logs, journals, and exception reports. Such recordings should be periodically and selectively examined both manually and through automated means looking for key indications of possible unauthorized activities. Such recordings on tape, disk, and sometimes paper listings should be archived for a reasonable period of time, and records should be kept to ensure that no reports are missing.

   For example, printed console logs should be on continuous forms. Any breaks in the forms should require signature indicating integrity of operation and no missing pages. In one computer installation, the console logs are examined on a sample basis monthly. All logs should be dated and timed with an indication of operational personnel on duty at the time the logs were produced. It may be necessary to keep manually written logs of some computer operation activities to compare with or complete the automatic logging of system activity.

4. Variables: Types and contents of activity recordings, mode of recording and archiving of records, archive cycling periods, analysis methods and frequency.

5. Strengths: Activity records may be important for evidence in litigation and insurance claims. Accountability of employees can be better assured. Recovery from contingencies can be facilitated.

6. Weaknesses: Large amounts of systems resources may be consumed in the recording and analysis. Large volumes of data may discourage manual inspection.

7. How to Audit: Periodic sampling and evaluation of recordings should be performed. Recordings represent an important audit trail for auditing various applications and computer usage.

8. Purpose: Detection

9. Control Area: Computer system

10. Mode: Computer operating system, computer application systems, manual procedures.

11. Area of Responsibility: Computer security, operations

12. Cost: Medium

13. Principles of Note: Control and subject independence, completeness and consistency, instrumentation, accountability.

1. Control Title: **Minimizing Numbers of Copies of Sensitive Data Files and Reports**

2. Objective: Prevent loss, modification, disclosures, or destruction of data assets.

3. Description:The number of copies of sensitive tape, disk, or paper files should be minimized. Destruction dates should be specified and destruction instructions followed. It may be advisable to destroy most paper copies of files on the basis that the information can be retrieved and reprinted from computer media when necessary. This is based on the concept that files stored in computer systems and computer media are generally often more secure than on paper. Normal backup procedures often require that several copies of computer media files be made and stored at different sites.

However, some files may be so sensitive that numerous copies in different locations may contribute seriously to their exposure. As many as 20 to 30 copies of computer-stored files may be produced in a single year in a large computer installation. The organization primarily accountable for highly sensitive information should have control and logs of all copies and their locations. Adequate backup must be balanced with the exposure danger or multiple copies and backup procedures.

4. Variables: Selection of data for special copy control, copy logging procedures, dating for destruction, assignment of responsibilities and accountability.

5. Strengths: Reduction in storage space and orderliness of facilities may be enhanced.

6. Weaknesses: Retention of minimum numbers of copies of records may weaken the backup capability.

7. How to Audit: Selective examination of storage areas looking for sensitive records and comparing to logging forms should be done periodically.

8. Purpose: Prevention

9. Control Area: Computer center

10. Mode: Manual procedures

11. Area of Responsibility: Operations, input/output, computer users

12. Cost: Low

13. Principles of Note: Simplicity, least privilege, completeness and consistency, accountability.

---

1. Control Title: **Data File and Program Backup**

2. Objective: Prevent loss, modification, disclosure, or destruction of data assets.

3. Description: The current form of every data file that may be needed in the future should be copied at the time of its creation, and the copy should be stored at a remote, safe location for operational recovery purposes. It may be advisable to store several copies, one immediately available in the computer center, another available some short distance away, and a third archived at some remote distance for longer term storage. Periodically updated data files should be cycled from the immediate site to the local site to the remote site by data file generations (father, grandfather, etc.).

   In addition, copies of the computer programs necessary to process the backed-up data files, documentation of the programs, computer operation instructions, and a supply of special printed forms necessary for production running of the programs should also be stored at a remote, safe location. This hierarchial arrangement of backup data files provides for convenient restarting of production runs in case of damaged or missing files. More serious problems that could result in loss of local backup data files can be resolved by using copies of remote backup data files. When a backup file is returned to the computer center for use, there must be assurance that it also is backed up safely with another copy.

4. Variables: Data files to be backed up, higher hierarchial arrangement in locations of backup files, cycling frequency and methods, archivable recordkeeping, security of backup facilities.

5. Strengths: Defensive depth of backup provides a significant increase in assurance of recovery that addresses small as well as large contingencies. Recovery from backup files is commonly done under abnormal conditions that usually accompany recovery efforts. These conditions increase the likelihood of loss of the backup files. Therefore, it is important to have at least secondary backup in addition to primary backup files.

6. Weaknesses: Operational complexity in moving backup files from one stage to the next at a multiplicity of backup sites may increase the opportunity for human errors or intentional acts of sabotage or theft. Multiple backups may produce complacency and cause degeneration of computer center procedures. There is an increased exposure to loss in transporting files to the remote sites.

7. How to Audit: An audit should periodically include the actual demonstration of recovery from each level of backup. Inspection of backup sites should be conducted to ensure their secure states.

8. Purpose: Recovery

9. Control Area: Computer center

10. Mode: Manual procedures

11. Area of Responsibility: Operations

12. Cost: Medium

13. Principles of Note: Defensive depth sustainability.

---

1. Control Title: **Disaster Recovery**

2. Objective: Recover from business interruption.

3. Description: Every computer must have a written disaster recovery plan and a recovery management team. Primary and backup managers must be assigned specific responsibilities for each aspect of recovery from all types of partial or complete disasters. Each aspect of the disaster recovery plan should have assigned a specific individual responsible for its execution. Separate individuals should be assigned to coordination, systems support, hardware recovery, facilities, administration, scheduling, communications, documentation and supplies, backup data files and security recovery funding, insurance, personnel, historical recording of events, and public affairs.

Priority processing needs of all time-dependent applications to be recovered after a disaster must be identified. This requires that all computer users specify the importance of their computer applications, processing requirements and alternative means of processing, and consequences of failure to process. Data processing management is responsible for meeting the critical needs of computer users in the best interests of the organization. Priorities will assist in the scheduling of processing when it is restored. A designated per-son should provide liaison with users informing them of special needs and the status of processing of their work. A detailed history of the recovery process must be documented and recovery activity verbally reported during the recovery process.

After recovery, the historical documentation should be analyzed to determine how future contingencies may be better handled and to handle insurance claims recovery and any litigation that may follow a disaster. Every job function should be analyzed relative to its performance during and prior to a disaster. Measures of criticality and priority of functions should be determined and documented in the plan.

4. Variables: Identification of anticipated disasters, applications and their priority for recovery, staff assignments, disaster and recovery plan, type of data processing backup site, documentation and distributions, identification or arrangement of alternatives, data processing capabilities during recovery, and arrangements for alternative services, such as communications, transportation, security guards, equipment, supplies, facilities, and personnel.

5. Strengths: Flexibility in plans facilitates meeting a wide range of contingencies. A documented recovery plan provides for a means of practicing and testing all recovery procedures. Potential threats that can provide a means of adding controls to reduce risk may be identified. Prioritizing applications provides users with perspective on the importance of better applications recovery needs. Application of limited area processing resources can be more effectively planned. Communication among recovery managers helps ensure smooth and minimum cost recovery. Documentation of recovery activities encourages responsibilities and accountability among managers and workers. Job function analysis facilitates management's quick mobilization of critical

personnel and resources in the event of a disaster. Management can more easily and effectively assign work to employees during recovery. A disaster plan reduces the likelihood of confusion. Use of a disaster recovery contact list provides for speedy notification of vendors, suppliers, and customers who can take appropriate action to assist or reduce loss.

6. Weaknesses: Documentation of a backup plan may produce complacency unless the plan is frequently reviewed and tested. Documented backup plans may also become quickly outmoded. Ranking of priorities of applications may cause ill will and disputes among computer users. The preparation of historical documentation may be distorted or incorrect and result in reduced capability to file loss claims with insurance companies or provide defense in litigation or governmental hearings. Documented recovery plans that have not been tested may quickly become too detailed or inappropriate for recovery.

7. How to Audit: Disaster recovery plans should be studied to ensure that they are still current. Proof of testing plans should be documented and reported. Scenarios of possible disasters can be generated and theoretically played against the disaster recovery plans to ensure their adequacy. Application priorities can be verified through auditors responsible for the audit of specific functions of an organization dependent on computer services. Examination of historical documentation recovery experience should be performed to note any changes necessary in disaster recovery planning for the future.

8. Purpose: Recovery

9. Control Area: Management

10. Mode: Manual procedures

11. Area of Responsibility: Management

12. Cost: High

13. Principles of Note: Simplicity, override capabilities, limit of dependence on other mechanisms, completeness and consistency instrumentation.

Baseline

1. Control Title: **Electrical Equipment Protection**

2. Objective: Prevent damage to equipment.

3. Description: Every item of computing equipment that is separately powered should have a separate circuit breaker in the electrical supply for that equipment. Alternatively, equipment may be supplied with other protective mechanisms from power failures or other electrical anomalies. Circuit breakers should be clearly labelled for manual activation. The locations of all circuit breakers should be documented and available in disaster and recovery plans.

4. Variables: Identified equipment, types of protective devices, assignments of accountability for activation, location, redundant transformers, documentation.

5. Strengths: Individual devices can fail and be switched off without having to cut power to other devices. Failures can be localized as well as more readily detected. Device configurations can be changed more readily, avoiding excessive time in diagnosing electrical problems and reconfiguring electrical systems to suit new equipment setups.

6. Weaknesses: Additional opportunity to tamper with equipment is possible.

7. How to Audit: Electrical switch boxes and circuit breakers should be periodically examined.

159

8. Purpose: Prevention

9. Control Area: Data center

10. Mode: Hardware

11. Area of Responsibility: Operations

12. Cost: Medium

13. Principles of Note: Override capability, limit of dependence on other mechanisms.

Baseline

1. Control Title: **Electrical Power Shutdown and Recovery**

2. Objective: Prevent damage to equipment.

3. Description: Emergency master power-off switches should be located next to each emergency exit door. The switches should be clearly identified, and easily read signs should be posted giving instructions for use of the switches. Activation of any of these switches should be followed with reports documenting the circumstances and persons responsible for their use.

   Alternative power supplies should be tested on a periodic basis. The power supply should be used during the test for a sufficiently long period of time to ensure sustained operation under emergency conditions. Fuel supplies for alternative power should be periodically measured, and the quality of the fuel tested. Pumps, switches, and valves for switching from alternative fuel tanks should also be periodically tested. In one computer installation having an uninterruptable power supply, two independent, separately located oil tanks are used. Either tank can independently supply the entire uninterruptable power supply. Each tank is filled by a different oil company. Two diesel generators and engines are also installed for backup purposes.

4. Variables: Number and location of master power-off switches, power-down and power-up operation instructions, frequency and extent of alternative power system testing, redundancy of power generators and fuel supplies.

5. Strengths: Easily identified power-off switches are valuable for firemen, rescue workers, and others in the event of emergencies. Testing facilitates preventive maintenance work and familiarizes staff with emergency procedures. Redundancies in alternative power supplies increase assurance of emergency recoveries.

6. Weaknesses: Unauthorized or accidental use of power-off switches can cause extensive damage to computer equipment and loss of data. Intentional use of power-off switches could assist in gaining unauthorized entry to computer facilities. Cutover to alternative power supplies may result in interruption of service and inconvenience to users. Redundancy increases the complexity of alternative power systems. This increases maintenance problems and likelihood of failures.

7. How to Audit: Periodically examine logs and question all switch activations. Ensure proper posting of identification and warning signs at switches. Observe testing of alternative power supplies and review testing logs. Review maintenance logs for excessive maintenance as an indication of possible problems.

8. Purpose: Prevention and recovery

9. Control Area: Data center

10. Mode: Hardware

11. Area of Responsibility: Operations

12. Cost: Medium

13. Principles of Note: Override capability, limit

of dependence on other mechanisms, instrumentation, sustainability.

---

1. Control Title: **Employees Identification on Work Products**

2. Objective: Detect unauthorized activities of employees.

3. Description: All computer operators and other employees should have standard identification in the form of official names, numbers, or passwords. This identification is to be entered into all records, data input, and activity logs and journals to identify workers associated with all work products. Identification can be accomplished by manual signatures or keying of identification into equipment keyboards. Data entry clerks should be required to initial all forms or batch control forms used for data entry and enter identification into computer input data. Computer operators should sign computer console printer listings or enter their codes through console keyboards indicating the starting and ending of work periods.

4. Variables: Form of employee identification, entry of identification, manual verification of correct identification activity.

5. Strengths: Manual identification on forms can be compared with identification entered into computer systems to match times and work products. Incentives for higher quality and quantity of work are possible when work ducts are identified by individual worker. Tracking of errors and unauthorized activities is facilitated.

6. Weaknesses: Possible forgery can result in errors in accountability for unauthorized activity.

7. How to Audit: Spotchecking of employee codes with immediate supervisors. Sampling of computer output by audit trail back to source data handling.

8. Purpose: Detection, deterrence

9. Control Area: Computer center, applications systems

10. Mode: Manual procedures, computer application system

11. Area of Responsibility: Operations

12. Cost: Low

13. Principles of Note: Control and subject independence, least privilege, instrumentation, acceptance by personnel, accountability.

---

1. Control Title: **Magnetic Tape Erasure**

2. Objective: Prevent compromise of data.

3. Description: Computer centers should have magnetic tape erasure devices, commonly referred to as *degaussers*. For the erasure of the contents of magnetic tapes. Such devices should be kept under strict control of the computer centers. Preferably, the device should be kept in a locked cabinet and authorized for use by selected individuals. The device should also be kept a significant distance away from magnetic tape storage areas. An erasure service should be offered to computer users, and an option for tape erasure should be made available on magnetic tape disposition forms providing a date upon which erasure should be performed. All magnetic tapes used for temporary storage (scratch tapes) should also be routinely erased before reuse. Dual control or separation of functions should be established to ensure that tapes containing valuable information are not mistakenly erased without authorization.

4. Variables: Location of equipment, procedure for use, erase disposition service.

5. Strengths: Routine erasure of tapes may prevent obsolete data from being used. Erasure of tapes can also be done at the time they are cleaned. High-speed degaussing devices, even when placed near magnetic tapes in storage, do not threaten magnetic media. A log can be used to record all degaussing.

6. Weaknesses: The ease with which large amounts of data can be lost requires great caution.

7. How to Audit: Examine documentation of procedures to erase sensitive information. Observe the handling of erasure activities.

8. Purpose: Prevention

9. Control Area: Computer center

10. Mode: Manual procedures, hardware

11. Area of Responsibility: Operations

12. Cost: Low

13. Principles of Note: Override capability.

---

1. Control Title: **Courier Trustworthiness and Identification**

2. Objective: Preventive disclosure, taking, or unauthorized use of documents.

3. Description: Couriers are frequently used to distribute computer output reports to computer users. Couriers must be especially trustworthy, have a background investigation similar to that for computer operators, and be bonded. A new courier should be personally introduced to all those persons to whom he will be delivering computer output and to all persons from whom he will be receiving materials for delivery. Couriers should be required to use signed receipts for all transported reports. Couriers should be required to keep all reports in their personal possession in properly locked or controlled containers. All users should be informed immediately upon the termination of any couriers delivering or picking up reports. Couriers should carry special identification to show that they are authorized to function in claimed capacities. Telephone calls in advance of delivery of highly sensitive reports should be made to recipients of those reports.

4. Variables: Courier background investigations, identification procedures, design of receipt forms, delivery procedures, logging procedures.

5. Strengths: Procedures ensure positive accountability by receivers and senders of reports as well as couriers.

6. Weaknesses: Because couriers are generally low-paid employees, their potential for trustworthiness sometimes is reduced. Bonding of such employees is imperative.

7. How to Audit: Couriers should periodically be followed in their delivery work and be observed. Their activities should then be compared to receipt documents.

8. Purpose: Prevention

9. Control Area: Computer center

10. Mode: Manual procedures

11. Area of Responsibility: Input and output, computer users

12. Cost: Low

13. Principles of Note: Control and subject independence, limit of dependence on other mechanisms, instrumentation, accountability.

---

1. Control Title: **Production Program Authorized Version Validation**

2. Objective: Prevent unauthorized program or data modification.

3. Description: The authorized versions or copies of production programs, according to identifiers, are checked with a list of authorized copies and changes made to the production programs to determine that the version of a production program to be run is authorized. Update of the list is part of the ordinary maintenance process of production programs. Separate test and production program libraries are maintained.

4. Variables: Identifiers, procedures, exception handling.

5. Strengths: Prevents unauthorized versions of the production programs from being executed when used in conjunction with other related controls. Accidentally running a test version or an old version of a production program can be prevented and detected using this technique. Unauthorized versions of production programs can be similarly detected and prevented from being run.

6. Weaknesses: Requires that the list of authorized change dates and identifiers be protected from unauthorized changes. Adds additional complexity to the maintenance and production running procedures. The process may have to be disabled for recovery or emergency purposes.

7. How to Audit: Logs showing all exceptions (compile dates that do not match) should be examined regularly; additionally, it should be determined whether action has been taken to follow up on all instances where a match between the list of authorized versions does not match identifiers.

8. Purpose: Prevention, detection

9. Control Area: Computer center

10. Mode: Manual procedures

11. Area of Responsibility: Operations

12. Cost: Low

13. Principles of Note: Minimization of exceptions, instrumentation, auditability.

---

1. Control Title: **Independent Computer Use by Auditors**

2. Objective: Prevent interference with auditing.

3. Description: Audit independence can be considerably enhanced by using a computer not associated with the data processing activities being audited. Otherwise, if the same computer is being used, then the computer should be used in isolation from all other activities. Where data tapes are being audited, they may be taken to a service bureau to perform audit activities.

4. Variables: Computer availability, computer system compatibilities, computer audit activity.

5. Strengths: Use of an independent computer may provide the EDP auditors with more direct computer operation experience, adding to

their capabilities. Audit computer use may avoid conflicts of overloading of the computer system being audited. The transportability of data from one computer to another can be validated.

6. Weaknesses: Unless a separate computer is readily available, the cost of audit may be prohibitive. Movement of sensitive data from the computer center may expose them to new vulnerabilities.

7. How to Audit: Investigate possible systems interconnections and ensure their independence.

8. Purpose: Prevention

9. Control Area: Computer system

10. Mode: Computer applications system, manual procedures

11. Area of Responsibility: Audit

12. Cost: Medium

13. Principles of Note: Cost effectiveness, least privilege, control and subject independence, limit of dependence on other mechanism, auditability.

**Selective
Large Production Systems**

1. Control Title: **Automation of Computer Operations**

2. Objective:Preventive unauthorized computer activities.

3. Description: Computer operations should be made as automatic as possible, using such capabilities as production, program and test program libraries, automatic tape library management, reduction of job control by punch cards, and computer operator activity logging.

4. Variables: Availability of computer operations software package, high volume of activity justifying use of automated methods, amount of routine production activity.

5. Strengths: Reduction of manual procedures generally results in improved control of computer operations activities. Reduction of staff reduces exposure to accidental or intentionally caused loss, provides motivation to use automated operations packages beyond other considerations of cost-effectiveness.

6. Weaknesses: Concentration of trust among fewer people may result in less exposure to loss but potential for larger losses if they occur. It becomes more difficult to separate job duties among fewer operations personnel.

7. How to Audit: Observe erasure activity and location of degaussing.

8. Purpose: Prevention

9. Control Area: Computer center

10. Mode: Manual procedures

11. Area of Responsibility: Operations

12. Cost: Low

13. Principles of Note: Accountability, instrumentation.

---

1. Control Title: **Separation and Accountability of EDP Functions**

2. Objective: Prevent loss of security support.

3. Description: Holding managers accountable for the security in the areas they manage requires that these areas be clearly and explicity defined

so that there is no overlap or gaps in managerial control of EDP functions. EDP functions should be broken down into as many discrete self-contained activities as is practical and cost-effective under the circumstances.

Besides being a good general management principle to maintain high performance, it also provides the necessary explicit structure for assignment of controls, responsibility for them, accountability and a means of measuring the completeness and consistency of meeting all vulnerabilities adequately. Separate, well-defined EDP functions also facilitate the separation of duties among managers, as is required in separation of duties of employees. This reduces the level of trust needed for each manager. The functions of authorization, custody of assets, and accountability should be separated to the extent possible.

4. Variables: EDP functions, accountability policy.

5. Strengths: This separation reduces the possibility of accidental or intentional acts resulting in losses. It forces the need for collusion among individuals who may attempt unauthorized activities. More efficient EDP functions are possible. The possible loss of control is inhibited from migrating from one function to another.

6. Weaknesses: Increased complexity of EDP functions could result from excessive separation of functions, making the application of individual controls more difficult. Small shops may not have adequate numbers of employees to support extensive separation of duties.

7. How to Audit: Managers of EDP functions should be interviewed and their charters examined to ensure adequate separation and effectiveness of functional interfaces. Interfaces should be reviewed for consistency and completeness.

8. Purpose: Prevention

9. Control Area: Management

10. Mode: Policy

11. Area of Responsibility: Management

12. Cost: Low

13. Principles of Note: Limit of dependence on other mechanisms, completeness and consistency, accountability.

Baseline

1. Control Title: **Computer Security Management Committies**

2. Objective: Prevent loss of security support.

3. Description: A high-level management committee is organized to develop security policy and oversee all security of information handling activities. The committee is made up of management representatives from each of the parts of the organization concerned with information processing. The committee is responsible for coordinating computer security, reviewing the state of security, ensuring the visibility of management's support of computer security throughout the organization, approving computer security reviews, receiving and accepting computer security review reports, and ensuring proper control interfaces among organization functions. It should act in some respects similar to a Board of Director's Audit Committee.

Computer security reviews and recommendations for major control should be made to, and approved by, this committee. The committee ensures that privacy and security are part of the overall information handling plan. The Steering Committee may be part of a larger activity within an organization to carry out the

165

function of information resource management. For example, in one research and development organization, an oversight council made up of representatives from organizations that send and receive data bases from the R&D organization was established. They are charged with oversight responsibilities for the conduct and control of the R&D organization relative to the exchange of data bases. Especially important are questions of individual privacy concerning the content of the data bases.

4. Variables: Level and participation of Steering Committee members, objectives and charter of the Steering Committee, powers and advisory capacity of the committee.

5. Strengths: A Steering Committee visibly shows the dedication and support of security by top management to the entire organization. Security activity is organized on a top-down basis. A committee that crosses organizational lines can better ensure the consistency of security across the interfaces and the consistency of attention to security in all information-processing-related functions. The Steering Committee can consider security and privacy within the context of other issues confronting the organization. Policies and procedures can be more effectively enforced. The committee approach can avoid the control of computer security by technologists who tend to be limited to technical solutions to security problems.

6. Weaknesses: A computer security management Steering Committee could add a level of undesirable bureaurcracy. Control procurements and decisions may become time-consuming and expensive because of approvals necessary from a high-level committee. Individual managers may attempt to avoid the responsibility for security by assuming that the Steering Committee absolves them of such responsibility.

7. How to Audit: Review decisions of the committee and its work products. The head of EDP Audit should be a member of the steering Committee.

8. Purpose: Prevention, deterrence

9. Control Area: Management

10. Mode: Policy

11. Area of Responsibility: Management

12. Cost: Low

13. Principles of Note: Completeness and consistency, accountability.

Baseline

1. Control Title: **Financial Loss Contingency and Recovery Funding**

2. Objective: Recover from business interruption.

3. Description: Self-insured organizations, such as government agencies, should be assured of readily available emergency funds for contingencies and recovery. Specialized EDP insurance is available and should be considered when insurance covering other types of losses in a business may not apply. Financial risk protection should cover asset losses, business interruption, and extra expense resulting from contingency recovery. Organizations not self-insured should bond all employees against fraud in high-risk areas of data processing activities. Blanket bonds will normally cover this activity.

4. Variables: Organization insurance practices, lines of credit and availability of emergency funds, size of potential losses, and deductible amounts.

5. Strengths: Protection against financial loss by sharing risks is an important business protection.

6. Weaknesses: Insurance must not be used as an alternative to good security.

7. How to Audit: The insurance or self-insurance program should be periodically reviewed. Assistance of experienced risk and insurance experts should be used.

8. Purpose: Recovery

9. Control Area: Management

10. Mode: Policy

11. Area of responsibility: Insurance

12. Cost: High

13. Principles of Note: Cost-effectiveness, minimazation of exceptions, limit of dependence on other mechanisms.

**Selective
Variable Data Sensitivity**

1. Control Title: **Data Classification**

2. Objective: Prevent compromise of data.

3. Description: Data may be classified at different security levels to produce cost savings and effectiveness of applying controls consistent with various levels of sensitivity of data. Some organizations maintain the same level of security for all data, believing that making exceptions is too costly. Other organizations may have only small amounts of data of a highly sensitive nature and find that applying special controls to the small amount of data is cost-effective. When data are classified, they may be identified in two or more levels, often referred to as general information, confidential information, secret information and other higher levels of classification named according to the functional use of the data, such as trade secret data, unreported financial performance, etc.

4. Variables: Amounts of data at various levels of sensitivity, potential controls, cost savings for no classifications or several levels of classification, policies concerning security for each level of classification.

5. Strengths: Separate security treatment of data at different levels of security can result in control cost savings when the volume and concentration of sensitive data warrant special treatment. Otherwise, savings can be made by reducing control exceptions.

6 Weaknesses: Classification of data can easily result in excessive complexities in data handling and processing.

7. How to Audit: Review classification policy and sample data for audit trail testing of controls.

8. Purpose: Prevention

9. Control Area: Management

10. Mode: Policy

11. Area of Responsibility: Management

12. Cost: Low

13. Principles of Note: Cost-effectiveness, simplicity, least privilege, minimization of exceptions, acountability.

**Selective
Internal Audit Resources**

1. Control Title: **EDP Auditor**

2. Objective: Prevent inadequacy of system controls.

3. Description: Organizations with internal audit resources should establish EDP audit expertise within the internal audit function. In small organizations, general auditors can acquire EDP knowledge and skills. In larger organizations, full-time EDP audit specialists should be established to carry out EDP audits and assist general auditors in financial audits.

4. Variables: Amount of audit resources, regulatory or legal requirements for internal audit.

5. Strengths: Management can be assured about adequacy of computer security and auditability of systems and be notified on a timely basis of vulnerabilities.

6. Weaknesses: EDP auditors may not be given sufficient responsibilities and resources to perform an adequate job. EDP auditors may fall behind in state-of-the-art EDP audit practices and tools.

7. How to Audit: Periodic external audits should report to management on the adequacy of internal EDP audit capabilities and practices.

8. Purpose: Detection

9. Control Area: Computer center, computer system

10. Mode: Manual procedures, computer application system policy

11. Area of Responsibility: Management

12. Cost: High

13. Principles of Note: Auditability, instrumentation, sustainability.

---

1. Control Title: **Computer Security Officer**

2. Objective: Prevent inadequacy of system controls.

3. Description: An organization with sufficient computer security resources should have an individual identified as a computer security officer. In small organizations, the individual appointed may share this responsibility with other duties. In large organizations, one or more full-time employees should be assigned computer security adminstration responsibilities. The computer security officer should ideally report to the protection or security department covering the entire organization. This provides proper scope of responsibility for information and its movement throughout the organization. For practical purposes, the computer security officer often functions within the computer department. Job descriptions are highly variable; examples may be obtained from many organizations with established computer security officers.

4. Variables: Computer security resources, functional and adminstrative position and reporting, job description.

5. Strengths: A computer security officer provides a focus for the formal development of a computer security program.

6. Weaknesses: Line management may attempt to transfer their responsibility for security to the computer security officer.

7. How to Audit: The computer security officer's activities should be audited according to his job description.

8. Purpose: Prevention

9. Control Area: Computer center, applications

systems, computer system, programming and maintenance, management

10. Mode: Manual procedures

11. Area of Responsibility: Computer security, management

12. Cost: High

13. Principles of Note: Control and subject independence, acceptance by personnel, sustainability, accountability.

---

1. Control Title: **Keeping Security Reports Confidential**

2. Objective: Prevent disclosure, taking, or unauthorized use of documents.

3. Description: Computer security requires the use and filing of numerous reports, including results of security reviews, audits, exception reports, documentation of loss incidence, documentation of controls, control installation and maintenance, and personnel information. These reports are extremely sensitive and should be protected to the same degree as the highest level of information classification within the organization. A clean-desk policy should be maintained in the security and audit offices. All security documents should be physically locked in sturdy cabinets. Computer-readable files should be secured separately from other physically stored files and should have high-level access protection when stored in a computer.

4. Variables: Security documents, safe storage containers, access authorization.

5. Strengths: The security function in an organization sets an example for the rest of the organization by appropriately caring for confidential information.

6. Weaknesses: Keeping security information under a high degree of protection makes the information difficult and time-consuming to use.

7. How to Audit: The auditors should periodically make an operational audit of the computer security program, including the safe storage of security documents.

8. Purpose: Prevention

9. Control Area: Management

10. Mode: Manual procedures

11. Area of Responsibility: Computer security

12. Cost: Low

13. Principles of Note: Completeness and consistency, accountability, least privilege.

---

1. Control Title: **Cooperation of Computer Security Officers**

2. Objective: Prevent inadequacy of system controls.

3. Description: Maintaining an effective computer security function can be enhanced by exchange of information with computer security functions in other outside organizations. Local computer security organizations can be developed within a city, a part of a city, or regionally. Monthly or other periodic meetings of computer security officers can be held to exchange useful information and experience. A hotline communication capability can be established for exchange of information on an emergency basis to provide warning of possible mishaps

or losses. It is important to limit the details of information exchanged to ensure that confidential controls information is not disseminated to unauthorized parties.

4. Variables: Identification of cooperating organizations, types of information exchanged, procedures.

5. Strengths: This cooperation provides an opportunity to share important experiences and information and develop professional relationships that strengthen the career path of computer security officers.

6. Weaknesses: Too much information regarding an organization's security may become known to unauthorized persons.

7. How to Audit: EDP auditors should become involved in such outside organizational activities.

8. Purpose: Detection

9. Control Area: Management

10. Mode: Manual procedures

11. Area of Responsibility: Computer security

12. Cost: Low

13. Principles of Note: Overt design and operation, least privilege.

BUILT-IN CONTROLS

Baseline

1. Control Title: **Responsibilities for Application Program Controls**

2. Objective: Prevent inadequacy of controls.

3. Description: The inclusion of controls in application programs should be explicitly ensured and documented starting with design requirements and continuing through specifications development, production, and maintenance stages. The responsibility for adequacy and types of controls should be shared among EDP auditors, systems analysts, computer programmers, users, and data owners. Explicit documentation of controls is essential to ensure completion of their implementation, test, development of operational procedures, to carry out the intent of the controls, and to ensure their integrity during change and maintenance.

4. Variables: Documentation procedures and forms, policy.

5. Strengths: It is difficult to document explicitly all controls that must be in application programs. However, establishing the procedures to ensure that controls are adequate and included in applications provides assurance that applications will be adequately controlled.

6. Weaknesses: Controls that are not adequately supported by computer program application users will not be effective, and sufficient budgeting of money and resources will not be provided to adequately complete the specified controls.

7. How to Audit: Auditors' participation in design requirements and postimplementation testing for compliance with specifications.

8. Purpose: Prevention

9. Control Area: Programming and maintenance

10. Mode: Manual procedures

11. Area of Responsibility: Development, computer users

12. Cost: High

13. Principles of Note: Completeness and consistency, instrumentation.

---

1. Control Title: **Compliance with Laws and Regulations**

2. Objective: Avoid violations of laws and regulations.

3. Description: A statement regarding the new or modified system's compliance with relevant laws and regulations must be provided in requirements and specifications. Direct quotes from laws and regulations regarding EDP security and privacy applying within a legal jurisdiction, or those that may apply, should be included.

4. Variables: Legal and regulatory requirements for inclusion of statutes, laws, and regulations.

5. Strengths: Provides management with increased assurance that an application system is in compliance with relevant laws and regulations, thereby reducing the chances that management liability and other sanctions might be applied.

6. Weaknesses: Unless reviewed by a lawyer or some other knowledgeable person and compliance assured by audit, the control can become merely a perfunctory piece of paperwork where the blanks are filled in regardless of compliance with laws and regulations.

7. How to Audit: Examine documentation for statements regarding compliance, i.e., did the system designers actually have cause to represent that the new system was in compliance? Discuss the applicable laws and regulations with corporate legal counsel and system designers.

8. Purpose: Prevention

9. Control Area: Application system

10. Mode: Manual procedures

11. Area of Responsibility: Legal counsel, development

12. Cost: Medium

13. Principles of Note: Simplicity, universal application, accountability.

---

1. Control Title: **Computer Program Quality Assurance**

2. Objective: Detect computer, application, and communications systems and operations failures.

3. Description: A testing or quality control group should independently test and examine computer programs and related documentation to ensure integrity of program products before production use. This activity is best authorized by software development management or by the quality assurance or test department. Excessively formal program development standards should be avoided. Basic life-cycle procedures should be established before more elaborate practices are required. However, compliance with the established standards and procedures should be strongly enforced.

4. Variables: Quality assurance resources available, procedures, staff charter and size, sign-off forms design.

5. Strengths: A consistent compliance with good controls design offsets computer programmers' resistance to independent observation of their work.

6. Weaknesses: Imposing too much discipline too quickly on applications programming staff may cause negative reaction. Quality assurance programmers are difficult to motivate.

7. How to Audit: Operational audits should be performed by EDP auditors with extensive experience and reputation as competent computer programmers.

8. Purpose: Prevention

9. Control Area: Application system

10. Mode: Manual procedures

11. Area of Responsibility: Development

12. Cost: High

13. Principles of Note: Acceptance by personnel, least privilege, accountability.

---

1. Control Title: **Computer Programs Change Logs**

2. Objective: Detect computer, application, and communications systems and operations failures.

3. Description: All changes to computer programs are logged in a permanent written document. The log can be used as a means of ensuring formal approval of changes.

4. Variables: Log content, assignments, and accountability.

5. Strengths: Review of the purpose, time, type, and individuals who made changes is facilitated. This control aids in researching problems that occur. Utility programs that maintain program libraries in the computer are useful; they can automatically log change activity.

6. Weaknesses: Enforcement to ensure completeness is difficult.

7. How to Audit: Visual review of logs and random verification of changes.

8. Purpose: Detection, prevention

9. Control Area: Development

10. Mode: Manual procedures

11. Area of Responsibility: Development

12. Cost: Low

13. Principles of Note: Accountability.

---

1. Control Title: **Secrecy of Data File and Program Name**

2. Objective: Prevent loss, modification, disclosure, or destruction of data assets.

3. Description: Names for data files and computer programs are necessary for computer program development and documentation. They are also necessary for job setup and in some cases for computer operation. However, file and program names need not be known by those people who are in a transaction relationship with the computer system and not concerned with programming of computer applications. Therefore, a different set of terminology, and naming of entities should be developed for documentation of users manuals and for transaction activities.

4. Variables: Selection of systems, naming conventions.

5. Strengths: The least-privilege or need-to-know principle significantly reduces the exposure of sensitive assets. Separation of duties must also include the separation of information.

6. Weaknesses: Having two sets of names for computer program application entities complicates communications between programmers and users.

7. How to Audit: Examination of computer program documentation and user documentation can indicate that different naming conventions are being used.

8. Purpose: Prevention

9. Control Area: Application system

10. Mode: Manual procedures

11. Area of Responsibility: Development

12. Cost: Low

13. Principles of Note: Least privilege, control and subject independence.

---

1. Control Title: **Participation of Computer Users at Critical Development Times**

2. Objective: Prevent inadequacy of system controls.

3. Description: Computer users, including those providing input data and using computer output reports, should supply explicit control requirements to systems analysts and programmers who are designing and developing application systems. Users should also be required to explicitly agree that necessary controls have been implemented and continue to function during production use of the system and programming maintenance.

4. Variables: Policies and procedures, forms for control requirements statements, responsibilities and accountability for adequacy of controls.

5. Strengths: Users' understanding of their own applications is enhanced significantly when control specifications are required from them. Users are placed in a position where they can make better decisions regarding the appropriate controls in some aspects of applications and determine recovery time requirements. Users become knowledgeable of and sensitive to the needs for computer security and privacy. Sharing of responsibility and accountability for control is enhanced. Separation of duties is also enhanced. Completeness and consistency of controls are more ensured.

6. Weaknesses: Users may not have sufficient expertise to identify necessary controls. Systems development procedures become more complex.

7. How to Audit: Review systems design and development procedures at points where users are to be involved. Interview users with respect to their participation, understanding of their role, and awareness of the potential for controls in applications systems.

8. Purpose: Prevention

9. Control Area: Systems development

10. Mode: Manual procedures

11. Area of Responsibility: Users, development

12. Cost: Low

13. Principles of Note: Independence of control and

subject, completeness and consistency, acceptance by personnel, accountability.

---

1. Control Title: **Programming Library Access Control**

2. Objective: Prevent unauthorized access to sensitive areas.

3. Description: Computer program libraries containing listings of programs under development and in production and associated documentation must be protected from unauthorized access. In larger organizations, a full-time or part-time librarian may be used to control access, logging in, and logging out all documents. the program library should be physically separated by barriers from other activities. Documents should be distributed only to authorized users.

   It may be necessary to enforce strict access control to programmers' offices as a means of protecting programs and documentation. Programmers should have lockable file cabinets in which they can store materials currently in use. A clean-desk policy at the end of each working day may be justified as an extreme measure. Program and documentation control is particularly important when using or developing licensed software packages because of the strict contractual limitations and liabilities.

4. Variables: Resources available for program library access control, barriers surrounding the program library and programmers' offices, policies and procedures regarding protection of documentation and program listings.

5. Strengths: Demonstrates the importance of computer program assets to the organization. Provides separation of duty among programmers to ensure that programmers have access

only to the documentation and programs within their areas of responsibility.

6. Weaknesses: Restrictions on access may stifle communications and creativity of the programming staff.

7. How to Audit: Observe operation of the program library, make unexpected visits and observations of programmer offices, review procedures and policies for restricting access.

8. Purpose: Prevention

9. Control Area: Programming and maintenance

10. Mode: Manual procedures

11. Area of Responsibility: Development

12. Cost: Medium

13. Principles of Note: Least privilege, control and subject independence, acceptance by personnel, accountability.

---

1. Control Title: **Requirements and Specification Participation by EDP Auditors**

2. Objective: To prevent inadequacy of system controls.

3. Description: EDP auditors should participate in the development of requirements for important applications systems to ensure that the audit requirements in applications systems are adequate and that adequate controls have been specified. EDP auditors should be required to sign off on all formalized application system requirements and specifications.

4. Variables: EDP audit resources, procedures

specifying EDP audit participation, forms for signoff.

5. Strengths: The auditability of application systems is strengthened and can reduce the cost of both internal and external audits.

6. Weaknesses: It may be claimed that excessive participation by EDP auditors could result in a loss of independence, since the EDP auditors must also evaluate the adequacy of implemented controls.

7. How to Audit: Audit management should periodically review EDP auditor participation and ensure that all significant application systems receive audit attention.

8. Purpose: Prevention

9. Control Area: Programming and maintenance

10. Mode: Manual procedures

11. Area of Responsibility: Audit

12. Cost: Medium

13. Principles of Note: Auditability, accountability, control and subject independence, completeness and consistency.

---

1. Control Title: **Vendor-Supplied Program Integrity**

2. Objective: Avoid inadequacy of controls.

3. Description: To the greatest extent possible and practical, vendor-supplied computer programs should be used without modification. Many new vendor-supplied computer programs have been developed with controls and integrity built into them. Any modifications to these programs will possibly compromise the built-in capabilities. Desired changes to the programs should be obtained from the vendor as standard program updates.

4. Variables: Selection of programs, authorizations.

5. Strengths: This control is a means of preserving the security and integrity built into vendor-supplied computer programs. It is also a means of holding vendors responsible for any deficiencies in the programs.

6. Weaknesses: Failure to modify computer programs to make them more responsive to user needs may encourage users to subvert or neutralize existing controls.

7. How to Audit: This control could reduce the frequency of changes to computer programs, thus facilitating director code comparison of production programs with master backup copies of programs. This should be done periodically to ensure that management policy is followed in restricting modification of vendor-supplied computer programs.

8. Purpose: Prevention

9. Control Area: Computer center

10. Mode: Policy

11. Area of Responsibility: Management

12. Cost: Low

13. Principles of Note: Accountability.

---

1. Control Title: **Technical Review of Operating System Changes**

175

2. Objective: Avoid inadequacy of controls.

3. Description: Whenever any change is to be made to the computer operating system programs, a review of the change is made. The intent is to make sure that the new changes are valuable and will not compromise controls and integrity, have an unanticipated impact on some other part of the system, or interfere excessively with vendor updates.

4. Variables: Review procedures, authorization assignment.

5. Strengths: Review helps prevent unnecessary changes and simplifies testing and understanding of the system.

6. Weaknesses: Slowdown of changes may occur. Loss of compatability with vendor's version may require costly, independent maintenance.

7. How to Audit: Review the logs of systems changes and compare with actual changes.

8. Purpose: Prevention

9. Control Area: Computer system

10. Mode: Manual procedures

11. Area of Responsibility: Operations

12. Cost: Medium

13. Principles of Note: Override capability, accountability.

Selective Processing of Personal Information

1. Control Title: **Separation of Personal Identification Data**

2. Objective: Prevent disclosure or unauthorized use of personal information.

3. Description: For data bases that identify individuals as well as contain sensitive information about individuals, the data base is separated into a file of personal identifiers and a file of data with an index linking the identifiers with the data.

4. Variables: Justification for separation, method of separation.

5. Strengths: Physical separation of data fields ensures that privacy of individuals will not be compromised, even if other controls are compromised. It is required by law (Title 28) in criminal justice agencies and possibly in other situations.

6. Weaknesses: The process is complex and requires significant administrative procedures. Special systems procedures may be needed.

7. How to Audit: Review how files are set up and check records that log destruction of link files.

8. Purpose: Prevention

9. Control Area: Application system

10. Mode: Manual procedures

11. Area of Responsibility: User

12. Cost: Medium

13. Principles of Note: Independence of control and subject.

Selective Personal Data Processing

1. Control Title: **Sufficient Personal Identifiers for Data Base Search.**

2. Objective: Prevent disclosure or unauthorized use of personal information.

3. Description: To reduce the probability that an erroneous match between personal data and identification will occur, a sufficient set of personal identifiers is required before searches are permitted. Using techniques for the location of a personal record involves the ranking of several matches or near matches on several fields, such as name, date of birth, race, and sex. Because the erroneous identification, such as a criminal history or other record for an individual, may involve potential harm to the individual, the probability of a correct match should be very high. One installation identifies a sufficient set as complete name including known aliases (or maiden name if applicable), race, sex, and date of birth.

4. Variables: Data files to be protected, identifier sufficiency.

5. Strengths: Increases the chances that records will be updated with valid information.

6. Weaknesses: Valuable processing may be precluded because the requisite search information was not obtainable. Special circumstances, such as a variable number of personal identifiers, increases complexity. Administrative costs may be increased if such strict rules are implemented and followed.

7. How to Audit: Examine data base search procedures looking for situations in which an individual could erroneously be associated with a record.

8. Purpose: Prevention

9. Control Area: Application system

10. Mode: Computer application system

11. Area of Responsibility: Computer users

12. Cost: Medium

13. Principles of Note: Simplicity, override capability, least privilege.

---

1. Control Title: **Cryptographic Protection**

2. Objective: To prevent compromise of data.

3. Description: A high level of data communications and storage protection can be obtained by using the Data Encryption Standard (DES). However, effective encryption key management is essential. Frequently, applications do not require this level of encryption, and much simpler forms of encryption may be used. Data compression is a particularly simple form of encryption that also increases the efficiency of data storage. Data compression can be achieved by eliminating redundant information (spacing, etc.) and by encoding data fields. The cryptanalysis work factor should be determined and compared to the value of compromising the data being protected.

4. Variables: Selection of data for encryption, selection of encryption methods and products, key management.

5. Strengths: Encryption provides varying amounts of protection to data in communication circuits and when stored in computer-readable form. Its strength depends on the work factor of cryptanalysis and the effectiveness of key confidentiality and administration.

6. Weaknesses: Weak encryption or powerful encryption but weak key confidentiality and administration may provide a false sense of security.

7. How to Audit: Periodic audits should be performed to determine the proper application of

cryptographic protection, the effectiveness of the key confidentiality and administration, and independent verification of unauthorized decryption work factor.

8. Purpose: Prevention

9. Control Area: Computer center

10. Mode: Hardware

11. Area of Responsibility: Computer security

12. Cost: High

13. Principles of Note: Least privilege.

---

1. Control Title: **Exception Reporting**

2. Objective: Detect computer, application and communications systems, and operations failures.

3. Description: Exception reporting on a timely basis should be built into the computer operating system, utility programs, and application systems to report on any deviation from normal activity that may indicate errors or unauthorized acts. For example, if a user defines a data file that allows public access, a message will be printed out warning the user, and possibly the operations staff, that the file is not protected.

   Exception reporting should occur when a specific control is violated, or the exception report may constitute a warning of a possible undesirable event. Exception reports should be recorded in a recoverable form within the system and when necessary for timely action, displayed to the computer operator, or, in case of on-line terminal use, displayed to the terminal user.

4. Variables: Actions requiring exception reporting, method of reporting exceptions, procedures for taking action on exceptions reported.

5. Strengths: This control is automatic and reduces the likelihood of human error in handling exceptions.

6. Weaknesses: Frequent or voluminous exception reports may result in lack of sufficient attention.

7. How to Audit: Tests that force exception reporting should be run, and actions taken should be reviewed.

8. Purpose: Detection

9. Control Area: Computer system.

10. Mode: Computer operating system, computer application system, manual procedures

11. Area of Responsibility: Computer users, operations

12. Cost: Medium

13. Principles of Note: Override capability, minimization of exceptions, instrumentation.

---

1. Control Title: **Input Data Validation**

2. Objectives: Prevent loss, modification, disclosure, or destruction of data assets.

3. Description: Validation of all input to a computer system should be performed in both applications and computer operating systems to assist in the assurance of correct and appropriate data. Validation should include ex-

amination for out-of-range values of data, invalid characters in data fields, exceeding upper and lower limits of data volume, and unauthorized or inconsistent control data. Program errors dependent on the content or meaning of the data can also be checked. For example, inconsistent criminal justice disposition data relative to previously entered dispositions can be flagged for manual checking and correction.

4. Variables: Validation checks, error actions to be taken, locations in processing sequences for validation activity.

5. Strengths: Early validation of input data can result in prevention of error propagation.

6. Weaknesses: Excessive computer resources may be used for infrequently occurring errors.

7. How to Audit: Review systems design documentation to determine that input data controls are appropriately designed into the system. Run tests using erroneous data to check on the functioning of validation controls.

8. Purpose: Prevention

9. Control Area: Application system, computer operating system

10. Mode: Computer operating system, computer application system

11. Area of Responsibility: Computer users, operations, input and output.

12. Cost: High

13. Principles of Note: Simplicity, override capability, minimization of exceptions, completeness and consistency, instrumentation, auditability.

---

1. Control Title: **Telephone Access Universal Selection**

2. Objective: Avoid computer access exposure.

3. Description: Limiting access to a computer and data files can be an important means of security. Several means of accomplishing this are possible. It may be possible and important to eliminate dial-up access to a computer. A computer interfaced to the dial-up public telephone network is exposed to access from any telephone in the world. There may be a trade-off in computer security by giving up or limiting the benefits of dial-up access. This can be accomplished by using only point-to-point wire or leased-line telephone access to the computer. An alternative is to provide dial-up access to a small computer for development or other timesharing purposes while reserving another computer for more sensitive production activity that is not interfaced to dial-up telephones. A control computer providing access to two or more other computers can also be used as a means of protecting them from dial-up access.

An alternative method of restricting access is to provide for dial-up access at limited periods of time of day. During periods of dial-up access, particularly sensitive files or applications would not be resident in the computer system or secondary storage. A variation is to remove all sensitive files from secondary storage except at the explicit times of use of these files. A partial degree of protection for dial-up access systems is to maintain strict need-to-know availability of the telephone numbers and login protocol for accessing the computer system. Most dial-up timesharing computer services have similar access protocols; therefore, a unique, very different initial access exchange of identifying information may be useful to limit access. the telephone numbers should be unlisted, different in pattern of digits, and have different prefixes from voice telephone numbers for the organizations that are publicly listed. Call back to verify the source of telephone access is also popular.

4. Variables: Type of communication service, selection of telephone numbers, log-in protocol, time limits, call back.

5. Strengths: Avoidance of exposure is a particularly strong means of simplifying and reducing the problems of securing computer systems. Limiting or eliminating dial-up access significantly reduces exposure.

6. Weaknesses: An important objective for computers is to make them easily and widely accessible. Eliminating or limiting dial-up significantly reduces this capability.

7. How to Audit: Access capabilities, review access logs.

8. Purpose: Prevention

9. Control Area: Computer systems

10. Mode: Hardware

11. Area of Responsibility: Operations

12. Cost: High

13. Principles of Note: Least privilege, limit dependence on other mechanisms.

Selective Multiple Transaction Terminal Access Systems

1. Control Title: **Limit Transaction Privileges from Terminals**

2. Objective: Prevent loss or destruction of assets, prevent unauthorized browsing of systems files, prevent "hacking" (trying commands just to see what will happen), prevent system crashes caused by unauthorized use of certain systems commands.

3. Description: In addition to controlling resources (files, off-line data storage volumes, etc.), the transactions that a particular user is permitted to initiate are limited. What the system commands that a user can use or is informed of is controlled by the user's job duties. Thus, the systems level and application commands, such as reporting who is currently logged into the system, are restricted on a need-to-know basis. Logs may be kept for all attempts to use an authorized system command; this can be used to determine who needs training or perhaps disciplinary action.

4. Variables: Transactions to be limited, assignment of privileges to users.

5. Strengths: Prevents users from performing unauthorized acts, including examination of file names of other users and other system-related commands. Without these systems transactions, compromise of the operating system and other such abuses are made significantly harder to accomplish. Because the system commands are monitored and controlled by the computer, they can be sustained and enforced.

6. Weaknesses: May unduly restrict users' ability to perform their jobs, especially if the users are programmers. Undue restriction may result in reduced productivity and increased levels of frustration. Determination of what commands should be restricted may be involved and time consuming.

7. How to Audit: Examine system commands permitted for certain groups of users for

reasonableness. Review requests for changes in systems command privileges for authorization and need. If available, examine logs for unauthorized attempts to use systems commands that certain users are not permitted to use.

8. Purpose: Prevention

9. Control Area: Computer systems

10. Mode: Computer operating system, computer application system

11. Area of Responsibility: Operations management

12. Cost: Medium

13. Principles of Note: Simplicity, least privilege, independence of control and subject, sustainability.

---

1. Control Title: **Privileged Information Display Restrictions**

2. Objective: Prevent unauthorized data disclosure.

3. Description: Programmers, users, and others who have access to computer data bases are allowed to view only the data that pertain to their own job functions. Other data that may be resident on computers, outside the purview of an individual's job duties, are not available, nor is the knowledge of such data available. For example, data base data item descriptions have only subsets of the data supplied to particular individuals. Assistance programs, system documentation, and the like are specially tailored to the needs of different groups of individuals with different duties.

4. Variables: Design of data base index and tables of contents displays, access administration.

5. Strengths: If users, programmers, and others with access to the data do not know that certain data types are available, then they are prevented from perpetrating abuses associated with these data. Similarly, if these individuals do not have documentation or other information regarding these data, although they know these data exist, they are prevented from perpetrating unauthorized acts.

6. Weaknesses: Time-consuming and expensive to maintain separation of reference information of the data resident on computerized systems. May not facilitate certain efficiencies to be discovered and implemented.

7. How to Audit: Review systems design documentation to determine that individuals are not provided with more than the requisite information. Review systems development guidelines. Test access controls.

8. Purpose: Prevention

9. Control Area: Application system, computer system

10. Mode: Computer operating system, computer application systems

11. Area of Responsibility: Computer security, development

12. Cost: High

13. Principles of Note: Simplicity, avoidance of need for design secrecy, least privilege, acceptance by personnel, minimization of exceptions.

---

1. Control Title: **Data File Access Subcontrols by Job Function**

2. Objective: Prevent unauthorized access to data.

3. Description: Different types of data base read and update privileges are given to employees with different job functions. Data field read privileges can be granted or not depending on user job function. Likewise, update privleges may not be granted, or may be granted only for certain data fields within certain types of records of a data base. For instance, clerks handling mailing-related matters would be permitted to update only the address field. This control results in division of labor and separation of duties.

4. Variables: Date file access control capability, identification and authorization of users, data files and fields within data files, administration.

5. Strengths: Collusion is made necessary and more difficult when privileges for file and field access are directly related to an employee's job duties. Employees are prevented from altering fields in records that do not come within the domain of their jobs. Privacy and confidentiality are preserved when persons who do not need to be able to access certain fields are prevented from doing so; browsing is prevented.

6. Weaknesses: Users must be uniquely identified with passwords and identification user words in order for this control to be applied. Significant system overhead may be associated with the authorization. If someone is unavailable, then another person who may not have the same privileges may need to perform the other's duties; this could lead to sharing of passwords and other circumventing of controls activities.

7. How to Audit: Ask employees to demonstrate certain system capabilities, if possible, asking them to do things that they properly should be prevented from doing. Care should be taken that internal system alarms triggered by such testing do not cause problems. Discuss with applications management and systems designers the segmentation of personnel duties within certain applications areas and the separation of duties enforced by the procedures.

8. Purpose: Prevention

9. Control Area: Application systems, computer systems

10. Mode: Manual procedures

11. Area of Responsibility: Computer users, management, development operations

12. Cost: Medium

13. Principles of Note: Least privilege, Independence of control and subject, accountability.

Selective
Computer Access Limited to Employees

1. Control Title: **Monitoring Computer Use**

2. Objective: Detect unauthorized activities.

3. Description: On a random or periodic selective basis, communications between the host computer and remote terminals are monitored. File names and contents are examined. Such monitoring must be limited to computer activity that is established for business purposes only to avoid privacy invasion. The usage is logged and analyzed to determine that the user is only doing actions that have been explicitly authorized.

4. Variables: Selection basis, monitoring and ex-

amination methods and assignments, exception reporting.

5. Strengths: Allows management to determine that computer/communications resources are being used as authorized. Allows management to take evidence of activities of persons they suspect of some wrongdoing. Allows management to determine how certain users interact with the system toward improving services (response time, application, ease of use, etc.). Useful as an audit tool. If users are aware that the activity exists, then they may be deterred from engaging in certain types of acts.

6. Weaknesses: Could be used by unauthorized persons to spy on and/or harass users.

7. How to Audit: Use the same procedures for other auditing matters. Identify individuals who engage in this activity and review their work.

8. Purpose: Deterrence, detection

9. Control Area: Computer system

10. Mode: Manual procedures, computer operating system

11. Area of Responsibility: Computer security, operations

12. Cost: Low

13. Principles of Note: Simplicity, independence of control and subject, instrumentation, accountability.

Selective
High Terminal Security

1. Control Title: **Terminal Identifiers**

2. Objective: Prevent unauthorized computer access.

3. Description: Automatic terminal identification circuits can be installed in or associated with terminals for identification in host computers. Terminal identifiers are used to indicate whether a particular terminal is permitted to initiate or receive certain transactions. This access control requires that remote terminals be physically secured and that only certain known individuals be able to access remote terminals. Cryptographic devices can be used as terminal identifiers. Certain record change requests must be handled by means other than the use of these remote terminals, such as through the mail to a central facility; in this way records integrity can be preserved. Unauthorized intentional or accidental use of applications programs is prevented. A log records all unauthorized attempts to use applications programs.

4. Variables: Selection of devices, host system controls, exception reporting and journaling usage.

5. Strengths: Users may not have to be bothered with log-in/log-off procedures.

6. Weaknesses: Requires that remote terminals be attended or physically secure 24 hours a day. Does not have users individually identified, hence accountability is hindered. Does not permit different users to have different privileges if only one terminal is available.

7. How to Audit: Examine records of access privileges to determine that users are not given privileges that they do not need in order to do their job. Examine all user privilege change requests and actions to determine that all the changes of user privileges are both justifiable and authorized. Use remote terminal to ac-

tually test the access control system and logging facilities. Examine exception report produced when unauthorized accesses occur to make sure that all unauthorized attempts were followed up.

8. Purpose: Prevention

9. Control Area: Computer system

10. Mode: Hardware, computer operating system

11. Area of Responsibility: Computer security, development

12. Cost: High

13. Principles of Note: Least privilege, instrumentation, auditability, accountability.

---

1. Control Title: **Passwords for Computer Terminal Access**

2. Objective: Prevent unauthorized computer system access.

3. Description: Secret passwords are commonly used for access to computer systems through terminals. However, there is wide variation in the procedures for password administration. Passwords are normally accompanied by a protocol of exchange of recognition between the user and the computer, including the input from the user of a project or account number and a password. Normally, one or more users are working with the computer under a single project or account number. Occasionally, only one password is used for a group of people as well. However, each user should have his own secret password. In some cases, each user may select his own password, and it is known only to him and stored in the computer system.

Others select their passwords but must receive approval of them from the computer security coordinator to ensure that they are appropriate and not easily guessed.

Some organizations use computer programs to produce appropriate, easily remembered, but somewhat random passwords. In other cases, passwords are chosen by a computer security administrator and assigned to users. And finally, passwords can be generated automatically by the computer system and assigned to users. Another variation is the assignment of a password to a user with instructions that he is to use his password for initial access, at which time he must then change his password in the computer system. He should be prevented from using the initial password again.

Frequently, privileged passwords are identified in the computer system so that systems programmers and others requiring password access allowing a wider range of system usage and use of special commands may carry out their work. It is generally accepted that passwords should be changed among a group of computer users who might share their passwords every time an individual leaves the immediate group by terminating his employment or given new assignments. Privileged passwords should be changed more frequently than others. Passwords should also be changed whenever there is any indication of possible system abuse or compromise.

If passwords are manually conveyed to users, it should be done in confidential, sealed envelopes personally delivered by a trusted employee or orally in face-to-face conversation in confidential surroundings. A receipt should be received from the user indicating that he has received and accepted a new password and agrees to keep it confidential. These receipts should be kept on file by the computer security administrator. It is best to keep no paper record of passwords, and the master password file in the computer system should be encrypted or otherwise protected. If a password is forgotten by the user, then it should be removed from the computer system and a new password should be assigned. The user should destroy any written record of the password once memorized, and severe penalties should be enforced for writing or revealing the password. An alternative is to keep a record of passwords locked in a safe place such as a vault. This can be done by the project leader for each group of users and is more desirable than having a centralized record of project numbers.

4. Variables: Password selection, password length, change frequency, recordkeeping.

5. Strengths: Secret passwords provide the equivalent protection of combinations for vault access that has long been accepted as safe access to valuable assets. The strength of the password system is primarily dependent on the length of passwords and the password administration.

6. Weaknesses: The primary weaknesses of password systems concern the administration and discipline with which passwords are used and kept secret by users and administrators and the characteristics of the log-in procedure that limits the likelihood of password compromise.

7. How to Audit: Auditors should periodically examine the journaling of password activity, looking for unusual patterns. They should observe the password administration to ensure compliance with procedural policy. They should also periodically observe terminal areas to ensure that controls are in place and working.

8. Purpose: Prevention

9. Control Area: Management

10. Mode: Manual procedures

11. Area of Responsibility: Computer security

12. Cost: Medium

13. Principles of Note: Least privilege, independence of control or subject, instrumentation, acceptance, accountability.

**Selective
Many Remote Terminal Users**

1. Control Title: **Passwords Generated and Printed by Computer in Sealed Envelopes**

2. Objective: Prevent disclosure of passwords.

3. Description: User passwords are provided by a computerized random number/letter generator and printed directly through sealed envelopes, using the same carbon paper in envelope techniques that are used for many direct deposit receipts. These sealed envelopes are delivered directly to the user without the password ever having been seen by humans. Because the user expects a new password at a certain time, a missing envelope will be noticed, and the previously generated password will be cancelled and reissued. Similarly, if an envelope is opened or has evidence of tampering, then the password is cancelled and reissued. Receipts are returned to ensure delivery.

4. Variables: Frequency, computer security during password generation.

5. Strengths: Prevents persons involved in the password administration area from using passwords without the user's knowledge. Ensures that passwords are distributed on a regular basis without compromise.

6. Weaknesses: Known techniques can be used

to read passwords within these envelopes without having to destroy the seal.

7. How to Audit: Witness the generation and distribution of sealed password envelopes. Examine the envelopes to determine the ease with which the passwords can be discovered without having to break the seal. Discuss with operations management the pros and cons of assigned versus user-chosen passwords.

8. Purpose: Prevention

9. Control Area: Computer system

10. Mode: Computer application system

11. Area of Responsibility: Operations, computer security

12. Cost: Medium

13. Principles of Note: Least privilege, independence of control and subject.

Frequent Terminal Usage Interruptions

1. Control Title: **Dynamic Password Change Control by User**

2. Objective: Prevent unauthorized use of passwords.

3. Description: Users are allowed to change their passwords any time once they have logged in to the system. A parameter can be set at login time or at any time during a logged-in session that prevents changing a password. This would be useful in the case where an individual logs in to the system, gets up and leaves the terminal for a short period of time, and does not want anyone to come along and change the password while he is away. The user must enter a new password twice to prevent an incorrect password entry caused by a typing error. If the second password is not the same, the user must begin again.

4. Variables: Password change protocol

5. Strengths: Provides flexibility for users.

6. Weaknesses: User motivation is difficult.

7. How to Audit: Conduct live test of the change procedure.

8. Purpose: Prevention

9. Control Area: Computer system

10. Mode: Computer operating system

11. Area of Responsibility: Computer security

12. Cost: Low

13. Principles of Note: Instrumentation, accountability.

---

1. Control Title: **Data Files Access**

2. Objective: Prevention of unauthorized access to, modification, destruction, and disclosure of, and taking or using data stored in computer systems.

3. Description: Every data file stored in a computer system that could result in a significant loss if compromised through modification, destruction, disclosure, taking, or use should be protected by having access restricted based on a secret password known only to authorized persons and computer programs. File access

should further be restricted by mode of access allowed: read only, append only, modify only, file name change, file access control change, or some combination of these modes.

Commercial file access control computer program packages are available for some makes of computer systems to provide this protective feature. The operating systems of some makes of computers have this capability integrated into the system. Specific resources such as magnetic tapes and disks can also be controlled. Access controls should also include the journaling of accesses to provide audit trails and should produce a set of journal reports and exception reports, for example, of all unauthorized attempts to access specific files. The administration of assigning access rights and password assignments is important for the effectiveness of internal computer controls.

4. Variables: Selection of computer program package or implementation of operating system programs, administration of access control, forms design, identification of data files to be protected, identification of authorized file accessors.

5. Strengths: Employees, knowing that their activities are controlled and monitored, are deterred from engaging in unauthorized activity. Journals and exception reports can be used to investigate suspected unauthorized activities or to obtain evidence of known or suspected activities.

6. Weaknesses: Computer program commercial packages or other programs for file access control may degrade system performance.

7. How to Audit: Review system journals and exception reports to determine that proper actions have been taken. Test file access control for effects of unauthorized access. Review file access control administration.

8. Purpose: Prevention

9. Control Area: Computer system

10. Mode: Manual procedures, computer operating system

11. Area of Responsibility: Computer security, operations

12. Cost: Medium

13. Principles of Note: Least privilege, control and subject independence, completeness and consistency, instrumentation, acceptance by personnel, accountability.

---

1. Control Title: **Computer Use Access Control Administration**

2. Objective: Prevent unauthorized computer access.

3. Description: People wishing to have access to a computer system or to change their mode of access and authorized privileges must go through a formal procedure administered by a computer user coordinator. Usually one or more special forms must be completed indicating the type of request and providing for authorizing signatures of appropriate managers. A specific document stating the conditions of access and privileges should accompany the authorization form. The person gaining access should be required to sign his name indicating that he has read and understands the conditions of access and limitations. The computer user, administrator, or coordinator may be in the data processing department or in a department where computers are being accessed.

4. Variables: Assignment of user coordinator, forms and agreements designed, authorization procedures, administration and record-keeping of access authorizations, coordination with computer operations staff for assignment of access in the computer system.

5. Strengths: Separation of duties between computer users and computer service providers is enhanced. The use of signed forms and agreements documents provides accountability and deterrent values.

6. Weaknesses: Adds complexity and bureaucracy, especially in small informal organizations.

7. How to Audit: Examine the coordinator's administrative activities and records to ensure proper management authorization of forms for access. Trace changes made to access authorization by interviewing computer users and operations staff.

8. Purpose: Prevention, deterrence

9. Control Area: Computer center, management

10. Mode: Manual procedures, computer operating system

11. Area of Responsibility: Computer security management, operations, computer users

12. Cost: Medium

13. Principles of Note: Override capability, least privilege, control and subject independence, instrumentation, accountability.

Baseline

1. Control Title: **Computer Terminals Access and Use Restrictions**

2. Objective: Prevent unauthorized use of computer terminals.

3. Description: Access to the use of all terminals owned or under the control of the organization should be restricted to authorized users. This can be done by physically securing rooms in which terminals are located and, where justified, by using metal key or electronic key locks to activate terminals. Terminals within security perimeters that are used frequently may be turned on at the beginning of the work day, then locked again at the end of the business day and left unlocked throughout the business day. Those terminals that are used only occasionally may be left locked except during use at any time of day. It may also be advisable to use various commercial locking devices to prevent terminals from being removed from assigned areas.

4. Variables: Physical security barriers around terminals, terminal locking mechanisms, procedures for locking and unlocking terminals and physical access areas, manual or automatic logging of usage at or within the terminal.

5. Strengths: The need for security can be impressed upon terminal users through secure locking capabilities.

6. Weaknesses: Physical security may sometimes be difficult to enforce in the informal environments in which terminals are frequently used.

7. How to Audit: Periodically observe terminal areas to ensure that physical security procedures are being used. Review the administration of key access control devices.

8. Purpose: Prevention

9. Control Area: Computer center

10. Mode: Manual procedures, hardware

11. Area of Responsibility: Security, computer security

12. Cost: Low

13. Principles of Note: Least privilege, limit of dependence on other mechanisms, instrumentation, accountability.

Baseline

1. Control Title: **Terminal Log-in Protocol**

2. Objective: Prevent unauthorized computer access.

3. Description: The protocol for logging into a computer system from a computer should be designed to reduce unauthorized access. The terminal response to a log-in should provide a minimum of information to avoid providing an unauthorized user with any assistance. No system identifying information should be provided until the full user identification process has been successfully completed. There should be no feedback aids to an unauthorized user at any time during the log-in process that would provide clues to correct or incorrect input. Incorrect input should result in no assistance, and the system should disconnect. When user identification and password are being typed in, there should be no intermediate feedback from the system during the typing of this information that indicates whether the system has accepted any partially completed identification input. This requires that a user enter the complete set of identification and password information before there is any indication of whether this information is correct or not.

Identification information should consist of the user name or other nonsecret identification such as account number, followed by input of the secret password. Display terminals should provide display suppression while the password is being typed in to avoid its observation by another person. Printer terminals should provide nonprinting character mode or provide underprinting and overprinting of the spaces where the password is printed on the page. Additional, personal questions may be posed by the computer system to be answered by the terminal user to further ensure correct identity. No more than three attempts at entry of an unacceptable identification or password should be allowed. Three unsuccessful attempts should cause a telephone line disconnect. Time delay after an incorrect identification or password input of several seconds should occur to increase the work factor of automated exhaustive search for passwords. Also, a limited amount of time should be allowed for entry of a password before a telephone disconnect is performed.

A variation of a password should be provided as a duress alarm. For example, if an individual is being forced to enter his password at a terminal he might interchange the last two characters that result in an immediate alarm at the host computer system that an entry is being attempted under duress. Any log-in that deviates from normal or accepted ranges of activity should be noted in an exception report at the host computer console in a timely manner for immediate action by a computer operator.

All log-ins, whether authorized or unauthorized, should be journaled for later audit trail analysis. A means of allowing an unauthorized terminal user to gain authorized access to the system under totally monitored conditions should be provided to assist in locating sources of unauthorized attempts. Unauthorized users can be provided enough benign services to keep them at the terminal long enough for other detection activity to take place. Each time authorized users log into the system successfully, they should be provided with information concerning the date and time of the last time they logged into the system.

Other information about their last sessions may also be summarized. Users can be made aware of any possible unauthorized use of their password in this manner.

4. Variables: Protocol information exchanges, nature and length of identification and password information, limit parameter values, journaling and exception reports, controlled unauthorized access mechanisms, computer operator procedures in the event of exceptional activity.

5. Strengths: Log-in controls can provide a means of positive identification of terminal users and motivate them to use good security practices.

6. Weaknesses: Inconveniences during log-in may discourage terminal users or tempt them to violate or test the log-in requirements. Excessive log-in requirements may cause many more log-in mistakes by authorized users.

7. How to Audit: Periodically test log-in procedures using out of bound, unacceptable activities to ensure exception recording effectiveness.

8. Purpose: Prevention

9. Control Area: Computer system

10. Mode: Computer operating system

11. Area of Responsibility: Computer security

12. Cost: Low

13. Principles of Note: Simplicity, override capability, least privilege, minimization of exceptions, instrumentation, acceptance by personnel.

---

1. Control Title: **Computer System Password File Encryption**

2. Objective: Prevent unauthorized computer access.

3. Description: The password file in the computer system contains master copies of passwords to verify correct identification and password input from terminal log-ins. This data file is one of the most sensitive in the entire computer system and therefore must be properly protected. Passwords in the file should be individually encrypted using a one-way encryption algorithm, i.e., the password can be encrypted but there is no reasonable means of decryption that would be computationally feasible given the current state of the art in switching speeds and cryptanalysis. When a password is entered from a computer terminal, it is immediately encrypted using the same algorithm and compared with the encrypted form of the master password for matching. In this manner, clear text passwords reside within the computer system for the shortest possible amount of time.

4. Variables: One-way encryption algorithm, change control of passwords in the encrypted password file.

5. Strengths: Unlimited levels of protection are possible, depending on the strength of the cryptographic algorithms.

6. Weaknesses: Modification of the encryption algorithm computer program could cause a total compromise of the system and would not be easily detected.

7. How to Audit: Analyze the cryptographic algorithm program to ensure its integrity.

8. Purpose: Prevention

190

9. Control Area: Computer System

10. Mode: Computer operating system

11. Area of Responsibility: Computer security

12. Cost: Medium

13. Principles of Note: Override capability, avoidance of need for design secrecy, least privilege

---

1. Control Title: **Remote Terminal User's Agreement**

2. Objective: Prevent assets responsibility loss.

3. Description: All remote users are required to sign a user's agreement before they are permitted to use system resources. The agreement covers who shall pay for systems-related expenses, identifies physical location and relocation of terminals, establishes maintenance and service of equipment, assigns training of users, states hours of usage, instructs on further dissemination of information obtained from the system, details proper usage of the system, assigns physical security of terminals and other equipment, states service provider rights to deny service and to inspect equipment, establishes insurance coverage and liability for losses and renegotiation of the agreement, and other related matters.

4. Variables: Form design and content, accountabilitiy for administration, period of agreement.

5. Strengths: Clearly delineates the rights and obligations of both the service user and provider. Serves as an authoritative source for resolution of disputes between users and service providers. Allows service providers to sensitize users to security and privacy concerns before users can do work on the system.

6. Weaknesses: Legality of certain provisions may be in doubt and may require attention of legal counsel. Certain users may believe that the agreement does not suit their circumstances and may wish to modify the agreement or eliminate it entirely. Agreements may need to be renegotiated in light of additional legislation, regulation or management decisions.

7. How to Audit: Examine user agreements for reasonableness and to make sure that they are still current. Consult with legal counsel about the enforceability of various clauses in the contract. Visit user sites to determine that the terms of the contract are being met.

8. Purpose: Deterrence, recovery

9. Control Area: Computer center, management

10. Mode: Manual procedures

11. Area of Responsibility: Legal, user, computer security, operations

12. Cost: Low

13. Principles of Note: Simplicity, independence of control and subject, accountability.

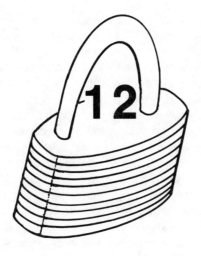

The Technology of Passwords

This chapter is taken from *The Uses of Passwords for Controlled Access to Computer Resources* by Helen M. Wood, published in 1977 by the National Bureau of Standards (NBS Publication 500-9).

Personal authentication may be required at any number of points along the path to accessing data. Such points include:

- ☐ Entry to building.
- ☐ Entry to terminal room.
- ☐ Enabling terminal.
- ☐ Encryption interface unit.
- ☐ Log-in.
- ☐ File access.
- ☐ Data item access.

Physical devices such as cards and keys are commonly used at the first three access points, while passwords, alone or in combination with other techniques, are commonly used at log-in, file access, or data access time.

In addition to authenticating users to systems, password schemes may provide some protection against other types of threats. In their report on information privacy, Peterson and Turn describe types of threats against which passwords may be effective. These include:

- ☐ *Browsing*—using legitimate access to a part of the system to access unauthorized files.
- ☐ *Masquerading*—claiming the identity of an authorized user after obtaining passwords or other authentication items through wiretapping or other means.
- ☐ *Between-lines entry*—penetration of the system when a legitimate user is on a communication channel but not using his terminal.
- ☐ *Piggyback infiltration*—interception of user-processor communications and the returning of messages that appear to the user to be from the computer system.

The degree to which passwords are effective

against such threats varies greatly. They provide good protection against browsing when implemented at the file or data level. Passwords are ineffective against the threats of between-lines entry and piggyback infiltration, however, unless used for every message in the former case, or when used as a means of reverse (i.e., processor-to-user) authentication (in the latter case).

Data encryption keys and the banking community's Personal Identification Number (PIN) are forms of passwords when used as a means to verify identity. An encryption key controls the algorithmic transformation (encryption) performed on data to render the data unintelligible. The PIN is typically a four-to-six-digit number assigned by the bank or selected by the cardholder. It is used in conjunction with a magnetically encoded card.

In order to be an effective deterrent to computer system penetration, a password should be:

☐ Difficult to guess.
☐ Easy for the owner to remember.
☐ Frequently changed.
☐ Well protected.

The degree to which a password scheme incorporates these features determines the difficulty of compromising the password.

The following sections discuss password-related techniques and mechanisms that can be combined to create the appropriate password scheme for a given system.

PASSWORD SCHEMES

Password schemes differ according to selection technique, lifetime, physical characteristics, and information content. In this section, the types of password systems are discussed along with the threats against which they are most effective. See Table 12-1.

PASSWORD SELECTION

A password may be chosen by the system user or assigned. User-selected passwords are far from secure, because people tend to pick words or numbers that have some personal meaning, such as a birthday, a child's name, or a street address, and consequently they are easy to guess. The primary advantage of a user-chosen password is ease of recall, alleviating the need for writing the word down.

Passwords may be assigned to users by the system security officer or by the computer system itself. Although assigned passwords are generally more secure than user-selected codes, their benefits may be nullified if they are written down by the user, taken from a discovered master list, or generated by a deducible algorithm.

Johnson examined the use of pseudorandom numbers as passwords and discovered that various "logistically attractive" periodic password generation systems are in fact vulnerable to simple number theory analysis. The generating systems he considered were of the type:

$$x_{n+1} = ax_n + b(\bmod 2^u), \ u = 40$$

where a and b are selected constants and x_n is the nth password generated. This type of generating system would be considered attractive, for example, in a large system in which it is not practical to use complex password schemes. To reduce vulnerabilities of such schemes, Johnson proposes new password generation and distribution strategies that would help to ensure a higher degree of security, without significantly increasing the system costs.

An example of a computer-generated password scheme is the random word generator developed to run on Honeywell's Multiplexed Information and Computer System (MULTICS). The random word generator forms pronounceable syllables and concatenates them to create words. A table of pronunciation rules is used to determine the validity of each construct. This system was developed to enhance the security of some MULTICS installations, such as the Air Force Data Services Center (AFDSC).

The motivation for a pronounceable password generator is to make the assigned words easier to remember, thus lessening the temptation to write

Table 12-1. Password Characteristics.

Password Scheme	Some Advantages	Some Disadvantages
Selection process: User-selected	Easy to remember	Often easy to guess
System generated	Difficult to guess	More difficult to remember; generating algorithm may be deducible
Lifetime: Indefinite	Easy to Remember	Most vulnerable to exhaustive enumeration and guessing attempts; difficult to tell if password stolen
Fixed	Easy to remember if time interval is fairly long (e.g., week or month); more secure than indefinite (shorter time interval, better the security provided)	Vulnerability depends upon time interval
One-time	Useful for detecting successful penetration of system; short lifetime prohibits exhaustive testing	Difficult to remember unless written down; valid user locked out if successful penetration occurs
Size and Alphabet:	Larger the password and alphabet, the more difficult to guess; less need for duplication of passwords	Larger the word, more difficult to remember and more storage required
Information Contents: (e.g., authorization information and check digits)	Could aid detection of penetration attempts if penetrator unaware of valid password structure	May cause passwords to be long and thus more likely to be written down; if scheme becomes known, passwords could be easy to deduce
Handshaking Schemes: (e.g., dialogs, user transformations)	Resistant to exhaustive enumeration attempts; provides some protection during transmission	May be time consuming; requires more storage space than single passwords

the words down. Of course, what is deemed pronounceable by one person may be considered gibberish by another, even though the rules of grammar for the particular language are adhered to.

In order to enhance pronounceability, generated words may be presented to the user in hyphenated form. Examples are *qua-vu, ri-ja-cas, te-nort, oi-boay,* and *fleck-y.*

Besides being easy to remember, the generated words may be hard to guess. This requirement is satisfied by giving the program the ability to generate a very large set of possible words in a random fashion.

The random word generator is capable of

generating words of any length. Words of five to eight characters are recommended, however. Longer words tend to be less pronounceable, while shorter words result in too few available passwords for a given system and its user population.

At the Air Force Data Services Center, the use of the password generator is not mandatory. To help lessen the problem of being given a password that to them is unpronounceable, a user can reject the assigned password and elect to provide another. After nearly 18 months of operation, it was observed that about 50 percent of the system users allow the system to assign their passwords.

Passwords that remain in effect indefinitely are the most susceptible to compromise. They are particularly vulnerable to exhaustive testing. Making the length of the password appropriately long, locking out log-on attempts after several tries and enforcing time delays between log-on attempts provide some defense.

Another shortcoming of passwords with indefinite lifetimes is the difficulty of detecting a successful compromise. Some systems prohibit a user from being logged on the system from more than one terminal at a time. Others, such as the Monitor operating system, inform the user at log-on and log-off of the presence of other users with the same user name or identification number, and hence the same password. Even if such system constraints are present, however, the odds of a system penetrator and the legitimate user trying to use the same account at the same time depend on the frequency and duration of access of each. Of course, to lessen the probability of detection in this manner, the penetrator may elect to use the system late at night when the legitimate user presumably is asleep.

As a deterrent against such threats, some systems include the last time logged on as part of the *banner*, the informative messages displayed the system when a user logs on. This presumably informs someone if such successful penetration has taken place.

Obviously, more frequent password changes are desirable. An example of a system that requires password updates at fixed intervals is the Air Force Data Services Center. In this system, users are re-quired to change their passwords every six months. The operating system enforces this requirement.

One-time passwords generally provide a higher level of protection. Successive passwords may be selected by the system from an internal list generated by a program or selected from lists or cards previously distributed to authorized users.

Anderson contends that if passwords are changed every time they are used, there is "no more risk in writing down the password than in carrying a key to a locked room." Should loss or theft occur, prompt reporting would minimize the risks involved. Of course, the legitimate user would have to access the system frequently to ensure the timely discovery of a successful penetration.

To further reduce the risk of carrying a password openly, Anderson suggests that the system print a list of passwords for each user. Only one word on the list would be the actual password, and the exact location of the valid password could vary from user to user. He also mentions the possibility of encoding the new password on a magnetic card.

The feasibility of using one-time passwords with magnetically coded cards was investigated by Richardson and Potter. In their design of a prototype system, the cardholder was required to key in a secret password in addition to that read from the card. Such combinations of authentication techniques may provide a higher degree of security than systems that incorporate only one such technique. Here, the use of a manually entered password is necessary to prohibit unauthorized use of a lost or stolen card. Likewise, the password is of no use to a would-be penetrator.

Lawrence Livermore Laboratory's OCTOPUS network uses a password scheme similar to one-time passwords, incorporating a changing counter. A computer generates and authenticates all passwords. At each terminal session, the counter increases the value of the password, and this new value is communicated to the user. The skipping of an expected value would suggest that someone else had used the combination.

One-time passwords are used in SWIFT (Society for Worldwide Interbank Financial

Telecommunications), the worldwide banking system developed by the Burroughs Corporation. When a terminal is connected, the operator uses a four-digit, one-time password taken from a list that is supplied in two lists sent separately. For example, from these lists:

List 1	List 2
1 2	4 5
3 7	9 8
4 6	3 5

the first password would be 1245.

Additional security features in SWIFT include message sequence numbers and the generation of a four hexadecimal digit authenticator result. This number is generated by running the entire message text through the SWIFT authenticator algorithm. In addition, at log-off time the operator specifies the next log-on time. SWIFT will refuse any earlier log-on attempts.

Major drawbacks to one-time passwords are the cost and difficulty of distributing the lists to large numbers of users and users who get "out of step" in a system with a heavy workload. Of course, in systems that incorporate counters or incremented passwords, the distribution problem is minimized.

One-time password schemes alone are not effective against the threat of between-lines or piggyback entry. For protection against these threats, message authentication by attaching one-time passwords to each message would be required. Encryption at the terminal level also is effective in this situation.

PHYSICAL CHARACTERISTICS OF PASSWORDS

A password's physical characteristics include its size and makeup—the alphabet or set of characters from which it is made. The number of different passwords possible in a given scheme is called the *password space*. The PIN system typically uses a four-to-six-digit number. Some computer systems accept passwords eight or more characters long, with letters, numbers, symbols, and other character permitted.

The likelihood that someone could systematically determine a password depends on the password's length, the size of the alphabet from which it is taken and the time over which the attempts take place.

It has been computed that a seven-letter password drawn from the English alphabet has a probability of no more than .001 of being recovered in three months of systematic testing. If you use the 128-character ASCII character set, a five-letter password will do the same.

Encryption keys are similar to passwords, but an adequate key size involves added considerations. The size of the key space should be as large as possible, not only to discourage trial-and-error attempts but to provide for frequent changes and large numbers of users.

The effectiveness of encryption does not depend solely on the chosen key. It also depends on the algorithm employed, when the encryption takes place, and the criteria used to select the key. If you use only four digits when your algorithm would support more, your space is effectively reduced.

Information Content

A password can provide more than just personal authentication. The University of Western Ontario's Generalized Information Retrieval System (GIRS) incorporates the use of assigned, functional passwords whose contents reveal the users' authorization levels. In particular, these passwords determine:

- ☐ Which subset of available processing functions can be exercised.
- ☐ Which parts of records can be operated on by these functions.
- ☐ Which records the user is privileged to work with.

In this system, an additional password is needed for authentication. The functional password is used by the information retrieval system to assess a a user's authorization level or capabilities. This is not indicate, though, that both functions could not be provided by one password.

Passwords also could be constructed to contain check digits or some other sort of self-checking code. Check digits already are successfully used in other environments. In one example reported by Alan Taylor, "The Pennsylvania Bureau of Sales and Use Tax some time ago adopted a Modulo-10 check digit to safeguard a seven-digit number. The technique it selected was to multiply the first digit by 10, the second by 6 and so forth until the last digit was multiplied by 1. It then used the Modulo-10 complement of the answer as the check digit and placed it after the seventh number."

Techniques such as this, combined with some elementary analysis, could help more sophisticated password systems discriminate between entry errors like transposed digits and actual penetration attempts, particularly those that use exhaustive testing.

HANDSHAKING SCHEMES

Other types of authentication schemes incorporate the execution of algorithm for authentication. Such procedures are referred to as *handshaking* or *extended handshakes*. Some of these procedures directly involve the use of passwords; others can only marginally be considered password schemes.

The ADEPT-50 timesharing system incorporates a handshaking scheme. To gain admittance to the system, the user must supply information that includes user identification, the password, and accounting data. The terminal identification also is compared against an authorization list.

In several systems, handshaking is accomplished by a dialog between the system and the user. In such procedures, the user may be required to ask questions (e.g., cat's name or astrological sign) asked in a semirandom fashion, or to supply additional passwords or account information. This is much like having several passwords, any of which may be requested in any order. It is even conceivable that the questions themselves could be chosen by the system user.

In another variation, the handshaking is accomplished by both the system and the user transforming a given number and comparing the results. The system presents the user with a pseudorandom number and requires that the user perform a specified mental computation, called T, on that number. It might be as simple as adding the hour of the day. The result is sent back to the computer, which performs a comparable transformation and compares the results.

Thus, if a user has performed T on a number x and transmitted the result, $y = T(x)$, an eavesdropper who monitors the transmission would at most see x and y. The computer's transformation need not match the user's; it can be any suitable calculation that tests whether the user has applied the right calculation.

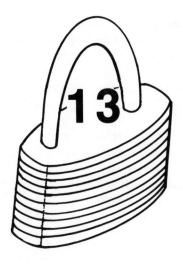

Badges and Other Identification Tokens

The material in this chapter is from *Guidelines on User Authentication Techniques for Computer Network Access Control* (Federal Information Processing Standards Publication 83).

The possession of a token, such as a key or a machine-readable card, is one of the basic ways to verify a person's identity. If the token provides machine-readable data, it may be used to provide the claimed identity; possession by the user is taken to verify the user's identity (assuming that it has not fallen into other hands). Alternatively, the user may enter a claimed identity by such means as a keyboard, numeric keypad, or combination dial, and then use the token to verify the claimed identity.

Computer terminals can be fitted with key locks or badge readers for use in this manner. Alternatively, the token-actuated device could be distinct from the terminal and could control the terminal's operation by some means such as controlling the power or communications lines. This might be more vulnerable, though, than incorporating the mechanism as an integral part of the terminal, using tamper-resistant construction.

A penetrator who succeeds in obtaining a token can use it as readily as the authorized user. Therefore it is advisable to include some type of password scheme to deter unauthorized use of the token.

The longer a security safeguard is in place, the more opportunity there is for would-be penetrators to become familiar with it and to devise a penetration scheme such as a duplicate key or counterfeit card. Therefore the coding should be updated at intervals, in such ways as replacing lock cylinders or reissuing cards with new codes. In the case of a card reader that reads and transmits a code, you can carry out the change by issuing new cards and updating the master control list. Rekeying the locks may be less convenient.

If a particular terminal is to be used by more than one authorized person, there should be ways to distinguish which person is using the terminal. This will enable the central facility to enforce the proper authorization for the particular user. If you use a lock and key, there will be no way for the computer to determine whose key is being used. The use of cards with unique codes for each user lets the computer determine which user is seeking access (or at least whose card is being used).

A variety of machine-readable cards has been developed for access control purposes. With some cards, the coding can be altered rather readily in the field; with others the coding is either permanently built in or requires special equipment for alteration. Many types of cards can include printed material and photographs and can serve as identification badges as well.

DESIGN OBJECTIVES

Several badge sizes are in common use. The selection is usually a compromise between a small, easily handled badge and a larger badge with more room for a photograph, color code indicators, and printed information.

Most commercially available coded credential systems use the standard credit card size, 54 by 86 mm (2 1/8 by 3 3/8 inches). This size is at best marginally acceptable for a picture badge. A slightly larger common badge size is 60 by 83 mm (2 3/8 by 3 1/4 inches). This is not much larger than the standard credit card, but it provides significantly more usable badge area when the badge is worn in a vertical position.

If none of the standard sizes is satisfactory, you may have to require that each employee wear a larger photo badge and carry a separate card to be used in electronic readers.

Preparing Badges

Ideally, badges should be assembled and laminated at the facility site. If not, you face delays, administrative overhead, and reduced security. A badge should be able to withstand daily use for five years with normal care. Some PVC plastic materials deteriorate rapidly when exposed to sunlight and become brittle when the temperature drops below freezing. Most common credit card materials exhibit these problems, but some PVC formulations are available that eliminate most of the. Poly-

ester-based badges are more durable, but take care in the selection process to make sure you can laminate them reliably and permanently.

Coded badges must be enrolled in the memory of the control processor after they are fabricated. For simple systems, enrollment is done on a keyboard at the control console. Provide for backup copies of the control processor's memory; otherwise, all badges must manually be re-enrolled after a power failure or equipment malfunction. This could be a serious problem for large installations.

Resisting Decoding and Counterfeiting

Any type of coded badge can be decoded and duplicated if you devote enough money and talent to the task. The major encoding techniques, from the easiest to duplicate to the hardest, are:

- ☐ Electric circuit code
- ☐ Magnetic stripe code
- ☐ Magnetic code
- ☐ Metallic strip code
- ☐ Capacitance code
- ☐ Passive electronic code
- ☐ Active electronic code

The first two types are easy to duplicate; the last six are significantly more difficult.

In general, it is not necessary to decode a badge to duplicate it. The degree of difficulty in decoding the badges is in approximately the same order as the list above. Often, the code data are cryptographically encoded or contain other internal checks. Counterfeiting a new badge then would require both decoding and understanding the internal check algorithm; this type of counterfeiting is much more difficult.

Resistance to decoding and counterfeiting is not as important if the badge is used in conjunction with a separate identity verification system based on a personal attribute. In this type of system, the badge number simply indexes a reference file where personal identification data are stored in a central computer. Access is allowed only if the personal identity algorithm is satisfied. In this case counterfeiting a badge will not, in itself, guarantee access.

Badge readers are vulnerable points at which to attack an entry control system. The readers should be equipped with tamper sensors. Further, protect communication lines between the badge reader and any central console or computer by line supervision, encryption, or both.

TYPES OF IDENTIFICATION TOKENS

A variety of machine readable cards has been developed for access control. These can conveniently be described by the methods used to encode information on the card. Listed below are the various types now in use.

Photo ID Badge. The most common credential is a color-coded badge with a photograph that can be checked visually by a guard. The common practice is to require that a laminated photo ID badge be used for access to controlled areas.

A badge exchange system reduces the possibility that a badge will be counterfeited, lost, or stolen. Duplicate badges are held at each controlled entry point. When an employee requests entry, a guard matches the individual to the photograph on the corresponding exchange badge held at the control point. If the individual passes the check, the guard exchanges the badges and grants the employee access. The employee's badge is held at the control point until the employee leaves the area, when the badges again are exchanged.

The exchange badge worn within the controlled area is never allowed to leave the area. However, this system would not prevent someone from using face makeup to match the image on a stolen badge.

Optical Coded Badge. This type of badge contains a geometric array of spots printed on an insert that is laminated into the badge. Photo detectors in the badge reader check the relative optical transmission of the spots. To make this badge resist tampering, the spots can be concealed so they can be detected only by infrared light.

Electric Circuit Coded Badge. This is a plastic laminated badge containing a printed circuit pattern that selectively closes electrical circuits when inserted into the reader.

For this type of badge, the reader is simply a card edge connector of the type normally used for a printed circuit board. The badge can be decoded with a simple electrical continuity tester, so it is easy to counterfeit.

Magnetic Coded Badge. This badge contains a sheet of flexible magnetic material on which an array of spots has been permanently magnetized. The code is determined by the polarity of the magnetized spots. The badge reader contains magnetic sensors that are checked electrically or magnetic reed switches that are activated mechanically.

The spots can be erased accidentally if the badge is placed in a sufficiently strong magnetic field, but in practice this has not been a serious problem. It is possible to build equipment that would recode or duplicate the pattern of magnetic spots and duplicate the badge. It is more difficult, though, to falsify this type of badge than to fabricate an electric circuit coded badge.

Magnetic Stripe Coded Badge. With this type of a badge, a stripe of magnetic material is located along one edge of the badge and is encoded with identifying data. A magnetic head reads the data. Magnetic stripe coding is widely used in credit card systems, and many vendors make equipment that is compatible with American National Standard Institute standards for this technique.

Forgery is relatively easy, because data from the magnetic strips can be decoded and applied to duplicate badges. All it takes is a common tape recorder.

Passive Electronic Coded Badge. The passive electronic coded badge is one into which electrically tuned circuits are laminated. The reader generates a radio frequency field and checks the frequencies at which significant energy is absorbed. These frequencies corresponded to identifying information encoded into the badge.

An important advantage of this technique is that the badge need not be inserted into a reader mechanism; all you need do is bring it near an antenna. On the other hand, the badges can be counterfeited with common radio frequency test instruments, and you are limited to only a few thousand unique code combinations.

Capacitance Coded Badge. This is a badge into which a small array of conducting plates has been laminated. Selected plates are connected, and the code is read from the badge by a reader that measures the capacitance of the plates and distinguishes which are or are not connected.

Metallic Strip Coded Badge. The metallic strip coded badge uses rows of copper strips that are laminated into the badge. The presence or absence of certain rows determines the code pattern, which is read by an eddy current sensor.

This technique was developed to be used with a Controlled Access by Individual Number System. The badges are durable and can be read reliably.

Each badge can be encoded with about 40 data bits.

Active Electronic Badge. This system consists of a portable, electrically coded badge and a stationary reading unit. The unit supplies power to the badge by magnetic induction. It then receives and decodes a credential number transmitted from the badge.

When the interrogation unit is placed at strategic locations, such as halls or doorways leading into controlled areas, it can automatically monitor, identify, and log every badge that enters or leaves the area. The employee needs to do nothing at all, because the badge is read automatically as you pass by a radio frequency field generated by the interrogation unit.

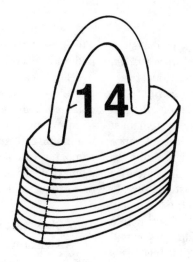

Verifying Personal Attributes

This chapter is based on material in FIPS Publication 83 (also cited in Chapter 13). There are inherent drawbacks in identification systems that depend on something a person knows or has. For that reason, much attention has been given to authentication methods based on something *about* a person.

Among the personal attributes being considered are hand geometry, fingerprints, signatures, and speech. This is an actively developing field, and it is premature to say that any particular technique is superior in security and economy at this time. For any given application, though, one of these techniques may have a natural advantage over the others.

The rapid growth in remote computer use and the increasing sensitivity of computer applications have combined to intensify the need for authentication methods that can positively establish the identity of users at remote terminals. At the same time, advances in instrumentation technology and low-cost processors, together with improved methods of signal processing and pattern recognition, have opened up new possibilities for automated identity verification based on unique aspects of personal attributes.

PROBLEMS OF MEASUREMENT

One of the chief problems in using personal attributes for identity verification is the difficulty of performing precise, repeatable measurements of the human body. This is true whether the attribute is a relatively static quality such as the fingerprint or finger length, or whether the attribute is dynamic, such as handwriting or speech. Because of the curvilinear nature of body surfaces and the plasticity of body tissue, it is hard to establish accurate reference points and good registration for taking measurements or matching patterns.

This lack of precise repeatability must be taken into account when testing and evaluating identity verification systems. In testing such systems, be prepared to vary all factors that are considered to have an influence on the attribute being used.

Two Kinds of Variation

The inability to repeat precisely the measurement for a given individual is called *intrapersonal variability*. The variation from one individual to another is designated *interpersonal variability*.

To allow for the statistical variations that result from intrapersonal variability, the system must have a certain amount of tolerance. If the tolerance is too great, though, you lose the ability to distinguish between individuals. An identity verification device can have an adjustable threshold you can use to tighten or loosen the tolerance. Tightening it improves the ability to discriminate between individuals, reducing the chance you will accept an impostor, but at the same time this raises the chance of incorrectly rejecting an authorized user.

Method of Operation

Devices to identify personal attributes generally operate the following way. The user inputs his or her claimed identity by entering a name, identification number, or other identifier. The user also may insert a token such as a magnetic stripe card that bears identification information in machine-readable form.

The device then prepares to verify the claimed identity. This will be done by comparing a reference profile of the attribute associated with the claimed identity with a measurement of the attribute as derived from the individual who seeks access. Depending on the device and the application, the reference profile may be obtained from a central file, from a local file in the device, or from a machine-readable token supplied by the individual.

An alternate method is to measure the attribute and send the measured profile to a central location for comparison with the reference profile. It may not be necessary to send the entire volume of measured data to the central location. Instead, a local processor can derive a set of parameters to represent the measured profile, and these features can be used for the comparison.

Another way is a sequential decision scheme that transmits information until a decision is reached at a specified level of statistical confidence. This makes the entry process shorter for the normal authorized user and longer for the impostor.

The measured profile then is compared with the reference profile and a measure of similarity is obtained. This generally results in an output signal from a comparator that has a value between some minimum and maximum. The resulting value is compared with a preset threshold, which results in a binary decision to accept or reject the individual, or to request more data.

Two Classes of Error

An identity verification device can make either of two types of error: a Type 1 error falsely rejects an authorized user, while a Type 2 error falsely admits an impostor.

In operation, an identity verification device carries out a series of measurements, processes this data, and compares the results with a reference profile. If the results match within a specified tolerance, the identity is considered to be verified. Because of the intrapersonal variation, the match will not usually be exact.

Figure 14-1 shows an analysis of such a process. The data from a series of measurements is plotted, matching a range of possible scores with the degree of match or mismatch. Ideally, all the scores for correct individuals would all be grouped at the right edge of the graph, indicating the highest scores, while those for impostors would all be grouped at the left edge.

In practice, the device does not operate in that ideal fashion; instead it might produce the results shown in Fig. 14-2. Here, the scores are spread out considerably, and some even overlap. There is no score you could safely use as a threshold that would reliably separate authorized users from impostors. You must compromise. You might set the score at the point in Fig. 14-2 where the two curves cross. This is known as the *equal error point*, at which the Type 1 and Type 2 error rates are equal.

You also could adjust the threshold to favor one type of error over the other. Move the threshold to the right, to a higher score, and you can improve

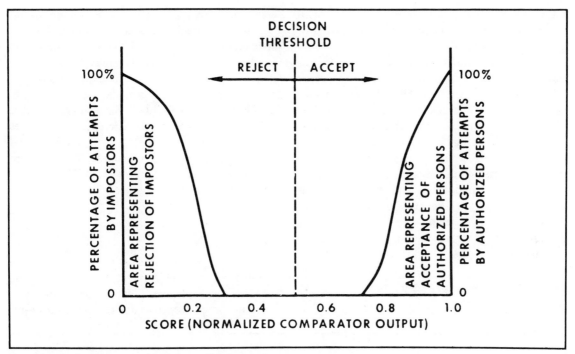

Fig. 14-1. Preferred output of identity verification device.

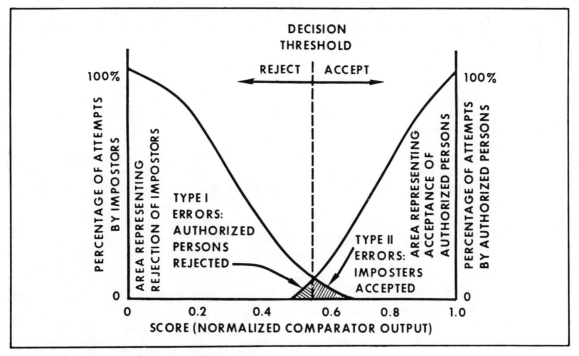

Fig. 14-2. Typical output of identity verification device.

the probability that you will reject an impostor. A lower score would do a better job of admitting all authorized individuals.

Part of this statistical problem arises from a physical one: Even when you are able to measure them accurately, a person's physical characteristics are subject to change. It has been found, for example, that tomorrow you can be as much as five pounds heavier or lighter than you are today. You lose a fraction of an inch in height during a working day as your spinal discs compress.

You must build enough tolerance into this system to allow for these variations and avoid the error of rejecting an employee with an important job to be done. This same tolerance makes it harder to identify impostors.

USING MULTIPLE ATTRIBUTES

It also is possible to improve an error rate by testing more than one attribute, as shown in Fig. 14-3. With two devices, you have two possible rules for making a decision. Rule 1 accepts the person if either device does so. It greatly reduces the chance of false rejection at the expense of an increased chance of accepting an impostor. Rule 2 accepts the person only if both devices agree that it should be done. This greatly decreases the chances of accepting an impostor but with an increased chance of false rejection. Of course, if each device has a variable threshold, these may be varied to achieve an acceptable balance.

Combining Methods

This analysis is based on using two personal attributes. It is possible, of course, to combine the use of different methods of verifying identification. A system might use one device based on an at-

	Assumed Values	
	Device A	Device B
Type I error rate	3%	4%
Type II error rate	1%	2%

Performance of Device A and Device B assumed to be statistically independent.

Rule 1: Access granted if accepted by either device—
     Probability of correct user being rejected: 3% × 4% = 0.12%
     Probability of impostor being accepted: 1% + 2% = 3%*

Rule 2: Access granted only if accepted by both devices—
     Probability of correct user being rejected: 3% + 4% = 7%*
     Probability of impostor being accepted: 1% × 2% = 0.02%

*Simplified calculations are shown, based on approximations which apply when both error probabilities are small.

Fig. 14-3. Combining two identity verification devices.

Illustrative Assumptions:
Type I error rate = 2%
Type II error rate = 1%

Statistical independence assumed among trials.

Rule 1: Access granted if either trial succeeds—
Probability of correct user being rejected: 2% × 2% = 0.04%
Probability of impostor being accepted: 1% + 1% = 2%*

Rule 2: Access granted only if both trials succeed—
Probability of correct user being rejected: 2% + 2% = 4%*
Probability of impostor being accepted: 1% × 1% = 0.01%

---

*Simplified calculations are shown, based on approximations which apply when both error probabilities are small.

Fig. 14-4. Allowing two trials to gain access.

tribute and other based on passwords or an identification token.

For example, the ATM system uses a combination of a magnetic stripe card and a PIN, which is a type of password. When identity verification based on personal attributes becomes established, a person could be asked to verify his or her identity both via an attribute and through one of the other methods.

Multiple Trials

The possibility of a Type 1 error has prompted many users to allow more than one trial to pass an access test. In one way, this process gives an impostor an extra chance or two to crack the system. Used properly, multiple trials can improve either a Type 1 or Type 2 error rate—but they cannot improve both at the same time.

There are some important conditions here. First, if a verification process is good to begin with, multiple trials can substantially improve its effectiveness in distinguishing between impostors and authorized users. Repeated trials cannot improve

performance that is poor at the outset, however. Also, the trials must be statistically independent. The outcome of any one trial should not influence the results of any repeat.

If you allow two trials to gain access, several decision strategies are available, as shown in Fig. 14-4. By allowing two trials, it is possible either to greatly benefit the correct users or to greatly enhance the rejection of impostors, but as usual, the improvement in one area comes at the expense of the other.

Rule 2 always requires two trials, increasing the time needed to carry out the verification process. With Rule 1, the process can be completed if the user passes the first trial. The likelihood of being rejected is small to start with, so only an occasional second trial will be needed.

Allowing More Than Two Trials

If you increase the number of trials, a greater variety of decision rules become available. It now becomes possible to improve the performance in both categories simultaneously. For example, with three trials the rule can be written to accept a person who passes one trial, two, or all three. The effects are shown in Fig. 14-5.

Note that for Rule 2, requiring at least two successful trials, the performance is greatly improved for both categories. In reality, the improvement would probably be less dramatic than this, but it still could be significant.

EXAMPLES OF PERSONAL ATTRIBUTES

Several methods have been developed to verify identity on the basis of personal attributes. No one technique has been identified as completely superior in all respects. They vary in accuracy, the length of time required, acceptance by users, cost, and other factors. Some of the equipment used still is in the early development stages, and that can affect performance.

Fingerprints

Verifying identity by manual fingerprint comparisons is a well-known technique. Fingerprints are compared mainly on the basis of *minutiae,* the ridge endings and bifurcations that can be identified by an examiner.

A fingerprint can contain up to 150 minutiae—40 to 60 is typical. These can be described in an X-Y coordinate system in which the coordinates of the minutiae are indicated along with certain feature information such as the angle at which the ridges lie at that point and the type of feature.

Illustrative Assumptions:
    Type I error rate = 2%
    Type II error rate = 1%

Statistical independence assumed among trials.

Rule 1: Access granted if a single trial succeeds—
    Probability of correct person being rejected: 2% × 2% × 2% = 0.0008%
    Probability of impostor being accepted: 1% + 1% + 1% = 3%*

Rule 2: Access granted if two trials succeed—
    Probability of correct person being rejected: 0.12%
    Probability of impostor being accepted: 0.03%

(The calculations for Rule 2 are a bit more difficult than for Rules 1 and 3, involving the tabulation of various possible outcomes.)

Rule 3: Access granted only if three trials succeed—
    Probability of correct person being rejected: 2% + 2% + 2% = 6%*
    Probability of impostor being accepted: 1% × 1% × 1% = 0.001%

---

*Simplified calculations are shown, based on approximations which apply when both error probabilities are small.

Fig. 14-5. Permitting up to three trials leads to this configuration.

Fingerprint impressions are invariably distorted. A skilled examiner can make allowances for these distortions and, given a sufficient number of features, can make a positive decision on whether two prints match. The distortions still are a source of variation, however.

More recently, research and development efforts have addressed the automation of fingerprint matching. Equipment has been produced that permits an image of the fingerprint to be obtained without using ink, and then to compress the image or details extracted from it into a reference file.

Two basic methods have been used. In the first, a direct comparison is made between the "live" print and a file print. This approach has the disadvantage of requiring a file of actual print images, with a mechanism for rapidly selecting and positioning them. It has the advantage of being relatively simple.

The second viewpoint relies on signal processing, such as on a digitized image, to extract information about the location and direction of the minutiae. It then compares this information with a list of characteristics from a reference file. A typical system requires a few hundred bytes of data for a print. Digital processing is used both to extract candidate records from the file and in the matching process.

It is feasible to scan a finger and carry out a comparison in about one second. To this you must add the time to key in a claimed identity or insert a card that bears this information, and the time to position the finger on the measuring device. In addition, if a match is not obtained the first time, it may be necessary to reposition the figure or to switch to an alternate finger. The number of retries can add significantly to the time, particularly if this happens very often.

An extensive test of an early automated fingerprint system produced a Type 1 error rate of 6.5 percent, a Type 2 error rate of 2.3 percent, and an average verification time, including retries when necessary, of 8.9 seconds. Later technology should be capable of much better performance, but it has not been as thoroughly tested.

Hand Geometry

The shape of a person's hand has been found to have enough interpersonal variability to distinguish one individual from another at a useful level of accuracy. The basic technique is to measure the length of the fingers, but it is a subtle process. The measurement starts at a point determined by the rounding at the end of the finger and ends at a point determined by the translucency of the web between the fingers.

In one form of this device, the user carries a magnetic stripe card on which an ID number and his or her finger length data have been recorded. The data on the card is scrambled to deter the unsophisticated. To use the device, the user places the card in a slot, then positions the hand on the measuring device with each finger resting in a slight groove.

The device then measures the finger lengths to obtain four three-digit numbers that are compared with the data deciphered from the card. The process takes less than a second, and the pass/fail output signal can be used for any purpose.

The identification data also can be stored in a central computer that makes the comparison. In this case, the user would enter an identification code at the device, and it would be transferred to the computer along with the readings from the hand.

Used on a remote terminal, such device could be used to establish the individual's identity as a proper user of that terminal. Be sure, though, to protect the data that is transmitted during the identification process.

The reliability of this process depends on the degree of repeatability for a given individual and the degree to which people's finger lengths tend to cluster around normal values. Most individuals produce results that are quite consistent, but a few individuals exhibit somewhat more variability. Typical of personal attribute identification devices, most errors occur among a relatively small group of individuals.

When you file the information in a computer, you also can provide for varied tolerance rates, based on the individual's characteristics. Recognize, though, that a clever penetrator will try to find out whose identification records call for the greatest tolerance. This means that any assessment of your computer security should be based on the most relaxed tolerances you allow.

Signature Dynamics

There recently have been several significant efforts to derive electrical signals from the process of writing a signature. These then could be analyzed to establish the writer's identity.

These efforts have demonstrated that the physical motions of writing a signature can be used with very reasonable error rates. The writing of a signature is a conditioned reflex, done with little conscious attention. While it is possible to forge a person's signature, it is hard to duplicate the dynamic motions associated with writing it. It requires conscious control, whose characteristics are different from reflexive behavior.

There are various ways to obtain signals that represent the dynamics of a signature. Qualities include positions, forces, and acceleration. The means to measure these could be designed into the writing instrument, the writing surface, or a combination. The instruments may be applied to one, two, or three axes of motion.

Time-variant position information can be derived by using an instrumented writing surface that can read out the coordinates of the stylus at selected times during the act of writing. It is important to measure the time as well as the positions. You also can measure force, such as the pressure applied to the writing surface or the drag forces along the surfaces.

Writing also is a jerky process, with rapid changes in velocity and acceleration. These can be measured with transducers mounted in the stylus.

One automatic signature verification system showed a Type 1 error rate of 1.9 percent, a Type 2 error rate of 5.6 percent, and an average verification time of 13.5 seconds. This was a relatively simple system that measured a single force on the writing surface. A more extensive system, which measures both pressure and acceleration, showed a Type 1 error rate of 1.7 percent, and a Type 2 rate of .02 percent. In a test of deliberate forgery attempts, the Type 2 error rate was 0.4 percent.

Speaker Verification

If all aspects of human speech are considered, the result is sufficiently complex and exhibits sufficient variation from one person to another to make it a potential technique for distinguishing among members of a large group. The computer is an effective tool for analyzing the many subtle distinctions between one person's speech and another's.

Speech may be viewed as a series of transitions separated by regions of varying duration in which the sounds are relatively steady. These regions are due mainly to vowels. The transitions have a "noisier" quality, coming from the various consonants. During the "steady" regions, the sound is influenced by the structure of the individual's vocal tract, throat, mouth, and nasal passages. This results in resonances, as well as a harmonic structure that is partly controllable and partly inherent to the individual.

In analyzing a person's speech for identity verification by a computer, the "steady" regions have most often been employed. While the steady regions contain most of the speech energy, most of the information about what is being said is contained in the transitions, and the way in which individuals use their tongue, lips, and teeth is lost. This drastically reduces the size of the data base at any given level of reliability.

A person to be enrolled first creates a reference file in the computer by repeating a "training set" of selected utterances a number of times. The resulting signal is digitized and sent to the computer. Various kinds of processing via special hardware may be done before or after the digitizing. The computer builds a reference file for each of the utterances in the training set. Thereafter, when the person wishes to verify his or her identity, the computer requests that he or she repeat these utterances, and it matches the new data against those in the reference file.

To prevent an impostor from simply recording a valid user's voice and playing it back to gain access, a specific strategy must be used. For example, the training set is made up of words from each of four categories, such as adjectives, nouns, verbs, and adverbs when the person enrolls. Then, when the person wishes to verify his or her identity, he or she is asked to repeat phrases made up of words selected at random from these categories.

A sample phrase might be, "Young Ben swam far." The words each have one syllable and have a prominent vowel sound. The computer can readily isolate the appropriate regions for making its comparisons. If another try is required, another random phrase is generated. Use of recordings is thus effectively thwarted for all but the most sophisticated penetrator.

The matching of features from speech by computer is done by processing algorithms that rely on a data base to characterize the desired response to an input. If a successful intrusion effort should be discovered, it would be possible, if a record has been kept of the original speech input, to analyze the successful deception, determine how it had been able to succeed, and refine the algorithms further to prevent a recurrence.

It also is possible to track a person's voice to adapt to slow changes, such as might occur with aging or with growing familiarity with the system. Recognition by voice generally will present problems when a person has a health problem affecting the voice, such as a cold or laryngitis.

Tests of one type or automatic speaker verification produced a Type 1 error rate of 1.1 percent, a Type 2 rate of 3.3 percent, and an average verification time of 6.2 seconds.

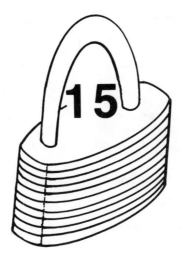

Securing Remote Devices

The material in this chapter is from FIPS Publication 83, also cited in Chapter 13.

Terminals and other remote devices can be equipped with circuits that will respond to an interrogation command and transmit an identification code for the device. This code may be a simple identification scheme that merely identifies the type of device, or it may be a security code that uniquely identifies the individual unit.

This can be a useful safeguard against an unauthorized terminal or device masquerading as an authorized one. There is more chance for this to occur on switched networks because of the ability to communicate between arbitrary points. However, even in a hard-wired network an impostor terminal might be attached by some means such as a wiretap.

The use of a built-in code to identify a terminal or personal computer does not provide much security if an eavesdropper can discern the code by prying into the terminal or by means of a wiretap. He could then falsify the code using a device of his own. The circuits that generate the code in the device therefore should be protected by a tamper-resistant housing, and the transmission should be protected by encryption.

THE ROLE OF ENCRYPTION

Encryption may be used to preserve the confidentiality of information being transmitted between computers and remote terminals, and it can aid in safeguarding against various threats such as wiretapping, electronic eavesdropping, misrouting, substitution, modification, and injection of messages. Data files also can be safeguarded by encryption techniques.

Encryption is achieved either through a secret process in which the data is transposed or substituted, or through a commonly known process that depends on a secret parameter, called a *key*. To allow compatibility of encryption processes within the typical variety of network components, the latter method is strongly recommended.

The encryption process is generally specified in an algorithm; *decryption* is the reverse process. Even with encryption it still might be possible for an impostor to imitate encrypted responses of a fixed nature if they are always the same. In a system, it is a relatively simple matter, however, to use numbering schemes in the dialogue that would cause identical information to be encrypted differently and in a manner that would be, in practice, impossible for an impostor to imitate.

Encryption is often appropriate for controlling access to computer networks. One use for encryption in this connection is to protect information that must be transmitted in order to verify the user's identity. Secret identification information such as passwords must be protected from disclosure. Nonsecret information such as signature characteristics must be protected from replacement and repetition.

Encryption algorithms also may be used to achieve "digital signatures" which are in effect a means to verify the identity of message senders and recipients.

Protecting Information for Identity Verification

When passwords or other information known to an authorized user are entered into a system, it is possible for a penetrator to intercept that information by wiretap or some other means. The penetrator then can use that information to impersonate the authorized users.

To guard against this threat, the keyboard or terminal used to enter the secret information should be safeguarded against tampering. Encryption then can be used to protect the information from the point where it leaves the keyboard or terminal and is transmitted to its destination. If you already are using encryption to protect the working information transmitted to and from the terminal, this same capability may be suitable for protecting the verification information.

The encryption process used to protect the verification information must provide for the information to be coded differently with each transmission. Otherwise, a penetrator might record the encrypted information from a point in its transmission path and spoof the system simply by injecting the same encrypted information without ever having to decrypt it. Encryption systems generally have provisions for achieving the required variability.

When a personal attribute is used to verify an identity, a set of measured values is obtained and digitized and used for comparison with a reference profile. This information, in clear form, can be used by a skillful penetrator to simulate the data obtained from an authorized user. To guard against this, the device that measures the attribute should be safeguarded against tampering so the measured data cannot be taken while it is in the clear. Encryption can be used to protect this information during transmission.

Verification systems based on personal attributes are configured in a variety of ways. In one configuration, the measuring device sends the measured values to a central system where the reference profile is stored and where the comparison takes place. In this case, the measured values should be encrypted for transmission to the central system.

In another configuration, the reference profile is sent to the measuring device with the comparison taking place in the device. In this case, the reference profile should be encrypted to prevent a penetrator from being able to inject a reference profile of his or her own.

Also, the device will produce a pass/fail signal, based on the results of the comparison, and this will be transmitted elsewhere, such as back to the central system that controls network access. This pass/fail signal also should be encrypted. Otherwise, a penetrator might be able to simulate this signal and produce a false pass response without ever having to deceive the measurement device.

The personal attribute sensing device generally will be either an integral part of a remote terminal or will be closely associated with such a terminal. Precautions should be taken to assure that equipment enclosures are tamper-protected and that there are no exposed leads that would let a penetrator tap sensitive information.

Digital Signatures

One form of authentication is the "digital signature," in which the sender of a message attaches a coded identification to the message, enciphered in such a way that only the intended recipient can decipher it and verify the identity of the sender.

One method for doing this is based on using individual station identifiers in the process of encrypting keys, which in turn are used to encrypt messages between the stations. Because of the hardware arrangements and operating procedures used with this system, it is possible for a sender to encipher a signature or any other message in such a way that only the prearranged recipient can correctly decipher it.

Digital signatures also may be achieved through public key encryption. In such a system, the encryption key differs from the decryption key, and knowledge of the encryption key does not result in knowledge of the decryption key. In a public key system, users may publicize freely the keys for encrypting messages that are to be sent to them; they keep secret the corresponding decryption keys.

The encryption and decryption procedures for some public key cryptosystems are inverses of each other. In normal practice, a message would first be enciphered for transmission and then be deciphered upon receipt to recover the information. The procedures in these systems may be applied in the reverse order, however, first using the decryption procedure to conceal the information, and then using the encryption procedure to recover it.

A secure digital signature can be achieved this way: assume that user A wants to send a secure digital signature to user B. A first passes the signature through A's own private decryption procedure, which in effect leaves it in unintelligible form. A then enciphers the signature in this form using B's public encryption procedure for privacy and sends it to B.

B first deciphers the signature using B's secret decryption procedure. B then applies A's public encryption procedure and recovers the digital signature. In practice, it is preferable to apply this process to entire messages rather than just the authenticating signature to keep a valid signature from being attached to a falsified message.

RANGE OF CAPABILITIES

Once the identity of a user has been established and authenticated, he or she may be granted access to the network and may request the use of various available resources. These resources consist of various entities such as host computers, areas of main memory, files, programs, auxiliary memory devices, and instructions. They often are referred to as *objects*.

Users must have proper authorization to be granted access to these objects. Each user has an associated set of access privileges to which he or she is entitled. This may be called the *capability profile*.

Similarly, each object has associated with it a set of requirements for its use, which may be called an *access requirement profile*. An access request is authorized when the requester's capability profile matches the objects' access requirements profile.

An object may have many ways in which it can be used, such as reading data from a file, writing data into a file, carrying out a transaction, executing a program, compiling a program, or invoking various operating system routines. Thus there is a range of capabilities associated with an object, not all of which may be authorized for use by every user.

It is possible to visualize this situation as a three-dimensional array, with users along one dimension, objects along another, and capabilities along the third, as shown in Fig. 15-1.

It is useful to visualize access control and privacy protection in three levels: memory, procedure, and logical. Access control at the memory level regulates access to memory in terms of units of memory. Concern at this level is with defined regions of memory rather than with its contents. This protection applies to the contents only while they remain in the defined region. Protected regions of memory typically are defined by the means of

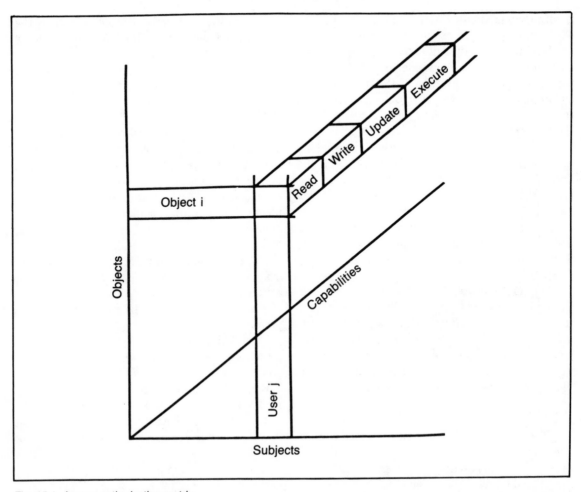

Fig. 15-1. Access authorization matrix.

memory-bound registers or storage protection keys that control access to the bounded memory regions.

Access control at the procedure level regulates access to procedures, where a procedure is a set of programs and associated data. Access control at this level is concerned with the conditions under which programs can pass control from one to another. That is, the execution programs must be monitored in terms of calls, returns, and the passing of parameters.

ACCESS AUTHORIZATION PRINCIPLES

Access control can be governed by a set of principles like those listed below.

Least Privilege. No requester shall have any access privileges that are not required to perform the function—in other words, a need-to-know standard. As a corollary to this, access to resources shall be compartmentalized whenever such separation adds to security.

Least Common Mechanism. There shall be minimal shared or common mechanisms, other than those that are there expressly for security purposes.

Reference Monitor Approach. Access control mechanisms must be such that they are always invoked, isolated from unauthorized alteration and accredited as being trustworthy.

Object Versus Path Protection. Protection can be provided to the object itself, the path to the object, or both. The network aspects are almost entirely path-oriented protection.

Composite Authorizations

Several entities are involved in nearly every computer transaction. These could include a person, a terminal, a host computer, and a process. Each of these entities must be authorized either to receive, process, or transport the information being handled.

The logical intersection of these authorizations will establish the level of information that can be sent by this sequence of entities, but a further step-by-step authorization check also is necessary to ensure that only the proper entity or entities are the ultimate recipients of the information. For example, one entity may be authorized to process, but not to copy, the information.

In some instances, the request will be connected to a host which will, in turn, need access to other resources on the requester's behalf. Authorization is a larger problem than authentication, because the latter is strictly binary at each intermediate requester. In contrast, the authorizations of each intermediate requester may differ, as may the authorization needs when information is processed at different nodes along the chain.

Two different approaches are possible. First, continually subsetting the authorizations as necessary so the final privileges are the intersection of those of the original requester and all intermediate nodes. This will ensure that no intermediate node gets any information for which it is not authorized.

Second, handling the authorization on a pairwise basis, so the nth level will provide an requested information for which the (n-1)th is authorized, and leave the burden of further controls on passing of data to the host. This procedure allows the use of so-called statistical programs, in which specific details are lost. For example, the system might respond with the average value of a group of data but not with a specific value within the group. Of course, you still would be vulnerable to a cleverly devised statistical request.

Access to the Authorization Mechanism

The authorization mechanism is called upon whenever a user presents an access request for an object. The mechanism must therefore be readily accessible for frequent use.

There also will be occasions when the mechanism must be modified to reflect changes in status for users and objects. This mechanism has a critical security function, and it must be properly protected from unauthorized modifications.

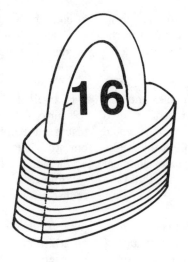

Principles of Network Security

This material in this chapter is from the introduction to *Design Alternatives for Computer Network Security* by Gerald D. Cole and Dennis K. Branstad (National Bureau of Standards Publication 500-21).

In recent years, computer usage has grown to the point that it influences almost every aspect of our commercial and military environments. Concurrent with this growth has been the need to share resources, to better utilize expensive equipment, to utilize and build upon the work of others, and to share work efforts. This need for controlled sharing has grown not only in terms of the number of people involved, but also in the geographic dispersion of these people and their need for rapid access to and interchange of information. Such growth has presented new technological and operational problems in many areas, particularly in system security.

The first generation usage of computers created security problems that could be solved by using conventional physical, procedural, and personnel control methods. Sharing was basically a matter of dividing the computer usage into

dedicated time-slots, with carefully controlled set up/tear down between jobs (or batches of jobs of the same security level). The development of multiprogramming methods provided a more efficient mode of hardware use by rapid context switching between jobs and by overlapping operations. This development required the machine to execute several jobs concurrently, thus adding a new dimension to the security problem due to the multiuser environment.

As software and data base resources began to grow in size and value, the need to share these resources also became evident, and added another dimension to the security control problem; namely, that of controlling access to the multiresources. The next logical step in this evolution was to share such resources across two or more machines (systems), which introduced yet another dimension to the security problem. These multisystem networks present a solution to the problems of sharing that involve a large number of persons who are geographically scattered, but who require rapid access and interchange of information. Such networks present formidable security problems due to the multiuser, multiresource, multisystem environment.

The purpose of our investigation is to define the security issues related to this complex network environment, and to determine the tradeoffs related to possible approaches and mechanisms that could resolve these issues. The end result of the study, as reflected in this report, is to be a predevelopment specification with the scope as defined in the statement of work:

Analyze several computer network configurations with respect to their ability to support end-to-end security (protection of information from originator to final destination) on all possible communication paths in the network. The effort shall yield specifications which include communication protocol, switching techniques, and protection techniques at such a level that a secure network development may be specified and initiated.

An excellent starting point for the investigation was available in the paper by D. K. Branstad, "Security Aspects of Computer Networks," which discussed many of the relevant issues. However, our study extended his efforts both in depth and by including a broader scope of issues.

Figure 16-1 is the general configuration of a secure network assumed for the purpose of this study. A set of computer systems (HOST computers), and terminals are to be interconnected via an arbitrary communications network, but under the control of a local Security Controller and cryptographic devices.

Assuming that each of the individual HOST systems is secure when operated in its own separate environment, we investigate the set of prob-

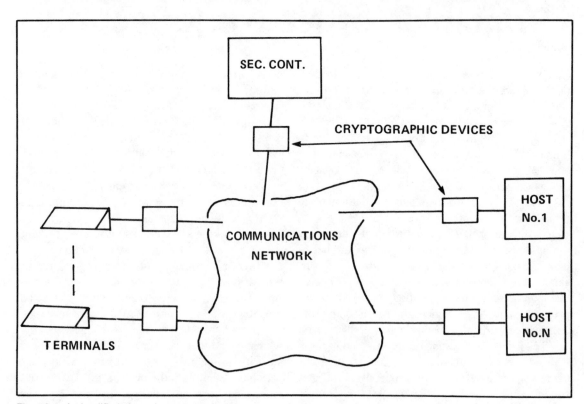

Fig. 16-1. A simplified view of a secure network.

lems that occur when they are integrated into a loose federation, with certain global constraints and controls being placed over these otherwise autonomous local centers.

The need for crypotographic devices is apparent, because the communications net is "open" to any would-be penetrators, but the cryptographic devices can provide much more than communications line security.

Unfortunately, many people feel that the use of cryptographic equipment solves the security problem, while in reality this equipment should be viewed as only one element of a larger total system design for security. An Air Force Security Study panel summarized this matter:

> Though considerable financial resources and management attention are drawn to the communications security aspects of networking (an important but well understood technology) the security problem of computer networking is not a communications problem but another more sophisticated instance of multilevel computer operating system security.
>
> Currently, most secure computer systems achieve their security integrity by prohibition of multilevel and multicompartment security operation. The computer is operated at a single, appropriately high security level for its needs, with all personnel and operating procedures controlled within the USAF/DoD established security framework. Networking ties two or more of these computer systems together; more often than not, systems dissimilar in equipment, configuration, purpose, management, and security control procedures. An example of the networking problem is the connection of the SAC SATIN network with AUTODIN network for both the receipt and transmission of information. Conceptually, the network can be viewed as a *supracomputer system.* The network security requirements then are different than most of its members because the supracomputer operates essentially as a multilevel, multicom-partment, multiuser computer system. The network's security vulnerability is that each network node (i.e., the computer system operated by a participating agency) is unprepared for multilevel, multicompartment use by users over which it exerts limited, if any, control. Furthermore, the problem often goes unrecognized since management erroneously assumes security integrity because the supracomputer interconnections are via secured (often crypto) communications lines.

As mentioned in the preceding quote, the real problem area in network security is lack of global control over users, where "users" must be interpreted as any combination of persons and systems operating on their behalf. This loss of control can be reflected in any of several security problems, including:

1. Problems due to the large number of possible combinations of persons operating from different terminal stations at different sites with different authorizations for different resources at different sites, each of which has different classifications and compartments, etc.

2. Nth party problems, in which processes operate on the behalf of a requester, perhaps many levels removed, and may spawn other subprocesses, etc. (perhaps on several different HOST's).

3. The autonomous nature of each network participant creates problems in that each domain of control may have differing methods, interpretations, etc. for providing security.

4. The problem that one compromised HOST may be used to penetrate yet another (the "domino effect").

5. The problems in which one operating system (or data base) may become faulty in a manner that spreads to other network HOST's (the network cancer problem, either accidental or malicious).

6. The potential problems related to a distributed attack on one system by two or more other systems (analogous to the asynchronous attacks on conventional multiuser systems).

These examples are by no means all of the network security problems, but represent the larger scope of the problems above and beyond that of individual resource-sharing systems. The examples also indicate that mechanisms are needed to prevent, or at least constrain, the spread of security compromises within the net. If this is not done, the network may not be any stronger than its weakest node, an unacceptable condition in any federation of entities. Network security must, therefore, be as independent as possible of the security of the separate autonomous nodes.

At this time, it seems appropriate to define what we mean by "computer network security." First, a computer network can be defined as an interconnected set of independent (or dependent) computer systems which communicate to share information and service resources in order to provide needed user services. Dependence among computer systems may come about in any of several degrees, e.g., either directly dependent processes such as in a distributed computer system (FAR-73) or more subtly when computer centers begin to become increasingly dependent upon each other for services that would normally have been provided locally. Another area of emphasis is the definition on meeting user needs: a mechanism is of questionable value unless it meets the needs of its ultimate users, and this is one of the fundamental concerns in the investigation and specification of a secure network.

The definition of security in the sense of a secure computer network involves three basic aspects of protection: (1) providing controlled access to resources, (2) providing controlled use of those resources, and (3) providing assurance that the desired level of protection is maintained. At this point we first encounter a question in defining the boundaries for network security, which also reflects on our definition of a network—are the HOST computers considered part of the network? In theory, one should answer this question with an une-quivocal "yes" (e.g., the supracomputer notion of the quoted ESD report); in practice, one must often segment the problem into data processing and data communication aspects due to the autonomous nature of the local computer centers, and/or the administrative separation of data processing and communication areas. This investigation of computer network security is based on the following:

1. Both the data processing and communications functions will be considered as generally as possible.

2. The investigation will focus on the interface between the data processing and communications functions; i.e., the intermediate layer of equipment required when separately secure HOST systems are to be interconnected via an "open" communications network.

3. The investigation will also consider the resulting impact on both the data processing and communications in order to provide this secure interconnection.

4. Globally defined network security mechanisms should augment rather than replace local (individual HOST) mechanisms. Aside from the "political" reasons (due to the autonomous HOSTs), augmentation rather than replacement also provides an evolutionary approach to network integration and the development of centralized security mechanisms, which can gradually assume more of the total security functions.

We are then faced with two questions: What global security-related policies must be developed to ensure nework security, and by what global and/or local mechanisms can those policies be implemented? The basic policy issues can be derived directly from our three-part definition of security:

Provide Controlled Access to Resources. All requesters of network services must be identified and authenticated, and their access request must be checked to ensure that it is authorized prior to establishing a connection (logical or physical) between the requester and the resource.

Provide Controlled Usage of these Resources. Although this is primarily the responsibility of the HOST providing the resource, the network interface must provide whatever functions it can to augment the HOST protective measures.

Provide Assurance that the Desired Level of Protection is Maintained. Two related areas of networking policy relate to maintaining a desired level of security: monitoring or survelliance of network usage, and ensuring the adequancy and integrity of the security mechanisms.

For each of these levels, one must consider all of the categories from the definition of security:

1. Identification/authorization.
2. Access request/authorization.
3. Access control: establishment of the connection.
4. Access control: usage of the connection.
5. Security monitoring (surveillance).
6. Security assurance (integrity).

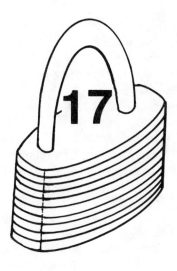

A System of Network Security

The material in this chapter is from *A Key Notarization System for Computer Networks* by Miles E. Smid (National Bureau of Standards Publication 500-54).

This paper proposes a Key Notarization System (KNS), which may be used in conjunction with a cryptographic device to provide increased data security. In 1977, the National Bureau of Standards published a completely defined encryption algorithm known as the Data Encryption Standard (DES), which became a Federal standard for the protection of unclassified data.

Since publication, several companies have produced hardware devices which implement the standard, and there has been an increased awareness that, in certain applications, encryption offers the only effective means of protecting information. The first applications of the encryption of unclassified data appeared in the area of electronic funds transfer, but the passage of the Privacy Act of 1974 (5 USC 522a) and Transmittal Memorandum No. 1 to Office of Management and Budget placed added responsibilities on Federal data systems for the protection of nonfinancial data as well.

Even before the DES was adopted, it was clear that there was more to cryptographic security than a secure encryption algorithm. Efforts were initiated by NBS to have additional standards, based on the DES, developed. An area which needed to be addressed was secure key management. DES keys are 64-bit binary vectors, individually selected to provide the unknown quantity necessary for security in the encryption algorithm. Key management involves the secure generation, distribution, and storage of cryptographic keys. If the key management is weak, then the most secure cryptoalgorithm will be of little value. In fact, a very strong cryptoalgorithm used in a weak key management system can give a false sense of security.

Previous work on key management systems may be found in Ehrsam, et al, and Everton. This paper develops a simple key hierarchy and a set of commands or protocols, which in conjunction with a secure random key generator and a strong encryption algorithm, may be used to generate and store keys as well as to encrypt and decrypt data. These commands have been devised for computer systems that employ key notarization facilities (KNFs). They are to be tested on the NBS Unix system, but they are not Unix-dependent. It is intended that the system be applicable to many different situations. On-line communications, file encryption, off-line mail, and digital signatures all are to be protected. Key notarization is presented to help provide security while maintaining the required flexibility.

REQUIREMENTS

The Key Notarization System (KNS) may be used in computer networks along with key notarization facilities (KNFs) to:

1. Securely communicate between any two users.
2. Securely communicate via encrypted mail (off-line).
3. Protect personal (nonshared) files.
4. Provide a digital signature capability.

Secure communication involves preventing the disclosure of plain text, detecting fraudulent message modification, detecting fraudulent message insertion or deletion, and detecting fraudulent replay of a previously valid message. The KNS must be consistent with these goals and yet operate at speeds sufficient for normal network communications.

With mail encryption, data is encrypted and then sent via mail or some means which cannot provide an immediate response. The data is stored in the encrypted form until decryption at some later time. In this situation, one cannot have an interactive system for exchanging keys because no real-time response is possible. Therefore, protocols must be devised so that the receipt of keys need not be immediately acknowledged.

Once encrypted, personal files can only be decrypted by the original owner. They are encrypted for secure storage rather than secure communication. In this case, encryption is used to protect against accidental disclosure, such as spillage, and intentional disclosure, such as scavenging.

It is often desirable that the data encrypting key be stored with the cipher for ease of recovery. Of course, the key would be encrypted under another long term key, which is kept for the user either in the KNF or in a secure location from which it may be entered into the KNF.

Digital signatures were developed in conjunction with public key systems. In such systems the decryption key is not equal to, and cannot be computed from, the encryption key. Encryption keys may be made public while decryption keys are kept secret. A digital signature is decrypted using the secret decryption key and sent to the receiver. The receiver may encrypt, using the public key, and verify the signature, but the signature cannot be forged since only the transmitter knows the secret decryption key. (The cryptoalgorithm must have the property that decryption of the signature followed by encryption equals the original signature.) Nonpublic key algorithms can also be used for digital signatures in conjunction with a *Network Registry*. In the KNS, a different method is proposed for implementing digital signatures with the DES nonpublic key algorithm.

THE NETWORK

The KNS is designed for computer networks that consist of host computers, user terminals, and key notarization facilities. Figure 17-1 shows a four-host network. The host controls the normal operation and communication of the terminals. Terminals have the capability of communicating with the host, with other local terminals through the host, and with terminals of other hosts via communication channels called *interchanges*. Each terminal will be able to use the host KNF by means of user commands. All commands will be implemented in the KNF, and every KNF will have the capacity to generate keys for distribution to other hosts or facility users.

Interchanges may be electronic communications lines, microwave links, courier routes, etc., or combinations of more than one medium. In Fig. 17-1, only host 3 shares an interchange with host 4. If host 1 shares a common interchange key with

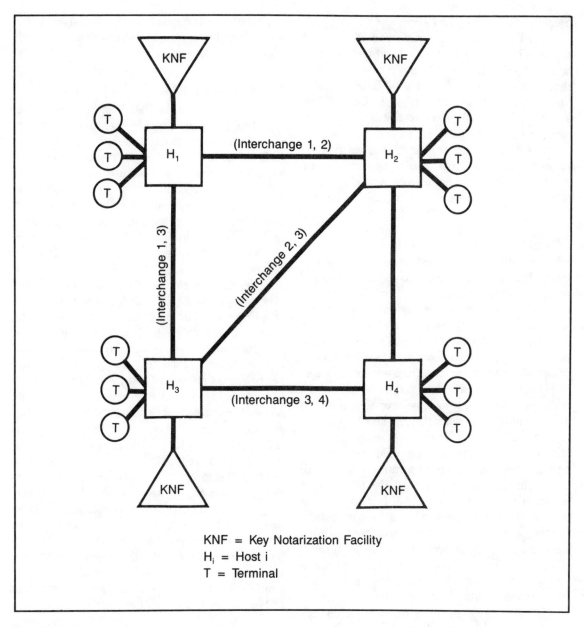

KNF = Key Notarization Facility
H$_i$ = Host i
T = Terminal

Fig. 17-1. A four-host network.

host 4, then host 1 may communicate with host 4 through host 3 without intermediate decryption and reencryption. Host 3 would merely act as a switch. This is known as *end-to-end encryption*. If host 1 does not share a common key with host 4 but does share a key with host 3, and if host 3 shares a key with host 4, then host 1 may communicate with host 4 via host 3. The cipher would have to be decrypted at host 3 and reencrypted in the key shared between host 3 and host 4. Care must be taken to ensure that the communications are not compromised when unencrypted. This method of encrypted communications is called *link encryption*.

The lines between the KNF and its host and the lines between each terminal and its host must be protected. They could be physically secured or they could be secured by the addition of cryptographic devices on each end of the links. When a user is editing a file in the host, it is in plain text form, and the host will have to protect the data from other users. Once the user has finished editing, he may command the KNF to encrypt the data and store the resulting cipher in unprotected memory or send it to a remote user over an interchange.

The Host

We will assume that the host computer has two types of memory: that which is not accessible to any user, called *system memory*, and that which is accessible to users, called *user memory*. User i's memory is core, disk, etc., where user i is permitted to store and recall data. Most computers have a means of protecting system memory from users, and some computers protect one user from another to a certain degree. We will rely on these protective features to the extent that the user should not be able to subvert the operation of the computer.

For example, the system must be able to maintain correctly the identity of the user once he has been authenticated and given permission to execute the commands. The system must also prevent one user from taking on the identity of another user and thereby obtaining access to his unencrypted data. In other words, encryption by itself does not solve the computer security problem. However, if properly used in a system with the necessary protective features, it can provide protection to stored and communicated data.

The encrypted keys of user i are stored in user i's memory, and encrypted passwords to which no user needs access will be stored in system memory. Nevertheless, we will assume that any user could gain read and write access to every encrypted password stored in system memory. Each user is expected to manage the encrypted keys that belong to him, but he will not know any clear keys. Yet, key encryption is not sufficient. A method is required to protect against key substitution and to ensure that each user correctly identifies the user with who he is communicating.

The Key Notarization Facility (KNF)

The KNF contains a DES encryption device. It will have a control microprocessor and memory to implement commands and data transfers. The KNF must also store the unencrypted interchange keys and the states of active users. An *active state* consists of a user identifier along with an initialization vector and an unencrypted data key for both transmitting and receiving data. A user is *active* as soon as his identifier is loaded into *active user memory* in the KNF. He may then proceed to load the rest of his state.

The KNF contains a key generator capable of generating unpredictable keys. At any time, a user should be able to predict the next key to be generated with only a $1:2^{56}$ probability of success. One possible key generator is proposed in the Appendix. Once the 56-bit keys are generated, the proper parity is determined and the entire 64-bit key is encrypted before it is returned to the host. Thus, no clear keys are known outside the KNF. The key generator is also used to generate 64-bit initialization vectors, which initialize the DES cryptoalgorithm. Since the KNF contains clear keys, the encryption algorithm, the commands program, and the key generator, it must be physically protected.

Cryptographic facilities containing a single master key are used to perform encryption and execute key management commands. Our key notarization facilities hold several keys and the key generator. They employ a different key hierarchy, a different set of commands, and are the enforcers of key notarization.

Distributed versus Centralized Key Generation

Network security centers (NSC) may be used for key distribution. Upon request, the NSC generates a key for use by each of the parties in a conversation. One copy is encrypted under a key shared between the NSC and the first party, and another copy is encrypted under a key shared between the NSC and the second party. The encrypted forms of the key are then sent to the appropriate receivers.

The KNS uses distributed rather than centralized key generation as employed by an NSC. In order to provide for off-line encrypted mail, the KNS gives each host the capability of key generation in its own KNF. Thus, two hosts do not even have to be electronically connected in order to communicate securely. The KNS requires fewer protocols because parties do not have to send a remote key generation request, and they do not have to respond to the receipt of a key. Fewer protocols mean fewer ways an enemy can attempt to trick or confuse the communicating parties by altering or playing back the protocol messages.

If a KNF is compromised, only communications involving the compromised facility are compromised. If an NSC is compromised, and there is only one NSC for the network, then the whole network is compromised. Finally, with a local key generator, one can encrypt personal (nonshared) files without having to depend on a remote site. The KNS approach has the disadvantage that the key generation capability and the KNF physical security has to be replicated at each host.

IDENTIFIERS AND KEY NOTARIZATION

A special feature of the KNS is the support of key notarization. This feature increases security, permits a simple system design, and provides a means of implementing signatures with a nonpublic key system. *Identifiers* are nonsecret binary vectors of up to 28 bits, which uniquely identify each user in the network. When a user first attempts to call the KNF he must submit his identifier along with the correct password to establish an active state in the KNF. Both the host and the KNF employ identifiers to "recognize" the users.

Key notarization is similar to the actions of a notary public who first requires his customer to identify himself via a driver's license, etc., before he seals (notarizes) the customer's signature on a document with his notary stamp. In addition to the notary's function of authenticating the creator of a message, the KNS authenticates the message itself and the person requesting decryption. Key notarization is similar to having a notary public on each end of a secure communication channel.

Let i and j be identifiers and k be a DES key. Then $(i \parallel j)$ represents the concatenation of i and j. K, a 64-bit key, consists of eight bytes, each with seven information bits and a parity bit. K XOR $(i \parallel j)$ is a special function defined as follows: The leftmost seven information bits of K are exclusive ORed with the leftmost seven bits of i. The eighth bit, a parity bit, is then appended so that the modulo 2 sum of all eight bits is odd. Then the next seven information bits of K are exclusive ORed with the next seven bits of i, and the correct parity bit is appended. This continues until the last seven information bits of K have been exclusive ORed with the last seven bits of j, and the final parity bit has been set. Therefore, K XOR $(i \parallel j)$ is a valid DES key with 56 information bits and eight parity bits.

All passwords and data keys are encrypted under K XOR $(i \parallel j)$ for some K and some i, j pair; in the case of passwords, $i = j$. This adds to security because one user cannot substitute his password or keys for those of another user and be able to authenticate or decrypt as that user. This will be explained in detail in Password and Key Storage. The security is also increased because both parties in a conversation must know the other's correct identity to communicate. Since the KNF only needs to retain keys for each interchange, instead of each user, the network design is simplified; and since only one user can encrypt with a given data key and only one user can decrypt with a given data key, a signature system may be devised similar to those used with public key encryption systems.

When key notarization is used, keys and passwords are sealed, upon encryption by the KNF, with the identifiers of the transmitter or key generator and the receiver. To generate a notarized key, the transmitter must identify himself to the KNF and provide proof of his identity by supplying his correct password. We call this *user authen-*

tication. He must also identify the intended receiver of the key.

Once encrypted, the correct key cannot be decrypted unless the correct identifier pair is again provided. To decrypt the key, the receiver identifies himself and provides password proof of his identity. The receiver must also supply the identity of the transmitter that may have been sent unencrypted. If the identification information is not the same as that provided by the transmitter to his KNF, then the decrypted key will not equal the original key and no information can be correctly decrypted. Thus, the receiver must know the correct transmitter and be the intended receiver.

USER AUTHENTICATION

Each user will have a password, used to authenticate the user and permit him to invoke user commands. The plain password is passed through an encryption function, that involves the user's identifier, and the result is compared with a stored value before the user is activated. Therefore, a user cannot exercise any other command until his identity has been authenticated. The password of each user is stored in system memory encrypted under the facility interchange key (See Key Hierarchy), combined with the user's identifier. Because it is assumed that the host can maintain the correct identity of a user once he has been authenticated,

the user need not resubmit his password for each key he generates while he is active. His authenticated identifier, which has been loaded into active user memory, will automatically be used as his identifier.

KEY HIERARCHY

Two distinct types of keys are used to form the key hierarchy, interchange keys (IKs), and data keys (DKs). Interchange keys encrypt passwords (PWs) and data keys, while data keys encrypt both data and initialization vectors (IVs). The key hierarchy is shown in Fig. 17-20.

Interchange Keys (IKs)

Interchange keys are used for the exchange of keys between users. One interchange key, called the *facility interchange key*, is used for communication within a facility and the encryption of facility user passwords. Other interchange keys may be available for the exchange of data keys between facilities or for special subgroups of a facility. IKs are generated outside the network and are entered, unencrypted, directly into the KNF. This permits two facilities to enter the same IK. One IK can be used to connect all the users of two hosts because a user may not decrypt a data key shared by two other users. This is because the identifiers of the

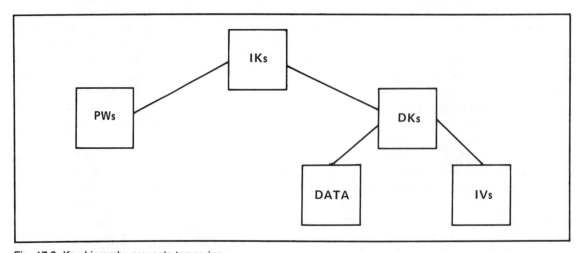

Fig. 17-2. Key hierarchy prevents tampering.

two parties are involved in the encryption of the shared key. Therefore, the number of keys that need to be stored in the KNF is reduced.

Data Keys (DKs)

Data keys are used to encrypt data belonging to one particular user or data shared between two users. DKs are generated by the key generator and are immediately encrypted under an IK XORed with the proper identifier pair. The identifier of the user requesting the key, who is also the transmitter, is always the left identifier, and the identifier of the intended receiver is the right identifier in the identifier pair. When encrypted, DKs may be sent, kept in unprotected memory, etc. Initialization vectors are employed by the DES algorithm in the cipher block chaining (CBC), cipher feedback (CFB), and data authentication (DAUT) modes of operation. All IVs are encrypted, before they leave the KNF, under the data key, which enciphers the corresponding data.

PASSWORD AND KEY STORAGE

Figure 17-3 shows how keys appear in KNF memory at host 1, in host 1 system memory, and in memory of user i at host 1.

KNF Keys

KNF memory contains both current and old interchange keys and active states of a limited number of users. When the interchange keys are changed, the old interchange keys are securely stored outside of the KNF along with their effective date. With the addition of another command, one could encrypt the IKs in the facility master key to reduce the number of clear keys needing protection. The current IKs become the old interchange keys, and the new interchange keys become the current IKs. After such a change, the passwords are reencrypted under the current (new) facility interchange key, and the users are told to reencrypt their data keys.

Passwords

System memory contains the encrypted passwords

for every user. Let $E[X](Y)$ indicate the encryption of Y under X in the electronic codebook (ECB) mode of operation. Thus, $E[IK1 \text{ XOR } (i \parallel i)]$ (PWi) denotes the encryption of PWi under IK1 XORed with user i's identifier pair, $(i \parallel i)$. IK1 is used because the encrypted passwords are from the system memory of host 1 and IK1 is the facility interchange key for host 1.

The password is encrypted under IK1 XORed with the appropriate identifier pair to protect against substitution. If identifiers were not used, system memory might appear as follows:

i. $E[IK1]$ (PWi)
j. $E[IK1]$ (PWj)
.
.

If user j could gain access to system memory, he might alter it as follows:

i. $E[IK1]$ (PWj)
j. $E[IK1]$ (PWj)
.
.

User j could then authenticate as user i by submitting his own password while claiming to be user i. If identifiers are used, then $E[IK1 \text{ XOR } (i \parallel i)]$ (PWj) would be calculated upon authentication, and it would not compare with $E[IK1 \text{ XOR } (j \parallel j)]$ (PWj), with was substituted as user i's encrypted password.

User Keys

User i's memory contains personal and shared data keys. Personal data keys are encrypted under the facility interchange key XORed with the user's identifier pair. Personal keys may be used to encrypt files and other private data, but cannot be shared. User i's memory also contains shared data keys encrypted under interchange keys XORed with the concatenation, ($\parallel$), of user i's identifier and another user's identifier. The expression ($i \parallel j$) uniquely identifies the communication parties. If ($i \parallel j$) were not used, another user could substitute

231

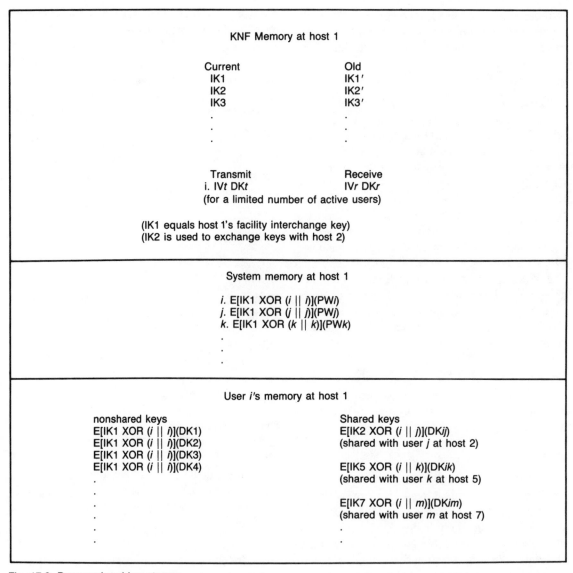

KNF Memory at host 1

Current	Old
IK1	IK1'
IK2	IK2'
IK3	IK3'
.	.
.	.
.	.

Transmit	Receive
i. IVt DKt	IVr DKr

(for a limited number of active users)

(IK1 equals host 1's facility interchange key)
(IK2 is used to exchange keys with host 2)

System memory at host 1

i. E[IK1 XOR ($i \parallel i$)](PWi)
j. E[IK1 XOR ($j \parallel j$)](PWj)
k. E[IK1 XOR ($k \parallel k$)](PWk)
.
.
.

User i's memory at host 1

nonshared keys
E[IK1 XOR ($i \parallel i$)](DK1)
E[IK1 XOR ($i \parallel i$)](DK2)
E[IK1 XOR ($i \parallel i$)](DK3)
E[IK1 XOR ($i \parallel i$)](DK4)
.
.
.
.
.

Shared keys
E[IK2 XOR ($i \parallel j$)](DKij)
(shared with user j at host 2)

E[IK5 XOR ($i \parallel k$)](DKik)
(shared with user k at host 5)

E[IK7 XOR ($i \parallel m$)](DKim)
(shared with user m at host 7)
.
.
.

Fig. 17-3. Password and key storage.

his own data key, encrypted under the interchange key and then be able to decrypt any subsequent cipher. Similarly, when user j receives E[IKp XOR ($i \parallel j$)] (DKij), he must know that he is communicating with i, over interchange p, to correctly decipher DKij. Thus, the transmitter is prevented from posing as someone else. Because several users may all use the same IKp to communicate, this protection is critical.

It should be noted that it is the system's responsibility to enforce any restrictions on the use of interchanges. For example, if user i is not allowed to use IKp, then the system must enforce this arbitrary restriction by not loading IKp for user i. User i should not be able to subvert the restriction by key substitution.

One could argue that substitution protection is not needed for system memory because if the system cannot protect system memory, it probably cannot prevent users from changing identity, from invoking system commands, or other security threats. This may be true, but encryption should not add additional possibilities for attacks. In user memory, the substitution threat is very real because many systems cannot protect one user's memory from another user, and even if they could, the encrypted keys will not be protected. Encrypted data keys may be stored with cipher on unprotected tapes and disks, and they may even be sent out over unprotected communications channels.

DEFINITION OF TERMS

When defining our commands, the terms initialize, reserve, load, store, generate, encrypt, decrypt, and reencrypt will be used. These terms should be defined so that the meaning of the commands is clear. The terms actually represent functions which operate on keys or passwords.

Initialize sets a password to a starting value that should be changed by invoking another command.

Reserve activates a user by loading his identifier into the KNF.

Load takes an encrypted key or encrypted IV from the user, decrypts it, and puts it into the active user memory in the KNF.

Store places an encrypted password in system memory. Operates on PW.

Generate calls the KNF random key generator which generates 56 unpredictable, random bits that are combined with eight parity bits, as required by the DES. The result is encrypted under an interchange key XORed with the appropriate identifier pair. IV generation provides a full 64 random bits before encryption. Operates on DKs and IVs.

Encrypt encrypts a DK or PW under an IK XORed with the appropriate identifier pair, and uses the ECB mode of encryption when operating on keys. "Encrypt" also refers to enciphering data in one of the approved DES modes.

Decrypt decrypts an encrypted DK or PW. "Decrypt" also refers to deciphering data in one of the approved DES modes.

Reencrypt decrypts an encrypted DK or PW and then encrypts it under a new IK XORed with the appropriate identifier pair in order to avoid the reencryption of data and the reinitialization of passwords when IKs are changed.

COMMANDS

This section describes the commands or protocols that need to be implemented in the KNF for key management and data encryption purposes. Besides encryption, decryption, and authentication, they are used to generate keys, which are given to the user, and to provide for the supersession of the keys controlled by the system. The commands are invoked by a command name followed by a parameter address list of passed and returned values. The user's identifier is shown as a parameter only when it must be supplied by the user of the command. For some commands, the system automatically supplies the KNF with the user's identifier. Interchange keys must be loaded into the KNF before commands are executed.

Initialize Password (IPW)

IPW: { pw }
pw = password

This command is used when a user is first put on the system. The password is encrypted and stored in host system memory. The original password is known to the user and the security officer. The user submits the original password when he first authenticates himself to the KNF, then he immediately changes his password to a secret value, known only to himself, by using the change password command, CPW. Only the security officer who is responsible for putting new users on the system should be capable of initializing the password.

Reencrypt Passwords (RPW)

RPW: {   }

The security officer executes this command

after the interchange keys have been changed. Each encrypted password stored in system memory is decrypted using the old facility interchange key and encrypted using the new facility interchange key. The result is then stored back in system memory. This permits a user to authenticate even though the interchange keys have been changed. After he is authenticated and active, it will be the user's responsibility to reencrypt his data keys before using them for encryption, decryption, or data authentication.

Reserve Active State (RAS)

RAS: { *ui, pw, ss, ua* }
ui = user identifier
pw = password
ss (system status) = *y* if active memory is available
= *n* otherwise
ua (user
authenticator) = O if *ss* = *n*
= *y* if *ss* = *y* and PW authenticates
= *n* if *ss* = *y* and no authentication

This command activates the user by loading the user's identifier into the KNF. Active user memory must be available and the user must authenticate before the identifier is loaded. No other commands may be executed by the user until he has successfully executed RAS. The authentication is for use of the KNF and is independent of the authentication for use of the system. Once authentication is complete, the system must ensure that other users cannot execute commands in place of an authenticated user.

Log Out Active User (LAU)

LAU: { *ui* }
ui = user identifier

This command may be used by the user when he has finished using the KNF. In this case, *ui* is optional. The command removes the user identifier from the active user list maintained in the KNF.

All active DKs and IVs belonging to the specified user are lost. The host may also keep a list of active users and the time of the last command executed for each one. If a user has not executed a command after a reasonable time period, then the host may use LAU to log out the user. The user may still be logged on the system, but he will have to repeat the RAS command to use the KNF. The system may also periodically decide to challenge a user by requiring him to reauthenticate. Whenever the user logs off the system, the LAU command should automatically be executed.

Change Password (CPW)

CPW: { *op, np* }
op = old password
np = new password

This command is used to change passwords. The old password is authenticated before any change is made. The user identifier must be loaded into active user memory, otherwise an error message is returned.

Generate Data Key (GDK)

GDK: { *in, sp, ed* }
in = interchange name
sp = identifier of sharing party
ed = returned encrypted data key

ex. (command executed by user *i*)
in = *p*
sp = *j*
ed = E[IK*p* XOR (*i* || *j*)] (DK*ij*)

This command is used to generate new keys. The identifier of the user invoking the command, user *i* in the example, is always the leftmost value in the concatenation of the sending and receiving identifiers. If the two identifiers are equal, then the key is personal and cannot be shared. This command may not be executed unless the user is active. Otherwise an error message is returned.

Encrypt Data Key (EDK)

EDK: { ui, dk, ed }
ui = user identifier
dk = data key
ed = returned encrypted data key

$ex.$
ui = i
dk = DK
ed = E[IK XOR ($i \| i$)] (DK)
IK = facility interchange key

This command is not used in the normal functioning of the system. It need only be used for communication with someone outside of the system who doesn't have the same key generation and encryption capability or for generating cipher encrypted under a particular key. Because this command violates the security criterion that no clear key be permitted outside of the KNF, it is recommended that only the security officer be allowed to execute it. It may be best not to implement this command at all.

Load Data Key (LDK)

LDK: { kf, in, sp, ed }
kf (key function) = t if key is for transmitted data
          = r if key is for received data
          = s if key is for personal use only
in = interchange name
sp = identifier of sharing party
ed = encrypted data key

$ex.$ (command executed by user i)
kf = t
in = p
sp = j
ed = E[IKp XOR ($i \| j$)] (DKij)

$ex.$ (command executed by user i)
kf = r
in = p
sp = j
ed = E[IKp XOR ($j \| i$)] (DKji)

$ex.$ = (command executed by user i)
kf = s
in = f (facility interchange identifier)
sp = i
ed = E[IKf XOR ($i \| i$)] (DKii)

This command loads a data key, either shared or personal, into the user's active state in the KNF. The key is stored at the transmit key address if kf = t, and at the receive key address if kf = r. If user i executed the command, then kf = s if and only if sp = i. Otherwise an error message will be returned. When kf = s and sp = i, the data key will be loaded into both the transmit and receive locations. The user must be active before this command can be executed.

Generate Initialization Vector (GIV)

GIV: { ei }
ei = returned encrypted initialization vector

$ex.$
ei = E[DK] (IV)

This command is used to generate new initialization vectors. The KNF key generator generates 64 bits, (56 random and 8 parity), and then encrypts them under the data key, which must be previously located at the transmit address in active user memory. The encrypted IV is returned to the user. The data key may be either personal or shared.

Load Initialization Vector (LIV)

LIV: { kf, ei }
kf = t if IV is for transmitted data
    = r if IV is for received data
    = s if IV is for personal data
ei = encrypted initialization vector

$ex.$
kf = t
ei = E[DK] (IV)

If kf = t then the data key at the transmit address is used to decrypt the encrypted IV. The IV is then stored at the transmit IV address. If $kf = r$ then the data key at the receive address is used to decrypt the encrypted IV, and the IV is stored at the receive IV address. When $kf = s$, the transmit data key is used to decrypt, and the IV is placed in both the transmit and receive IV locations.

Encrypt Initialization Vector (EIV)

EIV: $\{iv, ei\}$
iv = initialization vector
ei = returned encrypted IV

ex.
iv = IV
ei = E[DK] (IV)

This command is not necessary because one can always use the GIV command to obtain IVs. It may be used with the EDK command for communications outside of the system. Because, in the KNS, no unencrypted IVs are to be known by users, it is recommended that this command be restricted solely to the security officer or omitted completely. The IV is encrypted under the DK previously loaded at the transmit key address.

Reencrypt Data Key (RDK)

RDK: $\{kf, in, sp, ok, rk\}$
kf = t if data key is for transmitted data
r if data key is for received data
s if data key is for personal data
in = interchange name
sp = identifier of shared party
ok = old encrypted data key
rk = returned reencrypted data key

ex. (user j reencrypting a key sent to him by user i)
kf = r
in = p
sp = i
ok = E[IKp' XOR ($i \parallel j$)] (DKij)
rk = E[IKp XOR ($i \parallel j$)] (DKij)

IKp' = old interchange key
IKp = new interchange key

This command is used when interchange keys are changed. It reencrypts data keys under the new interchange key so that the data protected by the key does not have to be reencrypted. The user must be active. Also, $kf = s$ if and only if $sp = i$ and user i invoked the command.

Electronic Codebook (ECBE And ECBD)

ECBE: $\{pt, ct\}$
ECBD: $\{pt, ct\}$
pt = plain text (eight bytes)
ct = cipher text (eight bytes)

These commands are not required in the normal operation of the system. They are provided to accommodate future modes of DES encryption which, as yet, have not been considered or approved. ECBE encrypts eight bytes of plain text at pt and stores the result in ct. ECBD decrypts eight bytes of cipher at ct and stores the result at pt. Encryption uses the transmit DK, while decryption uses the receive DK. A data must be previously loaded into the appropriate active state.

Data Authentication (DAUT)

DAUT: $\{kf, da, nb, av, md\}$
kf = t if data is transmitted
= r if data is received
= s if data is personal
da = data
nb = number of bytes of data
av = returned authentication value (eight bytes)
md = CBC for CBC mode
= CFB for CFB mode

This command uses DES in the authentication mode to calculate an eight-byte authentication value on nb bytes of data at da. If $kf = t$ or s, then the data key and IV that have been previously loaded into transmit active storage will be used. If $kf = r$, the key and IV in receive key active storage will be used. The value of *md* indicates which of two DES encryption modes are desired.

Cipher Block Chaining (CBCE And CBCD)

CBCE: { *pt, ct, nb* }
CBCD: { *pt, ct, nb*}
pt = plain text
ct = cipher text
nb = number of bytes

For encryption, CBCE, *nb* bytes of data starting at *pt* are encrypted in the CBC mode, and the cipher is returned starting at *ct*. For decryption, *nb* bytes of data at *ct* are decrypted and returned to *pt*. If *nb* is not a multiple of eight, then the CBC mode is used until $b<8$ bytes remain. The final *b* bytes are encrypted by exclusive ORing them with the first *b* bytes of the next DES output block. DK and IV must be in the active user memory, otherwise an error message is returned. Encryption uses the transmit IV and DK, while decryption uses the receive IV and DK.

Cipher Feedback (CFBE And CFBD)

CFBE: { *pt, ct, nb*}
CFBD: { *pt, ct, nb*}
pt = plain text
ct = cipher text
nb = number of bytes

As described for the CBC commands, *nb* bytes are either encrypted or decrypted. Encryption uses the transmit IV and DK while decryption uses the receive values. If the required IV and DK values have not been loaded an error message will be returned.

DIGITAL SIGNATURES

Recall that digital signatures are possible with public key algorithms because one cannot decrypt another person's data even though anyone with the public key can encrypt data intended for that person. This is because the decrypt key is not shared. Because the KNF combines identifiers with inter-change keys for protection against substitution and employs separate encryption and decryption key storage, one cannot encrypt data in a key that was generated by another user. Therefore, signatures are possible. Suppose user *i* generates a key using the GDK command and sends it to user *j*. The encrypted data key would be of the form:

$$ED = E[IKp \text{ XOR } (i \parallel j)] \text{ (DK}ij)$$

where IKp is the interchange key for interchange p and DKij indicates a data key generated by *i* for transmission to *j*. Whenever *i* generates a key, his identifier is always leftmost in the identifier pair used in the encryption of the key. The only way user *j* can load DKij is by loading it as a receive key. Separate transmit and receive key registers are required. If *j* tries to load DKij as a transmission key for the encryption of data going to *i*, the cryptomodule will use $(j \parallel i)$ instead of $(i \parallel j)$ when decrypting ED. If *j* tries to load the key as a personal key, the $(j \parallel j)$ will be used. (See the LDK command.) When DKij is loaded as a receive key, only the decryption commands have access to it.

For example, suppose user *i* generates ED as before. He may then use the EIV command to generate an encrypted IV of the form:

$$EI = E[DKij] \text{ (IV)}$$

Next, he may encrypt a signature, S, under DKij and send ED, EI, and S to *j*. User *j* may load IV and DKij in the active receive state by the LIV and LDK commands, and decrypt the encrypted signature to recover S. There is no way that *j* can alter S to a particular S′and encrypt it under DKif because there is no way for *j* to get DKij, into the transmit data key active storage.

If user *j* generates his own encrypted data key, it will be of the form:

$$E[IKp \text{ XOR } (j \parallel i)] \text{ (DK}ji)$$

He may encrypt a signature S′under DKji but he cannot claim that it came from *i* because he could be challenged to decrypt the encrypted signature.

To do so j would have to load DKji by submitting E[IKp XOR $(j \| i)$] (DKji) to the LDK command with $kf = r$. The cryptomodule would not load the correct DKji because it would use $(i \| j)$ instead of $(j \| i)$ as the identifier pair. Thus, the signature would be garbled. Of course, user j may send a signature S to user i encrypted under the data key, DKji, in a similar manner as described above (Fig. 17-4).

Any message may be regarded as a signature. No additional keys or commands are required. All user j needs to do is keep E[IKp XOR $(i \| j)$] (DKij), E[DKij] (IV), and the encrypted signature in order to be able to prove that S was sent to him from i. User j may also wish to keep S as well.

The Authentication Value as a Signature

The signature, S, may be an entire plain text message, but it may be undesirable to store the cipher text of long messages. In such cases, one may use the DAUT command to calculate an authentication value that is a cryptographic function of every bit of data. This value could then be used as the signature. Signatures should be large enough to provide adequate security; at least 64 bits are recommended. S must be encrypted as in the previous example. Otherwise, the receiver could modify the message and calculate the correct signature for the new message using the DAUT command with the correct key in the receive active memory. This is because, unlike encryption and decryption, the DAUT command with $kf = t$ gives the same output as when $kf = r$ as long as the same key is used in both transmit and receive active memory.

If one is not concerned with proving that the receiver did not modify the incoming message, then the authentication value need not be encrypted. Suppose that it is only necessary that the receiver knows the correct transmitter of the message and that it has not been altered. The transmitter, user i, may generate E[IKp XOR $(i \| j)$] (DKij) and E[DKij)] (IV), and load DKij and IV into transmit active ;memory. He may then use the DAUT command with $kf = t$ to generate an authentication value, AV. User i may then send the following to j:

clear message, E[IKp XOR $(i \| j)$] (DKij), E[DKij] (IV), AV.

User j may authenticate the message by loading DKij and IV into active receive state and then using DAUT with $kf = r$ to calculate AV. If it matches, then the message must have come from i. If user k sent the message, the encrypted data key would have the form:

E[IKp XOR $(k \| j)$] (DKkj)

and the authentication value would be AV'. If j thought that it was from i, then when he executes LDK, $(i \| j)$ instead of $(k \| j)$ would be used to decrypt the data key. Therefore, the wrong data key would be loaded.

Nonpublic Key versus Public Key Signatures

A digital signature capability may be implemented in the KNS because the receiver of an encrypted data key can only load the key into his receive active memory and can, therefore, only decrypt with it. We have assumed that the KNF of each host is physically secured from all users and that shared keys are securely distributed. One must

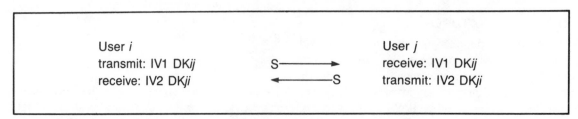

Fig. 17-4. Separate transmit and receive key storage.

guard against both disclosure and substitution of keys. If one could gain knowledge of the shared key, he could forge all signatures sent between both facilities. Of course, all keys encrypted under the shared key would also be compromised. Thus, the common key must be secured at the transmit and receive KNFs. With public key algorithms, the secret key requires protection against disclosure and substitution, while the public key must be protected from substitution. If a bogus key is substituted for the transmitter's public key, then false signatures can be sent to the receiver.

INITIALIZATION

Suppose cryptography were to be added to a computer network. First, each host would have to be provided with a KNF and the necessary interface. Then interchange keys would have to be generated and distributed. Once the interchange keys are loaded directly into the cryptofacilities and the authorized users are assigned unique identifiers and passwords, the security officer at each facility can initialize the passwords of the authorized users by using the IPW command.

The Transmitter

A user may then authenticate and become active by using the RAS command. He could change his password to a secret value known only to himself by the CPW command. Next he may want to generate data keys using GDK. Suppose he is on host 1, then GDK: $\{1, j, ed\}$ generates a personal data key and GDK: $\{1, j, ed\}$ generates a shared data key for use with user j at host 1. GDK: $\{5, k, ed\}$ generates a shared data key for use with user k over interchange 5. Interchange 5 may be the interchange between host 1 and host 5.

When he has an encrypted data key, say E[IKp XOR $(i \| j)$] (DKij), user i can load the key using LDK. LDK with $kf = t, in = p, sp = j$, and $ed = $ E[IKp XOR $(i \| j)$] (DKij) loads DKij into the transmit active key storage. The user must keep track of the fact that $kf = t$ and $in = p$ from the time the key is generated to when the key is loaded. If the key is stored for future use, then the values

of kf and in required by the LDK command should also be stored. User i may then generate an IV using GIV and load the IV into the transmit active IV storage.

After he sends the encrypted DKij and IV to j, he is ready to encrypt data intended for user j. Of course, if he is on line with user j, he must establish contact with j, identify himself, and send him the encrypted DKij and IV. If he is on line, he should require an appropriate response from j to ensure that he is being received. User i may encrypt in either the CBC or CFB modes. He should include a message number, the date, and the time in his plain text so that old valid messages from i to j cannot be played back to j. He may also use DAUT to calculate a digital signature, which is encrypted before transmission.

User i may use his personal encrypted key, E[IK1]XOR$(i \| i)$] (DKii) to encrypt a personal file and then store the encrypted key with the cipher or in a personal key file. Finally, he can log out of active status using the LAU command. If not, the system should automatically log him out after a specified time period or when he logs off the system, whichever comes first.

The Receiver

Once user j is active, and has received the encrypted DKij, IV, and data, he may use LDK and LIV to load the receive active storage. He can then decrypt and check the signature to ensure that it is correct. Note that the same data key may be used for both encryption and digital signatures. If j wishes, he can generate a DKji to communicate securely to i, but communications from j to i will not be encrypted with the same data key as communications from i to j.

Key Supersession

Interchange keys are generated in an unpredictable manner in a highly protected environment outside of the network. At key-change time, the current IKs are stored as old IKs and new IKs are entered as current IKs. The security officer uses RPW to reencrypt each user's encrypted password. The system tells each user when he becomes active to use the RDK command to reencrypt his data keys. When keys are changed, the old keys no longer stored in the KNF should be securely stored along with their effective dates. These keys may be needed to decrypt old files or to validate old signatures whose data keys were not reencrypted.

The Key Notarization System can provide secure authentication and encryption with limited protocol requirements in a variety of network configurations. Host operating systems must protect plain text and maintain user identity once authentication is complete, but the host need not protect keys from either disclosure or substitution. A set of KNF commands is defined for key management functions as well as for the approved DES modes of operation. The secure distribution of data keys is attained by encryption and the use of identifiers for key notarization. The system features on-line and off-line applications, local key generation, and a digital signature capability.

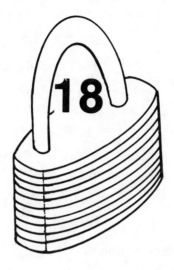

Security Auditing Guidelines

The guidelines in this chapter were published by the National Bureau of Standards to guide computer security audits—a formal process of evaluating the adequacy and effectiveness of a security program.

As you'll see, though, the standards that would guide an auditor also are much the same standards that should be used in planning and designing a security program.

This and succeeding chapters are based on the work of several study panels who compiled their reports for the National Bureau of Standards. They are taken from NBS publications 500-19 and 500-57, both titled *Audit and Evaluation of Computer Security*.

Computer security is generally considered a function of the environment in which the system operates. A dedicated system operating in a batch mode within a benign environment has altogether different security requirements from a shared automatic resource balancing computer network.

This session will address the various system en-vironments and identify the major aspects of each that the auditor must consider in conducting an evaluation of computer security. The consensus report that follows was developed, written, and reviewed by the entire membership of this session.

DEFINITIONS

The principal terms relating to computer systems security used in this report are defined as follows:

Environment means the physical facilities, systems architecture, and administrative functions which constitute an ADP system to be audited.

Security Audit is an assessment of the system of controls that ensure the continuity and integrity of the environment as defined by management. An assessment of the reasonableness of these controls is achieved by examining and evaluating controls over system access, accuracy, and availability.

System Access is the ability and the means

241

necessary to acquire, store or retrieve data; to communicate with or make use of any resource of an ADP system.

System accuracy is the state that exists when there is complete assurance that under all postulated conditions an ADP system implies (i) total logical correctness and reliability of the system, and (ii) logical correctness and completeness of the hardware and software necessary to implement protection mechanisms and to assure data integrity.

System Availability is the level or quality of service, as defined by the users, required to perform their primary functions.

AUDIT VERSUS DESIGN

The process of performing a security audit is closely related to the security determination study performed during the initial development stages of a system which is to be secured. This conclusion was reached as we attempted to develop a methodology based on an enumeration of all considerations applying to the audit of computer security in various system environments. We determined that specific computer-related, physical and administrative environmental descriptors required close examination. They are all interrelated and not readily separated. Our end result was the enumeration of those steps to be taken first by the design team and then with slight variations by the auditors.

This result should not prove too surprising if one examines the composition of an effective design team. To build cost-justifiable, comprehensive, and effective security into a system, at least one member of that team should have the auditor's viewpoint or be, in fact, a qualified auditor. Thus we see a two-pronged role to be played by the audit profession. First, the auditor must be an advisor to the design team providing essential inputs to the molding of the system; second, during the later, operational phase of the system the auditor must perform the traditional EDP auditor functions and reassess the effectiveness of the computer system security design.

We list below the steps necessary to arrive at an assessment of system security effectiveness, first for the design team and then for the audit team.

Steps a Design Team Must Take

Step (1) Define overall system requirements, objectives, and sensitivity.

Step (2) Specify the desired environment, based on results of Step (1).

☐ Specification of *physical parameters* such as:
—Location of system.
—Construction of "container" (building).
—Survivability of system under disastrous conditions such as flood, fire, bombing, etc.

☐ Specification of *system parameters* such as:
—Degree of information sharing (will there be one or multiple users).
—Batch or interactive processing.
—Centralized or distributed data bases, processes.
—Local or remote access.
—Application mix.

☐ Specification of *physical parameters* such as:
—Threat analysis.
—Personnel procedures.
—Organizational structure:
—Security requirements for:
(a) Access Control
(b) Accuracy
(c) Availability
—Insurance.
—System development procedures.

Step (3) Specify control techniques that can be used to enforce the environment in Step (2).

At this point, it may be helpful to point out the differences between security objectives, policy, and procedures. The objectives of the imposed controls in an operational environment are regulation of access, accuracy, and availability. The translation of the objective of access control into policy may take the form of personal accountability for all sensitive transactions. The translation of this policy into a procedure may take the form of logging into the system by way of a password, or manual logging into or out of a secure area.

Step (4) Perform a line-by-line cost/protection

analysis. This is by far the most crucial step in building a set of controls to protect the system within its environment. In this step we analyze each control line item specified in step 3 which could be employed to protect some aspect(s) of the system. The detailed cost/protection matrix will have hundreds or thousands of like items, dependent on the complexity of the system.

For each control requirement four judgments are made:

(a) Cost of implementation, development and operation of control.
(b) Effectiveness in regard to maintaining access control.
(c) Effectiveness in regard to maintaining accuracy.
(d) Effectiveness in regard to maintaining system availability.

The effectiveness judgments for (b), (c), and (d) are finally translated into (subjective) numeric values on a scale from 0 to 10, (0-noneffective, 10-supereffective). This conforms to the current state-of-the-art. However, a very desirable goal would be to devise instead an objective scale of measures of effectiveness.

The purposes of convenience, the designer may use a shorthand method or rating:

RATING = AC/A/AV

   where

   AC = numeric value assigned to effectiveness level of Access Control
   A = numeric value assigned to effectiveness level of Accuracy
   AV = numeric value assigned to effectiveness level of Availability

These ratings become part of the system documentation and are used in Step (5) and by auditors.

Step (5) Perform composite evaluation. After performing the line-by-line analysis described in Step (4), a specific subset of these controls is selected as the basis for the comprehensive set of safeguards. Management must concur that this subset provides the necessary depth, breadth and overlap of protection most cost-effectively for all aspects of the environment—physical, systems, and administrative. In other words, this is the stage at which the "risk assessment" is made and a "security" system is designed to meet the security objectives defined earlier.

Step (6) Incorporate the approved security controls. Reaccess this new Total environment in light of the additional features inserted into the three environmental (physical, system, and administrative) parameters. If these additions do not degrade the overall system effectiveness (meeting requirements and objectives, set down in Step (1)), the designers are ready to begin implementation. However, if after analyzing the total new system, it is found that the objectives are no longer effectively attainable, an iterative process must be initiated and the designers go back to Step (2), remolding the specifications of environment, etc., until all requirements set out in Step (1) are effectively satisfied.

Steps the Operational Auditor Must Take

Once the system has been designed and implemented, it can go into operation. The auditor is now called upon to assess effectiveness of security controls in an operational mode. As mentioned earlier, the steps of the initial design team and those of the operational auditor are very similar. In some steps, only the verb need be changed. For example, in Step (1) the designer defines systems requirements while the auditor reviews the stated requirements as set down by management.

Step (1) Review objectives, requirements, and sensitivity as documented by management for the system under audit.

Step (2) Determine the nature of the environment prevailing during actual system operation, independent of the organizational descriptions. The auditor's perceptions of the physical, systems, and administrative setup may be quite different from those that were specified during the design stage.

Step (3) Identify Techniques used to control the environment as perceived by the auditor in Step (2). Here we see a clear divergence from the design approach. Where the designer may have identified a large number of potential controls, the auditor is confined to examining only that subset of controls which are actually implemented. The auditor makes an independent examination and may, or may not, use systems documentation as a starting point for his/her identification of the system's security components.

Step (4) Perform line-by-line cost/protection analysis. As in Step (3), the auditor is not concerned with all possible safeguards, but only with those implemented and properly functioning within the system, as determined by his audit. While the designer may have given values to the components of the AC/A/AV ratings on an intuitive, nonobjective basis, the auditor will augment these judgmental determinations through hardware, software, and other sophisticated (where available) techniques to test the effectiveness of each component of the rating for meeting the stated security objectives.

Step (5) Perform a composite evaluation. The auditor now assesses the total effectiveness of the security system to determine whether it meets the objectives set by management. A comparison can thus be made of the designer's rating and that found by the auditor. Since the measures used by designer and auditor are perhaps different, this will be only a qualitative, albeit incisive, comparison.

Step (6) Prepare report of audit findings including recommendations for upgrading security where weaknesses are found,e.g., where the rating of the designer exceeds that determined through audit. It is also incumbent upon the auditor to recommend changes in overall security control requirements if the environment has changed from that assumed during the initial design or since an earlier audit.

ENVIRONMENT AND CONTROL

The key element of any systematic audit approach is a close link between the design and the audit processes while maintaining a separation of duties between designer and auditor. Care must be taken to insure that the same factors which influenced the design process are well understood and given appropriate consideration in the audit process. Two major factors must be considered. The first is the environment in which the system is to operate, and the second is the control techniques to be employed to enforce that environment. It is essential that the design process defines the environment in which the system is to operate and that the audit uses that same environmental description as a guide. If the operational environment has changed from that postulated at design time in a manner impacting security aspects of the system, this impact must be analyzed and the security control requirements must be reassessed as a part of the audit process in a similar fashion to the procedure initially used by the design team.

The approach being advocated here employs two rather sophisticated checklists and supporting material. The first checklist is used to establish, in considerable detail, the einvironment in which a system is to operate. In the case of a new system design, this is the list of desired system characteristics. In the case of an existing system under evaluation, this is the list of already existing system characteristics. We note that the process described in the previous chapter will work with either new systems being designed or existing systems being enhanced or merely being audited. In the audit process, the statement of environment is given. The auditor is encouraged to point out obvious inconsistencies in the environment, if he observes any, but the environmental checklist is his reference point from which he evaluates whether the control techniques specified by the designer are sufficient to enforce the given environment.

The second checklist is a description of the generic classes of control techniques which the designer may employ to enforce the environment in which his system must operate. As will be seen later, these range from physical locks and fences, through internal hardware and software access control checks, to administrative procedures. During the design process, after the system environment is established, the designer selects those measures from the control techniques checklist which he wishes to utilize to protect his system.

Each of the entries in the control techniques checklist represents a segment of a continuum. Each item contains a range of measures with two related variables: the degree of protection afforded and the cost. At the low range, little protection is achieved and usually cost is minimal; at the high range, a great deal of protection is achieved and the cost may be proportionately high. In the example of physical locks on doors, the range might be from a simple padlock through a sophisticated electronically controlled and centrally monitored door locking system, with proportionate cost ranges. Given the sensitivity of the information contained in the system (from the environment statement) the designer must select those control techniques he wishes to employ and the appropriate position on the protection/cost scale for each chosen technique to provide in the composite the necessary measure of security control.

From a security viewpoint, there are three basic criteria in determining the environment and in evaluating the suitability of control techniques to enforce that environment: access control, accuracy, and availability. Each of these factors must be addressed in the environmental assessment, and each of the control techniques being applied must be rated against all three factors.

Some control techniques will not apply to certain of these measures. For example, locks do not affect the accuracy of the information but they have a significant effect on access control and on availability of the system. In the environmental statement, the degree of protection needed in each of these areas must be stated and in the overall evaluation of the control techniques, a rating by the designer and the auditor of each of these measures must be calculated and compared against the environmental requirements.

Many of the entries in the control techniques checklist are complementary. If one measure is taken, another measure is perhaps not required. Investment made in one control technique will determine the extent of the investment needed in a complementary technique. The relationship between entries in the control techniques checklist is complex. To insure that sufficient measures have been taken to completely but not overly enforce the environment, the interactive relationship of controls within various environments must be explained in a guidelines book which should accompany the checklist (see section 5). The guidelines book will describe relative levels of effectiveness and cost of the various control techniques and will provide relative assessments of feasible tradeoffs.

The designer establishes both the environment in which the system is to operate and the appropriate control techniques. The process employed by the auditor in determining if sufficient control techniques have been applied is quite similar. The designer scans the control techniques checklist line-by-line, selecting appropriate items to be employed. Then he evaluates the achieved overall security of the system with an overall performance analysis determined by logically aggregating the selected effectiveness measures assigned to the line-by-line entries. If this overall analysis does not provide sufficient protection, or if it exceeds the constraining cost factors, then he reevaluates the control techniques or perhaps the environment itself, making such changes as necessary to achieve the security needed at a suitable cost.

The auditor, given the environment checklist, determines first that the actual operational environment is that assumed during the design stage. He then determines the control techniques which he believes appropriate to achieve this environment. He compares his control techniques checklist with that of the designer and weighs the differences so as to have a reference against which to perform his detailed analysis. He performs a line-by-line evaluation of the entries in the checklist and then an overall analysis similar to that done by the designer. Having completed the overall analysis he may go back and adjust his assessment of the individual control techniques based on a more complete understanding of the total system. The result of this audit process is an overall rating of how close the design comes to enforcing the security requirements of the operational environment. If this audit process produces a rating of sufficient protection then the system can be approved for use. If it yields an insufficient rating, then the designer must go back once again to the control techniques list or to the environmental checklist and make appropriate changes to insure the necessary security of the system.

The critical element in this process is the use of the same checklist information by both the designer and the auditor. This insures a common base from which to discuss related matters. It is this common starting point that is the crucial element of our methodology. The selection of elements from the control technique checklist and the degree of protection afforded to each element are often subjective, and the designer may wish to take issue with the auditor over specific ratings the auditor has given for some of these measures. The crucial point is that all elements of the design are understood by both the designer and the auditor in a common context. This complete and common listing of measures used by both the designer and auditor is an element that has been lacking in previous audits.

Checklists

Both the environmental and control techniques checklists are divided into three sub-categories: physical, system, and administrative. In the environmental checklist under the physical heading are those elements of the physical environment which materially affect security of the system. Included is the geographic location of the system, taking into account the susceptibility to natural and man-made disasters such as floods and crime, any special power or air-conditioning requirements, etc.

In the system environment list are those measures that describe the internal structuring of the system. In particular we find here those elements which affect the requirement to rely on internal hardware/software measures to enforce the security of the system. Under administrative measures are included such factors as the sensitivity and correctness of the information contained in the system, postulated threats to the system, etc.

The system environment comprises five physical and logical components or main categories:

1. Degree of Sharing: single versus multiple user(s).
2. Type of Service: batch versus interactive.
3. Organization: centralized versus distributed.
4. User Access: local versus remote.
5. Application: dedicated versus multipurpose.

The control techniques checklist is comprised of the same three categories: physical, system, and administrative. The physical controls include the traditional "put the system in a vault" measures, including perimeter control, hazard protection, and backup mechanisms. Systems controls include hardware/software access control techniques, program integrity measures, audit trail techniques, and failures response procedures. Administrative control techniques include what are commonly referred to as change control procedures. Each of the control techniques must be evaluated against each of the access control, accuracy, and availability factors and an overall score must be arrived at for each of those factors.

Guideline Book

A critical element that in the methodology described here is the background material that supports the checklist. This guideline will be composed of two sections. The first has a line-by-line description of the elements of the environmental and the control techniques checklists; in the latter case, the range of protection cost of each of the entries is given. The environmental checklist must be cross-referenced against the control techniques checklist to insure that if a particular element of the environment is specified, some range of control techniques can be applied.

Another element of the guideline book must deal with the interrelationship among control techniques. From it, both the designer and the auditor must be able to determine that if a certain control technique is employed, this may very well negate the need for another control technique. An obvious example is that if sufficient physical control measures are taken and if all personnel associated with the system have equal access to the information on the system, then reliance on internal software access control techniques may be significantly relaxed. This evaluation guideline is highly sensitive to the state of technology and will need to be updated frequently. Specifically, the relationship between cost and effectiveness of a particular form of protection will need to be revised frequently, and new techniques will have to be introduced as they are developed and become viable.

This overall methodology is a systematic approach to the problem of auditing a computer security installation. The approach is systematic since the designer and the auditor as well work from a complete list of both the environment in which the system is to operate and the control techniques which are to be employed to enforce that environment. By working from common lists, the designer and the auditor can more readily communicate differences in their evaluation and reconcile their evaluations.

A number of such checklists are already in existence; they can be used to form the basis of the environment and control techniques checklists. The establishment of a complete and accurate guidebook giving both the line-by-line descriptions and the element interrelationships is a crucial element of this overall methodology yet to be accomplished. For example, see *Data Processing Security Evaluation Guidelines* (Peat, Marwick, and Mitchell & Co., Certified Public Accountants; 345 Park Avenue, New York NY 10022).

GUIDELINES

In two previous sections we discussed audit methodology and the sequence of steps which an auditor will follow, preparatory to executing his audit function addressed here. Therefore, the purpose of this section is to discuss those considerations which comprise the "ideal" against which the auditor compares and measures data security in various system environments.

The "ideals" are derived from several sources,

including (1) information and experience which the auditor brings to his task, and (2) information and observations gathered by the auditor in his effort to understand more fully the system to be audited.

In this section we will not attempt to create an actual book on audit guidelines; several such reference materials exist already. However, we have attempted to identify significant *categories* of control techniques, as well as (in selected instances) some more specific security measures. While the various options within the control technique categories can be expanded upon by utilizing materials contained in reference works (and from the auditor's own knowledge and experience) we have chosen categories of control techniques which reflect major security options (in a general sense) that also provide an opportunity for analysis of the differences among selected system environment examples.

Our discussion indicated clearly that there are, theoretically speaking, many possible system environments, resulting from a combination of physical, administrative, and systems design points of view. In order to respond to the mandate given this group, we chose four sample systems which differed significantly from one another, representing four of the most prevalent kinds of systems existent in today's computer processing environment.

The description of the environment for each of the four sample systems is given in the [section titled "Four Examples" at the end of this chapter]. The method by which the constituent elements of an environment were ascertained, was discussed in the section on environment and control. The kinds of control techniques we have assigned as possible protective measures with respect to the four sample systems were briefly explained in that same section. However, our group took the further step of assigning subjective numerical scale values (ranging from a low of 0 to a high of 10) to the three categories of control techniques. Our choice for these values was derived from the group's consensus of whether such control techniques would be important with respect to the sample system. This importance factor was considered for each of the three basic categories of protection which our definition of "security audit" gave their AAA (AC/A/AV) rating: (1) access control, (2) accuracy, and (3) availability.

It is clear that there are certain general audit considerations which an auditor will utilize in determining the vulnerability of a given system. These are the experience items which the auditor must bring with him, to successfully complete the assigned task.

In the section "Four Examples," therefore, we considered only some specific aspects of the four sample system. We highlighted those that affect security considerations in a way that distinguished one system from another. Obviously, in a complete audit of security, one would exect an auditor to perform a much more comprehensive analysis. But we assumed that the purpose of the mandate given to our group was to focus upon specific problem areas in different system environments to which an auditor should pay particular attention. The more general case, as the proverbial textbooks explain, will be left as an exercise for the reader.

CONCLUSIONS

William C. Mair, co-author of *Computer Control and Audit,* recently observed, "DP auditors are not and cannot be policeman." He stated that the primary responsibility of the DP auditor is to act as an advisor to management, to emphasize the need for standards, which must be properly documented and communicated. Standards serve as the foundation on which everything else is built; they provide direction, predictability, and criteria for evaluation. Through these standards, the auditors establish systems controls which in turn help reduce adverse effects encountered in a basically hostile environment. In fact, the auditor is part of these controls.

Areas of vulnerability must be exposed to reduce risks to acceptable levels. The dangers confronting EDP systems include, above all, erroneous management decisions, but also embezzlement and fraud, loss or destruction of assets, excessive costs, and deficient revenues. Their impact can be severe, leading to competitive disadvantage, statutory sanc-

tions, even to economic, political, and military disasters.

We must not ever underestimate the power, ingenuity and perserverance of the "enemy". As we relate development of controls to potential exposures, we must follow a rather simple-minded approach: If we can think of it, someone else also can. Thus the auditor must be ingenious about gathering basic and detailed information, about evaluating the system's strengths and weaknesses, and about testing its design and performance. He must review all of its components individually and collectively according to a structural model specifically designed for that purpose.

A definitive, open-ended model has been developed to structure both initial internal design and the follow-up (external) computer security audits in various system environments. The model is predicated on the notice that for a system to be viable within a well-defined (and definable) environment, we must certainly maintain control over access to the system, must provide accurate services, and must assure the timely availability of these services to the users.

In making the audit, we assume the availability of standard guidelines for rating all identifiable system line items with regard to their contribution to access control, accuracy, and availability. A global measure of security audit can thus be derived from the line items' individual, local ratings. A number of algorithms have been suggested for converting the aggregate "local" into "global" ratings, but it appears as if only absolute and total compliance with the design specification ratings will be acceptable in the security environment.

In summary, we find that people are the critical element in all computer security audits. To attain perfect security, therefore, we are left with an obvious choice: Either we abolish computers or we abolish people.

FOUR EXAMPLES

To determine the effectiveness of the proposed methodology, four representative types of systems covering various facets of the system environment were partially analyzed. The results of the analyses are discussed here. See Tables 18-1 through 18-4.

System Selection

The four system types selected reflect at least one example of each category in the wide spectrum of possible system environments:

1. College computing center
2. Airlines reservation system
3. Electronic funds transfer system
4. Welfare check disbursement system

The objectives/requirements of each system were discussed and pertinent constraints and assumptions were indicated. As the analysis proceeded, further assumptions about the system objectives or constraints were required for clarification. For example, it was assumed that the college computing center was used strictly for training purposes and for nonsensitive research. No sensitive information (e.g., grades, payroll, etc.) and no critical applications (e.g., class scheduling) would be placed on the system.

Similarly, it was assumed that the airlines reservations systems had extremely high availability requirements but could tolerate errors to some "reasonable" extent. The electronic funds transfer system was assumed to be a network of individual processors located in separate financial institutions, retail outlets, etc. linked via cryptographically protected lines to provide for the transfer of funds between sites as one of their functions. The welfare check disbursement system was considered typical of large single-function dedicated funds disbursement systems much like a dedicated system to prepare corporate payrolls. It was assumed that inputs arrived on magnetic tape and one run per month was made to prepare the checks.

Determination of Environment

Physical. Two factors were selected as typical of physical environmental concerns which must be covered by the audit: location and survivability requirements of the system.

Systems. The systems environment was the main focus of this workshop. The five systems aspects to be considered are:

☐ Degree of sharing (single or multiple user)
☐ Type of service (batch or interactive)
☐ System organization (centralized or distributed)
☐ User access (local or remote)
☐ Applications mix (single-dedicated or multiple)

As indicated above, the four chosen systems together call upon each system environment aspect at least once.

Administrative. Two representative areas of administrative environmental factors were considered here: the sensitivity of the system and the postulated threats to the system.

After we selected the factors for analysis, the workshop members collectively discussed them and determined the corresponding implications for each of the four systems. Obviously, in an actual audit, many more environmental factors need be considered. Typically, appropriate elements will be selected for consideration from an exhaustive enumeration of security related factors.

Identification of Control Techniques

After the sample environmental factors had been established for each system, a representative sample of control techniques was developed by group consensus. Again, this work would typically be done with the help of an exhaustive list. Several techniques for each category (physical, systems, and administrative) were selected for evaluation.

Physical.
☐ Perimeter controls—this would be a composite (in this example) based on both people and "things". Various layers of perimeter controls would be considered (site, building, room, wall thickness, doors, locks, enclosure, etc.) and various aspects (ducting, filter, fire protections, air conditioning, TV monitors, guard forces, etc.)

Table 18-1. Example 1: General-Purpose Multiuser Programming System.

	ENVIRONMENT	CONTROLS	RATINGS *
PHYSICAL	LOCATION: College Campus SURVIVABILITY: Low	PERIMETER CONTROLS BACKUP SITES DISPOSAL CONTROLS COMMUNICATIONS PROTECTION	2 / – / 2 – / 0 / 0 0 / – / – 0 / – / 0
SYSTEMS	DEGREE OF SHARING: Multiuser TYPE OF SERVICE: Interactive SYSTEM ORGANIZATION: Centralized USER ACCESS: Remote APPLICATIONS MIX: Multiple	INTERNAL ACCESS CONTROLS PROGRAM INTEGRITY MEASURES ERROR DETECTION/CORRECTION AUDIT TRAILS FAILURE RESPONSE COMMUNICATIONS PROTECTION	2 / – / – – / 0 / – – / 0 / – 0 / 0 / – – / 4 / 4 0 / – / 0
ADMINISTRATIVE	TYPE: Non-sensitive THREATS: Denial of Service Theft of Service Spoofing Local	PERIMETER ACCESS PROCEDURES MAINTENANCE ACCESS PROCEDURES BACKUP PROCEDURES PERSONNEL PROCEDURES DEVELOPMENT PROCEDURES	2 / – / 2 2 / 2 / 4 – / – / 0 1 / 1 / 1 2 / 2 / 4

* Note: ACCESS CONTROL / ACCURACY / AVAILABILITY

Table 18-2. Example 2: Dedicated Data Base Management System.

	ENVIRONMENT	CONTROLS	RATINGS *
PHYSICAL	LOCATION: Multiple SURVIVABILITY: High SPECIAL: Dial-In Access	PERIMETER CONTROLS BACKUP SITES DISPOSAL CONTROLS COMMUNICATIONS PROTECTION	5 / – / 5 – / 3 / 7 4 / – / – 0 / – / 6
SYSTEMS	DEGREE OF SHARING: Multiuser TYPE OF SERVICE: Interactive SYSTEM ORGANIZATION: Distributed USER ACCESS: Remote APPLICATIONS MIX: Dedicated	INTERNAL ACCESS CONTROLS PROGRAM INTEGRITY MEASURES ERROR DETECTION/CORRECTION AUDIT TRAILS FAILURE RESPONSE COMMUNICATIONS PROTECTION	7 / – / 4 – / 7 / – – / 5 / – 1 / 6 / – – / 4 / 8 0 / – / 0
ADMINISTRATIVE	TYPE: Sensitive THREATS: Denial of Service Unauthorized Disclosure of Data Remote	PERIMETER ACCESS PROCEDURES MAINTENANCE ACCESS PROCEDURES BACKUP PROCEDURES PERSONNEL PROCEDURES DEVELOPMENT PROCEDURES	4 / – / 4 6 / 6 / 8 – / – / 8 2 / 8 / 5 4 / 7 / 9

* Note: ACCESS CONTROL / ACCURACY / AVAILABILITY

Table 18-3. Example 3: Distributed Multiuser Remote Access.

		ENVIRONMENT	CONTROLS	RATINGS *
P H Y S	I C A L	LOCATION: Multiple SURVIVABILITY: High SPECIAL: Encrypted Communication	PERIMETER CONTROLS BACKUP SITES DISPOSAL CONTROLS COMMUNICATIONS PROTECTION	6 / – / 7 6 / 3 / 6 5 / – / – 9 / – / 7
S Y S T	E M S	DEGREE OF SHARING: Multiuser TYPE OF SERVICE: Interactive SYSTEM ORGANIZATION: Distributed USER ACCESS: Remote APPLICATIONS MIX: Multiple	INTERNAL ACCESS CONTROLS PROGRAM INTEGRITY MEASURES ERROR DETECTION/CORRECTION AUDIT TRAILS FAILURE RESPONSE COMMUNICATIONS PROTECTION	9 / – / 5 – / 8 / – – / 8 / – 8 / 8 / – 8 / 8 / 4 8 / – / 3

A
D
M
I
N
I
S
	T
	R
	A
	T
	I
	V
	E
		TYPE: Highly Sensitive
		THREATS: Misuse
		      Denial of Service
		      Remote
			PERIMETER ACCESS PROCEDURES
			MAINTENANCE ACCESS PROCEDURES
			BACKUP PROCEDURES
			PERSONNEL PROCEDURES
			DEVELOPMENT PROCEDURES
				8 / – / 8
				8 / 8 / 6
				6 / 3 / 7
				8 / 9 / 7
				8 / 9 / 7

			* Note: ACCESS CONTROL / ACCURACY / AVAILABILITY	

Table 18-4. Example 4: Dedicated Batch Dollar Disbursement System.

		ENVIRONMENT	CONTROLS	RATINGS *
P H Y S	I C A L	LOCATION: Single Site SURVIVABILITY: Medium	PERIMETER CONTROLS BACKUP SITES DISPOSAL CONTROLS COMMUNICATIONS PROTECTION	4 / – / 4 – / – / 5 5 / – / – 0 / – / 0
S Y S T	E M S	DEGREE OF SHARING: Single User TYPE OF SERVICE: Batch SYSTEM ORGANIZATION: Centralized USER ACCESS: Local APPLICATIONS MIX: Single	INTERNAL ACCESS CONTROLS PROGRAM INTEGRITY MEASURES ERROR DETECTION/CORRECTION AUDIT TRAILS FAILURE RESPONSE COMMUNICATIONS PROTECTION	0 / – / – – / 5 / – – / 8 / – 0 / 8 / – – / 0 / 0 0 / – / 0
A D M I N I S	T R A T I V E	TYPE: Sensitive THREATS: Misuse Local	PERIMETER ACCESS PROCEDURES MAINTENANCE ACCESS PROCEDURES BACKUP PROCEDURES PERSONNEL PROCEDURES DEVELOPMENT PROCEDURES	4 / – / 4 3 / 5 / 3 – / – / 5 3 / 6 / 3 3 / 8 / 3
			* Note: ACCESS CONTROL / ACCURACY / AVAILABILITY	

□ Backup site-locations, security, availability, etc.

□ Disposal controls—control of output, shredding, etc.

□ Communications protection—link-by-link encryption, shielded conduits, etc.

Systems.

□ Internal access controls—hardware/software controls for identification/authentication, access authorization, enforcement methods, etc.

□ Program integrity measures—controls on self-checking, correctness, reliability, etc.

□ Error detection/correction—cyclic redundancy checks, redundancy, monitors, self-testing, etc.

□ Audit trails.

□ Failure response—software and hardware.

□ Communications—end-to-end encryption methods.

Administrative.

□ Perimeter access procedures.

□ Maintenance procedures—software and hardware.

□ Backup procedures—off-line and on-line.

□ Personnel procedures—training, indoctrination, bonding, etc.

□ Development procedures—standards, configuration management, certification, etc.

Control Analysis

Once the sample control techniques were enumerated, each system was evaluated on a scale from 0 (completely lacking) to 10 (maximum) against each control. Three criteria were used for each evaluation—the relative degree to which the control in that environment provided protection with respect to:

□ Access control to system.

□ Accuracy of system.

□ Availability of system.

All members of the workshop participated in the discussion of each item and an overall consensus was used to arrive at the results shown. Some results reflect our impressions of actual systems whereas others reflect possible "design objectives".

Composite Evaluation

The next step would be to derive an overall composite rating for the degree to which the system provides protection with respect to availability, accuracy, and access control; and to compare that with the security objectives determined by the system manager. This comparison must include analyses of tradeoffs between the various controls (i.e., good physical controls may permit relaxed systems controls or vice versa). It must also evaluate the "weakest link in the chain." A satisfactory technique for doing this must yet be developed.

One suggested approach would be to prepare parametric ranges or maximum values for each control technique line item as a function of a specific system environment under evaluation. These critical values then could be aggregated by subsystems to yield critical parameters for their assessment. For example, an acceptable critical value for a subsystem may be defined as the highest numerical parameter selected from the entire set of parameters which make up the line items for this subsystem.

Conceptually, we can continue this process of aggregation hierarchically until all microscopic levels of control adequacy on the (lowest) line item level have been translated into macroscopic parameters on higher subsystem levels. It is perfectly conceivable, even at this very preliminary stage of the investigation, that a "standard" scale for system security may eventually evolve from the crude beginnings postulated here.

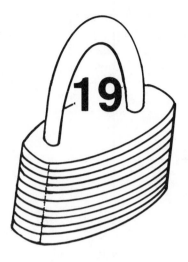

Managing Your Risks

This panel addressed itself to the identification of appropriate managerial control objectives and potential system vulnerabilities and exposures (risks) relating to computer system activities. We considered system vulnerabilities and potential control and security techniques from a management perspective for each of several organizational elements. We considered this appropriate because management must be considered to be accountable for system actions and misactions. Further, management must take an overall reponsibility to assure the existence of reasonable standards for system control and security, and undertake responsibility to assure that all system user personnel understand their responsibilities and duties in complying with such standards. See Table 19-1.

ORGANIZATIONAL ELEMENTS

In undertaking our task, we assumed a "worst case" environmental situation employing multiple use teleprocessing systems. Further, we restricted our considerations to those organizational elements of the hypothetical governmental agency structure designed by National Bureau of Standards which were assigned to us, and which included the following:

1. Operational divisions
2. Information systems project management
3. Data handling
4. Application program development
5. Data communications
6. Program validation

Operational Divisions

An operational division is considered to be an agency organizational unit responsible for one or more general agency functions. We assumed a management unit relating to the Information System Project Management and Data Handling Activities.

Table 19-1. Organizational Vulnerabilities and Controls.

Areas of responsibility

Risk (Impacts)	4. Operational divisions					5. Information systems project management	6. Data handling				7. Application systems development	8. Data communications	Horizontal frequency
	Long range planning	Short range budget planning	Systems contingency planning	Organizational communications	Personnel administration		Data input integrity	Exceptional (reporting) conditions	Information security management	Information product and output			
Tier 1: Organizational & Mission Impacts													
1.	x		x	x		x	x	x	x	x	x		9
2.			x	x	x	x	x	x	x	x		x	9
3.				x		x	x	x	x	x	x	x	8
4.	x	x			x	x		x	x	x	x		8
5.	x		x	x		x			x	x		x	7
Vertical frequency tier 1	3	1	3	4	2 [13]	[5]	3	4	5	5 [17]	[3]	[3]	41
Tier 2: Information Reliance Impacts													
6.	x	x	x				x			x			5
7.	x	x						x		x			4
8.				x	x					x		x	4

• Risks—

▶ = Will cause risk number.
◀ = Caused by risk number
□ Total for section/area

Tier 1: Organizational & Mission Impacts

1. Failure or unsatisfactory performance of mission and/or goals; financial loss or business risk; loss of relevant position.
   ◀ 2, 3, 4, 5, 6

2. Loss, alteration or destruction of data/assets/information; defalcation exposure; increased fraud exposure; unauthorized disclosure; erosion of security; ungraceful degradation of controls; violation of data integrity.
   ◀ 3, 11; ▶ 1, 3, 4

3. Misinformation and erosion of managerial decisions; data integrity and accountability; loss of confidence as effects both internal and external reporting requirements; unrecognized flaws and/or systems network violations.
   ◀ 2, 6, 10, 11 ▶ 1, 2, 4

4. Inability to comply with legal, regulatory, legislative requirements; incursion of statutory and/or judicial penalties; litigation.
   ▶ 1, 5

5. Waste, abuse or misuse of personnel, financial, time and/or organizational resources; decreased productivity effectiveness and potential; misallocation.
   ◀ 1, 4, 6-10, 11-14, 15-18

Vertical frequency tier 1

Tier 2: Information Reliance Impacts

6. Failure of current systems to satisfy operational requirements & short range goals/objectives and/or other informational needs; declining performance. ▶ 1, 3-5, 7, 8

7. Unsatisfactory reliability or inability to utilize information mechanisms in building toward longer term objectives.
   ◀ 6, 8, 9 ▶ 6, 11

8. Erosion of organizational confidence, internal as well as external, due to managerial and employee misunderstanding, miscommunication, frustration and dissatisfaction; inability to sustain internal organization communications.
   ◀ 6, 9, 10, 11, 13, 14, 16, ▶ 5, 6, 7, 9, 13, 16

Tier 2 (continued)

9. Insufficient basis for either monitoring or measuring performance and/or progress; uncontrolled systems environments; non-auditability of systems environments.
   ▲ 8, 14   ▼ 6-8, 10, 14

10. Premature failure or obsolescence of current systems; non-maintainable; unsatisfactory ability to reconstruct in timely and/or cost effective manner; unacceptable abridgement of planning.
    • 9, 11   ▼ 3, 6, 8

Vertical frequency tier 2

Tier 3: Control Disciplines

11. Impact of systems outage/interruption on operations, mission; or defalcation, degradation and recovery; on effectiveness of managerial control.
    • 7, 9, 11   ▼ 2, 3, 6, 12, 13 ▲

12. Cost overruns (uncontrolled) and exceeding of approved expenditure levels; negative performance.
    • 1, 5, 13 ▲ 11, 13

13. Unplanned duplication of systems development efforts; fragmentation of authority over standards and controls; costly over design: damaging under design.
    • 11, 12, 14 ▲ 8, 11, 12, 14

14. Incompatible and/or directly conflicting objectives across varying organizational units; significant and uncontrollable policy deviation.
    • 5, 8, 9, 13 ▲ 9, 13

Vertical frequency tier 3

Tier 4: Organizational Disciplines

15. Premature technical obsolescence of newly installed systems.
    ▼ 5, 13, ▲ 11, 18

16. Inadequate selection, identification, and assignment of personnel resources.
    ▲ 17, 18 ▲ 5, 8

17. Inability to correctly identify and adequately manage further organizational, functional environmental, and/or systems changes.
    ▼ 16, 18 ▲ 16, 18

18. Organizational mismanagement; managerial and staff incompetence: professional obsolescence.
    ▼ 16, 17 ▲ 15, 16,

Vertical frequency tier 4

Vertical frequency - total

255

Information System Project Management

This sub-element of an Operational Division was assumed to be responsible and have authority for the successful management of the hypothetical information system from the user's perspective. Its activities were considered to include ensuring that (a) all user requirements have been identified, (b) appropriate user specified controls are included in the system to assure accurate and timely results, and (c) system performance effectively supports the user's objectives as approved by general management.

Data Handling

This sub-element was considered to be responsible for all facets of data preparation, transport to and from input and output devices, and report distribution and storage.

Application Program Development

Under the assumed hypothetical agency organizational structure, all application program development and support are situated outside of data processing as a separate design activity even though many agencies place this function within data processing or within their organizational units. This element was, therefore, considered to include all facets of information systems analysis, programming and testing required to develop computer-based systems to support all levels of agency management operations. (As indicated by the hypothetical agency structure, we assumed that establishing standards for programming, testing and documentation of applications was not the responsibility of this group, but that we were required to assure that such standards were complied with.)

Data Communications

This element was considered as responsible for the movement of computer-encoded information by means of data transmission systems. We concentrated on questions of control and security of system transactions. We assumed that considerations

relating to specific communication system hardware and transmission path components would be covered by the technical panel groups established for that purpose.

Program Validation

This sub-element was identified as responsible for reviewing, validating, and approving all programs and program changes placed on the system. From a management perspective, we consider its activities as an inherent part of both the Information Systems Project Management and Application Program Development elements and did not retain it as a discrete and separate organizational group for purposes of this report.

OBJECTIVES

The panel believes that the objectives of a system of controls and the risks associated with a failure to achieve them can and should be identified. While these objectives and risks are not necessarily new, the panel believes they need to be reemphasized in all entities. In addition, the panel believes the following overriding control objectives must receive a higher level of attention that has been the case in the past.

1. Management has the ultimate responsibility for system controls. Therefore, they must have an appropriate comprehension and understanding of controls and where they can break down.
2. Users have a nonnegotiable responsibility for the controls in their systems. Clear definition of user controls and user understanding of those controls are essential to overall system controlability.
3. Short and long-term planning and budgeting within a properly designed organization structure is a key internal control. Without them, the entity will not be able to recognize, accept or manage the changes that take place within the entity.
4. An appropriate systems development methodology, which requires active management

and user participation and which results in a documented structure of systems controls, is essential to managing and maintaining the structure of control and to auditability.

Certain of the areas addressed by this panel, particularly with respect to the operational divisions element, such as planning, budgeting, etc., are very general in nature. However, we submit that these activities are basic and fundamental to the existence of strong management control over the line activities covered, and consequently to control and security of the computer related activities addressed by this report.

OPERATIONAL DIVISIONS

For purposes of this report, operational divisions are considered responsible for agency management activities relating to the information systems project management and data handling functions. They are responsible to top agency management for assuring that procedures have been designed and are utilized to provide reasonable assurance as to the control and security of data and data processing systems activities within those organizational units.

Long-Range Planning

Nature of the Objective. Procedures should exist for the preparation and periodic updating of a structured long-range plan, in order to assure, to the extent practicable, that current priorities as to organizational and systems activities are established in the light of projected agency directions. In preparing the long-range plan, its developers should give consideration to such internal and external factors as:

1. Agency and divisional goals and objectives.
2. Anticipated impact of technological developments.
3. Changing regulatory requirements.
4. Requirements for compliance with anticipated legislative actions relating to areas such as privacy, computer systems security, etc.

5. Management information requirements.

The long-range procedure should provide for periodic reviews of progress as to both the plan itself and the attainment of the established goals. The starting point for the plan should be clearly identified in order to provide a basis for periodic progress reviews.

Risks. In a general sense, the risk associated with an absence of long-range planning is that current activities, staffing, priorities, hardware and software acquisitions, etc., may be disorganized and misdirected. This could have severely negative effects on divisional performance. Examples include:

1. The division may fail to achieve its mission satisfactorily.
2. Agency and divisional resources may be wasted or misused.
3. The division may not be able to comply with regulatory or legislative requirements on a timely basis.
4. Installed systems may become technologically obsolete.
5. Agency and divisional management may not have sufficient information for measuring progress and performance.
6. The division may not be able to manage adequately its activities relating to organizational and systems changes.

Illustrative Control Procedures. A standardized procedure for structured long-range planning should be prepared and documented. It should be communicated to the organization and implemented. Planning responsibilities of all organizational components should be clearly identified at all levels, both as to preparation and periodic updating.

The plan should cover all activities, current and projected, of the organization. It should be consolidated for each organizational unit, for a division and for the agency as a whole. The completed plan should include a clear statement of the anticipated impact of projected changes on all organizational elements, and should be approved by top divisional and agency management.

Short-Range Planning (Budgets)

Nature of the Objective. A short-range plan or budget should be developed to set forth the goals and activities of the operational division and each of the sub-elements during the current fiscal period. It should be prepared giving consideration to present status, long-range priorities and directions as established by the long-range plan, and practical and affordable short term progress. It should clearly provide:

1. Appropriate allocation of available financial, personnel and other resources.
2. Recognition of the need for systems and operational modifications and projects to achieve them.
3. Identification of staffing and costs for continuity of current operations and systems.

Risks. The absence of a short-range planning and budgetary process could result in disorganized and non-productive activities in the current fiscal period. Specific negative results could include, among others:

1. The division may experience cost overruns and may exceed its funded expenditure levels.
2. Personnel resources may be inadequate.
3. Personnel and other resources may be non-productive.
4. Systems development activities may be wasteful or duplicative.
5. Progress toward achieving long-range objectives may be unsatisfactory or altogether lacking.
6. Current systems may become obsolete.
7. Current systems may fail due to an inability to satisfy operational requirements.

Illustrative Control Procedures. Control procedures for long-range planning also apply to short-range planning. The short-range plan should provide for a practicable plan, recognizing current constraints as to personnel and funding, and providing, as much as possible, some measure of progress toward achieving long-range goals. Each organizational unit's plan should be reviewed and approved by the next higher level management, as well as by appropriate functional management.

The plan should also provide for measuring current performance, on a period by period basis against the short-range plan. Adequate information should be provided for effective management analysis and control.

System Contingency Planning

Nature of the Objective. A formal and structured plan should be established to provide for operational continuity in the event of a major or extended failure of a system or system component. It should recognize the potential for system degradation at various levels and the potential impact upon operations at each such level, and clearly set forth policies and procedures to be followed to minimize such impact and provide for timely system recovery.

Risks. The risk associated with inadequate planning for system failures embodies the inability to discharge operational responsibilities satisfactorily during the period of outage. Certain operations are more critical than others and a failure to maintain highly critical operations could have severe effects upon agency and divisional financial and operational results. Examples include:

1. A severe and extensive system outage could result in a loss of effective management control of its operations, and in a worst case situation, failure of an agency mission.
2. Progress toward achieving short-range goals could be severely impeded.
3. Excessive personnel, outside contractor and other costs may be experienced.
4. Information and other assets may be destroyed or lost.
5. There may be increased exposure to fraud.
6. Personnel may be idle and, consequently, nonproductive.

Illustrative Control Procedures. A disaster or contingency plan should be established to recognize the potential for system interruptions and to provide formal and structured instructions and facilities for maintaining critical operations and providing for timely recovery. It should be specific, well documented, and should be explained to and understood by all appropriate personnel. Further, it should be approved by management. Documentation of the plan should be retained in secure, but readily available, on-site and off-site locations.

The level of detail in which the plan is prepared will vary, to a degree, depending upon the nature of, and criticality of agency operations. It should include, for example, provision for:

1. Levels of criticality of applications and activities.
2. Establishment of priorities.
3. Predisaster reduction of vulnerabilities.
4. Strategies for recovery.
5. Identification of people to be notified.
6. Identification of available hardware and software backup, including application programs and operating systems.
7. Procedures for recovery or replacement of data files.
8. Identification of need for and sources of forms.
9. Documentation of insurance coverage.

Depending upon the criticality of operations, it is often advisable to test the plan on a periodic basis to assure that it is practicable and understood by all appropriate personnel.

Organizational Communications

Nature of the Objective. This objective recognizes that the best intentions of management can fail to be achieved due to a lack of organization, dissemination and understanding of agency policies, procedures and responsibilities relating to security and control. Conversely, management at all levels is hindered in the effective discharge of its responsibilities if not kept fully informed on the results of day to day activities through appropriate and timely reporting techniques.

Management's policies relating to transaction and other authorizations, its approved procedures for transaction handling and processing, and its requirements for control and security should be formally and completely documented. Specific responsibilities of personnel at every organizational level should be clearly explained and a structured reporting system should be defined, implemented, and maintained.

Disseminated procedures should include identification of the organizational structure, and of upward, downward, and lateral unit interrelationships.

Risks. In general, the risk associated with inadequate organizational communication is a misunderstanding of objectives, policies, responsibilities, and procedures, as well as an inability to manage day to day activities effectively. Specific results might, for example, include:

1. A failure to achieve management's financial or other objectives due to a lack of understanding of the objectives.
2. Employee frustration caused by a lack of understanding of management's policies and plans.
3. The existence of incompatible or conflicting objectives at various organizational units.
4. A failure to comply with legal or regulatory requirements.
5. A failure to observe established management policies.
6. Weaknesses or gaps in the system of control and security.
7. An inability to monitor current developments.
8. Erroneous data and reports.
9. A misinformed management, and consequently, faulty decisions.

Illustrative Control Procedures. Management's policies and procedures should be documented in detail in official procedures memoranda or a procedures manual. With respect to the operational divisions considered by this panel, the policies should include, for example:

1. The organization and effective use of a management steering committee to establish system priorities, consider problems, review progress against planned objectives, consider short term needs, etc.
2. The requirement for user involvement in system design and user approval of all system modifications.
3. Clear identification of authorization requirements and specific exception procedures.
4. Definition of the responsibilities of the various organizational levels.
5. Reporting requirements and schedules.
6. A statement of management priorities.

Personnel Administration

Nature of the Objective. Personnel administration procedures should assure that personnel at all organizational levels understand their duties and responsibilities, are adequately trained in their duties, are effectively monitored, and are objectively evaluated as to performance.

Risks. The risks of inadequate personnel administration are many and varied. With respect to those areas considered by this panel, they could include, for example:

1. Low productivity due to inadequately trained or misinformed employees.
2. Employee frustration caused by a lack of understanding of responsibilities.
3. Employee dissatisfaction due to inadequate performance evaluation.
4. Abuse or misuse of agency resources.
5. Violation of data integrity as a result of misunderstanding control and security procedures.
6. Loss of data or system control due to poorly trained employees.
7. Organizational incompetence.
8. Organizational mismanagement.
9. Exposure to fraud.

Illustrative Control Procedures. Manage-

ment should establish specific policies and practices to be followed in personnel administration. These policies and practices should include, for example:

1. An agency code of conduct relating to all personnel which covers conflict of interest situations, gifts, expense accounts, relationships within and outside the organization, etc.
2. Employee interviewing, screening, hiring and termination practices.
3. Provision for adequate employee training.
4. Provision for rotation of duties, and job enrichment, as appropriate in the circumstances.
5. Adequate separation of employee duties in sensitive data handling areas.
6. An effective performance monitoring system.
7. A fair and objective performance evaluation system.

INFORMATION SYSTEM PROJECT MANAGEMENT

This organizational unit is responsible to the operational division to assure that all systems are successfully designed, implemented and controlled from a user management perspective. Risks associated with a failure to achieve system control objectives discussed below are considered generally applicable to all such objectives. Consequently, risks and illustrative control procedures will be discussed on an overall basis, rather than identified with a specific objective.

User Involvement in System Design

Procedures should exist to assure that users of a planned system are involved, in depth, in all phases of system design and development activities. Their involvement should encompass, for example, such responsibilities as:

1. Definition and identification of input data edits, file, field and report requirements, etc.
2. Proper documentation of such requirements.

3. Effective communication of requirements, in detail, to the system design activity.

User Specification of Controls

The system design methodology should assure that control requirements are specified in detail by system users and are included in system design. User responsibilities in this respect include the following, among others:

1. Definition of specific control requirements.
2. Documentation of all such requirements.
3. Effective communication of such requirements to the system design activity.
4. Continuing involvement with system design activity to assure that required controls are implemented properly in the system.

Continuing User Satisfaction

Procedures should exist for frequent user monitoring of operational systems performance and control to assure that the system continues to meet its objectives in terms of control and security.

User Compliance
With External Requirements

In connection with all system related activities, users should undertake to assure compliance with all external system requirements, including:

1. Legal.
2. Regulatory.
3. Interagency and intraagency.
4. Internal and external auditor needs.

Risks

The overall risk resulting from inadequate user involvement in system design activities is obviously the failure of implemented systems to satisfy agency needs and objectives in a controlled, cost effective and productive manner. Specific risks are many and varied. They include, for example:

1. A failure to satisfy one or more specific user

or external requirements.
2. Inadequately controlled systems.
3. Exposure to fraud.
4. Faulty system security.
5. Loss of accountability and the ability to reconcile data.
6. Unnecessary or excessive costs resulting from overdesign of a system or system reports.
7. Loss or misuse of resources.
8. Delayed implementation schedules.

Illustrative Control Procedures

Among many potential control procedures applicable to information systems project management, the panel believes the most important include the following:

1. An adequate systems development life cycle or other systems development methodology.
2. Adequate user responsibilities in systems development.
3. Adequate user responsibilities in systems changes and maintenance.
4. Adequately designed and implemented user controls.

System Development Life Cycle or Other Systems Development Methodology. The system development process should be organized into specific phases, such as:

1. Project definition and survey.
2. Preliminary system design.
3. System design.
4. Application software development and system testing.
5. Implementation.
6. Post installation review.

This concept of phased system development is covered, in depth, in available literature.

The requirements of each phase should be clearly spelled out and understood by all involved in the development process. Specific management checkpoints should be established during, and at the end of each phase, to assure that project goals and objectives are being realized and that costs to date, and projected for the future, are within established parameters.

User Involvement in System Development. The organization of each system project development team should provide for specific user involvement and participation throughout the development process. User responsibilities should include, for example:

1. Identification and documentation in detail of all user oriented system requirements.
2. Determination of the economic and operational feasibility of the project.
3. Establishment and documentation of project scope and objectives.
4. Project review and sign-off at specific checkpoints.
5. Involvement in system testing, user training and conversion activities.

User Involvement in System Changes and Maintenance. All changes to implemented systems should be approved by user management. User personnel should also participate in the testing process and authorize the implementation of the change.

Design and Implementation of User Controls. Specific control procedures for user personnel should be established, documented, communicated and understood by all involved personnel. These should cover, for example, such areas as:

1. Separation of responsibilities.
2. Authorization levels.
3. Responsibilities for master file changes.
4. Security of data and files.
5. Documentation and auditability requirements.
6. User responsibilities to specify application input, processing and output controls for data processing activity and to assure that implemented systems achieve the required level of control and security.

DATA HANDLING

The area of data handling constitutes those organizational entities directly responsible for transformation of external information into machine-usable data, and vice versa. These duties include data transcription, dissemination, storage and retrieval. The controls in data handling are direct, aimed at the physical integrity of the data and the organizational integrity of the information those data represent.

Maintaining Input Data Integrity

Nature of the Objective. The integrity of input data should be maintained at all times. The accuracy, completeness, and timeliness of the data being processed by the computer determines their usefulness to the organization. In computing, data is a raw material; any loss of data integrity will result in a flawed finished product. Procedures should exist to assure that:

1. All transactions are authorized by the appropriate person or persons.
2. Specific job functions include the ability to authorize certain input data within prescribed limits (dollar amount, geographic area, etc.).
3. All valid transactions are authorized by the system, and conversely, all invalid transactions are rejected so that all input batches are complete and error free.
4. Data are entered correctly and on a timely basis.
5. Edits assure that all data used are correct.
6. In on-line systems, each transaction entered is positively acknowledged to the enterer and is logged by the system to assure the data enterer that the system has accepted each item.
7. At the end of processing, all items are balanced against the day's total master file.
8. There is a transaction trail for all data entered to allow management to be able to recreate the path, both forward and backward, for all items in the system.

Correct and Timely Exceptions Reporting

Nature of the Objective. All exceptional conditions should be reported in a thorough and timely fashion. Since modern data processing systems are constructed on the basis of "management by exception," management can only exercise its function with regard to computerized operations if it is presented with meaningful information, where and when it is most needed. Procedures over exceptions should include the following:

1. Clearly established responsibility for responding to errors which the system identifies and positive actions to correct the exceptional condition.
2. Requirements for suspending transactions in cases in which errors cannot be immediately corrected, and methods for updating the suspense files in order to maintain financial control over errors.
3. Requirements for reconciling input to output once corrections have been made, to assure completeness and maintenance of financial and data controls.
4. Maintenance of accurate records of the number, type, distribution, and concentration of data handling errors to be used to develop statistics useful in identifying systematic and managerial weaknesses.
5. Resolution of exceptional conditions in an expeditious manner in order to avoid delays in error correction which could compound existing problems.

Secure Information Storage, Retrieval, and Use

Nature of the Objective. Information should be stored, retrieved, and used in a secure manner. Data should be protected against malicious and inadvertent destruction, modification and disclosure.

Data, and by extension, information, are organizational assets and as such must be secured against loss. The peculiarities of a data asset

necessitate all the awareness of security required for tangible resources, plus a number that are specific to data.

Procedures related to data security should include the following:

1. Identification and categorization of data elements by differing levels of sensitivity.
2. Delineation of individuals authorized to handle data, set forth in the same manner as security over the data.
3. Unique identification of users by the computer in order that their authority to access sensitive data can be verified prior to release of the data.
4. Storage in such a fashion, that data are protected against physical destruction, and are recoverable (or at least recreatable) if destroyed.
5. Design of systems to satisfy all statutory and regulatory requirements, e.g., privacy, nondisclosure, conflict of interest, etc.
6. Design and operation of systems in accordance with accepted organizational policies and practices, to reduce the overall exposure to litigation and statutory sanctions.
7. Monitoring systems regularly and continuously for breaches of security with all such events being responded to immediately.

Controlled Information Dissemination and Storage

Nature of the Objective. The information produced by the system should be disseminated and stored under suitable controls.

Output data may be either the end product of the system, or may be a report of its internal operations. In either case, these data are (or should be) produced for use, and thus should be used for their intended purposes, and only those purposes. Procedures for output data should include the following:

1. Review of all reports by supervisory person-

nel for reasonableness, accuracy, and exceptional conditions.

2. Designated supervisory responsibility to take appropriate action based on the content of those reports.
3. Distributing all output in a timely fashion.
4. Reconciliation of all output data to the input data entered originally, with checks on any transactions generated internally.
5. Distribution of output data only to those who have a demonstrated need for them, with such need being periodically reviewed and evaluated.
6. Secure storage of information while needed, with the information being properly destroyed when no longer required.

Risks

The risks associated with failure to manage and control the data handling area properly can expose the entity to many potential problems including, inaccurate or incorrect input data, improper output information, statutory sanctions, litigation, etc. Examples of risk include the following:

1. Admission of errors into the system in the form of erroneous or duplicated work, or outdated records.
2. Elimination of vital records from the files.
3. Introduction of unauthorized or possibly fraudulent transactions into the system.
4. Alteration, destruction, or disclosure of data in an unauthorized manner.
5. Susceptibility to fraud, statutory or regulatory sanctions, criminal and civil penalties, etc.
6. Production by the system of erroneous or out-of-date reports and other forms of output upon which management may improperly rely.
7. Failure of the organization to accomplish its stated objectives or its mission.
8. Exposure to direct financial loss.
9. Indirect financial loss arising from difficulties in reconstructing financial or other information assets.

Illustrative Control Procedures

Because the controls over data handling are inherently the controls over data processing in general, they have received considerable scrutiny by writers and researchers in EDP auditing and controls. These include:

1. Verification of input data.
2. Input batching and editing.
3. Run-to-run balancing.
4. Reconciliation of output.
5. Secure storage of input and output data.

It is strongly recommended that readers refer to the bibliography in Section 3, proceding, for identification of illustrative control procedures. Rather than illustrate many specific controls, the panel noted that it is critically important for the reader to realize that a suitable control structure must be developed and implemented as part of the systems development cycle.

APPLICATION PROGRAM DEVELOPMENT

This organizational unit is responsible to general agency management for the management and performance of all systems design, programming and testing activities required to support agency data processing requirements. Specific standards and policies relating to the techniques and approaches to be followed in discharging these responsibilities are expected to be established by the application interface unit of data processing. This unit is responsible for assuring compliance with such standards and policies.

Program Development Standards

Program development should adhere to established standards for coding and testing methodology, internal controls, documentation, and security.

System Development Life Cycle Check-Points

Systems should be reviewed at prescribed

check-points in keeping with the system development life cycle. At these points, both user and auditor approval should be obtained.

Coordination with Organizational Plans

The development of an application system should be linked to overall organizational plans.

Project Management System Control

All elements of performance in analysis, programming, and testing should be controlled and monitored by a project management system.

Testing and Review

All programs should be subjected to testing and review by developers, users, internal auditors, and systems validation (quality assurance) prior to implementation.

Risks

In an overall sense, the risks associated with inadequate control of application program design, programming and testing encompass a failure to satisfy management's information objectives and requirements effectively and productively. Specific risks include:

1. Organizational objectives with regard to resource allocation (general mission, time, money) may not be met.
2. Systems may be uncontrolled and unauditable, and as a result, may introduce errors into organizational records.
3. Systems may not satisfy internal and external requirements.
4. Systems will be difficult to maintain.
5. The organization may be susceptible to business risks such as interruption of operations, competitive disadvantage, and statutory sanctions.
6. Outputs generated by the system may be in error and may result in falacious internal and external reports.

Illustrative Control Procedures

Again, as in the preceding sections of this report, there are a variety of procedures available for use to satisfy the above objectives, all of which are covered in great detail in available literature. All four procedures outlined under Information System Project Management - Illustrative Control Procedures, also apply in this area. Other specific control procedures might include:

1. The existence of a formal methodology and procedure relating to program testing, including provision for test data preparation and retention.
2. Periodic reporting of progress against plan to senior management.
3. Adequate interface with the quality assurance function to assure compliance with requirements.
4. Adequate interface with internal and external auditors to assure satisfaction with auditability requirements.

DATA COMMUNICATIONS

The "worst case" environmental situation we considered implies the use of some one or combination of remote terminals or processing devices transmitting data over communication paths to another processing location. The control objectives and related risks applied to the other areas of this paper apply to the communication components of the system as well as any other components, and will not be repeated here. The existence of remote operations and transmission facilities, however, adds new dimensions to risks related to the integrity of data transmitted, and system security and reliability. Of these, certain result from the characteristics of the devices and of the communications paths utilized, and we have assumed that the technical panel groups, established for the purpose, would give adequate attention to these matters. Consequently, we have limited our comments in this section to the three objectives of integrity, security and reliability, extended risks in the teleprocessing environment, and illustrative control techniques.

Integrity of Data Transmitted

Nature of the Objective. The use of remote data terminals and communication facilities expands the potential for the introduction of incomplete or erroneous data into a system. All of the control objectives discussed under data handling, apply as well to the remote and communication aspects of the system. In addition, extended procedures should exist to assure that data are not lost or unintentionally altered due to the remoteness of access devices or the physical characteristics of the transmission paths.

Risks. Additional risks resulting from the online nature of the system relate to the entry or receipt of erroneous or incomplete data to or from a central system. These additional risks result from several factors:

1. Employees using access devices may not be adequately trained.
2. Input formats may be overly complex.
3. Terminals transmitted to may be out of operation.
4. Communication paths may be interfered with by natural disturbances, such as electrical storms, or by physical problems in some component.
5. Terminal transmissions may interfere with one another.

Illustrative Control Procedures. Management should establish specific policies and procedures to assure data integrity, including, for example, such as:

1. Adequate terminal users manuals.
2. Fixed terminal input formats.
3. Adequate data balancing controls.
4. Message numbering and logging.
5. Centralized control of communication networks, utilizing polling and specific device identification.

System Security

Nature of the Objective. Systems utilizing remote access devices and communications facilities can provide heightened opportunities for deliberate misuse of system files and data by employees and outsiders. Extended procedures should exist to help assure that the system and system data cannot be deliberately compromised or destroyed by employees or outsiders.

Risks. In an overall sense, the danger of an inadequately secured system is that unauthorized employees or others may gain access to the system. Specific risks include:

1. The system may be exposed to fraud.
2. Sensitive data, master files or programs could be examined or stolen by employees or outsiders.
3. The system or system data could be damaged or destroyed by disgruntled employees or outsiders.
4. Data confidentiality or privacy could be compromised.

Illustrative Control Procedures. Procedures designed to help prevent security breaches could include, for example:

1. Specific identification of users and terminals, under central system control.
2. Location of terminals in a secure physical environment.
3. The use of passwords to authorize system access.
4. System monitoring and logging of access attempts and transmissions.
5. System notification to security personnel of suspicious or unusual network activity.
6. Use of multilevel data file, data and transaction access controls.
7. Use of data encryption methods for highly sensitive transactions.

System Reliability

Nature of the Objective. In a multiple use teleprocessing system environment, the potential for system outage or inadvertent destruction c ꜣro-

266

grams or data is heightened due to the geographical dispersion of system components and the effect of natural disturbances on communication facilities. The objective, risks and illustrative control procedures related to system contingency planning, discussed in this paper, should be considered carefully in establishing a plan for system backup and recovery. In addition, system response times should be carefully monitored to avoid deterioration.

Risks. Additional risks related to system reliability in the teleprocessing environment include:

1. Terminal maintenance and repair may be disruptive and time consuming.
2. Failure of all or a part of communication facilities may render a system temporarily unusable.
3. System response times may deteriorate due to increased volumes, inadequate human factors at terminal sites, or equipment malfunctions.

Illustrative Control Procedures. Procedures to minimize the extended risks in this area might include:

1. A scheduled preventative maintenance program for remote devices.
2. Development of a plan for temporary voice telephone or other transmission of data during an outage period.
3. Provision of back-up equipment and/or communication facilities in time-critical situations.
4. Network and response time monitoring.

THE CASCADE EFFECT OF MANAGEMENT RISK

Following the panel's identification of the four major areas for systems management concern, we decided to examine the risks we have identified and associated with control objectives. By subjecting our sub-element vulnerabilities and exposures

("risks") to a frequency distribution, we have identified a critical, cascading or "Tier" effect of management exposure. Four principle risk levels are identified in cascading levels of importance.

Organization Mission Impacts. These are elements that will directly and negatively affect the unit's performance. Forty-one incidences of risk are identified in this Tier.

Information Reliance Impacts. These are elements of information dependency that will render executive decisions null over time. Nineteen incidences of risk are identified in this Tier.

Control Disciplines. These are elements of basic systems control subject to compromise, distortion and mismanagement. Eight incidences of risk are identified in this Tier.

Organization Disciplines. These are elements of basic managerial skill and organization analysis, especially those where a *lack* of sensitivity and comprehension will negatively impact the unit's mission delivery capacity. Four incidences of risk are identified in this Tier.

CONCLUSIONS

We find that if breaches or failures occur in any component of a higher tier, then several effects will follow in subsequent tiers. The importance of this chain effect should not be overlooked. Risks and increases in exposures run both upward and downward in cause and effect.

On our diagram which follows we have identified (across the top) major Control Objectives and (on the vertical side) Risk Tiers. This diagram illustrates several joint observations.

1. Data Handling, at the level of successful management of Tier 1, Organizational & Mission Impacts, is the most critical cluster. Seventeen incidences of risk are identified in Tier 1 alone for Data handling.
2. The opportunities to take preventative actions are more available to planning activities within Operational Divisions (19 of incidences risk) and to Information Systems Project Management (9 incidences of risk) than other areas.

3. Organizational Communications (mission, purpose, intents, facts, policy, events, directives, consistency, etc.) within operational divisions is the second most vulnerable managerial responsibility (eight incidences of risk).
4. Impacts affecting the integrity and reliability of a systems environment are influenced by the shorter range or tactical plans, leading us to conclude that long range business and systems plans are necessary to successfully support the shorter range budget process.
5. Although Tier 4, Organizational Disciplines, appears final on the chart and low in numeric value, we observed that if these elements fail in any permutation, the combined effect undermines the application of control disciplines.

Thus, this panel has concluded that it is important to reemphasize the critical, cascading effect of:

1. Management's overall responsibility for controls.
2. User's non-negotiable for controls in their systems.
3. Short and long term planning and budgeting.
4. An appropriate systems development methodology.

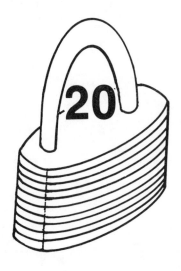

Securing Communication Links

This paper presents a set of guidelines that can be used when conducting a review of administrative and technical controls pertaining to a multiple user teleprocessing environment. The committee intends that this paper form the basis upon which auditors or security experts might review the degree of adequacy contained in the controls within a teleprocessing network.

In order to better understand what is meant by a teleprocessing environment, the preceding figure (Fig. 20-1) was developed to show examples of the alternative teleprocessing network configurations that might be available. These networks are among those that might be faced when conducting a security review in today's teleprocessing environment. It should be noted that there might be combinations of networks, where for example a multidrop configuration might have a local loop at each of the drops. Also, where this figure depicts "transmission lines" the audit and control expert reviewing the network might find various transmission media, such as satellite circuits, microwave transmission, fiberoptics, or copper wire pairs.

A computer security audit is an independent evaluation of the controls employed to ensure the accuracy and reliability of the data maintained on or generated by a teleprocessing network, the appropriate protection of the organization's information assets (including hardware, software, and data) from all significant anticipated threats or hazards, and the operational reliability and performance assurance of all components of the automated data processing system.

With regard to the communication component, all modes of data transmission and associated equipment should be considered. Specific vulnerabilities should be identified along with appropriate safeguards, e.g., interception of microwave transmissions, with encryption serving as the countering control.

THE CONTROL MATRIX

This paper presents a matrix that relates the various vulnerabilities to the specific controls that

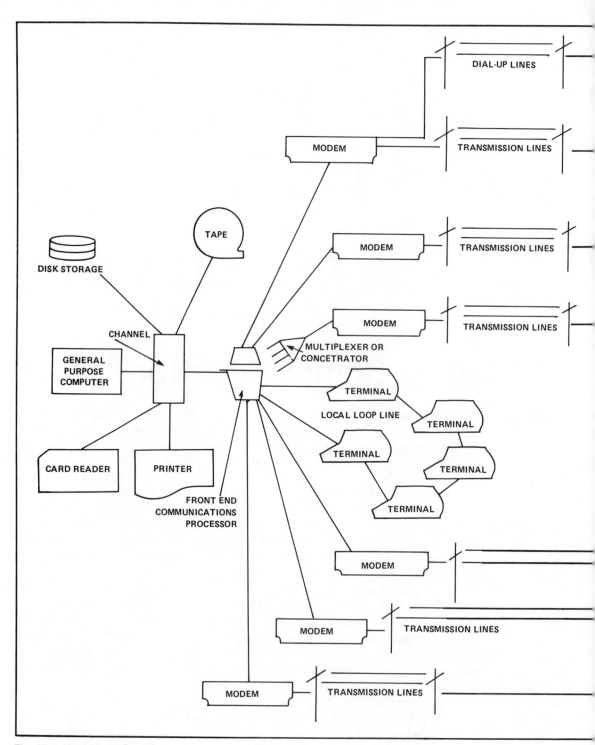

Fig. 20-1. Network configuration.

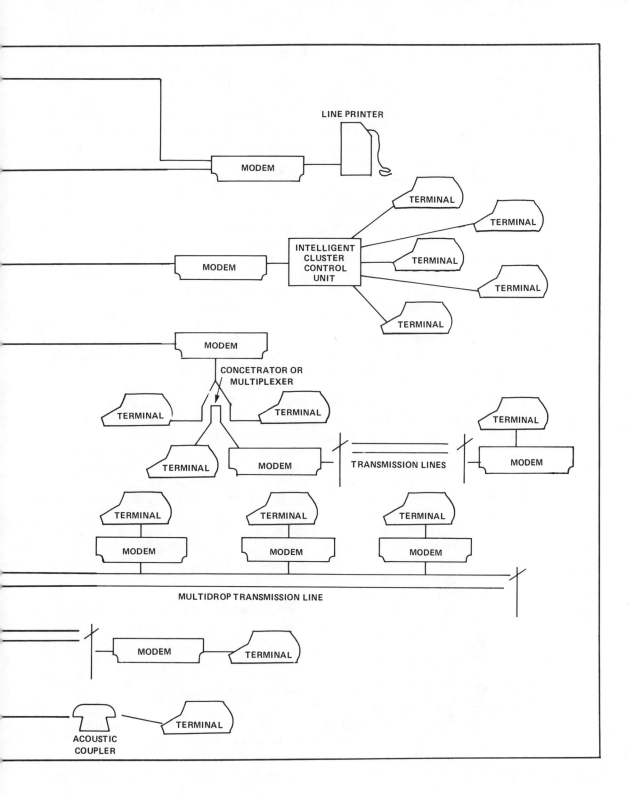

LINE PRINTER

MODEM

TERMINAL

TERMINAL

INTELLIGENT
CLUSTER
CONTROL
UNIT

MODEM

TERMINAL

TERMINAL

TERMINAL

MODEM

CONCETRATOR OR
MULTIPLEXER

TERMINAL

TERMINAL

TERMINAL

MODEM

TRANSMISSION LINES

TERMINAL

MODEM

TERMINAL

MODEM

TERMINAL

MODEM

TERMINAL

MODEM

MULTIDROP TRANSMISSION LINE

MODEM

TERMINAL

ACOUSTIC
COUPLER

TERMINAL

271

might be available to mitigate them (see Table 20-1, The Control Matrix). The vulnerabilities are listed across the top of the matrix and are defined in a later section of this paper. The controls are listed down the left vertical axis of the matrix and are also defined in a later section of this paper. Within the cells of the matrix there is either an X or an O whenever the control is an appropriate countermeasure to a specific vulnerability. An X indicates a primary control that can be used to mitigate the specific vulnerability; an O indicates a secondary control that might be useful in mitigating the specific vulnerability. To apply the matrix, first identify the vulnerability that may be present in your teleprocessing network. Next, proceed down the column of the specific vulnerability and identify whether the controls in the left vertical column are applicable.

The control matrix can be used in two other ways to assist the auditor. The first is to determine the exposures that will be faced by the organization whenever one of the vulnerabilities does, in fact, occur. These exposures are listed at the bottom of the matrix, below each vulnerability column. For example, if the vulnerability "Message Lost" occurred, then the organization would be subjected to exposures A, E, F, and G, defined in Table 20-2.

The second use to which the matrix can be put is to specifically identify the various components of the network where the controls might be most effectively located. To do this, the auditor would choose a specific control such as "Sequence Number Checking" and follow across that row to the right-hand side of the matrix, where there are some numbers, such as 9, 10, 17. These numbers indicate those specific components of a data communication network where the controls might be located. These 17 components are defined at the end of this report. See Fig. 20-1.

INTERRELATION OF SECURITY CONTROLS

The auditor should recognize that the security controls shown in the matrix have complex interrelations in solving certain security problems. There are no linear equations that show how these controls add to or subtract from one another. The security controls required in a worst case analysis of an intentional assault on a communication system constitute a highly structured set of interrelationships.

For example, encryption is a valuable security control in a communications system. It is not, however, a complete solution in and of itself. The security objectives of a communication system can only be satisfied when encryption is used in conjunction with several other controls. In particular, sequence numbers must be used to detect attempts to add, delete, or replay messages by a technically competent penetrator. A cryptographic error detection code must be used to detect alteration of messages. Encryption key management must be performed to ensure authentication of communicating devices.

In addition, message reconciliation must be performed during and at the end of every session to ensure that all messages transmitted have been received. Enamation controls prevent the loss of encryption keys and plaintext messages through undesirable electronic phenomena.

These constitute the necessary set of nondiscretionary controls required for secure communication. In addition, certain discretionary, human-oriented controls are required to support the encryption system. Physical security must prevent theft or unauthorized use of a device containing a valid encryption key. Maintenance and testing must ensure the correct operation of the controls. Documentation must explain how the controls must be used. Finally, the user must be educated and trained in the use of these controls.

DEFINITION OF THE VULNERABILITIES

The following list defines the vulnerabilities that are listed across the top of the control matrix. These vulnerabilities could be interpreted as the concerns or threats to which a data communication network might be subjected.

☐ Message Lost—Refers to a message that never reaches its intended destination.

☐ Misrouting—Is said to occur in a message-

Table 20-1. Control Matrix.

CONTROLS	MESSAGE LOST	MISROUTING	MESSAGE ALTERATION	DISRUPTION	DISASTER	DISCLOSURE	MESSAGE INSERTION	THEFT (Physical)	DUPLICATE MESSAGE	COMPONENTS WHERE CONTROLS ARE LOCATED
SEQUENCE NUMBER CHECKING	X	O					X		X	9,10,17
SENDING AND RECEIVING IDENTIFICATION	O	X				O				9,10,17
TRANSACTION JOURNAL	X	O	X	X	X		X		X	9,10,11,17
POSITIVE ACKNOWLEDGMENT	X	X	X	X			X		X	9,10,11,17
TIME AND DATE STAMP	X								X	9,10,11,17
PERIODIC MESSAGE RECONCILIATION	X		X	O			X		X	10,17
CHECK SUM ON MESSAGE ADDRESS		X								9,10,11,17
ERROR DETECTION CODE			X	O						9,10,11,12,17
ERROR CORRECTION CODE			X	O						9,10,11,12,17
KEY REDUNDANCY CODE			X	O						9,10,11,12,17
ECHOPLEXING	X	O	X	O			O		O	10
ERROR LOGGING	O	O	X	X					O	9,10
BACKUP EQUIPMENT AND FACILITIES				X	X					1,7,8,9,10,11,17
PHYSICAL SECURITY	O	O	O	X	X	X	O	X	O	1-17
RECOVERY PROCEDURES	O		O	X	X				O	1-17
COMMUNICATION POLICY	O	O	O	O	O	O	O	O	O	1-17
LIFE SUPPORT SYSTEM				X	X					4,8,9,10,11
DEVICE DISCONNECTION DETECTION	O							X		7,9,10,11
BUILT-IN DEVICE ADDRESS							X	O		9,10,11,17
ENCRYPTION	X	X	X			X	X		X	7,8,9,10,11,17
UNLISTED PHONE NUMBER (Dial-Up)						X	X			9,10,11
LOW ERROR RATE FACILITIES	X		X	X						1,2,3,7
SOFTWARE CONTROLS AND TESTING	X	X	X	X		X	X		X	9,10,11,17
DOCUMENTATION	O	O	O	O	O	O	O	O	O	1-16
EMANATION CONTROL						X				1-4,6-11,13-17
TRAINING AND EDUCATION	O	O	O	O	O	O	O	O	O	1-17
EXPOSURES (See Table I)	A,E,F,G•	A,D,E,F,I	A,D,E,G,H	C-I	C-I	F,G,I	B,D,E,G,H	C,E,G,H	D,E,G,I	

273

Table 20-2. Exposure Codes.

A. Erroneous Record Keeping
B. Unacceptable Accounting
C. Business Interruption
D. Erroneous Management Decisions
E. Fraud
F. Statutory Sanctions
G. Excessive Costs/Deficient Revenues
H. Loss or Destruction of Assets
I. Competitive Disadvantage

The above items A through I represent the various exposures that the organization faces whenever some sort of a vulnerability (threat or concern) takes place. In other words, the result of a threat might be one of these exposures.

switching network when a message intended for a destination, e.g. Node A is sent to another destination, Node B.

☐ Message Alternation—Refers to unauthorized (accidental or intentional) modification of an authentic message.

☐ Disruption—A temporary or intermittent service outage affecting one or more of the network components which may result in one or more of the following consequences: denial of service, misrouting, message alteration, messages lost, duplicate message, etc.

☐ Disaster—An interruption resulting in denial of service for an extended period of time as the result of an accident, natural catastrophe, or sabotage. The distinction between a disaster and a disruption is based upon the length of service outage and upon the permanence of the damage to the affected components.

☐ Disclosure (Privacy)—Unauthorized access to any data is disclosure. If the data is personally identifiable to an individual or legal person, then the unauthorized disclosure is a privacy violation.

☐ Message Insertion—The addition of an extraneous unauthorized message at any component in the network. This vulnerability is never

accidental and does not include duplicate messages.

☐ Theft (Physical)—Physical theft refers to unauthorized removal of any hardware component.

☐ Duplicate Message—The insertion or processing of multiple copies of an otherwise authorized message. This can occur accidentally or intentionally.

DEFINITIONS OF THE CONTROLS

The following list defines each of the controls listed down the left vertical axis of the control matrix.

☐ Sequence Number Checking—A method where all messages contain an integral sequence number for each level of the communication system. Vertification techniques must detect duplicate and missing numbers, reject duplicates, and report missing messages.

☐ Sending and Receiving Identification—A method where sufficient information is contained in the message to uniquely identify both the sender and the receiver of a message.

☐ Transaction Journal—A method of capturing sufficient system and message level data to

274

establish an adequate audit trail or to have an actual copy of each and every transaction transmitted in the network.

☐ Positive Acknowledgment—A method where the receipt of each message is positively confirmed back to the sender.

☐ Time and Date Stamp—An automatic procedure whereby each message contains time and data information for each major processing node.

☐ Periodic Message Reconciliation—System facilities to verify completeness of processing by periodically providing summary information to reconcile number of messages, dollar values, control totals, etc., both sent and received.

☐ Check Sum on Message Address—A procedure that vertifies the message address using hashing or other summing type of totals.

☐ Error Detection Code—A method of inserting redundant information for purposes of detecting any changed bit patterns.

☐ Error Correction Code—A method of inserting extra (redundant) bits of information to permit detection and correction of errors at the receiving equipment without retransmission of the original message.

☐ Key Redundancy Code—The insertion of duplicate information in key fields of the message stream (such as dollar amounts, description identifiers, quantities, etc.) which can be compared at the receiving equipment for correctness.

☐ Echoplexing—A verification procedure by which each character received by the receiving station equipment is transmitted back to the originating equipment.

☐ Error Logging—A software program that records error messages, by line, terminal, and

also type and frequency. This recording is to measure the degree of reliability and performance of the communication system. Statistical analysis and management reports are required for evaluation and corrective action to minimize error rates.

☐ Backup Equipment and Facilities—Duplicate or alternate equipment (power, air conditioning, etc.), software, and procedures to be invoked whenever a major outage occurs with the primary system. Also a physical facility located away from the primary site and capable of supporting the original primary site telecommunication function at an acceptable operational level.

☐ Physical Security—The ability to have proper physical security over the data communication facilities, software, and all other aspects of the teleprocessing network. This includes restrictive access controls over personnel, adequate fire protection, backup electrical equipment, and any other aspects of physical security with regard to maintaining the integrity of the data communication network.

☐ Recovery Procedures—A set of written procedures that clearly defines responsibilities and procedures for operational programming and supervisory personnel to allow for the orderly recovery of the system to operational status or to recover from excessive error rates.

☐ Communication Policy—A statement of agency or corporate policy regarding design, use, and maintenance of communication components including security objectives and penalties for not achieving these objectives.

☐ Life Support System—Equipment, techniques, and procedures that will eliminate or minimize damages caused by disasters, occurrences such as fire, power failure, flood, environmental changes, etc.

☐ Device Disconnection Detection—The use of

electrical control signals or other mechanisms to detect physical disconnection of communication system components.

☐ Built-In Device Address—The imbedding of a device address or identifier via hardware or software mechanisms in communication system components.

☐ Encryption—The transformation of data (cleartext) to an unintelligible form (ciphertext) through the use of an algorithm under the control of a key such as the federal Data Encryption Standard (DES) (FIPS Pub. 46).

☐ Unlisted Phone Number (Dial-Up)—The acquisition and use of unlisted telephone numbers for the communication system component that can be accessed via dial-up lines.

☐ Low Error Rate Facilities—The selection and use of data transmission facilities with characteristically low error rates such as conditioned lines or digital transmission lines.

☐ Software Controls and Testing—The procedures employed in development, installation, and maintenance of software in communication system components to insure the correctness, integrity, and availability of the software.

☐ Documentation—The generation, revision, and maintenance of manuals dealing with appropriate design, maintenance, and operational aspects of the communication system.

☐ Emanation Control—The use of shielding and associated techniques to suppress electromagnetic, acoustic, and radio frequency emanations from communication system components.

☐ Training and Education—The development, presentation, and periodic review of educational materials dealing with correct operation and maintenance of the communication system.

GENERAL DEFINITIONS OF COMPONENTS

The following list of items enumerates and defines the components of a data communication network. In some cases the item listed may be a characteristic of data transmission rather than an actual component.

1. Circuits—A circuit can be a single communication facility or a combination of different types of communication facilities such as:

   ☐ Satellite: a facility that uses ultrahigh frequency signaling relayed through a device orbiting the earth.

   ☐ Microwave: a facility that uses high frequency signaling which passes through terrestrial relay points.

   ☐ Fiberoptics: a facility that transmits signals through the use of optical media utilizing a fiberglass-like cable.

   ☐ Wire: a facility that transmits through a metallic conductor. This facility may utilize long-distance copper wire pairs, coaxial cable, or the copper wire local loop between a user premises and the telephone company's switching office.

2. Analog Transmission—Transmission of a continuously variable signal which has an almost infinite number of states (an example of an analog signal is a sine wave).

3. Digital Transmission—Transmission of a discretely variable signal such as discrete voltage levels (an example is signaling which is composed of either a positive or a negative voltage).

4. Carrier Switch/Facility—A communication facility supplied by a commercial vendor of telecommunication services that provides for the interconnection of transmission devices (an

example would be the telephone company's switching office or the Telnet Packet switches).

5. Configurations—These are the methods of connecting communication devices. There are many examples of communication configurations, some of which were shown in Fig. 20-1. Examples of these configurations might be as follows:

☐ Dedicated/private leased lines. These circuits are always available to the customer for transmission and generally are used with on-line and real-time systems.

☐ Dial/switch circuits. A circuit connection which is established by dialing a telephone or establishing a physical or logical connection before data can be transmitted.

☐ Point to point circuits. This method provides a communication path between two points. It can be a dial-up or a dedicated circuit.

☐ Multidrop circuits. This method allows for the sharing of a communication facility. It is similar to a party line telephone call because several input/output terminals share the same line. Only one terminal can be transmitting on the line at a time.

☐ Local cable. This method of connecting communication devices consists of a privately owned cable or wire interconnecting many terminals with the computer system.

6. Packet Switching (Value Added Networks—VAN) System—A type of data communication technique that allows for messages to be divided or segmented into packets and routed dynamically through a network to the final destination point.

7. Interface Unit—The device that connects a data transmitting (terminal) or receiving unit to the transmission facility. An example of this would be a modem, a digital service unit, or a device that converts voltage signaling to light signaling.

8. Multiplexer—A device that combines several independent data streams into one data stream at a higher signaling speed for transmission to a similar device that separates the high-speed signal into the original independent data streams. Note: Some of the multiplexers are software-driven and are similar to concentrators; however, most of them are non-intelligent hard-wired devices.

9. Concentrator—A programmable device that will perform the same function as a multiplexer with added functions such as data storage (buffering), message error checking, data flow control, polling, etc.

10. Front-End Communication Processor—A programmable device that interfaces a communication network to a host computer. Some of the functions that can be performed by a "frontend" are polling, code and speed conversion, error detection and correction, store and forward functions, format checking, data flow control, network statistics gathering, message authentication, communication routing and control, and the like.

11. Message Switch—A privately owned programmable device that accepts messages from many users, stores them, and at some time after receiving them transmits them to their intended destination. This device generally receives messages at slow speeds over dial-up lines.

12. Protocols—Software or hardware rules that facilitate the transmission between devices. Some protocols provide for error control.

13. Test Equipment (technical control facility)—
A combination of equipment that facilitates the physical monitoring, diagnostics, and restoration of communication systems should they fail. They can contain circuit patching, spare equipment, alternate switches, and might involve message text monitoring or quantitative measuring equipment.

14. Audio Response Unit—A unit that accepts analog, audio voice, or digital signals and converts them to digital computer signaling or can also convert digital signals from a computer into human understandable voice signals.

15. Auto Answering—A device that automatically answers a telephone and establishes a connection between data communication devices.

16. Auto Dialing Unit—A device that accepts computer signals and automatically dials the telephone number of a remote communication device.

17. Terminals—An input/output device that is used to enter messages into the system and/or receive messages from the system.

Index

OTHER POPULAR TAB BOOKS OF INTEREST

TAB TAB BOOKS Inc.

Blue Ridge Summit, Pa. 17214

Send for FREE TAB Catalog describing over 750 current titles in print.